EDIBLE PEOPLE

THE ANTHROPOLOGY OF FOOD AND NUTRITION

General Editor: *Helen Macbeth*

Eating is something all humans must do to survive, but it is more than a biological necessity. Producing food, foraging, distributing, shopping, cooking, and, of course, eating itself are all deeply inscribed as cultural acts.

This series brings together the broad range of perspectives on human food, encompassing social, cultural, and nutritional aspects of food habits, beliefs, choices, and technologies in different regions and societies, past and present. Each volume features cross-disciplinary and international perspectives on the topic of its title. This multidisciplinary approach is particularly relevant to the study of food-related issues in the contemporary world.

Recent volumes:

Volume 11
Edible People: The Historical Consumption of Slaves and Foreigners and the Cannibalistic Trade in Human Flesh
Christian Siefkes

Volume 10
Food Connections: Production, Exchange and Consumption in West African Migration
Maria Abranches

Volume 9
Food and Sustainability in the Twenty-First Century: Cross-Disciplinary Perspectives
Edited by *Paul Collinson, Iain Young, Lucy Antal, and Helen Macbeth*

Volume 8
Food in Zones of Conflict: Cross-Disciplinary Perspectives
Edited by *Paul Collinson and Helen Macbeth*

Volume 7
Liquid Bread: Beer and Brewing in Cross-Cultural Perspective
Edited by *Wulf Schiefenhövel and Helen Macbeth*

Volume 6
Consuming the Inedible: Neglected Dimensions of Food Choice
Edited by *Jeremy MacClancy, C. Jeya Henry, and Helen Macbeth*

Volume 5
Researching Food Habits: Methods and Problems
Edited by *Helen Macbeth and Jeremy MacClancy*

Volume 4
Drinking: Anthropological Approaches
Edited by *Igor de Garine and Valerie de Garine*

Volume 3
Food for Health, Food for Wealth: Ethnic and Gender Identities in British Iranian Communities
Lynn Harbottle

Volume 2
Food Preferences and Taste: Continuity and Change
Edited by *Helen Macbeth*

For a full volume listing, please see the series page on our website: https://www.berghahnbooks.com/series/anthropology-of-food-and-nutrition

EDIBLE PEOPLE

The Historical Consumption of Slaves and Foreigners and the Cannibalistic Trade in Human Flesh

Christian Siefkes

berghahn
NEW YORK • OXFORD
www.berghahnbooks.com

First published in 2022 by
Berghahn Books
www.berghahnbooks.com

First paperback edition published in 2026

Library of Congress Cataloging-in-Publication Data

Names: Siefkes, Christian, author.
Title: Edible People: The Historical Consumption of Slaves and Foreigners and the Cannibalistic Trade in Human Flesh / Christian Siefkes.
Description: [New York, New York]: Berghahn Books, 2022. | Series: The Anthropology of Food and Nutrition; volume 11 | Includes bibliographical references and index.
Identifiers: LCCN 2022019390 (print) | LCCN 2022019391 (ebook) | ISBN 9781800736139 (hardback) | ISBN 9781800736146 (ebook)
Subjects: LCSH: Cannibalism—History. | Slaves—Violence against—History. | Xenophobia. | Slave trade—History.
Classification: LCC GN409 .S54 2022 (print) | LCC GN409 (ebook) | DDC 394/.909—dc23/eng/20220714
LC record available at https://lccn.loc.gov/2022019390
LC ebook record available at https://lccn.loc.gov/2022019391

British Library Cataloguing in Publication Data

A catalogue record for this book is available from the British Library

EU GPSR Authorized Representative

LOGOS EUROPE, 9 rue Nicolas Poussin, 17000, LA ROCHELLE, France
Email: Contact@logoseurope.eu

ISBN 978-1-80073-613-9 hardback
ISBN 978-1-80758-081-0 paperback
ISBN 978-1-83695-987-8 epub
ISBN 978-1-80073-614-6 web pdf

https://doi.org/10.3167/9781800736139

CONTENTS

ILLUSTRATIONS

Figures

Maps

Tables

INTRODUCTION

Cannibalism has been called "the last taboo,"[1] "the strongest of all taboos,"[2] and "mankind's oldest taboo."[3] It can be doubted that no other taboos remain in modern society, and Reay Tannahill rightly rejects the last appellation, pointing out that "the tabu on eating human flesh is by no means the oldest tabu in the world."[4] But there can be no doubt that the taboo against practicing cannibalism is very strong—so strong, in fact, that it may seem as if "the taboo on cannibalism has become transformed into a taboo on thinking about cannibalism," as Robert N. Bellah observes.[5]

The back cover text of Lawrence H. Keeley's book *War before Civilization* includes the sentence: "Finally, and perhaps most controversially, he examines the evidence of cannibalism among some preliterate peoples." But why should evidence of cannibalism be more controversial than evidence of other violent and deadly practices? Cannibalism is a specific way of treating dead bodies—but in general, and quite reasonably so, people are more concerned with what happens to them while alive rather than with their body's fate after death. Considering this rightful concern over the treatment of living individuals, we should be much more shocked by the practice of burning supposed heretics and witches alive and by other cruel execution practices that were usual in the European Middle Ages than by the fact that, in some societies, killed enemies were subsequently eaten (rather than being left to rot or, maybe, "properly" buried or cremated). Just as we might ask why some societies considered certain cannibal acts as acceptable, we might ask why the practice is met with such a particular abhorrence in ours—a question to which we will return shortly.

In any case it is notable that the "taboo on thinking about cannibalism" seems to have caused many researchers and historians to shy away from the topic altogether, which has encouraged meta-discussions about talks about the practices instead of the analyses of actual cannibal practices. While human cannibalism has attracted considerable attention and controversy, discussions of the topic often focus on the question of whether descriptions of such acts are accurate or pure slander, or they treat cannibalism as a topic of discourse rather than an actual practice. Investigations of actual cannibal practices are largely limited to a few typical forms, such as famine cannibalism, the consumption of killed enemies in warfare, or of deceased relatives as a funerary rite.

Scant attention has been given to other aspects of the practice—aspects which are nevertheless well documented in the historical record. These include the connection between cannibalism and xenophobia, which is evident in the capture and consumption of unwanted strangers. Likewise ignored is the connection between cannibalism and slavery: the fact that in some societies slaves[6] and persons captured in slave raids could be, and were, killed and eaten. Other connections between cannibal acts and trade—the sale of human flesh or of corpses destined for consumption—are neglected as well.

Exploring these largely forgotten practices is the purpose of this book. It shows that cannibalism cannot be understood in isolation; rather, interconnections with other topics—such as the international slave trade in the nineteenth century and earlier—must be taken into account to get a comprehensive understanding of either topic.

Investigations of cannibalism—in particular, of violent practices, where people are killed and eaten, such as those studied in this book—are a part of examining the "darker side of humanity," as Shirley Lindenbaum remarks.[7] Are such investigations really necessary—is it not better to let this part of the past slide into oblivion? I do not think so. Science is always an enterprise of intellectual curiosity—an attempt to better understand the world as it really is and was. Shying away from certain topics because one considers them unpleasant and better forgotten violates the spirit of this enterprise. Moreover, true oblivion is unachievable—when the truth is not sought, all kinds of misconceptions start to flourish.

One such misconception is the idea that socially accepted cannibalism could never have existed anywhere. The idea that the cannibalism taboo is so strong that it *must* be universal and that therefore cannibalism as a socially accepted practice *cannot* have existed anywhere in the world has long been widespread in Western[8] thought, as we will see later. It may well have reached its pinnacle in the late 1970s and the 1980s when the spreading of postmodernism encouraged a way of theory-building that often seemed to be based more on personal preferences than on a careful evaluation of available sources and collected evidence. How and why *cannibalism denial*—which might well be considered a forerunner of other, more widely known denialisms such as climate change denial[9]—could, in spite of all contrary evidence, achieve for some time an astonishing popularity even in certain academic circles, is a question we will return to in the Conclusion.

Another misconception—often visible in movies or other popular accounts that try to depict cannibalistic societies—equates cannibalism with utter primitivity. One example is *Last Cannibal World* (1977),[10] one of the first and most successful movies made during a short-lived boom of exploitation films with a cannibal twist made around the year 1980. It features "a stone age tribe on the Island of Mindanao," the second largest island of the Philippines (not that cannibal peoples are documented in the Philippines). The movie cannibals live in a cave instead of constructing buildings of any kind; they lack a proper language, making just grunting and howling sounds ("these tribes don't use language as we know it," comments the hero); they have long and uncombed hair and highly uncultivated eating habits, ravenously tearing half-cooked (human) flesh out of each other's hands. In short, they are as primitive and uncivilized as any script writer can imagine a people to be.

A very similar depiction of a clan of cannibalistic cave dwellers is given in the film *Bone Tomahawk* (2015),[11] indicating that prejudices have not much changed during these nearly four decades. Such stereotypical cannibal savages have almost nothing to do with the cannibal peoples actually encountered by Western explorers in the Pacific Ocean, Africa, or elsewhere.

This book is an attempt to look beyond the misconceptions and understand certain cannibal practices as they really were. Actual cannibalistic societies were not particularly primitive—they had their social order and their own value systems, which were not necessarily less refined than the Western ones, though they were certainly different. Analyzing the principles that governed such societies is a part of the big endeavor of trying to explore the human condition—of exploring how humans lived (and died) under conditions that were sometimes so different from our own that they are difficult to even imagine. Investigating historical practices such as slave eating also reveals close interconnections between the consumption of slaves and captives in Africa and the international slave (and, as we will see, ivory) trade across the Atlantic and into the Arab world—an aspect of the history of slavery (one of the largest crimes of all times) that would remain unknown if we went on to ignore the historical record.

A Not Quite Universal Taboo and Its Origins

Before we plunge into societies where certain kinds of cannibalism were accepted, it may be worthwhile to reflect about contemporary viewpoints of the practice—which, however logical and "natural" they may seem, are actually a bit odd. In Western thought, the taboo against cannibalism is so strong and absolute that many believe that everyone, in any culture, must feel the same. One contemporary article, quite typical for this way of thinking, calls cannibalism "a universal taboo" and asserts that "no human society practices [or practiced] cannibalism." Instead, all reports of cannibal practices are considered "smears" used to justify "genocide, enslavement and cultural erasure" against the wrongly accused groups. Not only is the rejection of cannibalism supposedly universal but its usage for the purpose of vilifying others seems to be universal too—the author calls it the "universal demonization of an otherwise fictional entity."[12]

The belief that cannibalism is so obviously wrong that everyone must feel this—hence that socially accepted cannibalism exists nowhere—is not new. After observing the preparation of a cannibal meal in New Zealand in the 1820s, the British artist Augustus Earle comments that he had "witnesse[d] a scene which many travellers have related, and their relations have invariably been treated with contempt; indeed, the veracity of those who had the temerity to relate such incredible events has been every where questioned."[13] And the British admiral John Elphinstone Erskine writes after his visit to Fiji in the late 1840s: "The notion of using the bodies of our fellow-creatures for food is so revolting to the feelings of civilized men, that many have refused all belief in the systematic exercise of such a habit."[14]

It would be nice to imagine that such feelings are the result of a thorough acceptance of human rights and human dignity. But this seems doubtful, as the European taboo against cannibalism is clearly older than these notions from the Age of Enlightenment which only became widely accepted during the course of the twentieth century. Earle considers the death penalty an appropriate punishment for "thieves and runaways,"[15] and when he and Elphinstone were writing, slavery was still legal in the Southern United States, British India, French West Africa, the Portuguese territories and colonies, most of the former European colonies in South America, and many other parts of the world. While slaves in the Western world were not usually arbitrarily killed by their owners, their life expectancy was often severely reduced due to harsh working conditions. So-called refuse slaves, who because of illness or other factors failed to attract buyers, "were often left to die unattended on the quayside of the port of entry into the Americas"; if provisions on slave ships crossing the Atlantic became scarce, slaves could be thrown overboard with impunity.[16]

And yet the inhabitants of Western societies that tolerated such practices considered all cases of cannibalism as signs of primitiveness, depravity, or madness. While we might ask why certain cannibal acts were considered acceptable in some societies, we might equally ask why the practice is met with such a particular abhorrence in ours.

The answer seems to be connected to the Jewish-Christian notions of the bodily resurrection of the dead. According to the traditional viewpoint, people do not just have immortal souls, but their bodies will ultimately be restored and reunified with their souls. If a dead body is burned or a shipwrecked sailor is consumed by fish, this is considered a problem which God's omnipotence can overcome: surely, He knows where to find the pieces and how to reassemble them. But cannibalism poses a logical problem, since "you are what you eat" (as the proverb says) and Christian thinkers were aware of the worrisome consequences. Athenagoras of Athens (ca. 133–190), considered one of the "Fathers of the Church," wondered:

> How can two bodies, which have successively been in possession of the same substance, appear in their entirety, without lacking a large part of

> themselves? In the end, either the disputed parts will be returned to their original owners, leaving a gap in the later owners, or they shall be fixed in the latter, leaving in this case an irreparable loss in the former.[17]

More than a thousand years later, Thomas Aquinas (1225–1274) still thought about the same question. He decided that God can overcome even this challenge. Because "the flesh swallowed by a cannibal belongs to his victim by right . . . there will be a lack in the cannibal's body at the resurrection, but this will be filled by the infinite power of God."[18]

But even if God is capable of overcoming this challenge, the cannibal's attempt to mess with resurrection is far worse than anything else people can do within the realm of the living. "Because he claims for himself an extraordinary power over the circulation of atoms, upon which God will have to intervene with infinite power . . . , the cannibal is a diabolical figure in the most profound sense, an anti-Divinity," summarizes Catalin Avramescu on the traditional Christian viewpoint.[19]

Most contemporary Christians would certainly consider this kind of theological worry as quaint and beside the point. Nevertheless, the modern taboo against even thinking about cannibalism as anything other than madness or false accusation might well be an inheritance of this old discourse, at least to some degree. But certainly other factors play a role in keeping the taboo alive. One modern commentator states:

> Treating humans like cattle to be slaughtered and eaten goes against most of our instincts, because no matter how you spin it, everyone sees themselves as an individual. Everyone has their own hopes, dreams, fears, desires, and for all of that to be chucked away for the sake of a meal is, well, disgusting.[20]

This short remark mixes some insights into what makes cannibalism so particularly "disgusting" and unacceptable in our minds with certain misunderstandings (which are probably quite typical) about what cannibalism actually *is.* Indeed, it goes utterly against modern individualism to deny a human being all their individual traits and capabilities, treating them as nothing but edible matter. Being potentially edible is something that humans have in common with most animals and most plants. By turning this potential into actual edibility, the cannibals seem to add insult to injury, apparently denying the humanity of their victims. Humans are treated "like cattle"—and cattle, as everyone knows, are not treated very well.

And yet, from the cannibal viewpoint it may be exactly the humanity of their victims that matters—they know the difference between human flesh and beef (or whatever animal meat is available to them) and prefer, under certain circumstances and for whatever reasons, the former. Still, that is not the kind of appreciation of one's humanity that anyone who considers themselves an individual with individual preferences, experiences, and aspirations is likely to value. Besides this mutual misunderstanding between the modern individualist and the cannibal, it must also be pointed out that the idea that humans were treated by cannibals "like cattle" is only partially true. Slaves and captured enemies or foreigners were sometimes butchered for consumption—as we will see—but human beings were never systematically raised and bred for this purpose (as far as we know). Human beings were never used just as "livestock" (and nothing more). Instead, cannibalism was always linked to activities connecting humans with other humans, though often in adversarial and potentially humiliating ways—a fear or hatred of foreigners, slavery, warfare, sacrifice, or acts of punishment.

Which brings us back to the question of why warfare, human sacrifice, and slavery are not seen as quite as "disgusting" and shocking as cannibalism by the modern individualist. To be sure, the latter two practices will be strictly rejected by contemporaries, and most will agree that warfare is only acceptable in self-defense or in certain other, clearly limited circumstances, such as the prevention of severe human rights violations. But compared to cannibalism, these practices do not evoke a similar degree of shock and disgust, sometimes combined with an unwillingness to even *think* about such practices or admit that others could possibly have engaged in them. And yet, all the "hopes, dreams, fears, desires" of an individual are utterly ignored by those who enslave or sacrifice them, and war leaders similarly accept that a certain number of fighters and civilians on both sides will be killed, negating all hopes and dreams they might have had.

Clearly, there must be something besides the negation of individualism that shapes our feelings about cannibalism. Maybe it is an unconscious memory of the old Christian fear of the cannibal as anti-God? Or the humiliation of persons being treated (more or less) like animals? In any case, the rational interpretation of a violation of individualism and individual rights can explain part of our rejection of cannibal behaviors, but it cannot fully explain the strength of the taboo.

Who Is a Cannibal? And Why?

As with many terms, different people mean different things when talking about cannibalism. For the purpose of this book, a standard dictionary definition can serve as guideline: "the practice of eating the flesh of one's own species."[21] Some authors use a broader definition, according to which the consumption of any body part of a member of one's species makes one a cannibal. Thus, Paul Moon remarks that "someone who nibbles at their fingernail and then swallows it" is "technically" a cannibal.[22] Some even interpret the consumption of excretions of a human body, such as "mucous, excrement, and placenta" as cannibalism.[23] Such broad definitions are not used in this book, and neither is the drinking of blood from a member of one's species considered cannibalism (unless combined with other cannibal practices). At the same time, "flesh" in the above definition may be understood to refer not only to muscle tissue and body fat but also to edible organs such as brain, heart, liver, and intestines.

While the term *cannibal* is sometimes used with a pejorative meaning, I use it in a technical sense: a cannibal is someone who has at least once practiced cannibalism, as per the definition above, whether knowingly or not. Since people do not always know what exactly they are eating, it is possible to be a cannibal without knowing it. In the course of this book, we will encounter a few cases of persons unwittingly becoming cannibals, learning only later what they had eaten.

In our society, cannibalism might well be seen as the ultimate transgression, but clearly that was not the case in societies where cannibal acts were considered acceptable, maybe even expected, under certain circumstance. But we must realize that this is not a binary switch, a question of "nobody must be eaten!" versus "anybody may be eaten!" Any social practice is governed by rules controlling what is and is not allowed, and cannibalism is no exception. When cannibalism is a socially accepted practice, the most fundamental questions such rules must answer are: who may be eaten and under what circumstances?

Various cannibal societies differ to a large degree in how they answer these questions. If, for example, the corpses of deceased community members are ritually consumed by relatives and friends, cannibalism is a nonviolent funerary rite often known as *funerary cannibalism.* If, on the other hand, enemies killed or captured in warfare are eaten (*war cannibalism*), cannibalism is a violent act which may serve to humiliate and symbolically—as well as physically—annihilate one's enemies. In both cases, such acts are governed by rules, but the rules regulating who may be eaten and under what circumstances—in short, who is considered "edible"—differ and the meanings of the acts differ with them. Literally, *edible* means that something can be consumed and digested, when prepared in a suitable manner, without making the eater ill. But in a stricter sense it means that something is good to eat or meant to be eaten. I will put the term in quotation marks when this second meaning is intended.

It is important to keep in mind that societies which accepted certain cannibal practices were not "ruleless" or "lawless"—they merely had rules which differed, at least in this regard, significantly from ours. In the next chapter we will look more closely at which kinds of rules could typically be found in some of these societies.

Can We Trust the Sources?

Another important question concerns the reliability of sources. When looking for evidence of cannibalism, one quickly notices that it is well documented both in the archaeological record and in written sources. With the exception of China, however, local cultures in the regions which will be discussed in this book were largely oral—most written accounts therefore come from outsiders, often Europeans, who visited or had moved into these regions. How trustworthy are these sources? Some authors have suggested that they may often be mere fabrications or at least wild exaggerations, produced by colonialists to justify the oppression of local peoples[24] or by missionaries to convince their audience at home to support a good cause performed under the most difficult and dangerous circumstances.[25]

This may sometimes be the case and it suggests that we must take care, especially when relying strongly on a single source or on a small number of sources whose authors were in close connection to each other (say, by working for the same government or the same mission). The evidence which will be explored in the following chapters, however, comes from a wide variety of sources—not just from colonialists and missionaries, but also from travelers, anthropologists, and oral accounts of those who partook in such practices or heard of them from their ancestors. Moreover, those working for colonial governments were sometimes highly critical of these governments,[26] casting doubt on the idea that in the very same works they would have fabricated evidence supporting the government's actions; and among the accounts of missionaries are letters and diaries published decades after they were written and not originally intended for publication.[27] Sometimes accounts describing similar practices in the same region were originally written in different languages and published in different countries, making a deliberate collusion between their authors unlikely.

Paul Moon notes that when several independent observers give accounts of a practice, varying in details and circumstances but agreeing in certain common themes, this clearly points to descriptions of an actual practice. He concludes that, "in the absence of any evidence of collusion" or deliberate fabrication, such reports should be considered generally reliable, though there may be mistakes in the details or misunderstandings about motives.[28]

But maybe Westerners brought their stereotypical notions about cannibal "savages" with them and used them to "embellish" the reports of the cultures they encountered, thus creating a seemingly consistent but nevertheless false picture even without deliberate collusion? If this were the case, one would expect reports of cannibalism to cover all or most of the regions visited or colonized by Europeans more or less evenly. However, the evidence of cannibalism is limited to certain regions.

In the infamous European "Scramble for Africa," that continent was nearly completely colonized by European powers between the late nineteenth and early twentieth centuries. Yet, while a wealth of often quite detailed accounts refer to cannibal practices in certain central and western African regions (especially the Congo basin and Nigeria), similar accounts from northern, eastern, and southern Africa seem to be missing completely or to be limited to exceptional times such as severe famines. The situation in the South Pacific is similar—various detailed accounts come from certain islands and archipelagos (in particular, New Guinea, Fiji, and New Zealand), while elsewhere (for example, in Samoa and Tahiti) cannibal practices seem to have been unknown.[29] This highly uneven distribution is another hint that descriptions of such practices refer to actual local phenomena rather than to mere fantasies in the heads of their authors.

What You Will Find in This Book

This book is largely devoted to three topics which so far have received scant attention in the literature. Each of these topics explores the interconnections between cannibalism and a large-scale issue of current or of earlier times:

- The connection to slavery: the consumption of slaves and persons captured in slave raids—*slave eating* for short.
- The connection to xenophobia, a fear or hatred of foreigners: the kidnapping and consumption of individuals or small groups of people who have left the safety of their own community and may be seen as unwanted intruders or simply as convenient victims. I will use the term *foreigner poaching* to refer to this practice.
- The connection to commerce or trade: the sale of human flesh or of people or corpses destined for consumption. I will occasionally use the term *commercial cannibalism* in this context—arguably just a convenient way of speaking, as it was not the cannibalism itself that was commercial (people were not paid to eat human flesh), but the acts that enabled or facilitated it. In cases where slaves were deliberately bought for consumption, slave eating may also be regarded as a kind of commercial cannibalism. But not every commercial act that facilitated cannibalism was connected to slavery, therefore this topic deserves an independent investigation.

Each of these practices occurred in various regions throughout the world. In this book, each of them will be investigated in the context of a few regions where it has been particularly well documented. The selection of these regions is not arbitrary: it follows the sources by choosing regions for which a considerable number of preferably detailed sources can be found. References to similar practices in other regions will sometimes be made in passing or in endnotes, but such other regions are not the main focus of attention.

Before turning to individual topics and regions, I will in Chapter 1 consider under which circumstances and due to which motives cannibal practices occurred in general, in order to develop a taxonomy of such practices. Understanding the different aspects influencing cannibal behaviors will provide useful background knowledge regarding the context of the specific practices explored in this book.

Chapters 2 to 10 are all dedicated to slave eating—a well-documented, but so far deplorably under-investigated topic that may be considered the main focus of this book. Chapter 2 deals with the practice among the Maori in New Zealand; Chapter 3 investigates the Bismarck Archipelago near New Guinea and takes a look at Sumatra. Subsequent chapters are dedicated to the Congo basin, where the practice is particularly well-documented. Chapter 3 starts by exploring the interconnections between local cannibalism and the international trade in slaves and ivory. Chapter 5 investigates how two particular groups of foreigners—Swahilo-Arab slave and ivory traders from the African east coast as well as European officials of the colonial Congo Free State—benefited from and sometimes actively encouraged cannibal practices, without being cannibals themselves.

Chapters 6 to 8 aim to deepen our understanding of Congolese slave eating: Why, in which ways, and where did it take place? How did it work from an economic viewpoint and in which ways was it tied to commercial practices? How was it shaped by patriarchal social structures, and what were its connections to the exploitation of slaves in general? Finally, Chapters 9 and 10 are again dedicated to foreign—in particular, European—influences. Chapter 9 is a case study of a particularly well-documented and controversially analyzed example of the involvement of a European explorer in a case of cannibalism which took the life of a young enslaved girl. Chapter 10 takes a step back to consider more generally the question of European influences on cannibal customs elsewhere of the world—in Central Africa in particular. In this context we will also explore what is known about the beginnings and the end of Congolese cannibalism.

Chapters 11 and 12 are dedicated to foreigner poaching, the murder and consumption of unwanted foreigners. Three regions where such acts were common will be studied: New Guinea and the neighboring Bismarck Archipelago, Fiji, and Central Africa.

Chapter 13 investigates commercial aspects of cannibalism not directly connected with slavery—the sale of human flesh and of corpses destined for consumption.

Chapters 14 and 15 explore commercial and culinary aspects of cannibalism in China, where human flesh repeatedly appeared on marketplaces during times of famine and warfare, and where it was occasionally eaten even outside such times of hardship, sometimes due to culinary choice. While the rest of book deals with regions that were highly decentralized and, before the imposition of colonial regimes may well be considered as "stateless," China is a huge country with a very long tradition of statehood. These chapters will allow an understanding of how and under which circumstances the consumption of and the trade in human flesh could gain a certain social acceptance even in such a very different setting.

The Conclusion includes a review and a discussion of certain questions that arise when exploring cannibalism, including parallels and differences to meat eating in general and why and how cannibalism denial could, for some time, spread widely even in academic circles. A final topic is the pitfalls cannibalism poses for philosophic positions such as moral relativism.

Notes

1. The subtitle of Marriner, *Cannibalism.*
2. Korn, Radice, and Hawes, *Cannibal*, 10.
3. From the subtitle of Travis-Henikoff, *Dinner with a Cannibal.*
4. Tannahill, *Flesh and Blood*, 34.
5. In Sagan, *Cannibalism*, ix (foreword).
6. Some authors prefer the term "enslaved person" over "slave" in order to stress that being enslaved is a social condition, not an innate property. While this is a valid concern, I nevertheless often use the shorter term for convenience.
7. Lindenbaum, "Thinking about Cannibalism," 482.
8. The capitalized term *Western* (and related terms) is used in this book for peoples and cultures of predominantly European origin—including not only Europe but also large parts of the current population of the Americas, Australia, and New Zealand. This use of a cardinal point is, of course, purely conventional and has no geographic meaning (seen from Africa, Europe is in the north, from North America, it is in the east).
9. See Sahlins, "Artificially Maintained Controversies."
10. *Ultimo mondo cannibale*, Interfilm, dir. Ruggero Deodato, Italy.
11. RLJ Entertainment, dir. S. Craig Zahler, USA.
12. Nate Taskin, "The Cannibal: The Universal Boogeyman," *Massachusetts Daily Collegian*, 26 October 2017, accessed 25 September 2020, https://dailycollegian.com/2017/10/the-cannibal-the-universal-boogeyman/.
13. Earle, *Narrative*, 114–15.
14. Erskine, *Journal*, 256. A few decades later, Alfred St. Johnston made a similar comment (St. Johnston, *Camping among Cannibals*, 226).
15. Earle, *Narrative*, 121.
16. Thomas, *Slave Trade*, chapters 22 (quote) and 25; Lang, *Land*, 215.
17. Quoted in Avramescu, *Intellectual History*, 131.
18. Ibid., 134.
19. Ibid., 134–35.
20. Zoe Delahunty-Light, "Can We All Agree That Gaming's Evil Post-Apocalyptic Cannibal Trope Has to Stop?" *GamesRadar+*, 18 December 2017, accessed 25 September 2020, https://www.gamesradar.com/can-we-all-agree-that-gamings-evil-post-apocalyptic-cannibal-trope-has-to-stop/.
21. Oxford Dictionary on Lexico.com, "Cannibalism," accessed 28 September 2020, https://www.lexico.com/definition/cannibalism.
22. Paul Moon, "Are We Really Just Meat and Nothing More?" *The Spinoff*, 31 May 2017, accessed 28 September 2020, https://thespinoff.co.nz/books/31-05-2017/more-than-it-can-chew-a-new-book-about-cannibalism-lacks-meat-on-its-bones/.
23. Lindenbaum, "Thinking about Cannibalism," 479.
24. Kilgour, *From Communion to Cannibalism*, 148.

25. Davies, *Human Sacrifice*, 159.
26. See "Cannibal Stereotypes and Realities" in the Conclusion.
27. For example, Augouard, *28 années au Congo*; David Cargill as quoted in Hogg, *Cannibalism*; Jaggar, *Unto the Perfect Day*.
28. Moon, *This Horrid Practice*, 52.
29. Douglas L. Oliver notes that cannibalism was apparently not practiced in the Society Islands, in Hawaii, nor in most islands of Micronesia. In Melanesia it was widespread, but by no means universal (Oliver, *Oceania*, 316).

CHAPTER 1
A TAXONOMY OF CANNIBAL PRACTICES

Facets of Socially Accepted Cannibalism

The contexts in which cannibalism occurs and the forms it can take vary enormously—so much, in fact, that Shirley Lindenbaum has suggested "it might be better to talk about 'cannibalisms'" instead of using the term in the singular.[1] To tackle this diversity, different facets (or aspects) of the practice need to be considered. Not all combinations of relevant facets have actually occurred, but treating different facets separately makes it possible to better understand why certain combinations of facets (types of cannibalism) existed and in which ways they differed from each other.

One facet concerns societal views of the practice: is a cannibal act *socially accepted*; does it take place under *exceptional* circumstances (where the rules of normal social behavior are challenged or have broken down); or is it considered an *antisocial,* criminal act by most members of the society in question?

Another facet is the presence or absence of *violence:* was the victim killed or maimed, or did they die in an accident or of natural causes (illness or "old age")? Alexis Peri notes that Russian has two different terms for *cannibalism* depending on the absence or presence of deliberate violence: *trupoedstvo* means "eating flesh from an already dead human body," while *ljudoedstvo* means "killing and eating a human being."[2] The first term can be translated as *corpse eating* or *nonviolent cannibalism,* the second as *people eating* or *violent cannibalism.*

Note that even if cannibalism is preceded by violence (people eating), the cannibal act itself might not necessarily be the main driver of the violence. It is also possible that the subsequently consumed person was killed in a fight or executed for a crime. We might try to further distinguish *murderous cannibalism* (or "murder for meat": a person is killed just to be eaten) from other instances of violent cannibalism. However, such a distinction is sometimes hard to make: if a prisoner of war is killed and eaten, was the cannibal intent the reason for the execution? Or would the prisoner have been killed even if the captors had not practiced cannibalism? This poses a question about a counterfactual scenario, to which not even the captors might know the answer, let alone any outside observer.

A further facet concerns the relation between eaten and eater: did they belong to the same community (whose members understand themselves as positively related to each other in some way, however loosely) or not? Traditionally, the former case is known as *endocannibalism,* the latter as *exocannibalism.* However, these terms are problematic because they are frequently associated with further assumptions about the relation between eaters and eaten and about the context of the act. Endocannibalism is often associated with the nonviolent consumption of community members as a funerary rite,[3] while exocannibalism is associated with the consumption of enemies killed in war.[4]

Because of these overly restrictive associations, I propose to use the terms *intracommunal* instead of *endo-* and *extracommunal cannibalism* instead of *exocannibalism.* Violent cannibalism is more frequently extra- rather than intracommunal; while violence against community members with subsequent cannibalism occurs, it is relatively rare. Since this book is predominantly about forms of violent cannibalism (people eating), I will generally omit the term "extracommunal"—any cannibalistic act not explicitly labeled as intracommunal should be understood as extracommunal, unless the context clearly suggests otherwise.

The relation between eaten and eater does not end with the question of whether they belong to the same community. But to make further distinctions, we also have to take into account the facet of violence. Furthermore, the following discussion is restricted to cases of socially accepted cannibalism—the distinctions made below might not make much sense if applied to cases where a person eats another as an antisocial act or under exceptional circumstances.

If both belong to the same community and the eaten died without deliberate violence, the cannibal act is nearly always intended as a funerary rite: in some societies, the dead are buried, in others they are cremated, in some they are eaten. As mentioned, the term "endocannibalism" is sometimes considered a synonym for such *funerary cannibalism.*[5]

In general, for violent intracommunal cannibalism to be acceptable, there must be clear circumstances which allow, or even demand, the killing of a community member and their subsequent consumption. In some communities, this is the case if one or several of the following circumstances apply:

- The eaten is a newborn infant or young child killed because they are considered unwanted or unfit to live (*infanticidal cannibalism*).[6]
- The eaten is an old person killed by relatives or community members because they have reached the end of their "useful lifespan" according to the views prevalent in the community; often, such persons have

already become very weak and might be near their natural death (*senicidal cannibalism*).[7]

- A person who has committed a serious crime in the eyes of their community is killed and eaten as a punishment (*punitive cannibalism*).[8]

A fourth case of intracommunal cannibalism is the escalation of a conflict to such a degree that some community members kill and eat others belonging to the opposite side. This might be called *political cannibalism* since the cannibal act can be considered a "political" means of getting rid of the "opposition" as well as inflicting fear and terror among the survivors. If conflicts reach such an extreme, the community itself might be in danger of being torn apart. Such cases are therefore rare; they cannot occur during the normal, daily life of a community but only in times of distress.[9]

When it comes to extracommunal cannibalism, we must again distinguish whether or not the practice follows an act of deliberate violence. The term *corpse food* might be used for cases of nonviolent cannibalism (corpse eating) which are *not* motivated by an affectionate relation between eater and eaten—in such cases, human bodies are treated more or less like any other food. If, on the other hand, there *is* a positive affectionate relation, such acts usually have the meaning of a funerary rite (as discussed), but in cases of extracommunal corpse eating such a relation is usually absent (eater and eaten rarely even knew each other). Instead, in societies where the use of corpses as food is socially accepted, it often has a commercial aspect: corpses of foreigners who have died of whatever cause are purchased in order to eat them, or different communities exchange their dead to allow the other community to use them as food, without a deeper ritual meaning. Cases with such a commercial aspect will be covered in Chapter 13 of this book.

Persons violently killed and then consumed usually belong to one of three groups:

- Enemies killed or captured during acts of war (*war cannibalism*). Most peoples who practice war cannibalism eat only their enemies, but a few make no difference between the corpses of enemies and their own dead fighters, eating both.[10] And in some cases, warriors on a campaign captured, killed, and ate persons who did not belong to either of the warring sides, considering them a convenient food source.[11]

- Foreigners entrapped or hunted down in order to be used as food; usually the victims are lone individuals or small groups of people who have left the safety of their own community and can be captured or killed with a limited risk to the attackers (*foreigner poaching*). This practice will be covered in Chapters 11 and 12.

- Slaves purchased for consumption or already owned by a person who decides to kill them for food (*slave eating*). This custom will be explored in detail in Chapters 2 to 10.

In other cases, the relation between eater and eaten is less suitable for classifying cannibal acts since the victims may come from various groups, and yet a series of cannibal acts might have a similar purpose, or cause, without which they would (presumably) not take place. Two such purposes are specifically relevant to explain acts of cannibalism in different cultures around the world:

- *Sacrificial cannibalism*: one or more human beings are sacrificed in a ritual with a religious or spiritual meaning and subsequently eaten—the consumption may be part of the ritual, or it may follow. The victims may be slaves, captives, or, in some cases, they may belong to the community where the sacrifice is made.[12]
- *Medicinal* (or medical) *cannibalism*: human body parts are eaten out of a belief that this will improve the health of the eater or heal an illness from which they are suffering.[13]

Purposes such as these have the advantage of being comparatively easy to determine and of providing a single rationale for why an act takes place. Without a religious or spiritual ritual in which a human being is sacrificed, no sacrificial cannibalism can take place, and people will not practice medicinal cannibalism unless they believe in specific health benefits of the practice; such beliefs will often be common knowledge in the respective culture. Other motives might also play a role in such cases—the eaters might consider human flesh delicious, or its consumption might alleviate their hunger—but these additional motives do not in themselves explain the act.

Some authors attempt to distinguish between different types of cannibalism based on the motives of those involved, or the manner in which the act is practiced. Such distinctions are problematic because those involved might have several motives, and manners are mere outside appearance and usually insufficient to explain *why* an act takes place. One such problematic distinction is the category of "gastronomic cannibalism" used by several authors. Lewis Petrinovich defines it as cannibalism practiced to "provide a supplement to the regular diet"; according to Carole A. Travis-Henikoff, it takes place when "human flesh is dealt with and eaten without ceremony (other than culinary), in the same manner as the flesh of any other animal."[14]

Petrinovich thus considers a motive that might play a role in many cannibal acts, including cases of war cannibalism, slave eating, foreigner poaching, and even cases of intracommunal cannibalism such as the consumption of unwanted infants. But often, other motives will play a role as well: war cannibalism may take place to humiliate one's enemies and terrify the survivors, slave eating may be a way of celebrating and displaying one's wealth, and foreigner poaching may be a way of exercising one's strength and keeping outsiders out of one's territory. Neither does the label "gastronomic cannibalism" explain who the victims are and why the act can take place at all (without a suitable victim, there can be no cannibalism).

Travis-Henikoff's focus on the absence or presence of ceremony (the manner in which flesh is eaten) is equally problematic. Human flesh may be eaten like "the flesh of any other animal" but this does not reveal anything about how it ended up in the hands of the eaters in the first place. Foreigner poaching may somewhat resemble the hunting of animals, but even here other reasons—such as a desire to send a message to other foreigners that they rather stay away—may play a role. Warfare and slavery are specific institutions whose agents and victims are human, hence acts committed in such contexts differ considerably from the eating of animals. Just looking at the manner in which a cannibal act takes place is not sufficient to explain why and how it came about.

Terms such as *gastronomic* or *culinary cannibalism* can nevertheless be useful as shortcuts to refer to cannibal acts where this specific motive was clearly important. I will occasionally use the latter term to refer to occasions where human flesh was apparently eaten because it was considered good food, without other discernable motives such as revenge or a spiritual meaning. In a similar vein, I will occasionally use the term *commercial cannibalism* to refer to commercial acts which enabled or facilitated subsequent cannibalism: the sale or purchase of human flesh or of persons intended for consumption. But, depending on who the victims were, one may still group such acts of culinary or commercial cannibalism under war cannibalism, slave eating, foreigner poaching, or any of the other categories introduced above. These terms highlight a certain aspect of the practice, but by themselves they cannot explain how the practice could occur—and as for the *why,* they might just be a piece of a rather more complex picture.

This concludes the discussion of facets of socially accepted cannibalism. It is conceivable that additional groups of victims or additional purposes might have to be added to explain certain cannibal acts not covered by the categories discussed here, but doing so should be straightforward. I believe, however, that the categories listed here are sufficient to cover most cases.

Antisocial and Exceptional Cannibalism

So far we have discussed cases of cannibalism that are socially accepted. This does not necessarily mean that *all* members of a society approve of such acts (let alone participate in them), but that a large part of the population considers them as justified and appropriate considering the circumstances in which they occur. It remains to consider cases where this is not the case.

The opposite of socially accepted cannibalism is *antisocial cannibalism*—cannibal acts practiced by individuals that are met with disapproval by the vast majority of the population.[15] Since there is no society known (or even conceivable) in which *all* possible cannibal acts are considered legitimate, antisocial cannibalism can occur in any society, regardless of whether its members reject all (or nearly all) cannibal acts (as is the case in the modern world) or whether they consider some cannibal acts as appropriate. In a society where enemies killed or captured in warfare are regularly eaten, a person kidnapping and consuming their neighbor's child would still commit an antisocial act since neighbors are not enemies—they are not considered "edible."

Between socially accepted and antisocial cannibalism there are cases that take place under exceptional circumstances which cause a suspension of the rules of normal social behavior, at least in the minds of a certain part of the population affected. This is sometimes the case when a group of people is collectively threatened by starvation. Under these extreme circumstances, the normal rules of what is considered acceptable as nourishment are relaxed and people will eat things they would otherwise consider "inedible"—sometimes including human flesh (*famine cannibalism*).[16]

Because famine cannibalism is motivated by desperate hunger, the acquisition of victims tends to follow somewhat opportunistic lines. Instead of limiting their cannibalism to enemies, slaves, or other specific groups, desperate people tend to regard any dead body within their reach—or even anyone who can be killed with a limited fear of repercussions—as a potential source of protein. Therefore, the distinction made between intra- and extracommunal cannibalism and further distinctions based on the chosen group of victims often have little relevance for such acts—though it may still prove insightful to explore which groups of people practice such acts and which typically fall prey to them.

More relevant is the question of whether or not violence is used to acquire victims. If a person later eaten had died of starvation, illness, or other "natural" causes, even a modern audience is inclined to accept such acts of corpse eating as a sad necessity in cases where all other provisions are exhausted.[17] Cases of violent (or murderous) famine cannibalism (people eating), on the other hand, where individuals are deliberately killed so that others can eat their flesh, would today be met with nearly universal disapproval. This was not always the case: until the nineteenth century, it was widely considered acceptable for shipwrecked sailors to kill and eat one of their own to save the rest from starvation, as long as the victim was chosen by lottery (so that everyone of them had the same risk of serving as food for their more fortunate companions).[18]

This concludes the proposed taxonomy of "cannibalisms." Table 1.1 summarizes the discussed facets and the categories derived from them.

Comparison with Other Categorizations of Cannibal Acts

Like the approach developed here, Bruno Boulestin and Anne-Sophie Coupey distinguish between three types of cannibal acts based on societal views of the practice. They distinguish "survival cannibalism" or "cannibalism by

Table 1.1. Facets and Types of Cannibalism. (✓) means "sometimes."

Antisocial	Violent?	Intracommunal	Extracommunal	Victim/context	Category
		✓		Funeral rite	Funerary cannibalism
	✓	✓		Unwanted or unfit newborns	Infanticidal cannibalism
	✓	✓		Old or ill persons nearing death	Senicidal cannibalism
	✓	✓		Wrongdoers	Punitive cannibalism
	✓	✓		Enemies in a political conflict	Political cannibalism
			✓	Anybody (no affectionate relation)	Corpse food
	✓		✓	Killed or captured enemies (or other war victims)	War cannibalism
	✓		✓	Kidnapped foreigners	Foreigner poaching
	✓		✓	Slaves	Slave eating
	✓	(✓)	✓	Persons sacrificed in a ritual with a religious or spiritual meaning	Sacrificial cannibalism
	(✓)	(✓)	✓	Human body parts consumed to improve health or heal illness	Medicinal cannibalism
✓	(✓)	(✓)	(✓)	Potentially anybody (depends on perpetrator's choice)	Antisocial cannibalism
	(✓)	(✓)	(✓)	Potentially anybody (depends on situation)	Famine cannibalism (violent or nonviolent)

necessity" during times of famine (famine cannibalism) from "institutional" or "customary cannibalism" that is socially accepted and practiced regularly under certain circumstances (socially accepted cannibalism), adding that acts of "social deviants" (antisocial cannibalism) are excluded from their categorization. They further subdivide institutional cannibalism into endo- and exocannibalism, equating the former with "funerary cannibalism" (consumption of "one's own dead in the course of funerary rituals") and the latter with "war cannibalism" ("adversaries or enemies are consumed," usually with the intention of "annihilating them").[19]

Missing in their categorization are all cases of violent intracommunal cannibalism (such as senicidal and punitive cannibalism), as well as all cases of extracommunal cannibalism that do not involve warfare (foreigner poaching and slave eating). Medicinal and sacrificial cannibalism are missing as well. It might be argued that for the archaeological work undertaken by Boulestin and Coupey, the taxonomy developed in this book is too complex—it might, for example, be hard to distinguish between war cannibalism and foreigner poaching from the archaeological record alone (even if written records exist, there may sometimes be a gray area). But even if something is hard that does not mean it is impossible, and archaeologists should at least be aware of the various possibilities in order to attempt to distinguish between them where it is possible. Both war cannibalism and foreigner poaching have in common that the victims are violently killed outsiders. But if victims are usually found in small groups of one to three, this points to foreigner poaching; while indications that the victims were heavily armed and there was extended warfare, with destruction of buildings or other large-scale damage, point to war cannibalism.

If the eaten are old persons from the same community as the eaters, signs indicating that they were killed point to violent senicidal rather than peaceful funerary cannibalism. If remains of locally born infants that were killed and consumed are found, this points to infanticidal cannibalism—another possibility overlooked by Boulestin and Coupey. It might also be possible to determine "signatures" to identify other types of cannibalism, such as slave eating and punitive cannibalism. In any case, the knowledge that such practices did historically exist and may be relevant for understanding the archaeological record should be kept in mind.

Lewis Petrinovich distinguishes six types of cannibalism: "medicinal" and "sacrificial cannibalism" correspond to two types also proposed in this book; "survival" corresponds to famine and "mortuary" to funerary cannibalism. A further type, "gastronomic cannibalism," has been criticized above. His last type is "political cannibalism," practiced to "terrify one's neighbors or enemies by ruthlessly and publicly consuming those you capture and kill."[20] This final type corresponds to political cannibalism as used in this book if those to be terrified are indeed hostile "neighbors" who belong to the same community, and it corresponds to war cannibalism if enemies captured in warfare are eaten. But as in the case of gastronomic cannibalism, it is problematic to equate a suspected motive—to terrify—with the practice itself, since war cannibalism might also be practiced for other reasons, for example, as a convenient provisioning method.

Petrinovich would probably consider slave eating and corpse food instances of gastronomic cannibalism; punitive cannibalism—killing and eating wrongdoers—might be considered a kind of political cannibalism, if a desire to terrify other wrongdoers is the underlying motive. Infanticidal and senicidal cannibalism do not seem to fit anywhere in his taxonomy.

Like Petrinovich, Carole Travis-Henikoff distinguishes between survival, medicinal, and gastronomic cannibalism. She considers "'endocannibalism' or 'funerary' cannibalism" as synonymous terms, corresponding to his mortuary cannibalism. Because of this equation, all cases of violent intracommunal cannibalism (infanticidal, senicidal, punitive, political) are missing from her taxonomy. Equally problematic is her definition of "exocannibalism" as "the eating of one's enemies" (i.e., war cannibalism) since it ignores slaves, "poached" foreigners, and purchased or traded corpses as potential extracommunal victims.[21]

Similar to sacrificial cannibalism as used by Petrinovich and me is her "'religious' cannibalism," defined as "the actual or simulated partaking of human flesh as part of a religious rite." But since she includes mere simulations in this definition, she considers the "Christian Communion" a cannibalistic practice.[22] In my view, it makes more sense to speak of cannibalism only when human flesh or organs are actually consumed, excluding simulations and purely symbolic acts.

Her final category is "'ritual,' or 'token,' cannibalism[:] a specified part of an adversary, ruler, or family member is consumed, as in the eating of an enemy's heart, or the eyes of a previous chief eaten by an incoming chief."[23] This category seems to rest on the fact that only a small part of a human body is consumed. I would rather group such acts under war, sacrificial, or funerary cannibalism, depending on the circumstances, rather than relying on the specific body parts eaten. Otherwise, where should the line be drawn—would the consumption of hearts, livers, and possibly other choice parts of enemies still qualify as "ritual," or would it be something else? Moreover, "ritual cannibalism" implies that the consumption of larger parts of a human body is *not* accompanied by ritual, which would often be a wrong conclusion.

Thus, while previous categorizations have their specific qualities and merits, they are not sufficiently detailed to adequately capture all necessary distinctions. They may lead to "blind spots" in interpreting the evidence for cannibalistic practices, be it archaeological or anecdotal evidence taken from contemporary reports and diaries. The taxonomy of cannibalistic practices proposed here is intended to be exhaustive and sufficiently detailed to make the distinctions necessary for understanding these practices, without relying too much on motives (which may easily be attributed wrongly or be entirely inaccessible for certain regions and historical periods). It will be the foundation for the careful investigation of evidence in the rest of the book.

Notes

1. Lindenbaum, "Thinking about Cannibalism," 480.
2. Peri, *War Within*, 108. Трупоедство (*trupoedstvo*) is derived from труп (*trup*) = corpse; еда (*eda*) = food; -ство (*-stvo*) = similar to English-ness (creates an abstract noun); людоедство (*ljudoedstvo*) is derived in the same way from люд (*ljud*) = people, folk.
3. "Endocannibalism . . . is defined as the ritual consumption of deceased members from inside one's one family, community or social group" (Schutt, *Eat Me*, 90).
4. "'Exocannibalism' refers to the eating of one's enemies" (Travis-Henikoff, *Dinner with a Cannibal*, 24).
5. For an extensive treatment of funerary cannibalism in a South American society, see Conklin, *Consuming Grief.*
6. For examples, see Lumholtz, *Among Cannibals*, 134, 254, 273; Oberländer, "Die Eingeborenen," 279; Róheim, *Children of the Desert*, 71–72; Travis-Henikoff, *Dinner with a Cannibal*, 184, 196.
7. For examples, see Augouard, *28 années au Congo*, 1:320; Gero, *Cannibalism in Zandeland*, 41–42, 178; Meek, *Northern Tribes of Nigeria*, 56–57.
8. For examples, see Gero, *Cannibalism in Zandeland*, 39–40, 50, 66, 77, 111, 114; Hutchinson, *Ten Years Wanderings*, 63–66, 70–73; Junker, *Travels*, 148, 248–49; Knauft, *Exchanging the Past*, 13–14, 56; Knauft, *Good Company and Violence*, 57, 102–3, 118–21, 130–31, 200, 206, 210–11, 407n12; Wallis, *Life in Feejee*, 36–37, 47–49, 75, 92, 147–48, 153–54.
9. For examples, see Hinde, *Fall*, 208; Sutton, "Consuming Counterrevolution," 140–42, 146–50, 153–59, 163–65; Wallis, *Life in Feejee*, 110.
10. For an example, see Hinde, *Fall*, 134–35.
11. For an example, see Moon, *This Horrid Practice*, 135.
12. For examples, see Beatty, *Human Leopards*, 23, 31–32, 45–48, 58–60, 120; Castillo, *True History*, 75–77, 93, 112, 157, 174, 216; Erskine, *Journal,* 454–55, 472–73; Haberberger, *Kolonialismus und Kannibalismus*, 127–31; Harley, *Masks*, 19–20, 25, 28–29.
13. For examples, see Gordon-Grube, "Anthropophagy"; Korn, Radice, and Hawes, *Cannibal*, 90–91; Pettersson, "Cannibalism," 109, 112–18, 121–22, 167–79; Travis-Henikoff, *Dinner with a Cannibal*, 142–43.
14. Petrinovich, *Cannibal Within*, 6; Travis-Henikoff, *Dinner with a Cannibal*, 24.
15. Popular accounts of various cases of antisocial cannibalism can be found in Donnelly and Diehl, *Eat Thy Neighbour*, chapters 5–20, and in Martingale, *Cannibal Killers*.
16. For examples, see Korn, Radice, and Hawes, *Cannibal*, 79–85 (Soviet Union); Pettersson, "Cannibalism," 82–96, 129–59 (China); Simpson, *Cannibalism* (shipwrecked sailors); Tannahill, *Flesh and Blood*, 46–55 (Medieval Europe and Egypt).
17. See Korn, Radice, and Hawes, *Cannibal,* chapter 7.
18. See Simpson, *Cannibalism*, 144–45.
19. Boulestin and Coupey, *Cannibalism,* 120.
20. Petrinovich, *Cannibal Within*, 6.
21. Travis-Henikoff, *Dinner with a Cannibal*, 24.
22. Ibid.
23. Ibid.

CHAPTER 2
SLAVE EATING IN NEW ZEALAND

Slavery is the situation in which human beings are reduced to the status of commodities, of things. Enslaved persons usually had no, or very few, legal rights as persons. How far this rightlessness extended varied over different societies and times. In Ancient Roman law, people had to compensate the owner if they "unlawfully" (without the owner's permission) killed a slave or animal belonging to someone else, but it seems that slaves did not have a right to life that protected them from deadly violence by their owners. Only under emperor Hadrian (ruled 117–38 CE) did it become illegal for "an owner to kill his slave without the judgement of a court."[1]

Even the very limited protections granted to slaves in the later Roman Empire did not necessarily survive in later times. In the transatlantic slave trade, slaves could be thrown overboard with impunity. In 1781, the Liverpool slave ship *Zong* took longer than planned for its journey and "many slaves died or became ill" because of a shortage of water. Over the course of several days, the captain ordered the drowning of more than 130 slaves, who "were chained together and thrown overboard into a watery mass grave," since the "insurance compensation excluded sick slaves or those killed by illness."[2]

Since the insurers refused to pay for the drowned slaves, the case came to court. While the court sided with the insurers, the leading judge, William Murray, the Earl of Mansfield (1705–1793) stated that "they [the judges] had no doubt (though it shocks one very much) that the case of slaves was the same as if horses had been thrown overboard."[3] In 1783, this statement caused a scandal since the abolitionist movement had already become quite influential. In earlier times, similar things had occurred without causing an outcry. Subsequent attempts to prosecute the ship's crew for murder nevertheless came to nothing. While Britain outlawed the transatlantic slave trade in 1807, other European countries were much slower to follow and the deadly practice continued for decades. A petition made in 1825 claimed that "every year about three thousand negroes, men, women, and children" considered too ill or weak for sale were drowned by ship captains.[4]

Regardless of the legal situation, killing a slave was in most cases clearly wasteful: slaves were usually quite valuable commodities, and a dead slave can no longer work. And even when owners had the legal right to kill their slaves, the consumption of a dead slave's body was unthinkable in most regions where slavery was common, due to food taboos preventing the consumption of human flesh. But, while such taboos were widespread, they were by no means universal. In certain regions, where both slavery and cannibalism were accepted practices, slaves were indeed exploited as a source of food. In this and the following chapter we will investigate reports of such practices from the Pacific Ocean. Most of the available accounts come from two specific regions: New Zealand and the Bismarck Archipelago.

Punishment and Consumption of Slaves

In New Zealand, cannibalism occurred most often in the context of war. Dead enemies were eaten, and captives were often killed for this purpose.[5] A detailed analysis of Maori cannibalism, with a focus on war cannibalism, can be found in Paul Moon's book *This Horrid Practice*.

There are also reports of war parties killing and eating random people (unrelated to either of the warring parties) they just happened to encounter—acts explained as due to food scarcity on the march.[6] The ethnologist S. Percy Smith (1840–1922) collected various accounts of war campaigns told by participants. In several cases, the killing and consumption of women and girls spotted during travel is mentioned; convenience and a desire for food, rather than a preexisting hostility, seem to have been the motives.[7]

Most of the reports of war cannibalism are from a period known as "Musket Wars" (ca. 1807–1837), when warfare between Maori groups had become more intense and deadly because of the acquisition of muskets from European traders. Smith recorded a song cursing the "stranger from afar" who brought the "strange and powerful weapons, / That felled the mighty of this land."[8]

Captured enemies were either killed or enslaved; Maori warriors considered proposals to release them as stupid, arguing that they would only seek revenge at a later date.[9] Men were usually butchered and eaten. While many women and children met the same fate—women were often raped before being murdered, and European observers saw children of various ages spit-roasted whole over open fires—others were kept alive as slaves.[10] The Scottish surgeon and historian Arthur S. Thomson (1816–1860) notes that any captives not immediately killed were distributed among the victorious fighters. While slaves were usually captured in war, they were also objects of trade—they could be bought and sold—and sometimes they changed owners when a compensation for an injury was required. Their children became enslaved as well, at least if both parents had this status.[11]

The British artist Augustus Earle (ca. 1793–1838) once observed the return of a successful war party, which arrived by canoe with "quantities of plunder, human heads, human flesh, and many prisoners." The latter were "miserable creatures, women and children, torn by violence from their native homes, henceforth to be the slaves of their conquerors; some were miserably wounded and lacerated, others looked half-starved, but all seemed wretched and dejected." When Earle asked, "what they had done with the male prisoners," one of the warriors "coolly replied, they had all been eaten, except some 'titbits,' which had been packed up in the baskets and brought on shore, in order to regale particular friends and favourites!"[12]

While captives kept as slaves escaped immediate death, they were not always allowed to reach old age. The British merchant Joel Samuel Polack (1807–1882), who settled in the north of New Zealand in 1831 and spent the larger part of the next twenty years in the country, writes: "The victor or master has full power over the life and body of his servant." He adds that "slaves are liable to be put to death on the slightest fault committed by themselves . . . or at the caprice of their masters, in which case they are cut down, immediately dressed, cooked and devoured."[13] Thomson and the English-Australian missionary Samuel Marsden (1765–1838) agree that masters were free to kill their slaves if it pleased them to do so[14] and the politician and anthropologist Te Rangi Hiroa (1877–1951), son of a Maori mother and a white father, observes that slaves "were usually treated with kindness but . . . liable to be drawn upon to supplement the food supply."[15] The American anthropologist Andrew P. Vayda likewise notes that slaves were "liable to be killed in order to serve as a human sacrifice or as the relish in a feast."[16]

Polack reports of two female slaves who suffered this fate near his residence. Shortly after his arrival, a chief[17] named Te Táwoa ordered a "slave to prepare some . . . sweet potatoes" before starting for a "shooting excursion." He stayed away longer than expected; the food got cold and finally the woman ate it herself. She might have considered herself safe because she was his sexual consort, but when Táwoa returned and heard what happened, he "called the hapless woman to him, and without speaking a word, dispatched her with a blow on the forehead with a tomahawk." He invited all his friends, and "the body . . . was dressed, cooked, and on their arrival eaten." Polack heard of this feast from one of the participants, who assured him that the body had been completely consumed.[18]

The other case, Polack learned of from a European trader named Anscow who had been traveling along a nearby river, accompanied by a native crew, and attempting to sell "blankets, powder, and tomahawks." One evening, when he settled in a village for the night, an enslaved girl arrived, aged around fifteen and "remarkably handsome." Upon seeing her, an old woman started to loudly revile the girl, who apparently had been gone for two days "without leave." The woman then asked a man who stood nearby "to kill the girl immediately." Without hesitation, the man went to Anscow's boat, "and seizing one of the tomahawks, which had been brought for barter, he struck the miserable girl a blow on the forehead with the implement that cleft her head in twain." Anscow thought that he might have been able to purchase the girl "for a musket," thus saving her life, but events unfolded so quickly that he did not have time to intervene.[19] So he watched while the body was

> decollated, opened, and the entrails washed and placed in a basket, the limbs cut in pieces at the different joints, attended with circumstances at once horribly disgusting and obscene. The head was thrown to the children as a plaything, and these little miscreants rolled it to and fro, like a ball, thrusting small sticks up the nose, in the mouth, ears, &c. and latterly scooped out the eyes.[20]

Meanwhile, the flesh was washed in the river, "the ovens were heated, some vegetables scraped, and the whole was cooked in a half hour." Some of the flesh was offered to Anscow, "and he was derided for his refusal." Early the next morning, he attempted to leave, no longer caring for the hogs which the villagers had promised him in return for his trade goods. Instead, he packed his goods, including the tomahawk which had been used for the murder. But before he could leave, three villagers entered the boat, bringing with them "the remnants left uneaten of the cooked body, done up in some small baskets, as a present to be conveyed to their friends." Ignoring his protests, they accompanied him during the next part of his trip, until reaching another village where they "landed and carried the food to their friends." Anscow, too shocked to continue his journey, returned to the settlement from which he had started, there meeting Polack and telling him what he had witnessed.[21]

Other visitors had similar experiences. A few years earlier, Augustus Earle had spent nearly a year in New Zealand. He arrived on a ship that anchored near a village in which an English couple, Mr. and Mrs. Butler, had opened a trading post. Taking a "stroll through the village," he soon came around "the remains of a human body which had been roasted, and a number of hogs and dogs were snarling and feasting upon it!" Having already heard of local customs, he was "more shocked than surprised," but he went to Mr. Butler and asked him what had happened. The latter told him that a chief had ordered one of his slave boys "to watch a piece of ground planted with the koomera, or sweet potato, in order to prevent the hogs committing depredations upon it." But the "poor lad" had been distracted by the sight of Earle's ship arriving, ignoring the hogs which "soon made dreadful havoc." When his master saw this, "he instantly killed the unfortunate boy with a blow on the head from his stone hatchet. Then ordered a fire to be made, and the body to be dragged to it, where it was roasted and consumed."[22]

Later Earle settled for some time in a village in the Bay of Islands (near the northernmost tip of New Zealand and not far from where Polack would

Map 2.1. The North Island of New Zealand, showing places and towns (printed in **bold**) mentioned in the text. By the author, based on a map from FreeVectorMaps.com (https://freevectormaps.com/new-zealand/NZ-EPS-02-0001).

later stay) which "belonged to a [young] chief named Atoi."[23] While there Earle employed a local girl, aged about sixteen, for "carrying wood." When Atoi paid a visit, "he recognised [the] girl whom he said was a slave that had run away from him; he immediately seized hold of her" and some of his companions took her away. Earle did not make much of the incident at that time, but the next morning another European settler, Captain Duke, told him "that in the adjoining village a female slave . . . had been put to death, and that the people were at that very time preparing her flesh for cooking." Earle was dismayed when he realized that the victim might have been the girl who had been taken from him.[24]

Immediately they went to the village, where they spotted "a man preparing a native oven. . . . A hole is made in the ground, and hot stones are put within it, and then all is covered up close." Nearby stood a laughing boy, who, upon seeing the Europeans, "pointed towards a bush." In the bush, Earle "discovered a human head," and, to his "horror," he "recognized the features of the unfortunate girl I had seen forced from our village the preceding evening!" Near the oven, they met another man "preparing the four quarters of a human body for a feast; the large bones, having been taken out, were thrown aside, and the flesh being compressed, he was in the act of forcing it into the oven." The man did not seem nervous or embarrassed at being spotted by the Europeans; instead, he calmly told them "that the repast would not be ready for some hours!"[25]

Knowing that Atoi must have ordered this feast, they walked over to his house, "determining to charge [him] with his brutality." Arriving there, Earle "shuddered at beholding the unusual quantity of potatoes his slaves were preparing" for the meal. After initially claiming "that it was only a meal for his slaves," Atoi finally admitted that he would join in the cannibal meal, adding that such feasts were usually hidden from Europeans, who were known to react to them with "horror." But since secrecy had not worked, he promised to talk freely. Asked why the girl had had to die, "he replied, that running away from him . . . was her only crime." He showed them "the post to which she had been tied," explaining with a laugh that he had told her she would merely be flogged, but once she was secured to the post, he "shot her through the heart." Earle could hardly recognize the man whom he had known as "mild and genteel in his demeanour."[26]

Duke and Earle left him and returned to the oven where the girl's remains were roasting. They decided "to spoil this intended feast" and Earle went to call several other white men who stayed nearby, asking them to help.[27] Meanwhile, Atoi arrived with several companions, but they dared not stop the Europeans:

> We . . . dug a tolerably deep grave; then we resolutely attacked the oven. On removing the earth and leaves, the shocking spectacle was presented to our view,—the four quarters of a human body half roasted. . . . We collected all the parts we could recognise; the heart was placed separately, we supposed, as a savoury morsel for the chief himself. We placed the whole in the grave, which we filled up as well as we could, and then broke and scattered the oven.[28]

Afterwards, Earle felt proud of himself and his companions: "Six unarmed men, quite unprotected, . . . had attacked and destroyed all the preparations of the natives for what they consider a national feast," he writes, and yet, "no harm" had come to them. "It plainly shows the influence 'the white men' have already obtained," he concludes. But the next day, "King George," or Shulitea—a powerful regional chief and older relative of Atoi—appeared and dampened his elation. "You did a foolish thing, which might have cost you your lives," he challenged the Europeans, adding that they had accomplished nothing: after they left, the flesh was dug up again "and every bit was eaten"—a statement which Earle later verified, finding the grave empty.[29]

The self-styled king also disputed the Europeans' right to interfere in local traditions, and he forced them to admit that their own customs were not all that different: "'What punishment have you in England for thieves and runaways?' We answered, 'After trial, flogging or hanging.'—'Then,' he replied, 'the only difference in our laws is, you flog and hang, but we shoot and eat.'"[30] Shulitea then explained he had grown up before the introduction of pigs and potatoes[31] in an inland district where fish was unavailable, so "the only food they then had, consisted of fern roots and kumera [sweet potatoes] . . . ; and the only flesh he then partook of was human."[32]

But Earle does not want to write about his tales and justifications: "I will no longer dwell on this humiliating subject," he decides instead. He accepts, however, Shulitea's suggestion that an absence of other meats was the ultimate reason for cannibalism, adding that "nothing will cure the natives of this dreadful propensity but the introduction of many varieties of animals, both wild and tame." Earlier, however, he had mentioned that Atoi had sold four pigs to the Europeans the same evening he took the enslaved girl away to her death, observing that "he had not even the excuse of want of food."[33]

Admittedly, the continuation of a custom might be due to reasons other than those on which it was founded—we will later return to the question of motives and rationales. In the cases reported by Polack and Earle, the killings were always justified by some slight misbehavior of the slave: they had eaten food meant for their master, neglected their duties, left without permission, or tried to run away. Other witnesses describe similar incidents: for example, the Anglican missionary Henry Williams reports that in 1823 an enslaved woman "from Rangihoua, in the Bay of Islands, was killed and eaten for stealing potatoes."[34] These cases also have another thing in common: nearly always, the victim was a woman or a teenage (or possibly younger) girl or boy.

One exception where the victim was a man was recorded by Polack, who once tried to "purchase some hog's lard . . . for a lamp." He was about to buy a "calabash [of] adipose matter," when his young servant told him that it was "man fat." After closer inspection, he was sure that the substance was "neither the fat of dog, pig, nor bird." When he asked the vendor, the latter promptly told him: "It was the fat of a native man—of a slave," further explaining that the man had been executed for "adulterous intercourse with native women" and that his "body had been devoured."[35] Adultery, especially as it seems to have involved several wives of possibly important men, was apparently a sufficiently severe crime to justify the execution of an adult man—but in general they seem to have had a much better chance of being spared than female and juvenile slaves.

Richard A. Cruise, a captain of the British Army, who in early 1820 arrived in the Bay of Islands[36] (where Earle would stay a few years later) and spent the rest of the year in its surroundings, felt that reproaches raised against enslaved women were little more than pretexts for feasts of human flesh. "Instances occurred during our residence among them, and under the eyes of Europeans, of female slaves having been murdered for crimes too trifling to justify such severity," followed by the immediate cutting up, washing, and consumption of their bodies. The last act, he notes, usually took place out of the view of the Europeans—he knew only one sailor who had "witnessed the act of cannibalism" itself, but various missionaries who had seen its "immediate prelude."[37]

One specific case he mentions took place in the Bay of Plenty (in the east of the North Island). An enslaved woman had cursed her master for mistreating her. Immediately, and right in front of the house of a European settler, "he walked up to her, and with one blow of his mearée (or club) laid her dead at his feet." The body was then taken to a nearby "pool of fresh water" where "the entrails were taken out, it was divided into quarters, and washed perfectly clean. The chief [her master] then threw it into a canoe, and, with some of his tribe, crossed over to a neighbouring island to devour it." Several missionaries witnessed these events and later told Cruise about them.[38]

Cases Not Motivated as Punishment

In the cases discussed so far, the killing and consumption of slaves was explained as a reaction to a minor or not-so-minor misbehavior on their part. In other cases, it is unclear whether such a cause—or pretext—existed. In 1821, the Wesleyan missionary Samuel Leigh (1785–1852) met a man who was in the process of cooking a boy whose age Leigh estimated to be around fourteen. He saw the victim's body, which was complete, except for the head, and already "half roasted." In the nearby village, he "found a great number of natives seated in a circle, with a quantity of coomery [sweet potatoes] before them, waiting for the roasted body of the youth." They told him that the boy was a slave who had been killed for the occasion—if he had somehow misbehaved to provoke such an act, they did not say so.[39]

Leigh adds that he "prevailed on them to give up the body to be interred, and thus prevented them from gratifying their unnatural appetite."[40] It is unclear whether he was more successful in this attempt than Earle would be a few years later. In a similar case, the missionary Nathaniel Turner saw in 1823 "a cookey [slave] stretched out and partly roasted."[41]

In another case, relayed to Joel Polack by a trader who was nearby when it occurred, a man from the Waikato area (in the west of the North Island), "ordered a young female slave to make a very large oven, as he intended to regale his friends with a feast." Having done so, she "enquired what provisions should be put in; he peremptorily ordered herself to go into it." She pleaded with him, but to no avail: "the relentless wretch seized her, lashed her hands and knees together, and threw her in the oven alive. After the body was cooked, it was devoured by this monster and his friends."[42] No justification other than a desire "to regale his friends" is given. The claim of live cooking might sound too cruel to be believed, but there are other accounts of this practice. The English explorer and painter George French Angas (1822–1886) met a local chief who "boast[ed] of having roasted slave children alive, and then partaken of their flesh,"[43] and several sources mention that captives were occasionally roasted alive after battles.[44]

R. Skinner, the captain of the ship on which Richard Cruise traveled, did not believe that slaves' misbehaviors were responsible for them being killed: "There indeed appears not the smallest doubt but they frequently kill what they term their slaves, or persons taken in war, for the sole purpose of eating them," he writes, adding that "there were two or three instances of their eating human flesh while we were laying at the Bay of Islands."[45] That young children and babies were among the eaten also indicates such acts were not always meant as punishments. Polack reports that one of his acquaintances, a local chief, had a healthy appetite—so healthy, in fact, that he once consumed "nearly . . . a [whole] baby at a meal, without any after complaint of inconvenience and indigestion."[46] In his account of the conquest of the Chatham Islands by a group of Maori who killed or enslaved the Indigenous Moriori population, the politician and anthropologist Edward Tregear (1846–1931) mentions that one of their "leading chiefs" ordered six enslaved children to be slaughtered and cooked for a single meal held "to regale his friends."[47]

Generally, it seems that there were cases where the desire to give a feast, or celebrate a special event, was the primary motive for the consumption of slaves—though it is quite possible that those who had formerly displeased their owners stood a higher risk of being sacrificed at such occasions. According to the ethnographer Elsdon Best (1856–1931), in the eastern regions of the North Island a slave was sometimes killed for the "tattooing of a young woman of rank"—an important coming-of-age ceremony—"and the flesh of the hapless victim [was] the principal dish of the ritual feast." Best adds that he could not find any "religious significance" in the act—the body was simply "used as food," as some of the people who adhered to this custom explained it.[48] His account is confirmed by Te Rangi Hiroa, who writes: "Sometimes slaves or other persons were killed and baked on special occasions such as the tattooing of a high chief's daughter, a chiefly marriage, or the funeral of a high chief."[49]

The consumption of slaves at festive occasions might have been more common before the introduction of the pig, when—besides people—dogs, rats, and birds were the only sources of meat.[50] When Polack visited a *hahunga*—an exhumation ceremony held annually in honor of the dead[51]—at which a considerable number of pigs were served, he heard that formerly it had been usual to "sacrifice slaves" for the occasion, but that, due to "the scarcity in the slave-market of late years (their services being at a premium), the multitude are restricted from this much-esteemed food, and are now obliged to felicitate themselves on *only* a bit of pork."[52]

During the period of the Musket Wars, more persons were enslaved than in earlier times, but there was also an increased demand for slaves who were frequently employed to cultivate and dress flax for sale—often to Europeans.[53] It is therefore quite possible that they became more valuable, and owners preferred to exploit them for work purposes rather than sacrifice them for food, as Polack suggests. But it must also be remembered that pigs had not been known on the North Island until the turn of the century, and dogs and rats might have been considered too small and unpretentious to form the main course at important celebrations.

Samuel Marsden, who in 1815 opened the first Christian mission in New Zealand (in Rangihoua Bay, a smaller bay within the Bay of Islands), states: "I have heard of slaves being killed in cool blood as well as in moments of revengeful anger. One young woman was killed and eaten when I was there at this time, near my lodgings." In this context, "in cool blood" seems to mean an unprovoked murder, as opposed to one triggered by "anger" over a slave's perceived misbehavior. He adds: "When the chiefs return from battle and have any particular cause for rejoicing or mourning, they will kill a slave or slaves and eat them."[54]

In one case witnessed by several members of the Anglican mission at Kerikeri (today the largest town in Northland, the most northern of New Zealand's regions) "some slaves were killed and eaten" when Hongi Hika (ca. 1772–1828), the leader of the Ngāpuhi people (who live around the Hokianga estuary in the north of the North Island), returned from a successful war campaign.[55] And in a letter written in February 1822, Samuel Leigh states: "Hongi-Hika and his party have killed more than 20 slaves since their return from war . . . , most of whom they have roasted and eaten."[56] It is unclear whether this refers to the same incident—Leigh's Wesleyan mission was located at Kaeo, about twenty kilometers northwest of Kerikeri.

Polack also mentions the feasts held by Hongi Hika and his commanders, for which "many of those doomed creatures [slaves] were slaughtered and cooked."[57] Jacky Marmon (ca. 1800–1880), an Australian sailor, who deserted his ship in 1824 and from then on lived among the Maori of Hokianga,[58] freely admits to having eaten the flesh of slaves. He first did so at a feast held in honor of Hongi Hika for which several enslaved women had been butchered. Later he remembered that their flesh, "as served up by the Maori cooks was very passable. When chopped up with kumeras and potatoes it resembles a rather fatty stew."[59]

Slaves were not only eaten to celebrate victories, they were sometimes also taken along for war campaigns to provide food for the hungry warriors, as Andrew Vayda notes.[60] A group of Europeans sailors once saw how a successful war party on their way back home "killed a girl of their own party and ate her."[61] It seems likely that the girl was a slave or captive, as the warriors would certainly not have murdered one of their own daughters.

Earle estimates that a slave was more likely to be killed and "devoured by his brutal master" than to die a natural death—in the latter case, the body was not eaten, but "dragged to the outside of the village, there to be made sport of by the children, or to furnish food for the dogs." He also notes that it was not rare for slaves to be "sacrificed on the death of a chief."[62] He does not say whether those sacrificed at such occasions were consumed, but Percy Smith records the oral account of an unnamed Ngāpuhi warrior who said that, after the death of an important chief in a war campaign, "we conquered and took many slaves, with whom we returned to the place where our chief who had been speared lay, and there killed all the slaves as food for the mourners."[63]

Motives and Origins

Why were slaves eaten in New Zealand? The phenomenon probably cannot be understood in isolation from war cannibalism, especially since slaves were usually enemies taken in war. Moon argues that many wars among Maori groups can be understood as parts of an ongoing blood feud or vendetta. Eating one's enemies was considered necessary for retribution: if some members of your community had ended in the ovens, you had to kill and eat some persons from the offending community to make up for it. Consuming one's enemies was also a purposeful act of degradation and humiliation: they were deliberately treated like animals and literally reduced to feces.[64]

Moon also notes that war parties had to live off the land through which they moved, which usually meant a meager and meatless diet. By deciding to treat enemies as a source of food, warriors could alleviate this scarcity. Moreover, eating defeated enemies might have been "a satisfying opportunity to gorge on the piles of meat that were part of the spoils of war." This opportunity emerged only through the acceptance of cannibalism, which turned the bodies of dead enemies, as well as captives not considered useful for other purposes or thought too dangerous to keep alive, into exploitable resources.[65]

But when cannibalism was driven by a desire to overcome food scarcity or to make better use of dead bodies for which no personal sympathy was felt, it was no longer necessarily limited to hated enemies. Indeed, there are reports of war parties killing and eating random people from other communities they happened to encounter, giving food scarcity while on the march as motivation.[66] War might have helped to spread the idea that the consumption of others was acceptable—not just of enemies, but indeed of anybody who did not belong to one's own community.

Moon conjectures that cannibalism might originally have been a "ritualised, quasi-religious custom" directed only against enemies one wanted to humiliate.[67] Arthur Thomson mentions this humiliating effect as well, noting that it was still deeply felt in later times: being eaten was considered the ultimate disgrace, and claiming that someone's father had been eaten was a terrible offense.[68] Moon continues, however, that over time the consumption of others became widely accepted and evolved into a "simply expedient measure to supplement a slender range of food—as an occasional luxury." He concludes from the available information that in precolonial Maori society, cannibalism was regarded as "morally acceptable" and "perfectly normal," as long as no relatives were eaten. Being able to slaughter slaves or captives in order to regale one's friends and relatives was seen as a sign of wealth and generosity (rather than of criminal depravity, as it would be in the West).[69]

The status effect of cannibalism might also explain why such acts were not considered too wasteful—a dead slave, after all, can no longer work. But by showing that they could afford such a waste, individuals and communities could expose their wealth or military strength—insofar as slaves were often captured in wars rather than being purchased—in a striking manner. Such acts occurred, but it is also clear that they were relatively rare. The consumption of slaves seems to have been restricted to two situations: rare festive occasions such as coming-of-age or exhumation ceremonies as well as cases where a slave had supposedly misbehaved and was killed and eaten as punishment. Acts of punitive cannibalism were probably also targeted at the remaining enslaved population, showing them what might happen if they displeased their masters.

Hiroa agrees with Moon that "human flesh was eaten when procurable," without such acts requiring any specific justification.[70] Cruise reports that the locals he knew unhesitatingly talked about their cannibal customs, repeatedly expressing "their predilection for human flesh."[71] And Marsden notes that the Maori he spoke to practiced cannibalism without any sense of wrongdoing and "appear to have no idea that it is an unnatural crime." They were "surprised" when he "informed them that this was a custom unknown in Europe, and considered there as a great disgrace to the nation which practises it."[72]

Cannibalism was also considered justified by tradition. Shulitea reproached Earle for trying to prevent his relative Atoi and the latter's friends from eating the flesh of an executed enslaved girl, declaring: "It was an old custom, which their fathers practised before them; and you had no right to interfere with their ceremonies."[73] And acknowledging that things would have to change, but not yet willing to do so, Hongi Hika stated: "We are only following the institutions of our forefathers, which we cannot as yet relinquish. Our forefathers ate human flesh and taught us to do so."[74]

It seems that such traditions varied considerably between the northern and southern parts of New Zealand, since all specific examples of slave eating come from the North Island, and most from its northern regions. In the south, the practice was, if not unknown, then certainly much rarer than in the north. War cannibalism, on the other hand, was practiced in the South Island, though it may have been rarer than in the North Island.[75] The difference between north and south may be explained, at least in part, by the fact that slavery itself was much less common in the South Island.[76] Another factor that might have played a role is the disappearance of large edible animals, which happened quicker and more thoroughly in the north, as Anne Salmond points out. She notes that moas (huge flightless birds that could reach a weight of up to 230 kilograms) as well as elephant seals and leopard seals had become scarce in the South Island and largely extinct in the North Island in the fourteenth century; various other bird species had already disappeared completely. In the fifteenth century, more species died out or became very rare.[77]

The reasons are not entirely clear, but human behaviors such as hunting, the clearance of forests, and the introduction of dogs and rats are thought to be among the most important factors, though natural climate change might also have played a role. Around 1500, people on both islands started to build fortified villages (known as *pā*), warfare intensified, and "evidence of cannibalism begins to appear" in the archaeological record.[78] The archaeological evidence thus confirms that cannibalism was indeed a long-established practice and indicates that food scarcity—or more specifically a shrinking supply of edible animals—might have been a relevant factor in the emergence of the custom.

The consumption of people did not, however, start only after the complete extermination of large animals such as moas. Archaeologists found burnt bones of humans, moas, and dogs all intermingled in or near to ovens and middens, showing that both human and animal carcasses were prepared for consumption at approximately the same time, with their inedible remainders discarded as garbage in the same way.[79] If at that time people had only been eaten in the ritual context of revenge after war campaigns, it seems likely that human and animal remains would have been more clearly separated in the archaeological record, but this is not the case. Rather it seems that already before the full extinction of the moas, captives or slaves were treated similar to edible animals, being brought into or near to settlements and there butchered and dressed for consumption.

Salmond's observation that many animal species, especially the larger ones, quickly became rare or extinct, nevertheless makes it plausible that heightened competition over scarcer resources lead not only to increased warfare but also sparked the notion that killed or captured enemies could themselves be utilized as edible matter. An alternative conjecture is that some of the earliest Maori settlers, who arrived from eastern Polynesia in the thirteenth century,[80] were already accustomed to the consumption of human flesh. This has been proposed by Hiroa, who notes that "human flesh was eaten for its food value" in various Polynesian islands and therefore considers it "probable that some, at least, of the Maori ancestors brought the taste with them to New Zealand."[81]

This too is conceivable: while there is no archaeological evidence of cannibal practices in the thirteenth and fourteenth century, this does not prove that the practice did not exist at the time; maybe it merely left no traces which have been found. The rapid shrinkage of the animal population after the arrival of the first settlers might nevertheless have caused a practice which in earlier times was rare (if not unknown) to become more widespread and customary.

Hiroa acknowledges this too, writing that "the absence of pigs and the limited supply of dog's flesh may have been additional factors in inducing the Maoris to satisfy their hunger for meat with human flesh."[82] Shulitea, as we have seen, also pointed to the absence of animal meat as a reason for cannibalism, explaining (possibly with some exaggeration) that, before the introduction of the pig, "the only flesh" available to him and his compatriots "was human."[83] Before he heard this explanation, Earle had already observed a "total absence of quadrupeds"—though contrasted by an "abundance of birds"—and speculated that "to this dearth of animals may be attributed the chief cause of their ferocity, and propensity to cannibalism."[84]

Also noted by several witnesses is a clear preference for the taste of human flesh. In the Bay of Islands, Captain Skinner met people who spoke "with delight of eating human flesh, and appear to admire the flavour," leading him to conclude: "I really believe they prefer it to other food."[85] A European sailor who in 1829 witnessed the beheading and consumption of enemies captured in a battle came to the same conclusion: "They cut off the heads of the prisoners they had taken, then cleaned and washed the interior of the bodies and afterwards cooked them. The avidity shown by these savages, men and women, in that horrible repast, persuaded me that they preferred human flesh to all other."[86]

James Burns, a European who had permanently settled among Maori, says that "the natives find the smell [of human flesh being roasted] delicious."[87] And according to Thomson, the superior taste of human flesh over "that of all other animals" was proverbial among various Maori groups.[88] It is unclear whether this preference helped to spread the acceptance of cannibalism or whether it was a result of the latter becoming "perfectly normal"[89]—indeed, both attitudes might have supported each other.

It is notable that in most cases where personal details of eaten slaves are given, the victims were women or teenage or younger children. Why this was so is not—to my knowledge—explicitly addressed in the sources, except that some mention that the flesh of such victims was considered tastier than that of men. Cruise states that "the limbs only of a man are [considered] eatable, while, with the exception of the head, the whole body of a female or a child is considered delicious."[90] Nearly two centuries later, Carole Travis-Henikoff interviewed a Maori who told her that, according to his great-grandfather, "the hands and arms of young children made for the best eating."[91]

Even assuming that such preferences were real and not just a way of justifying the consumption of such victims, they can hardly be the whole story. Generally, it seems that gender distinctions were less clear-cut in Maori society than in Europe or in many of the highly patriarchal societies we will encounter in subsequent chapters. Both women and men played important roles in *whanau* (kin groups or extended families) and "Maori cosmology abounds with stories of powerful women."[92] Occasionally women became "tribal leaders," though more "often a woman's authority would be exercised by her husband or by male relatives."[93] The recklessness with which enslaved women and children were sacrificed for the culinary pleasure of their owners nevertheless indicates that their status must have been extremely low, even lower than that of adult male slaves who are rarely mentioned as victims.

Another theoretical possibility is that there were hardly any adult male slaves—after all, captured men were usually killed outright, while women and children were often enslaved.[94] But, aside from the fact that enslaved men are occasionally mentioned in sources,[95] this poses a logical problem: boys were evidently enslaved, so what happened to them once they grew up? They were certainly not freed—manumission seems to have been unknown in New Zealand—and while some of them were murdered and consumed, there are no hints that enslaved boys were systematically killed in order to prevent them from reaching adulthood.

In subsequent chapters we will see that in various societies the consumption of human flesh was predominately a male privilege. There is some disagreement on whether this was also the case in New Zealand. Hiroa writes that "most tribes . . . prohibited women from eating human flesh" and Thomson claims that "women were not permitted to eat human flesh," except in rare circumstances.[96] Vayda also concludes that women were in many regions not supposed to eat human flesh, but adds that this rule did not exist everywhere and that it seemingly was not always strictly adhered to even where it existed.[97] According to the ethnographer John White (1826–1891), in some places "a distinction was made between the flesh of enemies killed in battle and the flesh of slaves killed outside of war. Women could eat the latter but not the former."[98] The European sailor quoted above observed that both "men and women" ate human flesh with "avidity."[99]

It is noteworthy that in one of incidents relayed by Polack, it was an "old decrepid [*sic*] chief woman"—as he calls her—who ordered an enslaved girl to be killed for consumption.[100] In all other cases where a person responsible for such a deed is identified, it was a man. Polack does not state whether the old woman joined in the subsequent meal, but it sounds plausible. And when Samuel Leigh witnessed the cooking of an enslaved boy, one of those waiting for the meal was pointed out to him as the mother of the murdered child—he was told that she was obliged to join in the feast (possibly to prevent her from cursing the eaters?). It is not quite clear whether the rest of the potential eaters was mixed or all-male, but Leigh talks about "people" (rather than "men") and might arguably have mentioned it had she been the only woman in the group.[101]

All in all, it seems that, while customs varied between different regions, in Maori society cannibalism was less clearly associated with maleness than in some other societies we will encounter.

A negative result is also worth pointing out: some have conjectured that cannibal acts might have been motivated by a belief in the magical transmission of characteristics between eaten and eater, a belief that eating someone will make you as intelligent, strong, courageous, etc., as they were. However, Hiroa, Moon, and Thomson all agree that cannibalism in New Zealand was not motivated by a desire to acquire the eaten person's physical or spiritual properties.[102] We will later see that this negative result is also true of other regions where practices such as slave eating or foreigner poaching existed.

Notes

1. J. Gardner, "Slavery and Roman Law," 416, 433.
2. Thomas, *Slave Trade,* chapter 25; Shillington, *Encyclopedia*, 1376.
3. Quoted in Thomas, *Slave Trade*, chapter 25.
4. Quoted in Lang, *Land*, 215.
5. See, for example, Beaglehole, *Voyage*, 291–95, 818–19; Dillon, *Narrative*, 218–25, 233–35, 256; Earle, *Narrative*, 43–48n, 195–98; McNab, *Historical Records*, 1:307, 310–12, 398–99, 695, 697, 2:217–18, 283, 329, 401–3, 439; Polack, *New Zealand*, 1:166–68, 2:298–99, 317–20; Rickman, *Journal*, 59–66; Smith, *Maori Wars* (numerous references); Surville, *Extracts*, 40, 129, 166–67, 189–90; Tregear, *Maori Race*, 35, 328–29, 356–60; Vayda, *Maori Warfare*, 70–72, 79–80, 90–95, 104–5.
6. Moon, *This Horrid Practice*, 135.
7. Smith, *Maori Wars*, 64, 66, 100–2, 348.
8. Ibid., 400.
9. Moon, *This Horrid Practice*, 158–60; Vayda, *Maori Warfare*, 90–91.
10. McNab, *Old Whaling Days*, 44; Moon, *This Horrid Practice*, 142; Polack, *New Zealand*, 2:299; Smith, *Maori Wars*, 180; Vayda, *Maori Warfare*, 91–92.
11. Thomson, *Story*, 148–49. Thomson authored New Zealand's "first major written history" and has been called a "keen observ[er] of politics and race relations" (Te Ara—Encyclopedia of New Zealand, "Thomson, Arthur Saunders," accessed 9 September 2020, https://teara.govt.nz/en/biographies/1t95/thomson-arthur-saunders).
12. Earle, *Narrative*, 196–97.
13. Polack, *New Zealand*, 2:4, 105.
14. "No law or public opinion existed relative to the treatment of slaves," since according to the general "mode of reasoning," they had already forfeited their lives the moment they (or their ancestors) were captured (Thomson, *Story*, 149). "A slave has no security for his life. His master kills him whenever he pleases, and treats him in any way his passions may dictate" (Marsden, *Letters and Journals*, 386–87).
15. Hiroa, *Coming*, 402.
16. Vayda, *Maori Warfare*, 105.

17. The word *chief* is frequently used in older Western texts for local rulers, leaders, and influential men. In modern usage, it has often been replaced by more specific terms, such as *rangatira* in New Zealand or *big man* in Melanesia and Polynesia. Referring to Africa, the Ghanaian philosopher Kwasi Wiredu notes that the term *chief*, "though tainted with colonial condescension, has remained in general use even in the post-independence era by dint of terminological inertia" (Wiredu, *Cultural Universals and Particulars*, 184). In this book, the term is generally kept when it occurs in primary sources. Arbitrarily replacing it with alternative expressions could be misleading, since it is often unclear which exact role or function those termed *chief* actually had.
18. Polack, *New Zealand*, 2:4 (quotes), 5.
19. Ibid., 5–6.
20. Ibid., 6.
21. Ibid., 6–7.
22. Earle, *Narrative*, 12–14.
23. Ibid., 100.
24. Ibid., 112–13 (quotes), 117 (girl's age).
25. Ibid., 113–14.
26. Ibid., 115–17.
27. Ibid., 117, 118 (quote).
28. Ibid., 119.
29. Ibid., 53–54, 100 (on King George), 120–21 (quotes).
30. Ibid., 121.
31. Pigs and potatoes were first introduced to southern New Zealand in the 1770s by James Cook (1728–1779), the famous British captain and explorer. Around the turn of the century, they had reached the North Island and the Bay of Islands in its north. Cattle and horses arrived only in 1814 (Te Ara—Encyclopedia of New Zealand, "Kai Pākehā—Introduced Foods: Early Introductions," last modified 24 November 2008, https://teara.govt.nz/en/kai-pakeha-introduced-foods/page-1).
32. Earle, *Narrative*, 121–22.
33. Ibid., 115, 122.
34. Moon, *This Horrid Practice*, 97. For another case, see Cruise's account below.
35. Polack, *New Zealand*, 1:236–37. Polack also observes that human bones were used to make flutes, and that bones and teeth were used to decorate earrings (ibid., 184, 394–95).
36. Cruise, *Journal*, 5, 18.
37. Ibid., 287.
38. Ibid., 97. Ensign McCrae, a British soldier who served in the same regiment as Cruise, also described this incident (quoted in McNab, *Historical Records*, 1:539).
39. Leigh quoted in McNab, *Historical Records*, 1:574.
40. Ibid.
41. Quoted in Moon, *This Horrid Practice*, 97 (insertion in original.)
42. Polack, *New Zealand*, 2:320.
43. Angas, *Savage Life*, 235.
44. The ethnographer Elsdon Best notes that "cases are on record in which enemy prisoners were cooked alive . . . in a prepared, heated, steaming pit" (Best, *Maori*, 70). The Anglican missionary Henry Williams witnessed "how, in the heightened

frenzy of post-battle butchery, . . . some captured chiefs were actually thrown in the huge ovens whilst still alive" (Moon, *This Horrid Practice*, 102).

45. Quoted in McNab, *Historical Records*, 1:496.
46. Polack, *New Zealand*, 2:274 (italics removed).
47. Tregear, *Maori Race*, 357.
48. Best, *Maori*, 555.
49. Hiroa, *Coming*, 102.
50. Te Ara—Encyclopedia of New Zealand, "Kai Pākehā—Introduced Foods," last modified 24 November 2008, https://teara.govt.nz/en/kai-pakeha-introduced-foods.
51. Polack, *New Zealand*, 1:214; Te Ara—Encyclopedia of New Zealand, "Tangihanga—Death Customs: The Tangihanga Process," last modified 5 May 2011, https://teara.govt.nz/en/tangihanga-death-customs/page-4.
52. Polack, *New Zealand*, 1:225 (emphasis in original).
53. Te Ara—Encyclopedia of New Zealand, "Kai Pākehā—Introduced Foods: Pigs and Potatoes," last modified 24 November 2008, https://teara.govt.nz/en/kai-pakeha-introduced-foods/page-2.
54. Marsden, *Letters and Journals*, 409.
55. Ibid., 147 (on Kerikeri), 408 (quote).
56. Quoted in Smith, *Maori Wars*, 226.
57. Polack, *New Zealand*, 2:182.
58. T. Bentley, *Pakeha Maori*, 42–43.
59. Quoted ibid., 104.
60. Vayda, *Maori Warfare*, 80.
61. McNab, *Old Whaling Days*, 292.
62. Earle, *Narrative*, 124–25.
63. Quoted in Smith, *Maori Wars*, 108.
64. Moon, *This Horrid Practice*, 139–40.
65. Ibid., 135.
66. Ibid.
67. Ibid.
68. Thomson, *Story*, 146.
69. Moon, *This Horrid Practice*, 128, 134. Among the evidence considered by Moon is one of the three principal Maori myth cycles whose focus is a cannibal goddess, Whaitiri. The myth indicates that it is wrong to eat relatives (even if by mistake), but that the killing and eating of enemies and slaves is fine (ibid., 120–21).
70. Hiroa, *Coming*, 102.
71. Cruise, *Journal*, 286.
72. Quoted in McNab, *Historical Records*, 1:398–99.
73. Quoted in Earle, *Narrative*, 121.
74. Quoted in Marsden, *Letters and Journals*, 407.
75. Moon, *This Horrid Practice*, 89–90, 98.
76. One British settler estimated that half of the population of the North Island were enslaved, compared to less than ten percent in the South (Petrie, *Outcasts*, 84).
77. Salmond, *Two Worlds*, 39.
78. Ibid.
79. Moon, *This Horrid Practice*, 113, 115.
80. Te Ara—Encyclopedia of New Zealand, "Māori: Pre-European society," last modified 8 February 2005, https://teara.govt.nz/en/maori/page-2.

81. Hiroa, *Coming*, 102.
82. Ibid. Elsewhere he states about war cannibalism: "Without wishing to condone the practice, it must be borne in mind that there was a serious meat shortage in New Zealand before cattle, pigs, and sheep were introduced by Europeans. Hence it is not surprising that the Maori should have utilized what the battlefield provided" (ibid., 400).
83. Earle, *Narrative,* 122.
84. Ibid., 71–72.
85. Quoted in McNab, *Historical Records*, 1:496.
86. Quoted in Smith, *Maori Wars*, 414.
87. Quoted in Moon, *This Horrid Practice*, 136. Burns, who seems to have repeatedly witnessed the preparation of human flesh, describes the usual procedure as follows: "First, they separate the head, arms and legs from the trunk, draw out the entrails then roast the body exactly like the body of a pig, by filling it with stones heated in the fire. The limbs are roasted separately" (quoted ibid.).
88. Thomson, *Story*, 147.
89. Moon, *This Horrid Practice*, 128.
90. Cruise, *Journal*, 286.
91. Quoted in Travis-Henikoff, *Dinner with a Cannibal*, 109.
92. Mikaere, "Maori Women."
93. Te Ara—Encyclopedia of New Zealand, "Tūranga i te hapori—Status in Māori Society: Class, Status and Rank," last modified 5 May 2011, https://teara.govt.nz/en/turanga-i-te-hapori-status-in-maori-society/page-1.
94. See the section "Punishment and Consumption of Slaves" in this chapter.
95. For example, Earle, *Narrative*, 124.
96. Hiroa, *Coming,* 102; Thomson, *Story*, 145.
97. Vayda, *Maori Warfare*, 70–71.
98. Ibid., 71, referring to White.
99. Quoted in Smith, *Maori Wars*, 414.
100. Polack, *New Zealand*, 2:5 (quote), 6; see section "Punishment and Consumption of Slaves" for more context.
101. Quoted in McNab, *Historical Records*, 1:574.
102. Hiroa, *Coming*, 401; Moon, *This Horrid Practice*, 157; Thomson, *Story*, 147.

CHAPTER 3
SLAVE EATING IN THE BISMARCK ARCHIPELAGO AND SUMATRA

The Bismarck Archipelago

The consumption of enslaved persons is also documented in the Bismarck Archipelago, a group of dozens of islands which today belongs to Papua New Guinea. Sources from this region show some similarities but also clear differences with the situation in New Zealand. While the inhabitants of New Zealand all shared the same language—Maori—and had many cultural traits in common, Papua New Guinea is home to more than eight hundred languages representing a huge variety of peoples with often quite distinct lifestyles.[1]

Cannibalism was practiced by some, but by no means by all of these peoples, and among those who practiced it, customs governing who could be eaten and under which circumstances varied enormously. We will later see that foreigners could be "poached" and eaten in certain parts of New Guinea, the largest island in the region,[2] but no cases of slave eating have been reported from this island (to my knowledge). In the neighboring Bismarck Archipelago, most references to both slave trade and slave eating come from one specific region, namely the Gazelle Peninsula in the northeast of New Britain, the largest island of the archipelago.

From around 1884 to 1919, both northeastern New Guinea and the archipelago were claimed by Germany as a colony. Some years earlier, in 1882, the German branch of the Catholic Missionaries of the Sacred Heart of Jesus had set up its first mission station in New Britain (which was called *Neu-Pommern* at that time). One of the missionaries, Matthäus Rascher (1868–1904), notes that the inhabitants of the coastal regions of the peninsula captured many of the Baining people, who lived in the mountainous interior. Captives were either kept as slaves or killed and eaten; those killed in attacks were eaten as well. At special risk were small groups of Baining who had come to the coast in order to catch fish or to fetch limestone or salt water. Occasionally,

Map 3.1. The Bismarck Archipelago and eastern New Guinea (today's Papua New Guinea). Ethnic groups mentioned in the text are shown in *italics,* towns in **bold**. By the author, based on Wikimedia Commons (https://commons.wikimedia.org/wiki/File:Un-papua-new-guinea.svg).

however, whole villages were raided and both pigs and people taken away as bounty.[3]

Rascher reports that in a particularly large attack in September 1896, a group of Baining people were enticed by a promise of trade into visiting a nearby bay. Dozens of young, strong men were tricked into approaching the canoes of the attackers; suddenly, they were drawn into the canoes which immediately left, taking the Baining (who could not swim) with them. Those left behind were attacked by a group of fighters who had hidden in the bush; nearly all of them were killed. Rascher estimates that about fifty people were murdered, while about thirty young men were enslaved. Some of the killed were cut to pieces and distributed among the attackers, while the corpses of others were tied to poles and transported to the villages of the slavers for later consumption. To make escape impossible, the newly captured slaves were transported to Massava and Massikonapuka, two small islands north of the Gazelle Peninsula. Several of those killed were roasted and eaten on these islands in direct view of the captives.[4]

Rascher's mission station was on the coast near these islands, and he heard of these events from the slavers themselves. When he asked them if they had not felt pity for their victims, they told him that, "no, it was no big deal, since it had only been done to Baining people." They also implied that their victims were "so stupid" that they deserved what they got.[5] During his talks with the shore dwellers, Rascher found that they tended to regard the Baining as mere "animal[s], born without rights and only good for work. . . . They regard themselves as real people, as rich and clever people, because they . . . own boats, fish and especially tambu [shell money], while the Baining people have nothing of all this."[6]

This justification of both slavery and cannibalism due to one's own superiority and an outspoken disdain for the victimized people is something that seems specific to the region, with no known equivalents in New Zealand. In subsequent chapters we will occasionally hear similar statements from certain parts of Africa.

In common with New Zealand, on the other hand, was the notion of cannibalism as something self-evident and uncontroversial. While resting at a spring, Rascher's local companions told him that they used to wash the *virua*—the bodies of the slain—at this place. While they said that they no longer practiced cannibalism because of "the fear of the [colonial] judge and the difficulty of getting human flesh without attracting attention," they did not see anything bad or reprehensible in the custom.[7]

Albert Hahl (1868–1945), who from 1896 served as a colonial judge in the Gazelle Peninsula and later became the last governor of German New Guinea, observed that cannibalism was so ingrained in local customs that even people who had spent a long time among Europeans expected captives to be killed and eaten. Once he drew a little girl out of a battle zone to prevent one of his companions from killing her with an ax. Seeing this, "a boy, who had already spent nine years in the service of whites, exclaimed . . . : 'Sir, fine, I'll cook her, she'll make a good meal.'"[8]

In colonial times, though cannibalism could no longer take place as openly as earlier, Baining were still occasionally killed and eaten in the proximity of Rascher's mission. In 1897, a six-year-old who served as an altar boy in the mission church revealed that the day before he had eaten of the bodies of two Baining who had been spotted near the coast and killed with a spear by one of the men of the village. Another boy later confirmed the incident, which the adults had tried to keep secret from the Europeans.[9]

Rascher notes that in many attacks directed against groups of Baining people, including the large raid described above, unrelated Baining supported the shore dwellers as allies. The Baining themselves did not keep slaves, but practiced cannibalism when given the chance, and claimed some of the dead bodies as a reward.[10]

According to Rascher, slaves had been frequently butchered for feasts on the coast of the peninsula until a short time before his arrival in the region (in 1895). He claims that, according to local tradition, every sufficiently wealthy family was expected to slaughter one or more slaves in the spring and fall to regale their neighbors. The emerging trade with Europeans weakened this tradition; because of a higher demand for workers, more Baining were enslaved than ever before, and those who were useful workers now had a better chance of staying alive. Those captured in raids who were unable or unwilling to work, however, were still killed and eaten without further ado, as one of Rascher's confreres observed during his travels through the country.[11]

Rascher's informants told him that old people encountered in slave raids were usually killed and eaten—the men immediately, while the women were often raped before their death. Younger victims had a better chance of being left alive and sold into slavery, though there were some "archcannibals" who had all captive children slaughtered, seemingly enjoying their flesh more than the money they might otherwise have earned. As in New Zealand, women's flesh was considered better than that of men; brains were valued as special delicacies. Human flesh—like meat in general—was roasted between hot stones, then consumed together with taro and other vegetables.[12]

According to the British traveler Herbert Cayley-Webster, the flesh of slaves was still commonly served at feasts when he visited the Gazelle Peninsula in the 1890s. He met chiefs who told him, with evident pride, "how they have enjoyed their feast on the previous evening, which had been some portion of a human being." Some of them, he claims, butchered "every few days" one of their slaves "to satisfy their diabolical tastes."[13]

While this sounds exaggerated, the fact that slaves were sacrificed for feasts was also confirmed by liberated slaves themselves. When Albert Hahl became a judge, he declared slavery forbidden and postulated that all slaves be released. Since the slave owners ignored his request, he traveled through his district to liberate the slaves. While he was not usually very successful (the owners hid their slaves when he came), at Watom, a small island north of the Gazelle Peninsula, he forced a chief to free six young male slaves. One of them told Hahl that the slaves "had to work hard all the time," and also lived in constant fear for their lives: "When there was a big feast, the plumpest slaves were selected, killed and devoured." Other liberated slaves reported the same.[14]

Father A. Kleintitschen, who belonged to the same congregation as Rascher, notes that "the little Baining children" captured on the north coast of the peninsula usually did not survive for long because they were considered "choice delicacies." In 1890, he adds, the mission sent a boat along the coast in order to purchase and rescue enslaved children, but they managed to acquire only one four-year-old girl. "The shore dwellers regretted that they had not come earlier. A month ago they still would have had a lot of children to sell. But since they could not fish because of the frequent storms, they had eaten the little ones. For the next time, however, they intended to preserve some."[15]

In this case it seems that the children had been treated less as "delicacies" than as a food supply for difficult times. The last remark made by the shore dwellers indicates that this was not exceptional but might have been the fate of many enslaved children not considered valuable for other purposes. While the accounts of Rascher, Cayley-Webster, and Hahl leave the impression that slaves were eaten at lavish feasts held by the wealthy, Kleintitschen's account seems to suggest that the owners of enslaved children were poor fishers who might have faced hardship, possibly even starvation, if they had not slaughtered and consumed their human provisions. There may be truth in both versions—it is quite possible that slaves were considered "emergency rations" for times of food scarcity and also were sacrificed for sumptuous feasts held in times of plenty.

All reports so far are from the Gazelle Peninsula, which was clearly a hot spot regarding the consumption of persons who were considered slaves or had been taken in slave raids. Indeed Heinrich Schnee (1871–1949), the deputy governor of German New Guinea from 1898 to 1900, observes that slavery and slave trade existed as regular institutions only in the Gazelle Peninsula, where the Baining people were enslaved by the shore dwellers. Elsewhere in the Bismarck Archipelago and the nearby Solomon Islands, there was no organized slave trade, but (according to Schnee) war cannibalism was often practiced, and captives were occasionally kept alive for festive occasions—in some cases for years. During this time, they were exploited like slaves, but sooner or later all of them were butchered and eaten.[16]

While there might not have been a regular trade in living slaves outside of the Gazelle Peninsula, captives could be killed in order to sell their dead bodies, as the German settler Ludolf Kummer observed. Sometime after arriving in New Ireland (then called *Neu-Mecklenburg*), another large island situated northeast of New Britain, Kummer heard that a sixteen-year-old boy was about to be killed in a nearby village and his corpse sold for consumption to another village. Kummer hired the boy to work on his plantation, thus saving his life.[17]

Kummer, who settled on the island in the late nineteenth century, was told that until recently the fattening and slaughter of slaves (or, if Schnee's distinction is correct, of captives) had been fairly common in some areas. In his own time, human flesh was still served at festive occasions, as he discovered by accident. When visiting a village in 1900, he encountered the inhabitants in the progress of preparing a feast. Their chief invited him to join them. A large amount of a meat that looked similar to pork was served. Kummer was about to eat some of it when a villager he had talked to earlier quietly warned him that it was human flesh.[18] He does not say (and probably did not know) who the unfortunate provider of this meat was.

While Kummer discovered this by accident, the German traveler and author Stefan von Kotze (1869–1909) deliberately got himself an invitation to a banquet whose main course was a purchased woman. While in northern New Ireland, he heard of the upcoming cannibal feast from a "half-caste" friend. He convinced his friend, who was invited, to get him an invitation too—a privilege for which he paid a considerable sum of money. In preparation of the meal, the host, a local chief, bought "a young woman . . . from a foreign tribe"—it is unclear whether she had been sold by her own people or whether the sellers had captured her in a raid or battle.[19] Kotze's financial contribution likely went towards covering her purchase price, thus directly contributing to her death—but this does not seem to have bothered him.

Kotze did not see how the woman was killed, but he witnessed the subsequent preparation of the meal:

> Special pieces of the festive roast were reserved for the better gentlemen, myself included. A deep hole was dug and covered with red-hot stones. Certain soft parts of the body were carefully wrapped in banana leaves together with wild breadfruit, the package was put in the oven, several hot stones were placed on top of it, and the hole was filled with earth again. After about twenty-four hours, the word was: Messieurs sont servis![20]

While waiting for this moment, Kotze had drunk "a lot of cognac to calm my stomach." But when his reserved piece was served to him, "similar in appearance and consistency to a foie gras pâté," he felt overwhelmed with nausea and "had to leave immediately"—or so he writes.[21]

He adds that, while the earth oven was used for the parts consumed by the "better gentlemen . . . the plebs roasted the other parts, roughly carved, simply over an open fire." All the eaters were men, no women had been invited.[22] During his time in New Ireland he observed that women and children were generally excluded from the consumption not just of human, but indeed of any meat. He suspected that, because of a general rarity of meat, men preferred to get more for themselves and hence excluded other potential eaters.[23]

In neighboring New Britain, on the other hand, young boys were not generally excluded from cannibal meals. Rascher, as mentioned, knew a boy who at the age of six told the missionary that on three occasions he had eaten human flesh—the last time just one day earlier. Another boy confirmed that he too had attended the recent cannibal meal, though assuring that he had not eaten of the flesh "because the missionary had forbidden it."[24] Kleintitschen writes that eighty out of a hundred boys living in a mission-run orphanage admitted to having eaten human flesh.[25] There are, to my knowledge, no reports of women and girls eating human flesh in New Britain, which suggests that they might have been excluded from this food just as on the neighboring island. But boys seem to have been permitted to share in this "male privilege" at an early age.

In addition to the fact that cannibalism in the Bismarck Archipelago was apparently more clearly restricted to male eaters than in New Zealand, another notable difference is the absence of a punitive motive. In New Zealand, as we have seen (Chapter 2), the killing and subsequent consumption of slaves was often explained as a reaction to some kind of misbehavior on their part. While this might have been little more than a pretext, as some observers felt, it is notable that no such motive or pretext was ever given in the Bismarck Archipelago (to my knowledge). This also means that no underlying motive of keeping the remaining enslaved population at bay through disciplining terror is discernable here.

Sumatra

Later in this book (Chapter 13), we will turn to commercial aspects of cannibalism in the Bismarck Archipelago and elsewhere in the region collectively known as Melanesia. There is a certain overlap between such commercial transactions and the consumption of slaves, especially if a living person is sold with the understanding that the buyers will use them as food. It is therefore not surprising that that section will contain some material that might also have fit into the current chapter.

While the absence or rarity of a practice is harder to document than its presence, my impression is that slave eating was considerably rarer elsewhere in the Pacific Ocean than in the regions covered so far. However, one island outside of Polynesia (which includes New Zealand) and Melanesia (which includes the Bismarck Archipelago) for which the practice has been documented is Sumatra, often considered part of the boundary between the Pacific and the Indian Ocean.

The German author Sigwart Friedmann, who visited the island in the middle of the nineteenth century, notes that criminals and captured enemies were commonly eaten among the Batak people in the north[26]—a custom also documented by various other authors.[27] Friedmann adds that there were some wealthy men "who buy slaves, fatten them for a while like cattle and then slaughter them," but comments that most of the Batak disapproved of such purely culinary cannibal acts.[28] The German-Dutch botanist and geologist Franz Wilhelm Junghuhn (1809–1864), who in the 1840s lived for several years in Sumatra, agrees, noting that he knew of a Batak *rajah* (ruler) who from time to time had one of his slaves butchered for a feast—not as a punishment for crimes, but simply because he liked the taste. The *rajah* also regularly purchased slaves for consumption, paying a premium for fat ones. Junghuhn also notes that this man was an exception, "hated" by most of his neighbors.[29] Still it seems that those who wanted to buy slaves for consumption had no trouble finding sellers.

The consumption of the flesh of captives was less controversial than that of slaves. At the house of another *rajah,* Junghuhn was offered a soup with pieces of meat which turned out to be of human origin. He found out that the *rajah* had not had anything else ready and had not known, "in his guileless manner," that the European disapproved of such food. The flesh came from two captives caught some time earlier in an attack on their village and slaughtered just the day before. Junghuhn observes that human flesh was generally praised as very tasty—even better than pork.[30]

In earlier times, slave eating might have been more widely accepted in some parts of the island. The Italian friar Odoric of Pordenone (1286–1331) visited Sumatra in the early 1320s. He asserts that the inhabitants of Lamuri, a kingdom which existed in its north from around the ninth to the sixteenth century, "eat man's flesh . . . just as we eat beef." According to Odoric, slave traders from other regions brought children to sell to the people of Lamuri, "who buy them and slaughter them in the shambles and eat them." While Odoric does not claim to have personally seen this, he leaves no doubt that he visited Lamuri and talked with some of its inhabitants. The custom, he adds, was not due to hunger, because "the country in itself is excellent, and hath great store of flesh-meats, and of wheat and of rice."[31]

Henry Yule, who edited Odoric's account, notes that much of the latter's description of Lamuri and Sumatra is confirmed by other sources or contemporary evidence and concludes that the friar wrote down what he heard or saw while visiting the island, though every detail might not be based on personal observation.[32] An Arab collection of travel reports from the middle of the ninth century and the Italian merchant Marco Polo, who visited the island thirty years before Odoric, also state that human flesh was eaten in northern Sumatra, but without giving further details.[33]

As Odoric's more specific report is not confirmed by other independent sources, some doubts as to its reliability remain. But if essentially correct, it is one of the earliest sources documenting slave eating as a particular practice.[34] Odoric also points out that cannibals and non-cannibals worked together: in his account, merchants came "from far" to sell enslaved children to the cannibals, apparently not bothered by the subsequent fate of those they sold.[35] When we turn to Africa in subsequent chapters, we will repeatedly encounter similarly pernicious alliances between those who did and those who did not practice cannibalism.

Notes

1. "Papua New Guinea's Incredible Linguistic Diversity," *The Economist*, 20 July 2017, accessed 1 Apr 2020, https://www.economist.com/the-economist-explains/2017/07/20/papua-new-guineas-incredible-linguistic-diversity.
2. See Chapter 11, this volume.
3. Rascher, *Baining*, 114, 256, 281–82, 289.
4. Ibid., 289–91. This large-scale attack is also mentioned in Hahl, *Governor*, 26.
5. Rascher, *Baining*, 290.
6. Ibid., 245. A similar statement can be found on p. 286.
7. Ibid., 301.
8. Hahl quoted in Kleintitschen, *Die Küstenbewohner*, 311.
9. Rascher, *Baining*, 200–1.
10. Ibid., 287, 289.
11. Ibid., 293, 295, 301–2.

12. Ibid., 288, 301–2.
13. Cayley-Webster, *Through New Guinea*, 75.
14. Hahl, *Governor*, 27.
15. Kleintitschen, *Die Küstenbewohner*, 319–20.
16. Schnee, *Bilder aus der Südsee*, 213.
17. Kummer, "Kannibalismus auf Neu-Mecklenburg," 12.
18. Ibid., 14.
19. Kotze, *Südsee-Erinnerungen*, 145.
20. Ibid., 145–46.
21. Ibid., 146.
22. Ibid., 145–46.
23. Ibid., 149.
24. Rascher, *Baining*, 200, 201 (quote).
25. Winthuis, *Heidnische Greuel*, 27.
26. Friedmann, *Die Ostasiatische Inselwelt*, 46.
27. See Junghuhn, *Battaländer*, 156–61, and, for an overview, Leertouwer, "Cannibalism," 244–51.
28. Friedmann, *Die Ostasiatische Inselwelt*, 46.
29. Junghuhn, *Battaländer*, 162.
30. Ibid., 160–61.
31. Yule, *Cathay*, 85. An embellished version of Odoric's account was incorporated into the spurious travel report of John Mandeville (*Travels*, 127).
32. Yule, *Cathay*, 85, notes 2 and 4.
33. Kennedy and Toorawa, *Two Arabic Travel Books*, 27; Polo, *Travels*, 238.
34. For other early accounts from about the same time, but referring to western Africa, see Chapter 10, this volume.
35. Yule, *Cathay*, 85.

CHAPTER 4
IVORY, SLAVERY, AND SLAVE EATING IN THE CONGO BASIN

In the island regions we have visited so far, slavery was largely a regional institution—slaves were traded on an island or sometimes between neighboring islands, but rarely much further. Africa, on the other hand, became the source of most of the enslaved persons that were exploited in the Americas and elsewhere in European colonies and countries founded by Europeans. Throughout the Western world and possibly beyond, slavery became associated with blackness. The law governing slavery in the French colonies was known as *Code Noir,* its equivalent adopted in some Spanish colonies was named, in honor of the Spanish King Charles III, the *Código Negro Carolino.*[1]

Maybe because of the association, the consumption of slaves in Africa seems particularly hard to address. During times when the legitimacy of slavery was still a matter of debate, defenders of this "peculiar institution" sometimes argued that it was better to export Black Africans as slaves to the Americas because this spared them, at least, the fate of otherwise being eaten at home.[2] When we look at the historical record and find that slaves were indeed sometimes consumed in parts of Africa, does this not belatedly justify such a position?

This fear, while understandable, is nevertheless baseless: one wrong can never be used to justify other wrongs.[3] Moreover, we will see that the export of slaves to the Americas and their consumption within Africa were not alternatives, but in fact went hand in hand.

Much of the evidence of Central African cannibalism, however, comes from the late nineteenth century—a time when the transatlantic slave trade had already been outlawed and legal slavery was on its way of disappearing throughout the Western world. We will therefore start with exploring the connections between slave eating and the production of a good that at that time was considered a "legitimate" African export, suited to replace the export of slaves: ivory.

Since most of the available evidence of slave eating in Africa refers to the Congo basin, the focus of this and the following chapters will be on this region. Similar practices also existed in some other regions, parts of the Central and West African coast in particular, but it does not seem that they were as widespread as in parts of the Congo.

Ivory Trade and Slave Eating around the Ubangi River

Situated around the equator, right in the center of Africa, the Congo basin is a huge region covered with rain forests which are "interlaced with innumerable rivers."[4] The extent of the basin corresponds roughly to today's Democratic Republic of the Congo—often called Congo-Kinshasa after its capital, to distinguish the country from the Republic of the Congo (or Congo-Brazzaville), its smaller neighbor to the west. During the infamous European "Scramble for Africa," a predecessor of Congo-Kinshasa called the Congo Free State was founded in 1885 as a private dominion of the Belgian King Leopold II—a unique arrangement among all the European colonies in Africa. The neighboring regions of today's Congo-Brazzaville at that time belonged to the French Congo, a French colony founded in 1882.[5]

Ivory had traditionally been a substance of little interest in eastern and central Africa. Occasionally it was used for the insignia of rulers, and elephants were primarily hunted for meat, not for their tusks. But over time, the increasing demand of Western and Asian buyers turned ivory into a highly priced export. In the Western world of the late nineteenth century, it was considered a "legitimate" African export, suitable to replace the export of slaves which was no longer legitimate or legal. The demand for ivory, on the other hand, had continually increased. Most of it was exported to either Europe or India, where it "provided luxuries for the middle class—trinkets, billiard balls and piano keys."[6]

After the foundation of the Congo Free State, ivory quickly became its principal export good. Between 1888 and 1890 alone, "European traders exported approximately 140 tons of ivory from the Free State, worth nearly seven million Belgian francs."[7] This ivory, procured by local elephant hunters, often went through the hands of various interim traders before reaching its final destination. Various sources from the Free State and nearby areas indicate that this supposedly "legitimate" trade often went hand in hand with slavery and cannibalism: ivory was exchanged against slaves—slaves who were sometimes eaten by those who acquired them.

Dr. Sidney Langford Hinde (1863–1930), a captain in the army of the Congo Free State who arrived in the region in late 1891,[8] notes that the captains of steamers moving along the Ubangi River (the largest right-bank,

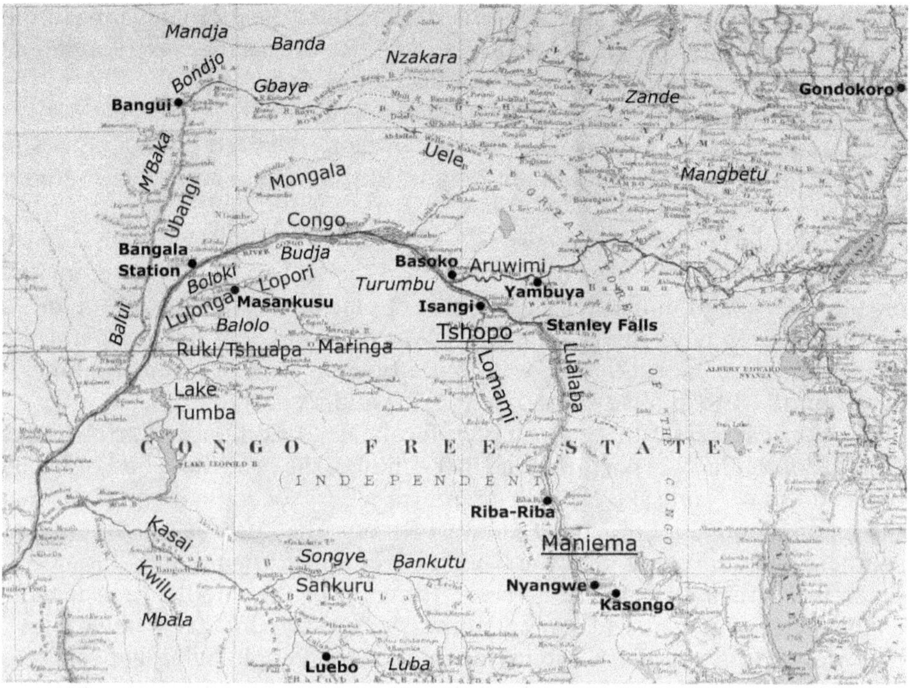

Map 4.1. The Congo basin and surrounding regions. Ethnic groups mentioned in the text are shown in *italics*, towns in **bold**. By the author, based on a map in Henry M. Stanley, *In Darkest Africa* (2 vols., New York: Charles Scribner's Sons, 1913, https://archive.org/details/indarkestafricao00henr).

or northern, tributary of the Congo) had serious difficulties securing provisions because "whenever they try to buy goats from the natives, slaves are demanded in exchange, and the natives often come on board with tusks of ivory or other money with the intention of buying a slave, complaining that meat is now scarce in their neighbourhood."[9]

The British journalist Edward James Glave (1863–1895), who spent most of his adult life in the Congo basin before succumbing to a tropical illness at the age of thirty-one, had the same experience. Traveling along the Ubangi, he was "asked on several occasions to barter a man for a tusk of ivory, and . . . at one village the natives urged me to leave one of my boat's crew in exchange for a goat. 'Meat for meat,' they said."[10] A Dutch trader sent to buy ivory on the same river complained that this was difficult to accomplish because "the natives asked him in return not for cloth, but for slaves from four to sixteen years old whom they intended to eat."[11]

In some cases, European traders seem to have been willing to satisfy such requests. John H. Weeks (1861–1924) was a Baptist missionary who arrived in the Congo in 1881 and stayed for more than thirty years, living most of the time among the Boloki on the central Congo River (a subgroup of a people commonly known as *Bangala*).[12] With disdain he notes that "the folk of the lower part of our district were procuring for their cannibal orgies the natives of a tributary of the Congo. They gave ivory and received human beings in exchange, who quickly found their way to the saucepan; and a white trader was the intermediary."[13]

The Hungarian anthropologist Emil Torday (1875–1931) likewise states that among those who, "for the sake of gain, . . . sell slaves to be immolated on the altar of an unnatural [cannibalistic] gluttony" was "a white man"—whether he refers to the same man as Weeks is not clear. He does not say more about him except that he was "not a Belgian" and "as far as I know, . . . is still [in the 1920s] alive and no doubt rich and respected."[14]

In other cases, as Torday also notes, locals acted as intermediaries in this kind of trade. Glave reports that in 1890—though the Free State had officially outlawed slavery and slave raids—there was a busy local slave trade between the Ubangi and the Lulonga (Lulungu) Rivers. The latter is a left-bank (or southern) tributary that joins the Congo River approximately 150 kilometers upriver (northeast) from the Ubangi. Roughly in the middle, between the confluences of these two rivers, another left-bank tributary, known along its lower part as the Ruki,[15] joins the main river. People living between the mouths of the Ruki and the Lulonga repeatedly ventured upriver along these southern tributaries (as well as smaller ones in between them), raiding the people who lived there and taking many of them captive. The victims of these raids were called Balolo by Glave and others—a tribal appellation that later fell into disuse.[16]

There was a division of work between these raiders and slave traders who lived around the mouth of the Ruki and farther downriver. The latter brought the newly caught slaves closer to their final destination—which often was death and consumption, according to Glave. During the course of ten days, he saw dozens of trading canoes return from the southern tributaries in order to resell the purchased slaves around the mouth of the Ruki or to transport them farther downriver and sell them along the Ubangi. In one such canoe, which might have been fairly typical, Glave counted "five traders, and their freight of miserable humanity consisted of thirteen emaciated Balolo slaves, men, women, and little children." Most of the captives were supposedly "sold in exchange for ivory" to buyers who had only their nutritional value in mind, subsequently slaughtering them "to supply some cannibal orgy"—only a few were purchased to be employed as warriors or become their buyers' "wives."[17]

Hinde gives a similar account, noting that the authorities of the newly established Congo Free State were confronted with "a wholesale human traffic" taking place between the southern and northern tributaries of the Congo. People living near the main river regularly organized raids, often

Figure 4.1. A slaver's canoe on the Ruki River. From Edward J. Glave's "The Slave Trade in the Congo Basin," *Century Magazine,* April 1890, 833.

along the Lulonga River. "When the raiders had collected a sufficient number of people to fill their canoes, they returned to the Congo, and carried them up the Oubangi [Ubangi], where they were sold to the natives to serve as food."[18]

Another account comes from the Baptist missionary William Bentley, who notes that the "human cattle" caught in raids near the Lulonga were sold on the Ubangi in exchange for ivory. "The purchasers," he adds, "would then feed up their starvelings, until they were fat enough for the market, then butcher them, and sell the meat in small joints."[19] Glave likewise notes that the purchasers, after paying with ivory, fattened their victims on "ripe bananas, fish, and oil" before killing them for consumption. He estimates that "hundreds" of the unfortunate Balolo fell victim to this process every month.[20]

The deliberate fattening of slaves has also been reported from the surroundings of the Ruki River. While traveling along a side arm of this river, the German officer Curt von François (1852–1931) saw a well-nourished, but bound man who, as his interpreter explained, was about to be slaughtered. After talking with the locals, the interpreter added that the man, whose "features pointed to the sufferings of prolonged slavery," had been "prepared for this act by rational fattening." François's attempt to purchase him failed, because the locals asked to be given three other slaves in return.[21]

While he does not mention fattening, the Baptist missionary George Grenfell (1849–1906) made a very similar experience during his travels along this river: "Grenfell came upon a group who were just about to kill a man and eat him. He tried without success to redeem him for a cash payment."[22]

Exchanges of "edible" slaves against ivory (or other goods) were not limited to the lower parts of the Ubangi River, they also occurred farther upriver, far away from the Congo River. In the late 1880s, a Catholic mission station was established at Bangui (today the capital of the Central African Republic), six hundred kilometers upriver from the mouth of the Ubangi. The French missionary and bishop Prosper Augouard (1852–1921), who spent part of his time at the mission, characterizes the "Bondjo" people living around the mission as accomplished elephant hunters who "willingly exchange their ivory, but only against slaves who are immediately put to death and devoured."[23] In a letter written in April 1893, he tells of the recent arrival of a canoe carrying enslaved children. "Eleven poor little slaves . . . were bought and immediately eaten by the terrible Bondjos." The missionaries generally tried to purchase enslaved children in order to save them, but when they heard of the incident, it was already too late.[24]

At that time, Bondjo (or Bonjo) was a generic name used by Europeans for various ethnic groups who lived around the Ubangi, especially on its upper part where it forms the boundary between the Central African Republic (formerly part of the French Congo) and Congo-Kinshasa (formerly the Congo Free State). Over time, various parts of this linguistically and culturally quite diverse group became known under more precise terms such as M'Baka and Gbaya, while the generic name disappeared.[25]

While it is conceivable that some of the victims of the "Bondjos" were shipped from as far away as the Lulonga or other left-bank tributaries of the Congo, most of them—or maybe all—probably came from more proximate regions. Many seem to have been caught and sold by ethnic groups who lived close to the "Bondjos" but were themselves less cannibalistic—indeed, since "Bondjo" was a generic term, it seems likely that not all the people to which it was applied were equally cannibalistic.

The French traveler Casimir Maistre, who visited the region in 1892/93, encountered a people called "Boubangis," who, he remarks (not disapprovingly), were "very commercial." They largely abstained from human flesh, though killed enemies were consumed and, from time to time, slaves were slaughtered and eaten at special occasions. But mostly they traded in living slaves, whether purchased elsewhere or captured in fights, whom they sold in return for ivory—most often to "the Bondjos of the Middle Ubangi, hardened cannibals who consider the slaves only as meat for slaughter."[26] The name "Boubangis" might refer to the Ngbandi, a people who live on the upper Ubangi River, east of those once known as "Bondjos."

The deadly trade between the two peoples is also mentioned by the French explorer Jean Dybowski (1856–1928), who explains that a small tusk of ivory weighting twenty-five to forty kilograms was exchanged for one slave who was "executed and consumed in due course," while two or more slaves were handed over for larger tusks.[27] The Catholic mission historian G. Renouard agrees with these accounts: "The Boubangis are the suppliers of their neighbors on the Ubangi, the Bondjo cannibals, and they know very well for what purpose their goods are bought."[28] Similar exchange ratios of slaves against ivory have been documented for other regions where cannibalism was absent or rare—in Equatoria (today part of South Sudan), a first-class elephant tusk was considered as valuable as a healthy young enslaved girl.[29]

Ivory as Export Good and the Role of Westerners

While many of the slaves traded around the Ubangi River were eaten—as all the sources agree—the ivory often given as payment inevitably ended elsewhere, as it was a valuable export good. Dybowski notes that tusks acquired in exchange for one or more "edible" slaves were resold downriver until finally reaching French or Belgian *factoreries* (offices of colonial agents).[30] From there they were shipped to Europe or the Americas. Considering that Dybowski and many other witnesses knew of the cannibalistic aspects of the trade, it seems unlikely that the European agents who acquired the ivory were clueless, but apparently this did not stop them from purchasing the highly priced good.

Were Europeans sometimes even more closely involved in this deadly trade? As mentioned, both John Weeks and Emil Torday knew of a white trader (conceivably the same man) who acted as "intermediary" in the exchange of ivory against slaves who were subsequently eaten. This may have been an exception, but it is notable that a Dutch trader, Edward Glave, and white captains known to Sidney Hinde were all invited to exchange ivory, or sometimes other goods, against "edible" slaves.[31] Dybowski made the same experience. When his group tried to purchase fruit or vegetables, the locals asked to be given a man in return, "and when we asked why they wanted him, we were told, 'But why, to eat him!' And they could not understand that we did not wish to make this exchange of fresh provisions."[32] Travelers visiting other rivers sometimes received similar offers.[33] If white men (with the exception of the one or two traders mentioned by Weeks and Torday) never agreed to such proposals, would not the locals quickly have stopped making them? If Western merchants did indeed join in the illegal and often deadly exchange of slaves against ivory, they certainly had reasons to remain silent, which would explain the absence of more evidence.

While the role of Western traders remains unclear, better documentation exists regarding the acts of Congo Free State officials. Not only did they often do little to stop slave raids, slave trade, and cannibalism on the territory they claimed to rule, some of them tolerated or actively facilitated cannibal acts among their own subordinates and allies. This is a point to which we will return later.[34] For now, however, it is interesting to note that the Western customers who ultimately used the ivory exported from the Congo also seem to have had a certain cavalier attitude regarding the origins of this product. At that time, the buyers of that luxury good did not yet care for the elephants that were killed to provide it, considering them an apparently inexhaustible resource. But the fate of the slaves who apparently were quite often given as payment for the tusks and subsequently slaughtered by their new owners should at least have given them pause, considering that the Congo region was not a minor player in the trade—in the late 1890s, almost half the world's ivory production was exported from the Free State to Europe.[35]

The connection between ivory trade and cannibalism might not have been widely known, but it was not a secret. First articles clearly documenting this connection were published in France and the United States in or before 1890,[36] when the practice seems to have been in full swing. Books published in the United Kingdom and France followed during the next seven years,[37] when it was probably far from over. Yet it seems that readers considered such accounts fascinating horror stories from a faraway world, unrelated to their own lives. It does not seem that anybody requested of the ivory importers to ensure that their products were untainted by such deadly exchanges or called for a boycott of items acquired under dubious circumstances.

Slave Trade, Raiding, and Cannibalism

From the sources discussed earlier, and others we will encounter later, there can be little doubt that slaves were sometimes bought directly for consumption (or for fattening and consumption), without any other purpose they were supposed to serve. How, we may well ask, had a situation developed where slaves were considered good for eating and were apparently readily available for this purpose? Why did cannibalistic buyers buy and why did slave raiders or other slave owners supply them? Why was such a custom not stopped by ethical or economic concerns?

These questions cannot be answered by considering the Congo basin in isolation. The region was part of a large trading network, reaching from the Americas in the west to the Arab world and Asia in the east, and the local custom of slave eating was closely intertwined with this trade, as we will see. Bogumil Jewsiewicki and Mumbanza mwa Bawele point out that slaves who permanently lived with this status were rare or unknown among most Central African peoples until approximately the first half of the nineteenth century. Oral evidence indicates that captives taken in wars were often killed and (in many regions) eaten. Women of childbearing age were frequently spared and forced into marriage with one of their captors; children were sometimes adopted into the families of their captors. Some other captives were already exported towards the African west coast, passing through the hands of various intermediary traders before finally being shipped across the Atlantic to the Americas.[38]

At that time, the consumption of killed or captured enemies already seems to have been quite common—at least, none of the later sources dealing with the practice suggests that it was new.[39] Sales of captives to others who would eat them might already have occurred as well. In fact, as Jewsiewicki and Mumbanza mwa Bawele found by investigating oral histories about these and later times, people generally assumed that anyone sold as slave would be eaten: "Because cannibalism was common, and slaves were purchased especially for such purposes, people assumed that slaves who were sold were probably sacrificed." Nevertheless, "incorrigibly troublesome" young persons were sometimes sold into slavery—a severe form of punishment that was expected to end in death: "One did not eat one's own relatives; instead, one sold them so that they might be sacrificed elsewhere."[40]

Nevertheless, these phenomena were limited in scope. Some people fell victim to wars and a few were sold by their own relatives, but the latter punishment was probably rare and warfare was by no means perpetual and ubiquitous.[41] But around the middle of the nineteenth century, the situation worsened considerably, because the Congo basin came under pressure as a supply area for both the transatlantic (or western) and Arab (or eastern) slave trade.

The transatlantic trade had developed and expanded over a long time. Already in the sixteenth century, in addition to ivory and copper, the most important exports of the coastal Kingdom of Kongo were slaves sent to the Americas.[42] Over time, the area where slaves were captured extended farther and farther into the Congolese hinterland, and increasing warfare and systematic raids spread with it. Around the year 1840, the area where slave raids were frequent reached the western regions of the Congo basin.[43]

Black slaves and white ivory were also in demand throughout the Arab world and Asia—in the nineteenth century, they were the two most important exports from East Africa towards these regions. Over time, the "catchment area" moved farther and farther inland, until finally reaching at least the northeastern quarter of the Congo basin.[44] During the second half of the nineteenth century, large parts of the Congo basin were therefore subjected to repeated and devastating raids organized to supply slaves for either the transatlantic or the Arab trade.

Wars "fought principally for the purpose of capturing slaves" became common, while in earlier times the taking of captives (some of whom were sold downriver towards the transatlantic trade) had been a side effect of warfare. But now raids against other villages were specifically organized for the purpose of enslaving as many people as possible. There was no strict separation between attackers and victims—any group who felt strong enough to get away with it might have raided nearby communities with whom no strong bounds of friendship or affinity existed. "When they were stronger they made us their slaves. But when they were weaker we were the ones who reduced them to slavery," a survivor later remembered.[45]

Raids usually took the form of a surprise attack on a village, often in the early morning. Those who resisted or were "too strong to make slaves of" were killed, while everyone else was taken captive and could potentially be sold—if there was a market for them.[46] But the demands of the international slave trade differed considerably from the supply acquired by taking everyone in a village. Paul Lovejoy estimates that about half the inhabitants of raided villages were teenagers and young adults in their "prime" (aged fourteen to thirty), while the rest were children up to thirteen (30 percent of the population) and "mature" adults above the age of thirty (20 percent). But among the slaves exported across the Atlantic, the huge majority where "prime" teenagers and adults (more than 85 percent)—there were considerably fewer children (less than 15 percent) and hardly any "mature" adults.[47]

Being of a suitable age was not enough to get a slave sold—European merchants preferred purchasing "the healthiest and strongest slaves," while a "sickly slave" was considered unsalable. And nearly all the children exported across the Atlantic seem to have been at least eight years old.[48] Some of those considered unsuitable for export were purchased by African buyers to be used as servants, laborers, or consorts, but local demand for very young and elder people was likewise limited or absent, hence "prices of infants and the old fell very low." Since raiders knew this, they often did not even bother with them: "old men and women, as well as children, were considered valueless and often killed." Joseph C. Miller estimates that in raids and war campaigns undertaken for acquiring slaves about as many persons were killed as were enslaved—either because they resisted or because they were considered unsalable.[49]

In regions where food taboos prevented the consumption of human flesh, the bodies of the killed were left to rot or feed wild animals. But in cannibal regions, the raiders had additional options: if they were not opposed to eating human flesh themselves, they could consume the dead rather than letting them rot. And if cannibals willing to purchase tasty humans in return for ivory or some other suitable compensation lived nearby, the raiders (regardless of whether or not they were cannibals themselves) could keep their otherwise unmarketable captives temporarily alive in order to sell them to those who just cared for their meat. Evidence from the Congo basin suggests that both these options were used. In passing it may be noted that this analysis might likewise apply to other regions where slaves were sometimes killed for consumption, such as Nigeria.[50] While the Congo and Angola were the single most important source of slaves exported to the Americas, Nigeria and neighboring Benin were not far behind.[51]

In the 1880s, when the first Westerners reached the inner parts of the Congo basin, the transatlantic slave trade was effectively over—more than seventy years of attempts to stop it, spearheaded by the British government, had finally paid off. But this was a very recent achievement. Until the 1870s, slaves had still been exported from the Congo basin across the Atlantic to Brazil, Cuba, and Puerto Rico in ships that ignored the illegality of the trade and managed to circumvent the British blockade. Even in the 1880s and beyond, slaves caught in the Congo basin were still sold downriver and along the African west coast. "Most of the European trading houses on the Lower Congo" still exploited slaves, noted the British explorer and colonialist Harry Johnston (1858–1927) a few decades later. Other Congolese slaves were sold to Angola and São Tomé Island (then Portuguese colonies), where they had to work on plantations.[52]

In general, colonial administrators turned a blind eye towards slavery, because "they needed the support of the chiefs, who were major slave-owners," therefore official prohibitions were widely ignored and "had little effect on the internal African slave markets." In the Congo basin, the relatively open trade in slaves "survived until about 1910," despite official proclamations that suggested otherwise.[53]

But why were some slaves sold towards the coast (and formerly across the Atlantic), where they often had to serve the needs of Western buyers, while others were traded locally for cannibalistic purposes? We already know part of the answer: European and American buyers were choosy, they spurned slaves who were very young, old, weak, or sickly. Johnston explicitly points out that cannibalistic and export slave trade went hand in hand: some of the slaves offered for sale around the Lulonga were sold downriver to the Ubangi or upriver to "Bangala towns" and other local destinations "where they were eaten"; others were shipped farther downriver and "resold as slaves for the white man." Ivory was also traded downriver, transported by the same intermediaries that bought and sold slaves.[54]

If these trades were connected, we may expect that the cannibals (or traders hoping to resell to cannibals) often bought those less wanted for export, as they would have been cheaper. From the sellers' viewpoint, selling otherwise unwanted slaves cheaply to cannibals was preferable to not selling them at all. There is indeed some evidence of such a division between different kinds of buyers. Among the slave markets visited by Glave was "the most important slave-trading center" in the region (as he calls it) in Masankusu (today Basankusu), a town at the source of the Lulonga River.[55] Tied to the poles of slave sheds or trees, he saw slaves of "all ages, of both sexes," including "even babies who cannot yet walk," offered for sale without their mothers.[56] This was certainly unusual—elsewhere infants were sometimes sold together with their mother, but they "added nothing to their [mother's] price," since buyers saw no reason to pay for "children who would need years of care" before becoming useful.[57] Visitors to slave markets outside the cannibalistic regions saw children from age six, eight, or ten exposed for sale—but none (or very few) younger.[58]

From the cannibal viewpoint, however, youth was not an impediment. On the contrary, it might have been considered a benefit, just as many modern meat eaters prefer lamb over mutton and veal over beef. Cannibal voices praising children as particularly tasty are not hard to find. The missionary and ethnographer Filiberto Gero (a pseudonym of Filiberto Giorgetti), who lived among the Zande at the northeastern fringes of the Congo basin[59] for almost forty years (from 1926 to the mid-1960s), heard from several of his local informants that the flesh of children had been preferred over that of adults because it was "very delicate."[60] When the German botanist and ethnologist Georg Schweinfurth (1836–1925) visited the neighboring Mangbetu people around 1870, he repeatedly heard that young children made "particularly tasty morsels."[61]

In Nigeria, where slaves were sometimes eaten as well,[62] the British anthropologist P. Amaury Talbot (1877–1945) found that those practicing cannibalism generally preferred young victims, explaining that "the younger the person, the tenderer are the 'joints.'" In some areas, "young children" were considered "the best [food] of all,"[63] and it seems they were sometimes deliberately fattened before being "baked" for the table.[64]

In the market at Masankusu, Glave talked with a woman exposed for sale who told him that she and her children had been captured in a raid on their village ten days earlier—her husband and several other men who had tried to resist had been murdered. She did not fear so much for her own immediate future, expecting to be sold to some neighboring people to "toil in the plantations" until she would become too "old and unfit for work." Only then, she added, "I shall be killed to celebrate the death of a free man."[65]

But she did not expect her children to be allowed to grow up. Two of them, she explained, "have already been purchased by the slave traders. I shall never see them any more. Perhaps they will sacrifice them on the death of some chief, or perhaps kill them for food." She could not know this for sure, but it is not implausible that these were typical fates of enslaved children who were too young to be exploited otherwise. Her third child was a baby, "clutching to her shrunken breast," which she expected to be taken from her the same day, since her owner was offering it for sale, independently of her, "for a very small price."[66]

The British adventurer and sculptor Herbert Ward (1863–1919), who spent the years from 1884 to 1889 in the Congo basin, also visited the slave markets on the Lulonga. He writes that it was not rare to see "upwards of a hundred captives, of both sexes and of all ages, including infants in their mothers' arms," exposed for sale in one of the "strongly fortified villages" where the raiders lived. He reminds us of the connection between these slave markets and the deadly trade in slaves and ivory that took place around the Ubangi River, pointing out that some of the buyers "came in large dug-out canoes" from the Ubangi in order to purchase slaves in return for ivory. While the ivory was subsequently resold downriver until it reached the markets of

Europe and the Americas, the slaves were taken to the Ubangi River, where "eventually, after having been deliberately fattened, they met their tragic fate, and their bodies were consumed."[67]

Ward adds that, in another part of the country (he does not say where exactly) he personally encountered whole "convoys of slaves that had been bought or captured" and were then "conveyed to tribes who purchase them as food, giving ivory in exchange."[68]

Consumption of the "Unwanted" and "Unfit"

Not everyone caught in a slave raid even made it to the nearest market. The enslaved woman whom Glave talked to stated that her husband and several other men had been killed. It is quite possible that their bodies had been eaten since (according to Glave) a successful raid was usually followed by a feast of human flesh. The raiders shackled only "the stronger portion of their captives ... hand and foot to prevent their escape"—the rest were killed and eaten, and the bodies of those killed in the attack served the same purpose. Old people in particular were rarely preserved for the slave markets; instead, they were murdered immediately after a raid: "their marketable value being very small, no trouble is taken with them." Before the surviving captives were brought to the nearest slave market, the fresh human flesh was consumed together with "all the bananas" found in the destroyed village.[69]

As bananas were a "staple food crop in the equatorial forest,"[70] it is not surprising that they are mentioned as a side dish to human flesh not just in this but also in various other accounts. Among the Songye people, human flesh was usually served with bananas or cassava, notes the renowned German ethnologist Leo Frobenius (1873–1938).[71] According to the Belgian author E. Carlier, the "Bondjo" people on the Ubangi liked to cook the flesh of executed slaves and war captives "in boiling water with cassava and bananas."[72] The famous Scottish missionary David Livingstone (1813–1873) once met a Swahilo-Arab slave trader who told him that he had recently seen human flesh cut up and "cooked with bananas" after a fight.[73] And after talking with a group of Bangala people about their customs, the Scottish traveler James Jameson noted in his diary that "they remove the inside [entrails]" of killed enemies or of "nice, fat, young women" purchased for consumption, "stuff them with bananas, and roast them whole over a big fire."[74]

To return to the coupling of slave raids with cannibalism, Herbert Ward agrees with Glave, writing that the raiders operating on the Lulonga and nearby rivers ate "those who are less suitable for the slavemarket" before selling the remaining captives.[75] And the British diplomat Roger Casement (1864–1916) comments: "The towns around the lower Lulongo River raided the interior tribes, whose prolific humanity provided not only servitors, but human meat for those stronger than themselves."[76]

The same practice of immediately consuming those considered unfit for sale seems to have existed among the Songye people living around the Sankuru, the longest tributary of the Kasai, which in turn is one of the largest left-bank (southern) tributaries of the Congo. Leo Frobenius heard from his local informants that young children caught in raids were "skewered on long spears like rats and roasted over a quickly kindled large fire" for immediate consumption. Adults (and supposedly older children) were usually kept alive and taken home, to be sold or eaten later.[77]

Raids undertaken for the double purpose of acquiring slaves (which were sold or employed locally) and victims for consumption are also documented in other regions. Adolf Friedrich, Duke of Mecklenburg (1873–1969), the leader of a German research expedition through the Congo basin, states that the Nzakara people (who live around a northern tributary of the Ubangi) regularly led raids, or war campaigns, against a neighboring people in order to "procure fresh slaves, and also human victims to satisfy their cannibal instincts." These raids still took place around the year 1910, when Adolf Friedrich was in the area. At that time the captured slaves were retained locally—in earlier times some of them might have been sold to traders for ultimate export across the Atlantic.[78]

The French botanist and explorer Auguste Chevalier (1873–1956), who had been in the same region a few years earlier, writes that the Nzakara "frequently undertake expeditions to supply their pantry" with human victims for consumption. He does not mention slave taking, but it seems plausible that (as Adolf Friedrich states) some captives were left alive and exploited as slaves. Chevalier adds that "women and children" were preferably eaten because they made "refined dishes"—likely a deadly expression of patriarchal dominance, though it is also conceivable that male slaves were in higher demand as laborers and hence had a better chance of being spared.[79]

An echo of Chevalier's statement comes from the Tshopo province in the northeast of the Congo basin, where a young chief explained to a Protestant missionary that "the flesh of the women and children is the best." With evident nostalgia, he remembered the good old times (which in 1903 had only just passed, it seems) when captives taken in raids could still be fattened for consumption.[80] While not mentioned, it seems quite possible that some of the captives were actually sold to the Swahilo-Arab traders who had been active in the area. The role of these merchants, who usually came from Zanzibar and nearby regions and traded in slaves and ivory destined for the East African coast and the Arab world, will be investigated later.[81]

According to Chevalier, children (though possibly not the smallest ones) and adolescents captured in raids or warfare could expect a somewhat better fate among the Mandja people, who lived west of the Nzakara. When Chevalier was in the area, children taken in raids were kept as slaves by their captors, while in earlier (precolonial) times, most of them were sold to Swahilo-Arab slavers. The corpses of killed enemy fighters were eaten, and adults taken captive were sooner or later killed and generally eaten too. Chevalier adds that human flesh was distributed equally among all families, except for "the heart and the liver," which were reserved for the chief.[82] The neighboring Banda people engaged in similar practices, but here the chief received "a leg or sometimes just a thigh" in addition to his regular share.[83]

Not only were slave raids deadly for many, the transport of slaves destined to be resold elsewhere or exported was often deadly as well. A captive who became too weak to move on was usually killed.[84] When asked what happened with slaves who were unable to walk, a Swahilo-Arab slaver replied that "[we] spear them at once! . . . For, if we did not, others would pretend they were ill in order to avoid carrying their loads. No! We never leave them alive on the road; they all know our custom."[85] It must be pointed out that this was a general custom practiced not only throughout Africa, but also by European captains who, on their route across the Atlantic, frequently threw slaves overboard if they seemed too ill or weak to "be sold to advantage."[86] But in regions where human flesh was considered edible, the practice could be applied with an obvious twist: from a cannibal viewpoint, even a dead slave was a useful resource.

While stationed in Luebo, a town in the Kasai region, William H. Sheppard (1865–1927) and Samuel N. Lapsley (1866–1892)—the first African American missionary in the Congo and his white companion[87]—heard from a friend "that some cannibals had killed a woman and eaten her, and that this woman had a little child who had also eaten of her mother." When told that the slave caravan where this had happened would pass nearby, Lapsley waited for it to show up.[88]

> Mr. Lapsley approached the head man, the chief, and . . . gently asked why they had killed and eaten one of the slaves.
>
> The chief explained, as a matter of course, that the woman's feet were swollen and she could walk no more, so they only did as they always do with those who are unable to march.[89]

To spare her the fate of further slavery and possibly a premature death, Lapsley then purchased and liberated the six-year-old girl who had involuntarily shared in her mother's flesh, paying with "some foreign cloth."[90] The slavers might have belonged to the Zappo Zaps, a group of Songye people known and feared as large-scale slave raiders and traders, since another time Sheppard notes that a group of "Zappo Zap (cannibals) . . . with a caravan of slaves to sell" had arrived in the town.[91]

Hinde reports that he repeatedly saw leftovers of cannibal meals on the roads in the Kasai region: "On the road—generally by the smouldering camp fire, or the blackened spot indicating where the fire has been—are the whitening bones, cracked and broken, which form the relics of these disgusting banquets."[92] While motives and contexts of such cannibal meals outside of settlements are unclear, some of them may well have been held by slave caravans after one of their captives had become too weak to move on.

Generally, there can be no doubt that the international slave and ivory trade and cannibalism in the Congo were not separate phenomena, but that they were interwoven, strengthening and complementing each other. There are hints, but not much direct evidence, that Western traders sometimes deliberately partook in transactions that they knew would lead to cannibalism. In certain other cases, the involvement of outsiders into Congolese cannibalism is much better documented. We will explore some of this evidence in the next chapter.

Notes

1. Sala-Molins, "Slavery in Law Codes," 212–15.
2. William Gilmore Simms (1806–1870), a writer and politician from South Carolina, claims that the typical slave was a "cannibal African . . . destined in his own country to eat his fellow, or to be eaten by him"—two equally unpleasant fates in his eyes, it seems (Simms, "The Morals of Slavery," 273).
3. For a discussion of why and for which reasons it makes sense to consider practices such as violent cannibalism and slavery as wrongs not just in our own value system but indeed cross-culturally, see the Conclusion, this volume.
4. Isichei, *History*, 103.
5. During its greatest extent, the French Congo covered the area of three modern countries: Gabon and Congo-Brazzaville to the west of the Congo basin, and the Central African Republic to the north.
6. Thornton, *Kingdom of Kongo*, xv; Lovejoy, *Transformations of Slavery*, 136; Isichei, *History*, 438 (quote).
7. Shillington, *Encyclopedia*, 306.
8. Hinde, *Fall*, 28.
9. Ibid., 67.
10. Glave, "Slave Trade," 832.
11. Bergemann, *Die Verbreitung der Anthropophagie*, 41.
12. Weeks, "Anthropological Notes," 435–36.
13. Weeks, *Among Congo Cannibals*, 70.
14. Torday, *Causeries Congolaises*, 83.
15. Along its whole course however, the Ruki is known as the Tshuapa, which is somewhat confusing since both names may be used interchangeably.
16. Glave, "Slave Trade," 832–33. The name Balolo may have been a generic term used for anyone who lived in the targeted area that was later replaced by other, more specific terms based on actual cultural or linguistic differences.
17. Ibid., 833.
18. Hinde, *Fall*, 66–67.
19. W. Bentley, *Pioneering on the Congo*, 211.
20. Glave, *In Savage Africa*, 191.
21. François, *Die Erforschung des Tschuapa*, 119–20.
22. Johnston, *George Grenfell*, 1:140.

23. Augouard, *28 années au Congo*, 1:423.
24. Ibid., 2:79. Augouard himself seems to have occasionally witnessed the consumption of human flesh (ibid., 578; Witte, *Monseigneur Prosper Philippe Augouard*, 46).
25. Samarin, "Linguistic World," 439.
26. Maistre, *A Travers l'Afrique centrale*, 24.
27. Dybowski, *La route du Tchad*, 122, 136 (quote).
28. Renouard, *L'Ouest Africain*, 132.
29. Moorehead, *White Nile*, 156.
30. Dybowski, *La route du Tchad*, 136.
31. See the beginning of the previous section, "Ivory Trade and Slave Eating around the Ubangi River."
32. Dybowski, *Le Congo méconnu*, 170–71.
33. François, *Die Erforschung des Tschuapa*, 116.
34. See Chapter 5, this volume.
35. Van Reybrouck, *Congo*, 67.
36. Froment, "Un Voyage dans l'Oubangui"; Glave, "Slave Trade."
37. Hinde, *Fall*; Maistre, *A Travers l'Afrique centrale.*
38. Jewsiewicki and Mumbanza mwa Bawele, "Social Context of Slavery," 73, 75.
39. Sources covering war cannibalism in and around the Congo basin include Chevalier, *Mission Chari–Lac Tchad*, 89, 99–100, 112–14, 232; Coquilhat, *Sur le Haut-Congo*, 217, 318–20; Evans-Pritchard, "Zande Cannibalism," 251–55; Fräßle, *Meiner Urwaldneger Denken*, 110–11, 114; Gero, *Cannibalism in Zandeland*, 38–39, 53, 68, 79, 110, 146, 153–55, 174–75; Hilton-Simpson, *Land and Peoples*, 131, 142–44; Hinde, *Fall*, 62–63, 69, 119, 124–25, 131, 134–35, 175, 208; Livingstone, *Last Journals*, 117, 127, 148; Schweinfurth, *Heart of Africa*, 18, 92–94, 222; Ward, *Voice from the Congo*, 203, 313–15.
40. Jewsiewicki and Mumbanza mwa Bawele, "Social Context of Slavery," 75–76.
41. Although, the British explorer and colonialist Harry Johnston asserts that small-scale wars were already a frequent occurrence throughout the Congo basin before the spreading of slave raids because shifting cultivation often led to violent conflicts over land (Johnston, *George Grenfell*, 2:625).
42. Thornton, *Kingdom of Kongo*, xv.
43. See map in Miller, *Way of Death*, 10.
44. Austen, *African Economic History*, 68–69.
45. Jewsiewicki and Mumbanza mwa Bawele, "Social Context of Slavery," 80, 82.
46. Glave, "Slave Trade," 829; Lapsley, *Life and Letters*, 216 (quote).
47. Lovejoy, *Transformations of Slavery*, 63–64.
48. Ibid., 62, 99 (quotes); Miller, *Way of Death*, 388.
49. Manning, *Slavery and African Life*, 93; Thomas, *Slave Trade*, chapter 19; Miller, *Way of Death*, 381.
50. For reports of slave eating in Nigeria, see Basden, *Among the Ibos*, 40, 107–8; Leonard, *Lower Niger*, 485. Slaves were also sacrificed at funerals, religious rituals, or state functions; in some regions, the bodily remains of the victims were subsequently consumed. For evidence of such practices in Nigeria and nearby West African countries, see Arnaud, "Notes," 250–52; Basden, *Among the Ibos*, 223–24, 228; Harley, *Masks*, 8, 17–20, 25, 28–29; Hecquard, *Voyage*, 74–75; Leonard, *Lower Niger*, 161–62; Talbot, *Peoples of Southern Nigeria*, 2:106, 3:828. In Southern Nigeria, slaves were still used "for human sacrifice in the early 1920s," with colonial

administrators turning a blind eye (Shillington, *Encyclopedia*, 1390). Slaves or captives could also be killed for consumption in today's Guinea, see Singer, "Woelffels Reisen," 315.

51. Thomas, *Slave Trade*, chapter 3
52. Johnston, *George Grenfell*, 1:139n (quote), 185.
53. Shillington, *Encyclopedia*, 304, 785.
54. Johnston, *George Grenfell*, 1:139n. Johnston adds that his account is based on "observations of Stanley, Grenfell, the present writer, and others" (ibid., 138n3).
55. The point where its two headstreams, the Lopori and Maringa Rivers, join each other.
56. Glave, "Slave Trade," 830–31.
57. Manning, *Slavery and African Life*, 99, 114.
58. Moorehead, *White Nile*, 25 (6+); Thomas, *Slave Trade*, chapter 32 (8+); Stanley, *Through the Dark Continent*, 5 (10+).
59. The region where the Zande live extends beyond the area once claimed by the Congo Free State (today Congo-Kinshasa) into a region known as Equatoria (today the southern part of South Sudan).
60. Gero, *Cannibalism in Zandeland*, 55 (quote), 67.
61. Schweinfurth, *Im Herzen*, 98; in the English translation (Schweinfurth, *Heart of Africa*, 93), the sentence containing this statement has been omitted.
62. See note 50, this chapter.
63. Talbot, *Peoples of Southern Nigeria,* 3:827, 839.
64. Hogg, *Cannibalism*, 93.
65. Ritual killings of slaves or wives during the funerals of important men occurred in various parts of Africa (Lovejoy, *Transformations of Slavery*, 180). In cannibal regions, some of the victims might have been buried together with their former master to serve him in the afterlife, while others were butchered for the burial feast (Johnston, *George Grenfell*, 2:657–58; Westmark, "Quinze mois," 23–24).
66. Glave, *In Savage Africa*, 191, 193.
67. Ward, *Voice from the Congo*, 310–11.
68. Ibid., 310.
69. Glave, "Slave Trade," 829–31. Glave had firsthand evidence from the slave markets only, not from raids, but since he talked to various captives, and presumably also to raiders, his description can probably be considered fairly reliable.
70. Shillington, *Encyclopedia*, 684.
71. Frobenius summarized in Volhard, *Kannibalismus*, 117. Frobenius visited the Kasai region in a research expedition undertaken in 1904–6. The official report of the expedition remains vague when it comes to cannibal practices (Frobenius, *Im Schatten*, 133, 161–63, 175), and while Frobenius's diaries have not been published, detailed summaries can be found in Volhard's book.
72. Carlier, "Les Bondjo," 416.
73. Livingstone, *Last Journals*, 148.
74. Jameson, *Story*, 31.
75. Ward, *Five Years*, 125.
76. Casement, *Correspondence and Report*, 44.
77. Frobenius in Volhard, *Kannibalismus*, 116.
78. Mecklenburg, *From the Congo*, 200.
79. Chevalier, *Mission Chari–Lac Tchad*, 232.

80. Quoted in Wack, *Story*, 305.
81. See Chapter 5, this volume.
82. Chevalier, *Mission Chari–Lac Tchad*, 112–14.
83. Ibid., 100.
84. Slade, *King Leopold's Congo*, 87.
85. Quoted in Swann, *Fighting the Slave-Hunters*, 49.
86. Lang, *Land*, 215; see also Chapter 2, this volume.
87. Edgerton, *Troubled Heart of Africa*, 116–17.
88. Sheppard, *Presbyterian Pioneers*, 65.
89. Ibid., 65–66.
90. Ibid., 66.
91. Ibid., 145. For more on the Zappo Zaps, see Chapter 5, this volume.
92. Hinde, *Fall*, 69.

CHAPTER 5
THE ROLES OF ARAB-SWAHILI MERCHANTS AND THE CONGO FREE STATE

Cannibalism among Allies of Swahilo-Arab Merchants

The preceding chapter mostly dealt with parts of the Congo basin closer to the Atlantic than to the Indian Ocean. From there, goods such as ivory were commonly exported to Europe and the Americas, and until the end of the transatlantic slave trade, slaves were sent from there to the Americas and the Caribbean. The eastern regions of the Congo basin were involved in a similar trade, but the slaves and ivory taken from there were usually sent eastward, towards East Africa, the Arab world, and sometimes farther destinations such as India.

In the late nineteenth century, the acquisition and transport of slaves and ivory from central and eastern Africa to the Arab world was largely organized by merchants from the island of Zanzibar and surrounding areas on the East African coast, where Swahili is widely spoken—either as mother tongue or as language of trade. Because only "some of them were pure Arabs, [while] others were of mixed African blood [or] African converts to Islam," they are now commonly known under terms such as "Swahilo-Arabs." In the European sources written at that time they were simply (but somewhat misleadingly) called "Arabs."[1]

Western traders usually acquired the slaves (and also the ivory) they intended to export "by purchase or negotiation with local rulers, merchants, or noblemen"—they rarely got their own hands bloody by organizing or participating in slave raids.[2] Many of the Swahilo-Arab merchants took a more active role. It was not rare for them to join forces with local people to raid nearby villages. Often, instead of paying their allies, they agreed to share the spoils in a mutually agreeable way. The consumption of human flesh is as strongly proscribed in Islam as in the Christian world, and there are no indications that these Muslim traders did not take this prohibition seriously—for themselves. Various accounts, however, reveal that at least some of them were willing to join forces with those who considered human flesh a delicious part of the spoils—provided that enough good-to-sell slaves remained for the Swahilo-Arabs.

These arrangements were not always free of conflicts. In 1863, the British explorer and officer Sir Samuel White Baker (1821–1893) met the party of a certain Ibrahim, a Swahilo-Arab trading in ivory and slaves. One of Ibrahim's men, who called himself Ibrahimawa, told Baker that they had for some years done business with the "Makkarika, a cannibal tribe"—a local name used for the Zande people.[3] He characterized them as "remarkably good people," who nevertheless had a "peculiar taste for dogs and human flesh."[4]

> They accompanied the trading party in their razzias, and invariably ate the bodies of the slain. The traders complained that they were bad associates, as they insisted upon killing and eating the children which the party wished to secure as slaves: their custom was to catch a child by its ankles, and to dash its head against the ground; thus killed, they opened the abdomen, extracted the stomach and intestines, and tying the two ankles to the neck they carried the body by slinging it over the shoulder, and thus returned to camp, where they divided it by quartering, and boiled it in a large pot.[5]

If this was the behavior of remarkably good people, one wonders what bad people might have done. Despite the disagreement between the Swahilo-Arab slavers and their local allies about the fate of captured children, the Arabs were evidently satisfied enough with the arrangement to keep the "Makkarika" as allies and porters. Though some children were killed, they apparently still got enough captives to make the joint raids a success for both parties.

A man employed by Baker told him that he had once seen a group of Swahilo-Arab traders, who brought with them a "great number of slaves" and were accompanied by a group of "Makkarika" porters, carrying the ivory the Arabs had purchased or robbed. When they stopped at Gondokoro, the town where Baker was at that time,[6] one of the enslaved girls tried to run away. Her owner (one of the Swahilo-Arabs) shot and wounded her, causing "a large lump of yellow fat" to exude from the bullet wound.[7] When the "Makkarika" saw this, they

> rushed upon her in a crowd, and seizing the fat, they tore it from the wound in handfuls, the girl being still alive, while the crowd were quarrelling for the disgusting prize. Others killed her with a lance, and at once divided her by cutting off the head, and splitting the body with their lances, used as knives, cutting longitudinally from between the legs along the spine to the neck.[8]

Fearing for their lives, "many slave women and their children who witnessed this scene, rushed panic-stricken from the spot and took refuge in the trees." But this incited the "Makkarika" to "give chase": they pulled several children from the trees (the mothers, it seems, were spared), slaughtered them, "and in a short time a great feast was prepared for the whole party." The man added that after witnessing this "horrible feast" he could not eat anything for the next three days.[9]

In other cases, the arrangements about dividing the spoils seem to have worked out better. Around 1870, the German botanist and ethnologist Georg Schweinfurth traveled for some time with a Swahilo-Arab ivory and slave trader named Mohammed—a man he considered his "friend."[10] Mohammed cleverly exploited the hostilities between different clans of the Zande, who are not a monolithic people but made up of various culturally diverse ethnicities or clans, only some of which practiced cannibalism.[11] Mohammed convinced one of these clans to join him in his "usual raid against the Babuckur" (or Babukur)—another Zande clan, though Schweinfurth apparently did not know this.[12] Mohammed sought to acquire both corn to feed his caravan and female slaves to sell. The Zande, by agreement, also got some of the captured women, whom they used in various ways: "the youngest were destined for their houses [as servants and consorts], the middle-aged for their agriculture [to work in the fields], and the eldest for their caldrons [*sic*]!"[13]

Schweinfurth reports that he personally saw how, after the raid, Zande warriors "were bestowed with old unfit women—for eating." A few days later, he purchased the fresh skulls of several of these women for the Anatomical Museum of Berlin.[14] That, by paying for the bodily remains, he might have given an incentive for further cannibal killings does not seem to have concerned him; instead he comments: "as I was not able to bring the poor [women] to life again I saw no reason why I should not purchase their remains in the interests of science."[15]

Schweinfurth does not say what became of the men killed or captured in the raid. According to Filiberto Gero, who spent several decades among the Zande, male captives had often been killed and eaten quickly—they might have been considered too dangerous to keep alive.[16] While younger women were kept alive as slaves, the Zande saw no reason to raise their babies, as Schweinfurth learned shortly after the raid. In a local farmstead he met

> an old woman . . . sitting surrounded by a group of boys and girls, all busily employed in cutting up gourds and preparing them for eating. . . . Midway between the two huts a mat was outspread; upon this mat, exposed to the full glare of the noon-day sun, feebly gasping, lay a new-born infant: I doubt whether it was more than a day old.[17]

When he inquired why they did not take better care of the baby, the locals told him that, cooked together with the gourds, it would soon make "a dainty dish." The mother, they explained, was "one of the slaves who had been captured in the late raid," but her baby had been taken from her "because its nurture would interfere with her properly fulfilling her domestic duties." Young servants, insofar as they were desired, could be captured—there was no need to raise them from birth. Schweinfurth was so appalled that he "felt ready to shoot the old hag" who was calmly organizing the preparations for the meal. But (he adds) "I was swayed by the protestations of the Nubians [Swahilo-Arabs] ringing in my ears that they were powerless in the matter, and that they had not come to be lawgivers to the Niam-niam [Zande]," and so he decided to leave the women and the baby to their respective fates.[18]

His comment refers to a repeated discussion he had with his Swahilo-Arab companions:

> Often I reproached the Nubians of my retinue with allowing such abuses to go on before their eyes, and under the sanction of the flag bearing the insignia of the Holy Prophet; but just as often I received the answer that the Faithful were incompetent to change anything, but must submit to the will of God; it was impressed upon me that the Niam-niam were heathen, and that if the heathen liked to eat each other up, it was no concern of theirs; they had no right to be lawgivers or teachers to cannibals.[19]

Considering that their own leader, Schweinfurth's friend Mohammed, had organized the raid and convinced the Zande warriors to participate in it, this absence of "concern" is certainly remarkable. But this attitude seems to have been quite typical for Swahilo-Arab traders who came into Central Africa and enlisted local help. They were likely morally strict in their own behavior towards other Muslims, but they disclaimed all responsibility for the actions of nonbelievers, including their own allies. Schweinfurth also observes that they were not at all keen to spread the Islamic faith in the regions they visited, since believers had to be treated as "brothers" and could no longer be legally enslaved.[20]

The neighboring Mangbetu people also repeatedly accompanied Swahilo-Arab merchants on their raids, and here similar arrangements were made. Schweinfurth talked with several Swahilo-Arabs who told him they had seen their companions "cut [human] flesh into long strips and dry . . . it over the fire in its preparation for consumption." He heard that the corpses of all enemies killed during fights were dried and taken home for consumption; many prisoners claimed by the Mangbetu were subsequently eaten too.[21] The Swahilo-Arabs were apparently quite willing to let the Mangbetu keep any children too young to make useful slaves; while Schweinfurth stayed at the court of King Munza, he heard persistent rumours "that nearly every day some little [captive] child was sacrificed to supply" the royal table. Even though he repeatedly visited the king, he was never allowed to join his meals or indeed to observe any Mangbetu eating. Munza frankly told him that since he knew of the European's "aversion," he had ordered that any cannibal acts had to take place "in secret" during his stay.[22]

Schweinfurth nevertheless once spotted a human arm being smoked over a fire. Another time he saw "a number of young women who had a supply of boiling water upon the clay floor in front of the doorway of a hut, and were engaged in the task of scalding the hair off the lower half of a human body"—a sight that reminded him "of the soddening and scouring of our fatted swine."[23]

The Italian explorer Gaetano Casati (1838–1902), who visited the Mangbetu more than a decade later, received similar information about the fate of children captured in their regular raids against neighboring peoples. He notes that, while adult captives were kept as "slaves to be employed in the fields, . . . it is said that very young ones are still destined to satisfy cannibal taste."[24] Adults could usually expect a better fate, but only as long as they behaved. By then, Munza had been succeeded by his brother and, in contrast to Schweinfurth, Casati saw the court officials dine (he does not say whether he was invited himself) and was "horror-struck" when the "roasted leg of [a] woman" was served. It turned out that the leg had belonged to an enslaved woman, who, "weary of long-continued service, left her master's house, and went to stay with some friends." Punishment was swift and harsh: she was executed and her body donated (or sold?) to the royal court for consumption.[25]

The Raids and Exploitations of Tippu Tip

The most successful of all the Swahilo-Arab merchants in the Congo was Hamad bin Muhammad el Murjebi (1832–1905), better known under his nickname Tippu Tip. His men intruded deeper into the Congo basin than those of his competitors, and from 1887 to 1892 he even served as a governor of the newly established Congo Free State. While Tippu Tip held considerable power for some time, his main goal, shared with the other Swahilo-Arabs, seems to have been the augmentation of his wealth through the acquisition and resale of slaves and ivory. One of his subordinates told the British adventurer and sculptor Herbert Ward that, from the first expedition he undertook for Tippu Tip, he had been instructed "to obtain as many slaves and tusks of ivory" as possible.[26]

In the early 1880s, the German explorer Hermann Wissmann (1853–1905) encountered a large Swahilo-Arab camp near the Lukushi River, a tributary of the Lualaba, the largest headstream of the Congo. In the camp, he estimates, were about five hundred Swahilo-Arab slave raiders, accompanied by an even larger number of local "cannibals" they had recruited as allies. They were led by a young man named Said who worked for Tippu Tip.[27] After visiting the camp, several of Wissmann's soldiers returned

> livid with fear and loathing, reporting that Said . . . had for a long time practised firing with a revolver, making a target of [a group of wounded] prisoners, until they had dropped down after many shots. He had then

Figure 5.1. Said shooting at prisoners. Drawing from Hermann von Wissmann's *My Second Journey through Equatorial Africa from the Congo to the Zambesi in the Years 1886 and 1887* (London: Chatto & Windus, 1891), opposite p. 202.

handed over his dead victims to his auxiliary troops, who had cut them in pieces and dragged them to the fire to serve as their supper.[28]

While Said's cruelty might have been exceptional, dealings between Tippu Tip's slavers and local cannibals were not. In 1887/88, Ward and his Scottish companion James Sligo Jameson (1856–1888) stayed for a year at Yambuya, a village situated on the Aruwimi River, a right-bank tributary in the eastern Congo basin. They belonged to the so-called Emin Pasha Relief Expedition, organized by the (already famous) explorer Sir Henry Morton Stanley (1841–1904) for the purpose of sending relief, or additional support, to Emin Pasha, the governor of Equatoria. Today the southern part of South Sudan, at that time Equatoria was an Egyptian province, but it had been cut off by an insurrection led by Muhammad Ahmad, a self-proclaimed "Mahdi" who had established an Islamist regime that would last for almost twenty years.

Since Stanley did not find enough porters to carry all the equipment and goods he had brought along, he left six Europeans and some of the porters he had already hired behind as a "rear guard." They had to wait at Yambuya while Stanley went to Equatoria with an advance guard of about four hundred men. According to an agreement between Stanley and Tippu Tip, the latter was to provide the missing porters, but apparently he was not keen to keep his part of the bargain. Therefore Ward, Jameson, and their companions were stuck at Yambuya, surrounded by Tippu Tip's fighters who repeatedly raided the neighboring peoples for slaves.[29]

During this time, Ward recorded a talk with the leader of Tippu Tip's men: "Had a chat with Selim bin Mohammed this morning about cannibals. He told me he had frequently seen the natives he used to have with him in these parts… kill a slave, cut it [*sic*] up, and eat the flesh in front of him."[30]

Selim added (apparently finding nothing wrong with these arrangements) that Tippu Tip commonly paid his native carriers by "divid[ing] the slaves they catch *en route*. Tippoo Tib takes one-half, and the carriers the other portion, whom they kill and eat."[31] One month later, Ward talked with two other Swahilo-Arab leaders who were equally frank:

> They told me that these friendly tribes who live around the Arabs' camp generally accompany them upon their raiding excursions, and appropriate all the dead and wounded, who they cut up and divide, drying the greater portion for future use. They said they had seen heaps of human flesh three feet high, cut up into serviceable joints.[32]

Despite these frank admissions, the members of Stanley's rear guard were on friendly terms with the Swahilo-Arabs. Neither were they deterred by the latter's raids against nearby villages, which are repeatedly mentioned in the diaries of the two men.[33] Once a porter came to Ward, "looking very scared" and explaining that "he had seen a lot of Selim's Manyemas eating and cooking the flesh of the natives they had just killed."[34] Another time, Ward was invited by the Swahilo-Arabs to a "village of cannibals" with whom they were on friendly terms.

> On arriving there, almost the first man I saw was carrying four large lumps of human flesh, with the skin still clinging to it, on a stick; and, through Fida [a local woman serving as interpreter], I found that they had killed a man this morning, and had divided the flesh. Subsequently I came across a party of men squatting round a fire, before which this ghastly flesh, exposed on spits, was cooking.[35]

During one of his other journeys through the Congo basin, Ward complains in another book, "when camping for the night with a party of Arab raiders and their followers, we were compelled to change the position of our tent owing to the offensive smell of human flesh, which was being cooked on all sides of us."[36]

He notes that a state of permanent warfare prevailed around the Aruwimi River. This situation, he suspects, was exacerbated, if not created by the Swahilo-Arabs' frequent raids for slaves and ivory.[37] The British journalist Edward Glave reflects that the Swahilo-Arab slavers accepted the cannibalism of their allies because it served their purpose, allowing them to "enlist . . . tribes in [their] behalf, paying them for their services as fighting men and guides by a share of the 'meat' obtained in the raids—being the human beings killed by these brutes." He points out, however, that Westerners were likewise to blame, because they provided the Arabs and their followers with guns and because they often purchased the ivory acquired in their raids, ignoring all the "atrocities" committed to get it.[38] Again it is clear that Congolese cannibalism was not a local phenomenon, but tied to the world market—and contemporary witnesses had noticed this.

Tippu Tip himself was not so stupid or careless as to openly admit that he or his subordinates rewarded their allies with human flesh. But in his dialogues with his biographer, the German author Heinrich Brode, he admits to cooperating with cannibals at least once—in his version, mainly for purposes of revenge. One of his expeditions (he told Brode) had ended in disaster—his uncle and sixty of his men had been killed and "devoured by the cannibal natives," somewhere west of Kasongo, a town in the east-Congolese Maniema region. To get revenge, as well as more slaves, he organized a huge campaign, gaining a party of Maniema warriors as allies.[39] What happened then is described by Brode:

> Killing and burning, as usual, they marched from place to place, and the cruelties elsewhere practised were enhanced by all the male prisoners being devoured, at which the victors developed a hearty appetite, two of them eating up a whole man. Tippoo Tib endeavoured to put a stop to these doings—less out of love for his neighbour than because the sickening smell of the slaughtered human flesh upset him. The Manjema, however, paid little heed to his representations. "If," they replied, "we are not to eat men's flesh, do you refrain from goat's flesh." In face of this reasonable argument things remained as they were.[40]

Cannibal Acts Tolerated or Ignored by the Congo Free State

In 1885, the Belgian King Leopold II had managed to gain control over the Congo as his "private colony" by suggesting that his purposes were entirely disinterested and philanthropic, but nothing could have been further from the truth. While "suppression of the slave trade . . . and an improvement in the well-being of Africans" were among the declared goals of the Free State, in practice these principles were all but ignored.[41] Instead, the Free State government soon got busy extracting as much commercial gain from the Congo region and its inhabitants as possible. The British diplomat Roger Casement notes: "The Government, so far as I could judge, is conducted almost exclusively on commercial principles, and, even judged by that standard, it would appear that those principles are somewhat short-sighted," with short-term wealth extraction being favored over long-term improvement of the country.[42]

Because anything that did not help to improve the earnings of the administration was neglected, the suppression of slavery and cannibalism ranked low among the priorities of Free State officials. In 1902, slaves were still "almost daily" openly "exposed for sale" in some cities.[43] Nor were cannibal acts consistently prosecuted. Edgar Canisius (1865–?) and Guy Burrows (1861–1912) were two Free State officials who later turned whistleblowers, writing a book that documented the ultra-exploitative mode of operations of the government. Burrow writes that, when he was stationed near the Mongala River, a right-bank tributary which joins the Congo about four hundred kilometers upriver (northeast) of the Ubangi, he and his colleagues "were well aware that scores of slaves were being sold to supply meat to the people on the other side of the river. They were smuggled up a small creek called the Dolo, in the neighbourhood of which the consumption of man-meat was said to be enormous."[44]

Burrows would have liked to stop the deadly trade, but he failed to convince the government to take action. Most other officials, and likewise the private companies licensed to work in the area, were busy extracting as much rubber as possible, he complains. They cared little what the natives did to each other as long as they continued to supply it. And so, even after more than ten years of colonial rule, "the ancient traffic in slaves for the shambles flourishes unhindered."[45]

Around the same time, adds Canisius, the Budja (or Budza) people—a Bangala subgroup like their neighbors, the already mentioned Boloki[46]—were still "known to be exceedingly fond of human flesh, and the number of slaves annually killed among them for food must be very large." The government, considering them too warlike to get into conflict with, tended to leave them alone, instead "preferred to wage war upon the weaker and more docile of the tribes," who could more easily be subdued and exploited for commercial gain.[47]

Free State officials did not just turn a blind eye towards cannibalism among the population, they also accepted such acts among native fighters recruited into their army or considered as "auxiliaries." In 1892, conflicts between the Swahilo-Arab merchants and the Free State administration about who should control the eastern parts of the country erupted into open warfare. After two years the fighting ended with the victory of the Free State troops.

A detailed description of the war was published by Sidney Hinde, who had participated as a captain of the Free State Forces.[48] Both sides relied largely on native forces who in some cases were accustomed to cannibalism. Hinde describes this frankly, even highlighting the positive aspects he found in the habit, noting that, by "dispos[ing] of all the dead, leaving nothing even for the jackals," the cannibals "saved us, no doubt, from many an epidemic."[49] After fights, all the killed and wounded left on the battlefield were routinely "cut up to furnish a banquet in the evening to the victorious survivors." To his "disgust," Hinde found "that the camp followers and friendlies made no difference in this respect between the killed and wounded on their own side or the enemy's." Eating one's own relatives was forbidden, as he observed in one incident. Another time he witnessed how those who had accidentally eaten the dead wife of an important chief were executed and consumed as punishment. In general, however, enmity was no precondition for cannibal acts.[50]

Like Hinde, many Free State officials seem to have accepted the cannibal acts of their allies and supporters as something that was unfortunate, but that had to be accepted for the time being. Oscar Michaux, a Belgian official already accustomed to local customs, had to calm down another European after the latter, "straight out from Europe," had seen "a human leg being cooked."[51] Subsequently, he wrote that he "explain[ed] as well as I could that I knew it was horrible, but still, for the moment, we had to pretend not to see it, so as not to be obliged to interfere."[52]

Nyangwe is a town in the Maniema region which had been one of the main centers of the Swahilo-Arabs. The conquest of this town was followed by days of cannibal feasting, in which hundreds of the slain were consumed, as Hinde graphically describes.[53] Sometime later, riots broke out among the surviving population, which were quickly and brutally suppressed. Emile Lémery, another young Belgian official stationed in the town, wrote home that "certainly a thousand people were killed in a few hours [in retaliation]. Happily Gongo's men, cannibals *par excellence,* ate them up at the same rate. It's horrible but exceedingly useful and hygienic. . . . I should have been horrified at the idea in Europe! but it seems quite natural to me here."[54]

Considering this almost positive attitude, it is not so surprising that in the years that followed the Free State administration seems to have done little to stamp out cannibal customs even among the native soldiers it employed. And the brutally exploitative regime established by the administration gave soldiers with such customs new opportunities to satisfy them. In the early 1890s, a system of forced labor, justified as a head tax, was set up whereby all native inhabitants of the colony had to regularly deliver certain quantities of rubber—one of the most valuable resources that could be found in the region—to the government.[55]

If the quota was not met, the Free State military was summoned to terrorize the population into submission. The required work was so extensive that it was often nearly impossible to deliver the requested quota, but that only increased the wrath of the government officials. In some cases, whole villages were ravaged by punitive expeditions.[56] Edmund Dene Morel (1873–1924) was a British journalist who wrote a series of articles and books that helped to expose the crimes of the Free State government to the European public.

In the 1890s, he had acquired firsthand knowledge of the local situation while working as a clerk for a Liverpool shipping firm that did business with the Free State; additionally, he asked missionaries who had been allowed to work in the Congo to send him their accounts.

Kenred Smith of the British Baptist Missionary Society wrote him that, in June 1898, he visited a village that had just been hit by a punitive expedition because its inhabitants had not fulfilled their rubber quota. He "saw mutilated bodies or parts of bodies representing some twenty people, and new-made graves bringing up the number to at least thirty." The survivors told him that at least two hundred people been killed in this and and some nearby villages and that "a cannibal feast [had] followed the slaughter." He reported this to the local administration but did not receive any response.[57]

Five years later, another group of Baptist missionaries arrived in a village on the Congo River that had been "occupied by a party of Congo Government soldiers under two white officers." As one of them reported to Morel, they saw "the native soldiers of the administration, under the very eyes of their officers, engaged in mutilating dead bodies of natives who had just been killed." They were in the process of dismembering several bodies, one of them a child, "and human limbs were lying within a few yards of the [mission] steamer as she sought to make fast. . . . A State soldier was seen drawing away the legs and other portions of a human body. Another soldier was seen standing by a large native basket in which were the viscera of a human body." Two officers who were present quickly ordered the missionaries to leave the beach and move on.[58]

Human Flesh as Reward

In the accounts considered so far, Free State officials did at least turn a blind eye to cannibal practices, but it is unclear whether they actively approved or facilitated them. In other cases, some of them went farther than that, giving cannibal allies or subordinates opportunities or at least tacit approval for such acts. In 1903, Roger Casement traveled through the Free State to investigate the alarming rumors that by then had reached the European public. His resulting report[59] played an important role in turning the public opinion against Leopold's reign of terror.

Among the locals interviewed by Casement was a girl who lived near Lake Tumba, a lake situated near the Congo River opposite the confluence of the Ubangi. When soldiers arrived in her town in order to punish the inhabitants for their noncompliance with the tax demands of the government, she and her little sister tried to hide. But they were discovered by soldiers who immediately killed her sister, stating that she was too young to keep up with them and carrying her would have meant too much trouble. The older girl, whose name Casement abbreviates as S S, was taken to a neighboring town, together with two other prisoners, among them "a very old woman." A group of "soldiers asked C D [a white officer] to give them the old woman to eat, and C D told them to take her. Those soldiers took the woman and cut her throat, and then divided her and ate her. S S saw all this done."[60]

The murder and consumption of the old woman had taken place not only with the knowledge of the white officer, but with his explicit permission. S S later managed to run away. She had had at least four siblings, but when Casement talked to her, she was the sole survivor of her family: "S S's mother was killed by soldiers, and her father died of starvation, or rather, he refused to eat because he was bereaved of his wife and all his children."[61]

Other survivors had similar experiences. David Van Reybrouck quotes a man whose village was attacked because the villagers had failed to fulfill the demanded rubber quota. He reported that the village chieftain was murdered immediately, together with two of his wives and a child that "was cut in two." The bodies were then eaten by the soldiers. Ten men, who had tried to flee, were caught and killed as well. When the soldiers left, they deliberately left parts of a human body behind, "chopped into pieces and mixed with banana and manioc, in plain sight, to frighten the villagers."[62]

A woman remembered how, when she was a young girl, soldiers had come into her village and started to arbitrarily shoot at people "because of the rubber. My father was murdered: they tied him to a tree and shot and killed him, and when the sentries untied him they gave him to their boys, who ate him."[63]

Another work that helped exposing the crimes of Leopold's government was *The Curse of Central Africa* (1903) by the two whistleblowers Guy Burrows and Edgar Canisius, already mentioned. Burrows had worked for six years for the Free State government, ultimately as a district commander; Canisius had spent five years working for the government and for one of the concessionary companies which had received exclusive licenses to exploit the country's resources. After their return both decided that they could not remain silent about the things they had witnessed in the Congo.

John George Leigh, the author of the book's introduction, claims that "it is notorious that the Congo native troops were living for the most part on the flesh of prisoners taken on the road and on the corpses of the Dzande people killed in the skirmishes." In 1896, during a punitive expedition against a village accused of "massacring two white men and fifty native soldiers . . . a woman and infant captured in the bush were brought into camp and taken before the commander and his Belgian staffs."[64] Though the mother pleaded for the life of her child, "at a sign from the [Belgian] leader of the expedition," one of the soldiers "took the child from its mother, and, holding it up by one leg, disembowelled and afterwards cut its throat before the eyes of the wretched mother, who in her turn was murdered and very probably devoured by the soldiers."[65]

One year earlier, a troop led by the Belgian officer Hubert Lothaire was sent to suppress a rebellion on the Lomami River, a left-bank tributary of the

Congo. They captured "a dozen men and women" who were "butchered with small knives. . . . Their corpses were afterwards passed as food to the native auxiliaries."[66]

Burrows explains that soldiers were deliberately stationed far away from their own villages, to extinguish feelings of relationship and neighborly concern. This allowed them to be used in the "punitive raids" which the Free State army repeatedly undertook against villages that had "not sent in enough rubber or ivory" to fulfill the demands of the government. Villages who had not made the quota were often "wiped out" to make an example of them. Men and women who tried to escape or resist were shot; the rest were taken captive and distributed among various state stations and farms for employment as forced laborers. "The children are drafted down to the Catholic missionaries to be educated in the rudiments of Christianity and civilized vice."[67]

If the desperate situation led to open resistance or rebellion, the state reacted with even bloodier raids, in which men, women, and children were arbitrarily killed. The measure of "success" of each squad was the number of dead enemies. For each killed warrior, his spear and shield were collected and counted, while a small stick was collected for every killed unarmed woman or child. Almost all the victims were civilians—usually there were about ten "sticks" for each "spear." Even children who tried to hide from the approaching soldiers were shot without mercy.[68]

Children captured alive were sometimes handed over to native allies who still practiced cannibalism and might well have regarded them as a source of food. The Free State finally decided to take military action against the Budja people, not because (as mentioned above) they were still openly cannibalistic, but because they evaded the oppressive tax regime and had "massacred" a group of soldiers who tried to impose order.[69] Canisius, who took part in the resulting punitive expedition, writes that his soldiers captured three infants from one of the attacked villages, who had "been lost or abandoned" when the villagers fled from the upcoming attack. Not knowing what to do with their young captives, they passed them on to a Budja chief who had decided to take the side of the government. "Very possibly they later on found their way into that dusky diplomat's cooking-pots," he adds.[70]

In this case, at least, it is unclear what became of the captive infants—maybe they were adopted into families and reached an old age. In other cases, Free State officials openly rewarded their auxiliaries with booty which included human bodies and human flesh. The anthropologist Robert B. Edgerton writes about a group "known as Zappo Zaps after the sound of their rifles," that state officers "paid [these] heavily armed men from the cannibalistic Basongye [Songye] tribe to enforce their trading policies. . . . [W]henever a village failed to produce enough rubber, these men would attack, raping and eating their victims before cutting off their hands."[71]

In September 1899, more than seven hundred Zappo Zap fighters raided and burned several villages near the mission station where the Presbyterian missionary William Sheppard was employed. Sheppard immediately visited their camp to find out what had happened. In his diary, he documented his talk with their chief, M'lumba N'kusa. "I don't like to fight, . . . but the state told me if the villages refused to pay to make fire," the latter told him. Accordingly, he had asked "all [the] chiefs, sub-chiefs, men and women" of the peaceful Pianga people to visit his camp for a "palaver." They appeared for what they expected to be a round of peaceful talking, but after their arrival, N'kusa closed the fence around the camp and "demanded all my pay or I would kill them." When they refused, almost all of them were killed; only a few managed to escape though breaches in the fence. N'kusa estimated that "between 80 and 90" persons had been killed right in the camp. Subsequently he sent his fighters to attack the helpless villages of the murdered chiefs, where many more were killed.[72]

Walking around the camp with the chief, Sheppard saw three naked corpses "with the flesh carved off from the waist down," leaving only the bones. "My people ate them," explained the chief. One of the dead was a headless man—the forehead had been turned into a "bowl . . . to rub up tobacco and dimba in," the chief added.[73] Altogether, Sheppard counted forty-one bodies, many of them partially or fully defleshed. He was told that there had been more victims but that the rest had been completely consumed (their bones apparently discarded somewhere he did not see). Most of the dead were men, but he also saw a woman whose limbs had been totally defleshed. The partially defleshed bodies of several persons hung from trees; Sheppard observed that one of them had been "tied with ropes," indicating that the victim had been alive when bound to the tree. He also saw sixty living women who had been taken captive.[74]

Lachlan Vass, another clergyman, sent by the mission to verify Sheppard's findings, "counted fourteen incinerated villages and forty-seven corpses, some of them partially eaten."[75] After the missionaries reported the incident to the Free State authorities, the captured women were released and M'lumba N'kusa was temporarily jailed. He resented this treatment, complaining to the *chef du zone,* a Mr. DuFour: "You have sent me to do this and yet you have put me in chains." DuFour was never charged with anything.[76]

Though the Free State officially forbade slavery, it employed forced laborers on the state-owned farms whose status could hardly, or not at all, be distinguished from that of slaves. Burrows writes that "case[s] of slave-raiding by the Belgian officials and officers . . . are frequent throughout the Congo, [and] the example set by the State is only too readily followed by the companies" licensed to work in the Free State.[77] Once he met a Luba woman named Ilanga who had been enslaved a few weeks ago. She told him that a large group of Free State soldiers, led by a white officer, had come into their village, seized all the people, and carried them off as captives. They had no idea what—if anything—they had done wrong. The soldiers forced the villagers to carry "baskets of food," some of which contained "smoked human flesh." The group of captives to which the women belonged were made to work on the state-run plantations around Burrows' post.[78]

Sometimes there were disputes between the state and the concessionary companies about how to share the spoils. In one such dispute, "the State and company's agents mutually accused each other of having purchased rubber with human flesh, of which, it was said, a quantity had been found in one of the capita posts." Burrows comments that "it is very certain that one or the other, and perhaps both, had been guilty of this awful barter." Indeed, he considered it quite likely that the state had participated in the cannibalistic trade, since the "region had been almost depopulated by the agents of the State," and he saw no reason to assume that the agents had more respect for the dead bodies of the natives than for their lives. But as the state ran the legal system, the blame was squarely put on low-ranking members of the company. "One black capita [head man]" was arrested, while "his white employers, of course, were left unmolested."[79]

In 1901, Burrows investigated accusations of misconduct brought forward against the employees of another concessionary company, the "Isangi Company, which has a monopoly in the district" where Burrows was district commissioner.[80] At that time, the company controlled a trading station with the same name; today, Isangi is a town in the northeastern Tshopo province of Congo-Kinshasa. According to several witnesses, a company assistant named M[r]. Hottiaux had been involved in the death and subsequent consumption of several people. A local chief stated under oath that a man who had killed two others in a dispute was first whipped by Hottiaux and then "handed . . . over to . . . chief Massanga to be eaten."[81] Two eyewitnesses reported that Hottiaux had sentenced a young man employed as his "boy" to death merely for returning to his village without permission, afterwards giving the dead body "to the natives of the neighbouring village to be eaten."[82]

Another chief, Liamba, stated that in return for materials he supplied for constructing the company buildings and for work performed by his men, he "was paid with the corpses of the prisoners killed by M. Hottiaux." Liamba himself had been present when Hottiaux ordered the captives in question to be killed. Another time, Hottiaux gave him live captives, "six women and two men . . . in payment for rubber which I brought into the station," telling him to "eat them, or kill them, or use them as slaves—as I liked."[83]

Hottiaux's carpenter confirmed that he had repeatedly seen prisoners being brought to the post. "Some of them were given to the natives to be kept as slaves, or to be eaten, at the will of the chief." He also saw how nine men and two women were killed by cutting their throats upon Hottiaux's orders. Subsequently Hottiaux gave their corpses to some of his workers as payment, telling them to "cut them up" for consumption.[84] After hearing these witnesses, Burrows concluded that all charges were "satisfactorily proved"; he added that such charges "are by no means uncommon in the annals of Belgian administration."[85] He does not state which punishment Hottiaux received.

Some years earlier, Burrows was present during an inquiry into a "massacre of 150 natives who had been killed" in a punitive expedition. The Free State troops had motivated a large number of native auxiliaries to participate in the attack by promising them "the bodies to eat," as well as "loot and women."[86] Burrows does not say whether the inquiry led to any convictions.

The Congo Free State was not the only European colonial regime erected in Africa that tolerated or occasionally even facilitated cannibal acts of local auxiliaries or allies. While visiting the Ubangi region in the early 1890s, the French traveler Jacques d'Uzès says how a group of Nzakara "auxiliaries" supporting the French troops "massacre[d] some women and some children" during a punitive expedition against a local village. Then they took the bodies of those they and the French had killed, and "in the evening . . . engage[d] in a great cannibal feast that we [did] not have the means to prevent. They roast the bodies of their enemies. After removing the skin and sending their children to wash the innards in the river, they put the pieces of meat in their pot, add spices, and enjoy it."[87] The French missionary and bishop Prosper Augouard heard of similar events from French soldiers who were present when they took place.[88]

In the late nineteenth century, today's Sudan and South Sudan belonged to Egypt, which was treated by the British as a protectorate, though officially it was still a part of the Ottoman Empire. In the 1870s and early 1880s, the British army repeatedly sought the help of local allies, among them Zande and Mangbetu fighters, to crush rebellions. British as well as outside sources indicate that these allies not infrequently ate killed or captured enemies.[89] Gaetano Casati writes that, while trying to contain the Mahdist rebellion, the British deliberately handed over "seventy Arabs . . . accused of hostile feelings towards the besieged people to the Sandeh-Bombe [a Zande clan], who had hastened to help the Government; and the victims, having been slaughtered like cattle, were eaten by the hungry anthropophagi."[90]

In the 1910s, when Cameroon was a German colony, a German military commander rewarded his local allies who had helped in suppressing a rebellion with "human flesh, that of the enemies killed in battle" and with "slaves (women and children) . . . destined to be 'stocked' and eaten later," as archived documents show.[91]

Still, nowhere did the cooperation between colonial forces and local cannibals seem to have been as widespread as in the Congo Free State. Two factors likely played a role here. On the one hand, cannibalism was widespread, and many locals were used to it—especially men from warlike ethnic groups which the state liked to employ as auxiliaries or regular soldiers. On the other hand, the state's reckless exploitation of local resources and the native population seems to have encouraged an "anything goes" mentality among many of its officials; and the same is true of at least some of the employees of the large European concessionary companies licensed to exploit the country's resources in return for considerable fees.

There are no indications that cooperation with cannibals or acts such as giving away human bodies as a reward were condoned by official government policy, but neither were they strictly condemned and consistently sanctioned. When inquests took place, it seems to have been largely due to external pressure (say if missionaries had got wind of a massacre and threatened to expose it, which would have resulted in bad publicity) or if a few righteous officials such as Burrows took the initiative. Even then, it is unclear whether any white Free State or corporate official even received a serious punishment; rather, it seems that the blame was usually put on native subordinates or allies such as the "black capita" mentioned by Burrows and the Zappo Zap chief interviewed by Sheppard.

Notes

1. Van Reybrouck, *Congo*, 31–32. While Van Reybrouck uses the adjective "Swahilo-Arab," Elizabeth Isichei calls them "Arab/Swahili merchants" (Isichei, *History*, 442).
2. Thomas, *Slave Trade*, chapter 19.
3. An early edition of the *Encyclopedia Britannica* lists "Makaraka" as one of the names under which the Zande were locally known (Encyclopedia Britannica [1911 edition], "Niam-Niam [Zandeh, A-Zandeh]," https://en.wikisource.org/wiki/1911_Encyclop%C3%A6dia_Britannica/Niam-Niam). Ibrahimawa mentioned that the Makkarika lived about two hundred miles west of his meeting point with Baker (a town named Gondokoro), which fits into the area settled by the Zande.
4. Baker, *Albert N'yanza*, 278.
5. Ibid., 278–79. A similar method of carrying children destined for consumption has been reported from eastern New Guinea: "In the case of a child one hand was tied to one foot, and a warrior would sling the body over his shoulder as a hunter might a wallaby's. Usually, perhaps always, the victim was dead before he was bound in this manner" (F. Williams, *Orokaiva Society*, 172).
6. Situated on the eastern bank of the White Nile (one of the two main tributaries of the Nile) in Equatoria (today southern South Sudan).
7. Baker, *Albert N'yanza*, 279.
8. Ibid.
9. Ibid., 279–80.
10. Schweinfurth, *Heart of Africa*, 171.
11. Evans-Pritchard, "Zande Cannibalism," 252–53.
12. Filiberto Gero concludes from Schweinfurth's description that the attackers (Mohammed's allies) belonged to the Amadi or maybe the Adhuga clan (Gero, *Cannibalism in Zandeland*, 116–17).
13. Schweinfurth, *Heart of Africa*, 222.
14. Schweinfurth, "Dr. G. Schweinfurth's Reise," 139.
15. Schweinfurth, *Heart of Africa*, 223.
16. Gero, *Cannibalism in Zandeland*, 79.
17. Schweinfurth, *Heart of Africa*, 223–24.

18. Ibid., 224. In another account of his journey, Schweinfurth writes that he saw "babies" (in the plural) exposed in this manner before being butchered for food, indicating that while this was certainly the first such scene he witnessed, it might not have been the last (Schweinfurth, "Dr. G. Schweinfurth's Reise," 139).
19. Schweinfurth, *Heart of Africa*, 223.
20. Ibid.
21. Ibid., 93, 94 (quote).
22. Ibid., 63, 93–94 (quotes).
23. Ibid., 93.
24. Casati, *Ten Years in Equatoria*, 68.
25. Ibid., 119.
26. Quoted in Ward, *Voice from the Congo,* 102.
27. Wissmann, *My Second Journey*, 194–95.
28. Ibid., 202–3.
29. Jameson, *Story*, 261.
30. Ward, *My Life*, 68.
31. Ibid. As seen here as well as in later quotes, several variants of the spelling of Tippu Tip's (nick)name were in common use.
32. Ibid., 81–82.
33. Ward, *My Life*; Jameson, *Story*.
34. Ward, *My Life*, 88.
35. Ward, *Five Years*, 162.
36. Ward, *Voice from the Congo*, 309.
37. Ward, *Five Years*, 159–60.
38. Glave, *In Savage Africa*, 230–31.
39. Brode, *Tippoo Tib*, 91.
40. Ibid., 92.
41. Shillington, *Encyclopedia*, 306.
42. Casement, *Correspondence and Report*, 2.
43. Benedetto, *Presbyterian Reformers*, 141.
44. Burrows and Canisius, *Curse of Central Africa*, 210.
45. Ibid., 210 (quote), 211.
46. Weeks, "Anthropological Notes," 457.
47. Burrows and Canisius, *Curse of Central Africa*, 91.
48. Hinde, *Fall.*
49. Ibid., 69.
50. Ibid., 62–63, 134–35 (quotes).
51. Slade, *King Leopold's Congo*, 110.
52. Quoted ibid., 110–11.
53. Hinde, *Fall*, 174–75. For more on cannibalism during this war, see ibid., 119, 124–25; Edgerton, *Troubled Heart of Africa*, 102.
54. Quoted in Slade, *King Leopold's Congo*, 115 (italics in original).
55. Shillington, *Encyclopedia*, 306.
56. Van Reybrouck, *Congo*, 88–90.
57. Quoted in Morel, *Red Rubber*, 46.
58. Ibid., 62.
59. Casement, *Correspondence and Report.*

60. Ibid., 73–74.
61. Ibid., 74.
62. Quoted in Van Reybrouck, *Congo*, 90.
63. Quoted ibid., 91.
64. Burrows and Canisius, *Curse of Central Africa*, xx–xxi.
65. Ibid., xxi.
66. Ibid., xxiii.
67. Ibid., 23, 35–36.
68. Ibid., 111–12, 114.
69. Ibid., 83.
70. Ibid., 91, 127.
71. Edgerton, *Troubled Heart of Africa*, 111.
72. Quoted in Benedetto, *Presbyterian Reformers*, 122–23.
73. Quoted ibid., 123.
74. Ibid., 123–25.
75. Shaloff, *Reform*, 77.
76. Quoted in Benedetto, *Presbyterian Reformers*, 126n6.
77. Burrows and Canisius, *Curse of Central Africa*, 256.
78. Ibid., 249–52.
79. Ibid., 172–73.
80. Ibid., 262.
81. Quoted ibid., 265.
82. Quoted ibid., 266.
83. Quoted ibid., 267.
84. Quoted ibid., 267–68.
85. Ibid., 264.
86. Ibid., 269.
87. d'Uzès, *Le voyage*, 268.
88. Augouard, *28 années au Congo*, 2:277–78.
89. Wilson and Felkin, *Uganda*, 168, 187; Junker, *Travels*, 398, 449.
90. Casati, *Ten Years in Equatoria*, 204.
91. Copet-Rougier, "Tu ne traverseras," 469.

CHAPTER 6
UNDERSTANDING CONGOLESE SLAVE EATING

In the preceding chapter we explored the interconnections between Congolese cannibalism and other practices such as the ivory and slave trade and the highly exploitative regime of the Congo Free State. We have seen that there was no insurmountable chasm between "cannibals" on the one hand and "everybody else" on the other. Many of those who did not practice and who in theory might have condemned cannibalism still benefited from the practice by selling or giving people to those who would use them as food, or by joining forces with people eaters and letting them have human flesh as part of the "spoils." While so far we have thus looked at cannibalism largely from the outside, we now have to approach the practice in itself: Under what circumstances and for what reasons were slaves or purchased captives consumed? Why were people eaten at all—why not (just) eat animals or vegetable matter instead?

These questions are not easy to answer because we have no direct accounts from the people eaters themselves. All the available evidence has been recorded by persons who did not practice cannibalism and who usually clearly rejected the practice; most of them were also outsiders who had a limited understanding of the cultures in which such acts occurred. Occasionally they have recorded literal statements from the cannibals, but this is not often the case. And even then we cannot be sure how much was lost or distorted by misunderstandings between the speaker and the reporter, or whether speakers did not deliberately frame things in a way that they thought would be easier to understand or accept for the listener, while their true motives and considerations might have differed considerably.

While these caveats must be kept in mind, the large number of accounts from the Congo allows to form at least a broad picture of why and how cannibal acts took place. Details sometimes require speculation—which will be marked as such—and it is always possible that further evidence will require changes to some parts of the picture. Nonetheless, the available evidence enables us to draw a number of conclusions with a certain confidence that most of the subsequent analysis will stand the test of time.

Food for Feasts

In today's highly industrialized countries, meat is often eaten more or less on a daily basis. This was not the case in most earlier societies. Human flesh, in particular, seems to have been eaten relatively rarely throughout most of the Congolese societies practicing cannibalism. (We will later discuss some evidence of possible exceptions.) When Edward Glave traveled along the lower Ubangi River, the people he met proudly displayed the skulls of the victims they had eaten. Once he "asked one young chief, who was certainly not more than twenty-five years old, how many men he had eaten in his village, and he answered me thirty. He was greatly astonished at the horror I expressed at his answer."[1]

Despite Glave's horror, the answer also indicates that cannibalism was by no means a daily affair. The young man had (if his statement is correct) participated in the consumption of about thirty victims—he had certainly not eaten them all by himself. Assuming that he had started eating human flesh around the age of fifteen, this would mean that his village was able to get a single human body (whether of a purchased slave or a captured enemy) about three times a year; if he had already eaten it as a child (a question to which we will return later), such occasions were even rarer.

John Weeks notes that "cannibalism was very general" along the north bank of the Congo from the mouth of the Ubangi to about four hundred kilometers farther upriver—the region where the people generally known as Bangala live. Still, he adds, cannibal feasts were relatively rare, because "slaves were dear, and bloody fights [which provided dead enemies for consumption] were infrequent." While the inhabitants of the towns near Weeks' mission station "bought slaves to eat" when they could afford to do so, this was not often the case, since a male slave cost about seven times as much as a goat.[2] It seems that human flesh was a treasured luxury item, certainly not an everyday fare.

The most detailed report of a slave-eating feast held in this area comes from the Belgian officer Camille-Aimé Coquilhat (1853–1891), who had helped set up Bangala Station (today Makanza), one of the earliest outposts of the later Congo Free State on the Congo River. In October 1884 (a few months before the Free State was officially founded), he noted in his diary:

> Mongonga, the chief of Mongwele, had bought at Bolombo a native of Irebu [about 300 kilometers downriver of Makanza], who had been caught in the act of conversation, unauthorized by the husband, with a local woman. This morning, he broke his arms and legs with a sledgehammer in order to eat him tomorrow.[3]

This remark indicates that local laws could be very harsh. Just *talking* to another man's wife without her husband's permissions seems to have been enough to get a man convicted to slavery and possible death! During the following night, writes Coquilhat, the victim was "exposed . . . still alive, to soak in the river, the head alone coming out of the water." The purpose of this treatment "was to make the black skin easier to remove," he explains. In the morning, the man was beheaded, skinned, and dressed for consumption.[4]

> The head was boiled in a separate jar. As for the body, it was dismembered and put in the pot with goat quarters, palm oil and salt. Large quantities of chikwanga [cassava bread] were also cooked. Twenty jars of cane beer were assembled. Friends were invited, including Longenga, the chief of Mokolengila upstream.
>
> The feast was superb. About five o'clock the guests embarked in a large canoe, in the center of which was placed the remaining half of the steamed man in an enormous pot. They are going to continue the party at Longenga's, who has made a fine supply of beer.[5]

Mongonga decided to stop at Coquilhat's post—for a friendly chat, it seems—but the latter did not let him.

> I strictly forbade him to land, fully expressing my horror at his cannibalism. The chief of Mongwele was frankly surprised at my revulsion.
>
> "You're joking, aren't you?" he said.[6]

Only when Coquilhat told his soldiers to aim their weapons at Mongonga, the chief realized that he was serious,

> but he still did not understand it.
>
> "Why is the white man angry with me?" he asked his friends. "When he kills a goat, I do not interfere. This man whom I put to death was my property; I had neither robbed nor captured him, but bought him for fine cloth."[7]

Coquilhat's report shows that cannibal feasts could be highly social affairs. Neighbors visited and friends were invited, with the human flesh shared among all. The practice was not considered controversial—the chief organizing the feast was genuinely surprised when Coquilhat expressed his disapproval. The status of an enslaved person seems to have been similar to that of an animal; Mongonga did not understand what was bad about killing a slave, if killing a goat was acceptable.

Coquilhat confirms Weeks's observation that human-flesh meals were not frequent. He was aware of three such meals held in his "immediate vicinity" during the course of five months but adds that the actual number was likely higher, since the locals soon started to hide the practice after they had learned of the European's disapproval. Nevertheless, he estimates that not even the powerful and wealthy Mongonga was able to enjoy human flesh twenty times per year.[8]

Another account of a slave-eating feast comes from Weeks, who worked in approximately the same area as Coquilhat. The inhabitants of a village near his mission station decided

> to have a great feast. They bought as fat a slave as they could procure, broke his legs and arms, and fed him for three days, while they made a great quantity of sugarcane wine. I made every possible endeavour to save him, but utterly failed to do so, and on the third day he was killed and the horrible orgy was held.[9]

Like Coquilhat's, his account shows that such feasts were communal affairs in which a whole village might join. This is also confirmed by Herbert Ward, who in 1886 had become commander of Bangala Station, the government post cofounded by Coquilhat. The first time he witnessed cannibalism, he writes, he "saw a group of perhaps forty or fifty men gathered in a circle around a large fire" on which human flesh was being roasted.[10] According to Ward, cannibalism was still quite common when he was in the area: "almost weekly some savage act of cannibalism would be brought to my notice." Like Coquilhat and Weeks, he notes that both enemies killed in war and purchased slaves were eaten.[11]

That human bodies were a welcome addition to festive occasions has also been reported from other regions. Disasi Makulo (ca. 1871–1941) belonged to the Turumbu people who live near the confluence of the Aruwimi into the Congo River.[12] As a child, he had been kidnapped by a group of Swahilo-Arab slavers who worked for Tippu Tip. Later, he was purchased and freed by Henry Morton Stanley and became a helper of the Baptist missionary George Grenfell.[13] As he was born in a region where cannibalism was widely accepted, but educated by Europeans who strongly condemned the practice, Makulo experienced the mismatch between local and Western attitudes most clearly. In his mid-twenties, he visited the village of his birth which he had not seen for more than ten years. Once his relatives recognized him, the joy was great.

> By way of welcome, the gongs were sounded from one end of the village to the other. The next day a great feast was organized. Goats and dogs were slaughtered, and two slaves were seized to sacrifice them too. Seeing this, I was greatly indignant at the persistence in my tribe of those barbarous customs of slavery and cannibalism! But before the decapitation order was executed, I intervened and told my parents that what they wanted to do was the worst possible act. I myself went to untie these slaves.[14]

Though he had spent his first twelve or so years in this village, his compatriots no longer understood him, nor he them. "Many of them wondered with astonishment how and why I pitied these slaves, and others reproached me for having prevented them from eating the delicious flesh of man." The feast was nevertheless a success, with two days of uninterrupted dancing.[15]

But Makulo was unable to convince the villagers to change their ways. During a later visit, he saw a female slave "tied up, arms and legs, ready to be beheaded" and slaughtered for consumption. He freed her by cutting her ropes, but again it seems doubtful whether his act led to any lasting change.[16]

All these accounts indicate that human flesh was not a daily food; nor was it eaten just at occasions that had a special religious or spiritual meaning. Rather it was considered the proper food for feasts—not altogether different from animal meat, but somehow better, for reasons that we will continue to explore in subsequent sections. This observation is in agreement with an account from Sidney Hinde, who repeatedly went hunting with various Bangala men. He observed that they "always break the legs and wings, or arms, as the case might be, of birds and monkeys before killing them"—the same procedure that slaves had to undergo prior to their death and consumption, as described by Coquilhat and Weeks. When Hinde criticized their cruelty, they explained "that it was better to let the bird [or other animal] linger, as it made the flesh more tender."[17] Queried further, several Bangala men told him, independently of each other, that when they were

> at home and about to prepare a feast, the prisoner or slave who was to form the *pièce de résistance* had always his arms and legs broken three days beforehand, and was then placed in a stream, or pool of water, chin-deep, with his head tied to a stick to prevent him committing suicide, or perhaps falling asleep and thus getting drowned. On the third day he was taken out and killed, the meat then being very tender.[18]

While both animals and human victims were submitted to the same cruel treatment in order to supposedly improve the taste of their meat, it seems that birds and monkeys were considered good enough for everyday fare—but when a proper feast was called for, the centerpiece had to be a "prisoner or slave."

The same procedure, apparently meant to serve the same purpose, has been documented from the Ubangi area. The Catholic mission historian G. Renouard describes the last hours of enslaved children as follows: "the arms and legs of a child are broken, and the child is left for long hours at night in the water of the river, in order to macerate the meat and make it more tender." With some pathos he adds: "The tortures and horror, the mad agony felt by the child do not move the hardened souls of the executioners.... What do the lives of others matter, provided they can add some enjoyments to theirs!"[19]

Conspicuous Consumption and Prestige

Throughout large parts of Africa, slave ownership was an important sign of status—slaves often "represented the most striking manifestation of personal wealth," notes Hugh Thomas.[20] Killing slaves could give their owners even more prestige, since it showed that they were able to waste resources and still remain wealthy. Slaves could not only be killed or buried alive at funerals, but in some regions (where cannibalism was not practiced) agreements between chiefs were confirmed by killing a slave "on the spot to mark the agreement."[21]

In some parts of Nigeria, the sacrifice and subsequent consumption of slaves at funerals and ceremonies held in honor of the dead was common throughout the nineteenth century (and probably in earlier times as well); sometimes the victim was subsequently eaten.[22] David Northrup observes that "slaves were . . . perceived as the embodiment of capital which could be destroyed as a display of wealth, particularly by killing them at funerals." He concludes that the deliberate and unprovoked killing of healthy slaves in order to display and celebrate the wealth of their owners might be considered "conspicuous consumption carried to an extreme, although there is evidence that troublesome or infirm slaves were more likely to be sacrificed than others."[23]

It is not implausible to consider the eating of slaves in the Congo as a similar case of, quite literally, "conspicuous consumption"—at least in certain regions. Slaves and captives could, in general, also have been exploited economically or sold for commercial gain. By doing neither of those, but butchering them for feasts to which one's friends and followers were invited, one could prove that one was wealthy (if slaves were usually purchased) or powerful (if captives were usually taken in warfare) enough to do so. Especially in the Ubangi region, several sources agree that holding cannibal feasts was a way for influential men to improve their standing. Ward notes that "a chief's position is esteemed according to the number of slaves he is able to kill" for the purpose of consumption.[24] Prosper Augouard agrees: "A chief is all the higher regarded the more often his people eat human flesh."[25]

So far, we have noticed that cannibal feasts were usually rare events, held only from time to time. Several sources indicate that slaves were occasionally sacrificed and eaten at funerals—similar to the human sacrifices held more commonly in Nigeria. This has been reported from the Nzakara,[26] the Ndolo on the Lulonga River,[27] and the Bangala.[28] More common, however, seems to have been celebrations held for more profane reasons, such as—in the case of Makulo—to celebrate the return of a long-lost relative.

On some parts of the upper Ubangi, cannibal meals seem to have taken place more frequently than elsewhere, possibly because the prestige associated with cannibalism motivated chiefs to try to outdo each other by providing human flesh on a more or less regular basis. The accounts of the French missionaries active in the area suggest that many (maybe most) of the victims were children—possibly because they were easier to get or less risky to handle. According to Father Allaire, a missionary who traveled extensively along the Ubangi, some chiefs owned so many children kept for future consumption that he felt himself reminded of "herds [of] sheep or geese."[29] Renouard claims that "the fattening of these children for slaughter" was a continuous operation in some areas, "and there are villages where they eat seven or eight of them per month."[30] Augouard gives a comparable number, mentioning "villages where several slaves are killed [and eaten] every week." In a letter written in May 1889, he even expresses his dismay at having "learned that in a village which I know well, a child aged ten to twelve was sacrificed every day to serve as food for the chief and the principals of the area."[31]

Though the reports of the French missionaries certainly have a factual basis, their estimations of victim counts must be treated with suspicion. They bought enslaved children they considered in danger of being eaten in order to save and liberate them—and, less altruistically, to raise them as Christians. Since they otherwise seem to have had very limited success at gaining local converts, they certainly had reason to exaggerate the risks threatening enslaved children in order to justify their ongoing purchase.

But Ed[mond?] Froment, the head of a French colonial post on the lower Ubangi, likewise reports a high number of victims, though his estimation is somewhat lower than those made by the French missionaries (who worked farther upriver). In some of the surrounding villages, he writes, "there is hardly a week that is not marked by an execution" of a slave sacrificed for food.[32] Similar to what we have heard from other observers,[33] he explains that the local people (known as Balui) sold their ivory only in return for slaves who inevitably ended their lives in the "slaughterhouses."[34]

It seems that, because human flesh was held in high esteem, people sometimes expected to receive it—rather than some other, lesser good—in return for services well-performed. The French explorer Jean Dybowski tells that when another European, Mr. Nebout,

> dismissed the four guides he had been given by the chief of a village near the river mouth, they blamed him for not killing a few men when they were on the upper [Ubangi] river for them to eat in their village when they returned home and celebrated. This lack of respect on Mr. Nebout's part seemed to them to be a sign of dissatisfaction which, they said, they did not deserve.[35]

The distribution of meat to one's followers was a way to express wealth and power and to ensure loyalty; this was a general principle, by no means specific to cannibal regions. Along the lower parts of the Congo River, closer to the West African coast, "large amounts of meat were distributed to the participants at feasts of different kinds, for example at funerals and installations of political chiefs." In this area, where cannibalism was unknown or at least rare, the meat came generally from pigs, goats, sheep, or chickens.[36] But around the Ubangi River, it seems that human flesh in particular had become a favored way of expressing appreciation and securing loyalty—Nebout's guides would likely still have been disappointed had he given them a few goats instead of human beings.

Slaves as Property and Persons of No Concern

While animal meat has been eaten in most societies, the social acceptance of cannibalism has been documented for only a few. How did Congolese cannibals see the people they ate? How did they take the humanness of their victims into account? Did they more or less ignore it, essentially treating their victims as just another kind of animal? Or did they eat them in spite of their humanness—or even because of it?

Camille-Aimé Coquilhat, as we have seen, had talked with a Bangala chief who had been genuinely surprised at the European's rejection of cannibalism, arguing instead: "When he [Coquilhat] kills a goat, I do not interfere. This man whom I put to death was my property," which he had rightfully "bought" and could therefore utilize in any way he liked.[37] One month after the slave-eating feast described by Coquilhat, a group of "boys" (native assistants) working for George Grenfell saw the preparations of a cannibalistic meal in a nearby village. In vain they tried to save the male victim from being beheaded. Reporting the incident, Grenfell describes the same way of thinking:

> The natives could not, or at least appeared not to understand why the white man and his people should take exception to their proceedings. "Why," said they to one of our boys, "do you interfere with us? We don't trouble you when you kill your goats. We buy our *nyama* (meat) and kill it; it is not your affair."[38]

The same attitude of astonished surprise, combined with the "property" argument, has been recorded by the Swedish explorer Theodor Westmark, who writes that the Bangala "have never been able to grasp our complaint" about cannibalism, instead "assuring us that they had certainly done nothing reprehensible, and that the men or women they had killed and eaten belonged to them in full ownership."[39]

The argument that slaves were property and that people could use their property in any way that pleased them seems to have been specific to the Bangala region. In later times, many Bangala would become merchants, sometimes traveling wide and far to conduct trade[40]—it seems they often showed a commercial focus which might have shaped their ways of thinking about slavery and cannibalism.

On the other hand, the equation of slaves—and of "edible" outsiders in general—with animals or simply with "meat" has also been recorded from other Congolese regions. In the early twentieth century, the Hungarian anthropologist Emil Torday stayed in a settlement on the Kwilu River, a tributary of the Kasai. He notes that not only "enemies slain in war are eaten" in this region, but that slaves were purchased and killed for this purpose. Once the local chief sent him as a gift "a so-called 'antelope leg,' which I instantly recognised as a portion of a human thigh." When Torday reproached him that "such proceedings were most improper," the chief "did not follow my reasoning," instead making it clear that he saw no reason to "distinguish between the practice of eating the flesh of goats and that of human beings."[41]

In this, adds Torday, "he took up the position of [a] vegetarian friend" of his in Europe—except that the cannibal and the vegetarian drew opposite conclusions from the shared point of view.[42] Torday observes that the inhabitants of this region did not see their cannibal practices as something that was wrong or needed any special justification: "They are not ashamed of cannibalism, and openly admit that they practise it because of their liking for human flesh."[43] Elsewhere he notes that, while cannibalism was practiced in the Congo for various reasons, including a desire to humiliate the enemy and convenience during wartime, "the most common [reason] was simply gastronomic: the natives loved 'the flesh that speaks' and paid for it."[44]

Statements equating slaves or other outsiders with edible animals were also frequently expressed around the Ubangi. While traveling along this river, Grenfell was repeatedly asked "to sell some of his Luango or Kru boys from off the steamer. Coming from the shore of the great salt sea they must be very 'sweet,' very appetizing. When he protested, they would say, 'You eat fowls and goats and we eat men; what is the difference?'"[45] On the same river, Glave was repeatedly asked "to barter a man for a tusk of ivory." And when he tried to purchase a goat to feed his party, the sellers asked for one of his crew members in return. "'Meat for meat,' they said."[46]

The Belgian author Albert Chapaux asserts that slaves were commonly referred to as "meat": "In the Ubangi, these slaves literally serve as meat for slaughter, and when the natives are asked whether they are slaves, they simply reply: 'Te, niama!' 'No, they're beasts, it's meat!'"[47] Augouard once got the same reply when asking a local chief about the name of one of his slaves: "'Nyama!' *It's meat!*"[48]

Farther east, among the Mangbetu and Zande people, similar attitudes seem to have prevailed. Not only were persons taken in slave raids and warfare often killed and eaten, if they were not considered useful to keep alive as slaves,[49] but, as we will see later (Chapter 12), unrelated foreigners were frequently kidnapped and eaten too. A widespread viewpoint seems to have been that those weak enough to be exploitable in such a manner deserved no better. In 1934, when Filiberto Gero mentioned his Zande "boy" in a conversation with a Mangbetu man, the latter reacted with disdain. "The

Azande were our meat," he explained, evidently regretting that the good old times were over. Members of different Zande clans seem to have sometimes regarded each other in the same light. A member of the Amadi told Gero that his people had formerly hunted and consumed persons belonging to the nearby Babukur clan. "They were our chickens," he remembered proudly.[50]

Similar comparisons with species of edible animals have been recorded from other ethnic groups in the vicinity. The French mission historian Jehan de Witte writes that the Kele people, who likewise live in the northeast of the Congo basin (in today's Tshopo province), "systematically" raided the neighboring Mbole for "human flesh . . . , cynically" calling them "their antelopes."[51] That neighboring groups who were raided, killed, and eaten were disdainfully called "our game" has also been reported from other parts of the world, such as New Guinea.[52]

When Gero compiled a vocabulary of Madi, the language of the Amadi clan, he noticed that the words for "stranger" and "meat" were identical and that the word for "wild game" differed by just one vowel.[53] The famous English anthropologist E. E. Evans-Pritchard (1902–1973) talked with an old Zande man who told him that, in former times, enemies and strangers were eaten simply because they "made good meat." They could be eaten without regret and without any specific justification, because, as a Zande might ask rhetorically, "What was a stranger to him?"[54] Nothing, it seems, but meat.

Similar to Gero's observation about the Madi language, the anthropologist Kajsa Ekholm Friedman points out that various Bantu languages spoken in the Congo region use the same word for "fallen enemy" and "game." She concludes that enemies and other outsiders "are not real human beings and can therefore be placed in the category 'game,' that is, among other delicious creatures that roam in the forest."[55]

While there is clearly some truth in this statement, it may nevertheless be somewhat misleading, since it presupposes a concept of a "(real) human being" that, from the cannibal viewpoint, might simply not have been relevant. Throughout the Congo (and elsewhere), enslaved women were not only exploited sexually, but they were also often forced to become wives or consorts of their captors or owners and bear them children. The cannibals no doubt knew they could interbreed with their slaves or captives and hence, in this sense at least, form a common species. It rather seems that, when it came to the question of who or what was "edible," this did not matter to them. Slaves and captives could be equated with "game" and "meat" not because they were thought to be members of a different species, but because they were persons of no concern.

Writing about the Bangala, Weeks states that—as far as he could discover—their concepts of morality and "being good" were only concerned with the proper behavior towards relatives, neighbors, and superiors. Stealing from neighbors or otherwise harming them was wrong, but "in dealing with an alien it would not be considered wrong to rob, beat, abuse, or even murder him, unless he had come on a visit, for trade or other purposes, to some one in the town." Strangers did not belong to any category of beings that morally mattered. Since they knew this, persons traveling in small groups in places where they had no friends "would hide by day and travel by night" to avoid being spotted; if they were, they could be captured and enslaved, or killed and eaten, without anyone considering such deeds as wrong or objectionable. Concerning the consumption of killed strangers, enemies, and slaves, Weeks comments that "I do not think they regarded the eating of human flesh with any more concern than they did the eating of a goat."[56]

Regarding the Ubangi area, both Froment and Augouard stress that the local people were not mean or intentionally cruel—but also that they routinely treated their slaves in the same way as goats or other animals, apparently not considering the fate of the former as more relevant than that of the latter. Cannibalism, remarks Froment, is practiced "in broad daylight, not cynically, but as a natural thing." It was not motivated by hate or a desire for revenge—most of the victims, after all, were purchased slaves rather than enemies. "It has no other motive and no other origin than the unbridled love of meat: one eats man as one would eat buffalo or wild boar."[57]

Augouard observes that the "Bondjos," despite their love for the flesh of enslaved children, were not aware of doing anything bad or evil: "It is with the greatest amiableness [French: *bonhomie*] that they kill a poor slave, butchering and eating them as if they were an ox or a sheep." They did not understand why the missionaries criticized their consumption habits, instead wondering "why we don't eat such a delicacy."[58]

Other sources likewise indicate that the eating of human flesh and the killing of slaves for this purpose were seen as "natural" and uncontroversial things. Hinde writes that, while he was employed on the Sankuru River, a young Songye chief borrowed the commandant's knife, which he then used to "cut the throat of a little girl-slave belonging to him." When he was subsequently spotted "in the act of cooking her"—likely in preparation of a feast, as he had certainly not planned to eat the whole girl all by himself—he was arrested and imprisoned, though only for two months.[59] It does not seem that he had acted out of spite, but rather that to him such a usage of enslaved children had been part of the traditional and natural order to things.

When Ward once asked, "Do you people eat human bodies?" upon seeing what he suspected to be smoke-dried human flesh, he got the surprised reply: "Yes; don't you?"[60] He adds that "upon more than one occasion portions of human flesh were actually offered to me with the utmost cordiality" in a gesture of hospitality.[61] Weeks reports the same. He once saw a large group of fighters return after a successful attack on a neighboring village, bringing prisoners, plundered goods, and "the limbs of those who had been slain in the fight" with them.[62]

> Some had human legs over their shoulders, others had threaded arms through slits in the stomachs of their dismembered foes, had tied the ends of the arms together, thus forming loops, and through these ghastly loops they had thrust their own living arms and were carrying them thus with the gory trunks dangling to and fro.[63]

In the evening, "cannibal feasts" were held in the village where Weeks had his station as well as in neighboring ones, "and the next morning they brought some of the cooked meat to the station, and thinking they were doing us a favour, they offered to share it with us—the meat looked like black boiled pork."[64] Weeks's companion W. H. Stapleton, who also documented the proceedings, adds that "one of our workmen eagerly joined . . . in disposing of the dainty morsels."[65]

When Coquilhat tried to argue with a group of Bangala, expressing his conviction that the consumption of human flesh was "horrible," he got the reply: "On the contrary, it's delicious, when eaten with salt."[66] His argument, meant to be about ethics and the boundaries of acceptable behavior, had been misunderstood as a claim about taste.

A Feeling of Superiority

Like Coquilhat, the Belgian explorer Edouard Lamotte argued with Bangala men about their cannibal customs. He attacked not their custom of occasionally eating slaves—which was essentially risk-free for those who did so, as long as they were not enslaved themselves—but the consumption of killed or captured enemies, by pointing out that "you, too, could one day be made prisoners and eaten by your enemies!" The reply he got was: "We know . . . , but it is the fate of war; so much the worse for him who falls!" It was especially warfare that made cannibalism worthwhile—conquering, killing, and consuming your enemies was the most complete victory over them you could ever achieve.[67]

Coquilhat confirms this view, noting that the warriors he met "believe it glorious—and humiliating for the vanquished—to eat prisoners made in war. 'In this way,' they say, 'the enemy who makes a counter-attack no longer finds any traces of his own.'" He adds that, since slaves were eaten as well, this cannot have been the sole reason for cannibalism. Observing that "a meal of human flesh is [considered] a treat," he concludes that cannibal acts were also driven by a strong "desire for meat."[68] But war cannibalism was likely older than slave eating, at least as a widespread custom,[69] and some of the feelings of superiority and the celebration of "glorious" victories associated with war cannibalism may well have remained even when the person being eaten was a purchased slave rather than a captured enemy.

Just as among the Bangala (see the previous section), ethical concerns of those who lived near the Ubangi River seem to have been largely limited towards the well-being of their own community members. When it came to outsiders, it was a matter of strength and superiority to determine who might dominate and exploit (or even kill) whom. Traveling along this river, Glave was repeatedly invited by warriors to join them in attacks against neighboring peoples. "They said, 'You can take the ivory, and we will take the meat'—meaning, of course, the human beings who might be killed in the fight." They could not understand why Glave's party did not use their superior weapons to attack villages, robbing all valuables and taking the inhabitants as slaves. They certainly knew that, if unlucky, they themselves might have fallen prey to such attacks. Still, they seem to have thought that anyone who had the power to do something also had the right to do it, and they considered Glave "very eccentric" for refusing to make use of such opportunities.[70]

In these cases, the right to subjugate, enslave, or eat others was considered a consequence of one's own physical or technological superiority: being able to conquer others gave you the right to treat them as it pleased you. But the Mangbetu people in the northeast seem to have framed their own superiority in racist terms, if Georg Schweinfurth is to be believed. He writes about them:

> Surrounded as they are by a number of people who are blacker than themselves, and who, being inferior to them in culture, are consequently held in great contempt, they have just the opportunity which they want for carrying on expeditions of war or plunder, which result in the acquisition of a booty, which is especially coveted by them, consisting of human flesh.[71]

Gaetano Casati, who had visited the Mangbetu a decade earlier, remarks that they considered the people they raided "an inferior race, hunted to supply the slave trade or to pander to the anthropophagous taste of their masters."[72] How much of these notions of subjugating others because of their "racial" and cultural inferiority or even their darker skin color came from the Europeans—among whom racist prejudices were widespread and largely considered self-evident at that time—and how much from the Mangbetu themselves? That Casati and Schweinfurth both, independently of each other, write about the supposed inferiority of the raided makes it likely that they did indeed hear some explanations of that kind while among the Mangbetu. It is conceivable that the latter justified their behavior in terms they thought the Europeans would understand.

Better Than Animals

In the modern viewpoint, it is generally considered acceptable to eat certain species of animals (though ethical vegetarians and vegans disagree) but never members of our own, human species—people like us who are intelligent, who talk, make plans, have dreams. (Of course, animals might have dreams too, but we cannot be sure of that and so find it easy to ignore it.) Surprisingly, while we regard the intelligence and language capabilities of others as an argument against eating them, some of the Congolese people eaters explicitly took the opposite viewpoint. Albert Chapaux notes that "the Bangalas are convinced that human flesh is a noble food, because man has more intelligence than an animal, as well as speech."[73] Coquilhat tried his best to convince them that eating others is wrong and harmful, arguing:

> You understand the difference between a man and an animal; one has intelligence and the other does not; the former is of the same kind as you; he has a name; he speaks to you at the moment when you are going to kill him; he did not hurt you. You eat him because he is a slave or a captive. Don't you feel ashamed to consider man as food?[74]

But far from feeling ashamed, the people he talked to replied: "Everything you say proves how refined it is to eat human flesh, a meat that had a name and that spoke. It is a noble food, while the animals furnish only vile food."[75] Ward records a similar reaction from a Congolese man (he does not say of which ethnic group) who told him: "We eat men because it is good to eat meat that talked. It is our custom."[76] Apparently it was precisely the humanity of slaves and captives that made their flesh a "nobler" kind of food than that of mere nameless, unintelligent animals.

Why this is so is not explicitly said—after all, once a person is dead, intelligence, language capabilities and other specifically human qualities are gone. Nor did people believe that eating human flesh would transmit some of the desirable properties of the eaten to the eaters. Such a belief is never recorded, and some commentators explicitly note that they could find no traces of it.[77] The notion has sometimes been suggested as an explanation for cannibalism, but it seems to be nothing but a myth, never confirmed by the cannibals themselves. This is not particularly surprising—eating rabbits does not allow us to run faster, nor does eating beef give us the ability to digest large quantities of grass. The idea that cannibals did not know this might have been just a subtle (and probably unconscious) attempt to declare them stupid. The actual absence of such a belief has also been noticed from other parts of the world where cannibalism was practiced.[78]

But why, then, the particular preference for the flesh of humans? A possible explanation is that eating flesh is a demonstration of superiority over who (or what) you are eating. Eating a cow is nothing to be specifically proud of, but by eating a human being you demonstrate your strength and cunning (it you defeated an enemy or foreigner) or your wealth (if you can afford to purchase and kill a slave).

According to Torday, human flesh was likewise known as "the meat that speaks" among the Mbala (Bambala) people on the Kwilu River—a region where slaves were occasionally killed "to provide a cannibal feast," and where enemies and convicted criminals were eaten as well.[79] In spite of using this term, however, people do not seem to have considered the fact that the meat providers had been able to speak as particularly important, instead explaining the practice as due to "a sincere liking for human flesh." Torday notes that they spoke about the custom freely and without shame, "display[ing] no reticence except in the presence of state officials."[80]

That human victims were seen as something different from and better than mere animals in, at least, parts of the Congo basin is also indicated by the fact that their execution was celebrated in elaborate ceremonies among some of the peoples who lived north of the Congo River. In this region at least the death of adult male victims seems to have been considered a special occasion quite different from the simple slaughter of an animal; it is unclear whether such ceremonies were also held for women and children.

Renouard recorded one such event in detail, based on the descriptions of the French missionaries employed on the Ubangi. The people of a village had decided to hold a feast (for what reason is not said). They had purchased a slave and fattened him for some time. All the inhabitants of neighboring villages were invited, and everyone was soon drunk on palm wine. While the crowd dances around him, the victim "sits on a log, . . . hands and feet immobilized with a forked piece of wood deeply buried in the ground . . . ; the head is attached by a liana to a flexible, curved pole, which, upon being released, must toss it into the air."[81]

Then a "witch-doctor" starts to sing "a death-song, which the crowd repeats after him." He beheads the slave with a knife, causing the pole to spring back and throw the head into the crowd. Immediately, "the women rush forward, chopping up the corpse, pulling off pieces and throwing them into the pot," where they are cooked quickly and then consumed. "The scene continues in a disgusting orgy," Renouard concludes.[82]

In spite of the chronicler's revulsion, the description makes it clear that the sacrifice and subsequent consumption of a human victim was a special event celebrated by the whole community. There are no reports that animals intended for consumption were ever "executed" in a similarly elaborate manner.

During his visits to Balui villages on the lower part of the Ubangi, Albert Dolisie (1856–1899), an explorer who later became lieutenant governor of the French Congo, saw various places used for the ritual execution of slaves and captives:

> Here and there, there are small, well-understood facilities to conveniently cut people's necks. They consist of a seat made of a block of clay soil on which the subject is seated. On each side there are two poles on the ground, to which the arms are attached; a third pole serves as a backrest and the patient is fixed there. In the ground, about two metres backwards,

> there is a long pole with a flexible end, fitted with a solid vine in order to stretch the neck.[83]

In one village, Dolisie was shown the "fresh" skulls of four captives who had been executed and consumed a few days earlier. A young enslaved boy, kept around to be beheaded and eaten at the next suitable occasion, approached him, "trembling all over and deeply ashamed," and asked for his protection. Dolisie pleaded with the chief who allowed him to take the boy away.[84]

Guy Burrows saw similar "execution grounds" in or near many villages around the Mongala River, farther in the east. In this area, "the slave destined for the cooking-pot is made to kneel," otherwise the procedure was the same: "A stout sapling . . . is bent down and attached with a cord to the head of the victim. When the executioner's knife descends, the sapling reverts to its upright position, causing the severed member to fly high into the air."[85]

While such elaborate decapitation ceremonies are documented only for areas north of the Congo River (to my knowledge), in the south the murder of a slave for consumption could be accompanied by the "beating of drums and outbreaks of excited mirth," indicating that such an event was seen as something extraordinary and worthy of celebration. Glave witnessed this in a village on the Ruki in early 1890. As in other regions, the inhabitants saw no reason to hide their cannibal customs. One of them told Glave that they ate all parts of the human body, including the head, after putting it "in the fire to singe the hair off."[86]

So, even if purchased people were referred to as "meat," it seems clear that their consumption was considered something special—their death was (at least in some cases) celebrated in elaborate rituals and their flesh was considered a dish for feasts, not something eaten on a routine basis. Why was this so? In addition to the occasional explanations that explicitly refer to the humanness of the victims—they had names and were able to speak, in contrast to mere animals—there was also a very widespread explanation of a more profane nature: human flesh, cannibals throughout the Congo (and also in many other regions) agreed, had an excellent taste.

When Augouard asked the "Bondjos" why they practiced cannibalism, they assured him "with great conviction that human flesh is far above all other meats."[87] The German ethnologist Leo Frobenius notes that, among the Gbaya (one of the peoples formerly known as Bondjos), "it is openly stated that no meat is as excellent as that of humans."[88] Hinde states that the people he encountered around the Ubangi River "seem fond of eating human flesh; and though it may be an acquired taste, there is not the slightest doubt in my mind that they prefer human flesh to any other."[89]

Investigating why the Bangala practiced cannibalism, Weeks "could never obtain any other reason for eating human flesh other than that 'it is very nice and better than any other meat.'"[90] In the second part of the same article, published a few months after the first, he confirms that the Boloki (a large Bangala subgroup) "ate human flesh for the pleasure of it," but adds that health concerns might have been an additional motive: "Although they did not believe that the qualities of the person eaten were imparted to them, yet they thought that human flesh had a beneficial effect on those who ate it, for if a person had bad ulcers he would quickly lose them after eating such flesh."[91] There are, to my knowledge, no other statements attributing Congolese cannibalism to health concerns; the motive might have existed, but it was certainly not the most important one.

Praise for the taste of human flesh, on the other hand, could be heard in many regions. In Maniema, the Scottish missionary David Livingstone met a fighter who told him that he looked forward to "eat[ing] those killed" in battle because "human flesh . . . is better than goat's."[92] When Casati visited the Zande people, their king offered him the meat of a freshly killed ape with the words: "Eat it; the flesh is very nice . . . as good as man's." And a chief of the neighboring Mangbetu was full of praise for the delicate flesh of chimpanzees, calling it "as good as human flesh"—in his eyes, the ultimate commendation.[93] Gero heard from his Zande informants that human flesh is "very sweet, even more so than monkey meat."[94]

Similarly doubtful praise could be heard in certain West African regions. Referring to southern Nigeria, where slaves were sometimes eaten as well,[95] the British anthropologist P. Amaury Talbot notes that "human flesh is preferred above all for its succulence, and that of monkey is generally considered to come next." Among the Igbo people, he adds, "human flesh was prized above all other kinds of meat." And from Ekoi people (an ethnic group living in the southeast of Nigeria and the southwest of Cameroon) he heard that "man's flesh was sweeter than any other meat."[96] Farther in the west, the German traveler Walter Volz observed that the Kpelle people in northern-central Liberia (whom he visited in 1906/7) considered the "flavor and tenderness" of human flesh as superior to the meat of any animal, preferring the former as a matter of course whenever they could get it.[97] No cases of slave eating are known from this region, but foreigners were sometimes kidnapped and eaten.[98]

Among the Fang people, who live west of the Congo basin in today's Equatorial Guinea and Gabon, foreigners could suffer the same fate and corpses were widely traded as food, as we will see.[99] The missionary and medical doctor Albert Bennett talked with a Fang man who admitted to have eaten human flesh—though only once, he claimed—and described it as "much superior to goat."[100] The English travel writer Mary Kingsley found that, though the Fang had become unwilling to openly confess to practicing cannibalism, they still had the highest praise for this kind of dish: "Man's flesh, he says, is good to eat, very good, and he wishes you would try it."[101]

One American who took this wish to heart was the journalist William Seabrook (1884–1945), who seems to have been disappointed when he found out that the people he visited in Liberia in the 1920s had recently abandoned their cannibal habits. While in France, he convinced a hospital intern to give him "a sizable rump steak, also a small loin roast . . . of a freshly killed man, who seemed to be about thirty years old" and had died in an accident.[102]

Seabrook cooked the pieces, commenting that "the cooking odors, wholly pleasant, were like those of beefsteak and roast beef" and that the pieces also looked like beef, though, while raw, they were "slightly less red." After eating the flesh, he declared that it tasted "like good, fully developed veal, not young, but not yet beef. . . . It was mild, good meat with no other sharply defined or highly characteristic taste such as for instance, goat, high game, and pork have."[103] While not quite as enthusiastic as some of the other cannibal voices we have heard, his confession is a curious addition to the choir of those who praised the taste of human flesh.

To return to the Congo basin, it is notable that sentiments in the southern Kasai region likewise seem to have been somewhat less euphoric than elsewhere. According to Frobenius, the Songye considered the taste of human flesh as "very pleasant, similar to pork"[104]—similar, but not necessarily better. Nor are there other voices from this region praising the particular taste of human flesh, it seems. What this apparent difference in attitudes might mean will be discussed later.

When Coquilhat noticed that his pleas not to eat their fellow humans failed to move the Bangala he talked to, he tried to appeal to their material interests instead. He pointed out that eating a human being meant "destroying an instrument of wealth" and that the Bangala could make better use of their slaves by "forcing [them] to work," for example, as fishers, cultivators, or weapon makers. While the individuals he spoke with admitted that this was true, they did not see it as a sufficient reason to give up their custom, arguing that they would lose "a special enjoyment, that of eating an excellent meat 'of a peculiar taste.'" And they added, in a not-so-subtle criticism of the European settlers' materialism, that "we are not accustomed, like the white man, to give up a great pleasure to make a doubtful gain."[105]

What was the underlying reason for the widespread praise for human flesh? Was it just by chance that the eaten whose flesh was praised so much belonged to the same species as the eaters? Or did the cannibals—maybe subconsciously—enjoy the feeling of superiority they received from eating others and thus totally subjugating them to their own will? Did the humanness of the victims inform the cannibals' sense of taste or had, conversely, the perceived excellent taste of human flesh helped to make cannibalism more acceptable? Since taste is a subjective matter and since, by definition, nobody except cannibals knows how human flesh tastes, it seems impossible to really untangle these questions. All that can be said is that, from the people eaters' viewpoint, taste mattered—and they generally saw it as an argument in favor of their custom.

Regional Differences

While there can be no doubt that cannibalism in general, and slave eating in particular, were quite widespread in some parts the Congo basin, it is equally clear that they were not practiced everywhere. A large part of the reports of slave eating comes from the northwest of the country, referring to certain tributaries (such as the Ubangi, Lulonga, and Ruki) and a stretch of the main Congo River (the area where the Bangala and related peoples live). Other reports refer to the Mangbetu people and some Zande clans in the northeast, the region around the Aruwimi River in the east, and to the Kasai and its tributaries in the central west. This leaves large areas—including the whole south and parts of the east—where slave eating seems to have been unknown, or at least very rare. But there were also more locally focused differences—it seems that cannibals and non-cannibals lived sometimes side by side. This is notable in the case of the Zande, where several sources leave no doubt that some clans did practice cannibalism, while others did not.[106]

Elsewhere similar local differences seem to have existed. While the European writers of that time tend to speak about "cannibal" and "non-cannibal tribes," such labels must be regarded with great care. Who became known as a "tribe" or ethnic group often depended on decisions made by outsiders, whether Europeans or neighboring peoples. Often those who spoke the same or similar languages were treated as a unit, even if in their culture and their customs they might have been quite diverse.[107]

It is therefore not surprising that the patterns of who did or did not eat human flesh do not clearly fit the tribal labels used by Europeans. "Balolo" was such a label used for those who lived along the upper parts of the Ruki, the Lulonga, and their headstreams[108]—people who, as we have seen, are repeatedly mentioned as victims of their more "powerful" and violent neighbors, "who are continually making raids upon them, capturing and selling them into slavery, and eating those who are less suitable for the slavemarket," as Ward writes.[109] But the distinction between raiders and raided might not always have been as clear-cut as that. A photograph published in the Belgian colonial magazine *Le Mouvement Géographique* in 1897 shows a group of naked children and several armed men guarding them. It is entitled "Children captured near the Lulonga by Balolo cannibals"; the accompanying text explains that the photograph was taken in 1889 and represents "a party of Balolo marauders returning from a raid and leading a convoy of young prisoners destined to be exported to the Ubangi as meat for slaughter."[110]

It is possible that the (anonymous) author of this article made a mistake and it was actually the children, not their captors, who belonged to those generally known as Balolo. But it is also possible that Balolo men sometimes decided to do some raiding of their own if they saw a suitable opportunity. Those who had suffered under earlier raids may also have been motivated by a desire for revenge to launch counterattacks against the attackers or their allies. While it is unclear what really happened here, it seems unwise to assume that the boundaries between "perpetrators" and "victims" were always clear-cut and impermeable.

While Ward does not say whether Balolo sometimes undertook any raids of their own, he observes that some subgroups showed a clear "desire of eating human flesh" and practiced cannibalism when given the opportunity, while

Figure 6.1. "Children captured near the Lulonga by Balolo cannibals (based on a photograph by Mr. De Meuse)." From the Belgian colonial magazine *Le Mouvement Géographique*, 1897, 181–82.

other Balolo groups "denied all participation in such practices"—credibly, as Ward judges, noting that such statements were sometimes made during the first contact with white people, when the latter's "abhorrence" could hardly have been known.[111]

Elsewhere too, the boundaries between cannibals and non-cannibals did not always follow the tribal appellations used by Europeans. Torday calls it a "striking difference" that the northern groups of Mbala (Bambala) people on the Kwilu River liked to eat human flesh (and sometimes sacrificed slaves for this purpose), while the Southern Bambala "abhor cannibalism." He suspects that the northern groups had adopted the practice under the influence of their neighbors, and conjectures more generally "that cannibalism is spreading through retaliation, for people coming in contact with cannibals see those who have fallen in war eaten by their enemy, and it is a natural act of revenge to eat the first prisoner that falls into their hands." But he also observes that cannibalism could spread through imitation, with curious people who saw others eat human flesh inclined to try it themselves if given an opportunity.[112]

Referring to the Kwese people (Bakwese) who likewise live in the Kwilu area, he notes that a "small section [of them] have adopted this habit [cannibalism] in the last few years in consequence of contact" with cannibal neighbors—whether in imitation or revenge he does not say. He adds that "non-cannibal Bakwese do not despise" those who had started to eat human flesh, "but there seems no tendency to imitate them."[113]

It will need more detailed studies to explore how cannibal customs spread and why some groups refrained from engaging in such acts, while others saw them as uncontroversial and even desirable. Did the Balolo subgroups who refrained from eating human flesh do so by choice? Or was it rather the case that people whom Ward calls "oppressed and persecuted . . . timid and inoffensive"[114] simply lacked the opportunity to acquire human flesh?

Torday speculates that war cannibalism may have spread through revenge, with those who saw their own fallen comrades eaten deciding to retaliate against their enemies by treating them in the same manner. Slave eating must have spread in other ways, since the slaves themselves are in no position to retaliate; moreover, it requires access to slaves that are considered sufficiently "surplus" that they can be slaughtered for food. For those not directly engaged in slave raiding, it also requires a certain wealth or access to goods against which slave traders are willing to sell. As we have seen, many of the Congolese slave eaters were either raiders themselves or they were elephant hunters who had ivory to sell—a precious material in the Congo at the time. Furthermore, the practice requires a certain attitude towards cannibalism: slave eaters must regard human flesh as "edible" even outside of specific situations of hatred or a desire to humiliate one's enemies.

It is clear that all the conditions required to make slaves "edible" were fulfilled in some parts of the Congo basin, but not everywhere. But when people did not engage in the practice, it is not so easy to figure out why. Were they strictly opposed to all kinds of cannibalism? Did they eat the flesh of vanquished enemies (or other specific groups), but not that of slaves? Were they unable to acquire slaves, or did they find them too expensive to "waste" for food? Presumably, each of these answers might have applied to some of the Congolese groups who did not participate in such acts. But the absence of a custom is harder to reliably detect than its presence, and clarifying the reasons for this absence is even more challenging.

Similar question may be asked about the participation in slave raids: some groups of Congolese people were apparently quite willing to engage in slave raids, either accompanying foreign (often Swahilo-Arab) raiders or else raiding on their own and then selling the captives to foreign (often European) merchants. Others so did so rarely, or not at all. What was behind these different behaviors? Did they depend mostly on opportunity—access to potential allies and buyers, good weaponry, military experience? Did some peoples deliberately refrain from such activities out of ethical concerns? Were those who did get involved mostly driven by a desire to overpower enemies and settle old scores? Or did they participate for financial or other reasons?

More research will be necessary to provide satisfying answers to these questions, and much may turn out to be unknowable due to a lack of sufficiently detailed credible sources. In this book I do not try to answer these questions—but it must be kept in mind that customs and behaviors varied.

Cannibalism and slave eating have been reported from certain Congolese regions, but how widespread and generally accepted they were in these regions is hard to judge, and among neighboring groups behaviors and attitudes might have been quite different.

Notes

1. Glave, "Slave Trade," 832.
2. Weeks, "Anthropological Notes," 121.
3. Coquilhat, *Sur le Haut-Congo*, 269.
4. Ibid., 270.
5. Ibid.
6. Ibid.
7. Ibid.
8. Coquilhat, *Sur le Haut-Congo*, 273 (quote), 274.
9. Weeks, *Among Congo Cannibals*, 104.
10. Ward, *Voice from the Congo*, 316.
11. Ward, *Five Years*, 128, 132 (quote).
12. Van Reybrouck, *Congo*, 29.
13. Ibid., 42–45, 68–69.
14. Makulo, *La vie*, 57–58.
15. Ibid., 58.
16. Ibid., 72.
17. Hinde, *Fall*, 53–54.
18. Ibid.
19. Renouard, *L'Ouest Africain*, 135.
20. Thomas, *Slave Trade*, chapter 3.
21. Harms, *River of Wealth*, 149, 150 (quote).
22. See Chapter 4, note 50, this volume.
23. Northrup, "Ideological Context," 110–11.
24. Ward, *Five Years*, 119.
25. Augouard, *28 années au Congo*, 2:100.
26. Johnston, *George Grenfell*, 2:657.
27. Ibid., 2:657–58; Ward, *Five Years*, 138.
28. Westmark, "Quinze mois," 23–24.
29. Quoted in Witte, *Monseigneur Prosper Philippe Augouard*, 45–46.
30. Renouard, *L'Ouest Africain*, 297.
31. Augouard, *28 années au Congo*, 1:516, 2:100.
32. Froment, "Un Voyage dans l'Oubangui," 208.
33. See Chapter 4, this volume.
34. Froment, "Un Voyage dans l'Oubangui," 208.
35. Dybowski, *La route du Tchad*, 181.
36. Ekholm Friedman, *Catastrophe and Creation*, 43.
37. Coquilhat, *Sur le Haut-Congo*, 270.
38. Quoted in W. Bentley, *Pioneering on the Congo*, 95. The episode is also mentioned in Coquilhat's diary (Coquilhat, *Sur le Haut-Congo*, 298).

39. Westmark, "Chez les Bangallas," 435.
40. Van Reybrouck, *Congo*, 215.
41. Torday, *Camp and Tramp*, 68 (quotes), 69.
42. Ibid., 68.
43. Ibid., 177.
44. Torday, *Causeries Congolaises*, 80 (quote), 81.
45. Johnston, *George Grenfell*, 1:399.
46. Glave, "Slave Trade," 832.
47. Chapaux, *Le Congo*, 545.
48. Quoted in Witte, *Monseigneur Prosper Philippe Augouard*, 46.
49. See Chapter 5, this volume.
50. Gero, *Cannibalism in Zandeland*, 54, 60n24. Georg Schweinfurth had likely witnessed a raid by Amadi people against their Babukur neighbors; see Chapter 5, this volume.
51. Witte, *Monseigneur Prosper Philippe Augouard*, 105.
52. D. Gardner, "Anthropophagy," 30.
53. Gero, *Cannibalism in Zandeland*, 55.
54. Evans-Pritchard, "Cannibalism: A Zande Text," 74.
55. Ekholm Friedman, *Catastrophe and Creation*, 221.
56. Weeks, "Anthropological Notes," 122, 445–46.
57. Froment, "Un Voyage dans l'Oubangui," 208.
58. Augouard, *28 années au Congo*, 2:70, 100.
59. Hinde, *Fall*, 63–64. Two weeks after his release, the young chief was again arrested due to rumors among the Free State soldiers that he still ate human flesh. "He had a bag slung round his neck, which on examining we found contained an arm and a leg of a young child." Accordingly, he was considered "an incorrigible," sentenced to death and shot (ibid., 64).
60. Ward, *Voice from the Congo*, 309.
61. Ibid., 316.
62. Weeks, *Among Congo Cannibals*, 69.
63. Ibid.
64. Ibid., 69–70.
65. Quoted in W. Bentley, *Pioneering on the Congo*, 257.
66. Coquilhat, *Sur le Haut-Congo*, 271.
67. Lamotte, *Chez les Congolais*, 110.
68. Coquilhat, *Sur le Haut-Congo*, 271.
69. See Chapter 4, this volume.
70. Glave, "Slave Trade," 832; *In Savage Africa*, 219.
71. Schweinfurth, *Heart of Africa*, 92–93.
72. Casati, *Ten Years in Equatoria*, 168.
73. Chapaux, *Le Congo*, 545.
74. Coquilhat, *Sur le Haut-Congo*, 271.
75. Quoted ibid.
76. Ward, *Voice from the Congo*, 307.
77. Such as Coquilhat, *Sur le Haut-Congo*, 271; Evans-Pritchard, "Zande Cannibalism," 255; Torday, *Camp and Tramp*, 84; Weeks, "Anthropological Notes," 457.
78. For example, Seligmann, *Melanesians*, 552, regarding New Guinea; regarding New Zealand, see the end of Chapter 2, this volume.

79. Torday, *Camp and Tramp*, 83, 202.
80. Ibid., 83.
81. Renouard, *L'Ouest Africain*, 136.
82. Ibid.
83. Quoted in Chavannes, *Albert Dolisie*, 43.
84. Ibid.
85. Burrows and Canisius, *Curse of Central Africa*, 211–12.
86. Glave, "Slave Trade," 832.
87. Augouard, *28 années au Congo*, 2:79.
88. Frobenius, *Und Afrika sprach*, 189.
89. Hinde, *Fall*, 67–68.
90. Weeks, "Anthropological Notes," 121.
91. Ibid., 457.
92. Livingstone, "Fragment of 1871 Field Diary."
93. Quoted in Casati, *Ten Years in Equatoria*, 120, 133.
94. Gero, *Cannibalism in Zandeland*, 46.
95. See Chapter 4, note 50, this volume.
96. Talbot, *Peoples of Southern Nigeria*, 3:827, 842, 850.
97. Volz, *Reise*, 103.
98. Ibid., 101–2, 104.
99. See Chapters 12 and 13, this volume.
100. Bennett, "Ethnographical Notes," 84.
101. Kingsley, *Travels*, 268.
102. Seabrook, *Jungle Ways*, 184 (quote); *No Hiding Place*, 306.
103. Seabrook, *Jungle Ways*, 185–86, 188.
104. Frobenius in Volhard, *Kannibalismus*, 117.
105. Quoted in Coquilhat, *Sur le Haut-Congo*, 273.
106. See Chapters 5 and 13, this volume.
107. Isichei, *History*, 97, 106.
108. Ward, *Five Years*, 137.
109. Ibid., 125.
110. "Le cannibalisme au Congo," *Le Mouvement Géographique* 1897: 181–89 (picture and quoted text: 181–82).
111. Ward, *Five Years*, 138–39.
112. Torday, *Camp and Tramp*, 83, 201–2 (quotes); see also previous section, "Better Than Animals."
113. Ibid., 223.
114. Ward, *Five Years*, 125.

CHAPTER 7
COMMERCIAL AND ECONOMIC ASPECTS OF CONGOLESE CANNIBALISM

Sale of "Edible" Slaves to Neighboring Peoples

In this chapter we will explore the connections between commerce and cannibalism and the economic aspects of the custom. We have seen that slaves were purchased for consumption—something that was, of course, only possible because there were traders willing to sell under such terms. In some cases, the owners of slaves might simply not have cared what would happen to those they sold; in other cases, people seem to have made a deliberate business out of catering for the needs of cannibalistic neighbors.

While camping near a Balui village in late 1886 on the way to his mission station, Augouard "saw in the middle of the [Ubangi] river something which appeared and disappeared as it struggled. Assuming an accident, we wished to go to the rescue of the castaway; but the natives, guessing our thoughts, seized their light canoes, and went to collect a poor child that was frightfully lean." The rescued girl turned out to be a slave owned by one of the villagers who had planned to sell her, maybe after some fattening, to "the cannibalistic Bondjos." But because she had become "sick and too thin," he had "thrown her mercilessly into the water" rather than wasting further food on her. On hearing this, Augouard bought her from her owner for "a piece of cotton, valued ten francs."[1]

While cannibalism was not unknown among the Balui themselves,[2] some of them apparently regarded the ownership of slaves as a business opportunity rather than an occasion for a feast—just as has been reported for the "Boubangis," who lived further upriver.[3] The fate of slaves was considered of no concern—when Augouard purchased the nearly drowned girl, the villagers were utterly amazed, "wonder[ing] what we wanted to do with such a creature. If we had not purchased her, she would certainly have been thrown back into the river."[4] That his intent was to save the child's life was not something they could understand.

According to Augouard, this case was no exception since enslaved children circulated as a kind of "common currency" in the Ubangi region. Even children too young to make useful workers were accepted as payment by cannibals and non-cannibals alike, the latter knowing that potential buyers who might seek them for "feasts" were never hard to find.[5] Without particularly mentioning children (who may have been more or less discounted based on their age and size), Glave notes that "the standard of value on the Ubangi was human life—human flesh."[6]

In addition to children, women seem to have been sold for consumption as well. The French ethnographer Dr. Poutrin states that some groups of the M'Baka (often subsumed under the "Bondjo" label) made a business out of selling "young and healthy" women across the river where they were "killed and eaten." These transactions took place "in times of peace," when human flesh was otherwise hard to get. Poutrin might have heard of this from French soldiers who once rescued a group of women sold for this purpose.[7] While he does not say so clearly, he seems to think that the victims had been born in the village that sold them. But unless they had done something which had seriously offended their community, this seems doubtful. There are reports that community members considered guilty of serious wrongdoing were sometimes sold as punishment even in the knowledge that they would probably be eaten,[8] but there is no conclusive evidence that "innocent" free individuals were ever subjugated to such a fate.

One possible exception is an account of the British officer John Hanning Speke (1827–1864), who claims that the Bembe people (Wabembe) in the northeast of the Congo basin, "when they cannot get human flesh otherwise, give a goat to their neighbours for a sick or dying child," because "such flesh" was considered "the best of all."[9] Since he heard this from others about the Bembe, it might have been nothing but a rumor. Nevertheless, it is possible that poor parents were sometimes willing to sell a child whom they considered dying and lost to them anyway even if they knew that the victim was destined for consumption. The women mentioned by Poutrin, however, were "young and healthy."

Several sources also indicate that parents were sometimes driven by poverty to sell their children into slavery and that some of these children, after passing through the hands of several interim traders, were purchased by cannibals who might well have used them for food—but in these cases the parents did not know what would happen to their children and will certainly have hoped for a less sinister outcome.[10]

While a few might have been sold by their own parents or communities, most of the slaves who circulated in the Ubangi region likely were the victims of raids, warfare, or kidnapping. Many seem to have been children, possibly because they were considered easier to handle or because of a preference for their tender young flesh[11]—"four to sixteen years old" was the preferred age range according to the Dutch trader cited earlier.[12] Several of the children purchased and liberated by the French missionaries said that they had been resold more than twenty times.[13] G. Renouard adds that these children, once freed by the missionaries, often had trouble adjusting to their new situation: having known, sometimes as far back as they could remember, that their bodies were "only valuable according to the state of their fat" and that their lives were "worth less than a quarter of a hippopotamus or of a buffalo," they found it hard to develop any sense of self-respect. Sometimes they could scarcely believe that they would be allowed to grow up and old, considering the missionaries' attempts at educating them just another cruel delay of a fate they had been forced to accept as inevitable.[14]

Children also seem to have made up a considerable part of a cannibalistic slave trade that took place in the Kasai region, farther in the south. According to Sidney Hinde, the Songye people (Basongo) in his vicinity, while not opposed to eating human flesh at suitable occasions, increased their wealth by shipping "slaves and children" downriver to the Basongo Meno (another Songye group) who purchased them "for food." The reference is certainly to be read as "adult slaves and enslaved children"; there are no indications that the Songye were desperate enough to sell their own offspring to people who might eat them. Observing that the victims were often children—maybe because for adult captives it was easier to find non-cannibal buyers elsewhere?—the local Free State commissary reacted drastically, ordering "the sentries on the river to take, or fire on, any canoes descending the river with children on board, and, after catching a few, succeeded in stopping the traffic."[15]

Leo Frobenius notes the central Songye groups were more martial than those living near the borders of their region. Both, he adds, preyed on the neighboring Luba people, but while the central groups raided whole villages, the peripheral groups preferred capturing lone individuals or purchasing slaves captured by others. Victims were exploited as laborers, killed and eaten, or both.[16] Those called "Basongo Meno" by Hinde might well have been one of more peripheral groups who bought victims from the more active raiders who lived in his vicinity. The Presbyterian missionary Samuel Lapsley mentions them as well, calling them "the awful Bassonge Mino, saw-toothed cannibals," but adding that they "were friendly and peaceably disposed towards the white man."[17]

A trade in slaves that were subsequently consumed has also been reported from the Aruwimi River in the east of the Congo basin. The German Catholic missionary Josef Fräßle (1878–1929) was stationed near Basoko, where this river joins the Congo. He writes that the Turumbu people (to whom Disasi Makulo belonged)[18] living across the river received twice a week a shipment of "slaves, women and captives," brought in an "ultra-long dugout. . . . Those unhappy people were bound to poles [in the river], with their ankles dislocated, and sticking up to their heads in the water. After four days their flesh was tender for the kitchen and they were slaughtered."[19]

Figure 7.1. "A cannibal scene with human flesh roasting over the fire," somewhere in the Aruwimi area. Drawing from Herbert Ward's *Five Years with the Congo Cannibals* (London: Chatto & Windus, 1891), 161.

As in other regions, for a long time the Free State was apparently unwilling or unable to stop the deadly trade—in 1906, however, the trader responsible for most of the cannibalistic shipments was finally arrested and executed, according to Fräßle. (He does not say anything more about this trader except that he was responsible for the semiweekly delivery of slaves for butchery, so it is not known to which ethnic group he belonged or whether he was a foreigner.) But this does not seem to have changed people's attitudes towards their slaves, at least not quickly. Like their French companions on the Ubangi, the missionaries bought enslaved children in order to free them and raise them as Christians, but doing so was expensive. Fräßle complains that the owners of such children were unwilling to sell them for twenty-five or even fifty marks, arguing that "their meat, their labor is worth more than that."[20] Butchering purchased children for meat or exploiting them as workers—both were still valid options.

The practice of soaking people for several days in the river prior to slaughtering them has also been reported from the Bangala people and the Ubangi region.[21] Around the Ubangi and among the Bangala this practice was combined with the breaking of legs and arms, according to these sources, while Fräßle writes that the victims' ankles had been "dislocated" (German:

verrenkt), which indicates that they had at least been deliberately sprained, if not outright broken.

Prisoners caught in battles or raids were in some regions subjected to the same treatment, as Ward reports (based on personal observation) from the Lulonga River.[22] He explains the practice as due to "a prevalent belief . . . that the flavour of human flesh is improved by submerging the prospective victim up to the neck in the water for two or three days previous to sacrifice."[23] Fräßle, Hinde,[24] and Renouard[25] all explain it as motivated by a desire to make the flesh more tender, while Camille-Aimé Coquilhat writes that it made the "skin easier to remove."[26] Whatever the exact motive was, it seems clear that the additional suffering this cruel treatment caused their victims did not concern the cannibals. Apparently, they were not deliberately sadistic, but neither did they care.

An episode reported by Léon Roget, a captain of the Free State army, indicates that the sale of persons for consumption was not always free of risk for the sellers. Roget, who like Fräßle was employed near the Aruwimi River, describes a conflict between two villages in this area. One of them (called L—) had purchased a woman from the inhabitants of the other village (called M—). The buyers had slaughtered the woman and started to cook her flesh in eighteen pots; the villagers might have distributed the dismembered body among themselves with each family taking their part home for cooking, hence the many pots. But a dog belonging to M— strolled through the village and ate some of the flesh from one of the pots. The buyers felt cheated and sent a group of armed men who kidnapped a young girl from the other village. The girl was killed, and her flesh added to that of the purchased woman.[27]

When the sold woman had apparently been a slave, maybe caught in a raid elsewhere and deliberately sold, the girl seems to have been a random victim. Hence it is unlikely that she too had been a slave or captive; more likely she had belonged to the village community and her parents and relatives must have felt devastated by losing her. Yet collectively the villagers merely argued that "by taking a little girl of that size, L— had compensated itself too amply," since her body had yielded "more meat" than what was stolen by the dog. They had retaliated by kidnapping and consuming someone from the other village in return, triggering a small war in which several more persons on both sides suffered the same fate.[28]

When hearing of the conflict, Roget volunteered to act as "arbitrator" and restore peace between the villages, but Albert Chapaux, who recorded this account, does not tell whether and how he was able to do so. According to Roget, cannibalism was frequent in the region, with this case just "one example among thousands."[29] The case indicates that responsibility was held collectively and that the inhabitants of a village were held responsible even for acts of their animals. Promising human flesh and then not delivering enough of it, or taking some of it back, was dangerous, since it left a debt of human flesh which the buyer was entitled to have settled.

Human Flesh as a Commodity

We have seen that, at least in parts of the Congo basin, the owners of slaves were under no obligation to keep them alive: they were free to sacrifice them or use them for food, if it pleased them to do so. Wealthy men used this to regale their friends and followers with human flesh, thus increasing their prestige and ensuring loyalty. We will turn to the question of prices in the next section, but it seems pretty clear that buying a whole slave was an expensive proposition, usually out of reach of the common people. Those less wealthy who had cannibal tastes could therefore only hope to get invited to such a feast, or get human flesh in some other way, say as a fighter taking part in a war campaign. In some regions, however, it was not necessary to buy a slave or fight in a war to get access to human flesh, because this flesh was also a commodity offered for sale.

Like slave eating in general, it seems that such transactions were considered quite natural along parts of the Ubangi River. In a letter written in late 1887, Augouard complains that "the people are cannibals to the highest degree who, without shame, offered us a human thigh or arm for ten or fifteen sous!" In another letter he adds that "human flesh is an ordinary butcher's article. They sell an arm or a leg for a value of one franc and take their gourmandism so far that they prefer the parts that are most greasy and devoid of nerves."[30] A few years later, Maurice Musy (1865–1890), a French explorer and colonialist who founded the French governmental post of Bangui (today the capital of the Central African Republic), met a Mr. D—, the manager of a French *factorerie.* The latter told Musy that during a former journey along the same river he had accidentally purchased human fat and used it for cooking, discovering too late the origin of the substance. Both of them had been offered pieces of human flesh for purchase. Such incidents were "not rare" and one soon "does not even pay attention" anymore, Musy comments.[31]

Some of the offered flesh might have come from killed or captured enemies or from "poached" foreigners. Referring to some clans of the Zande farther in the east, Gero writes that they used to sell the flesh and fat of killed strangers and enemies to neighboring villages; the victims' fat was extracted by slowly boiling their bones.[32] But regarding the Ubangi area, the Baptist missionary William Bentley notes that, while "people did not as a rule eat their own townsfolk and relatives"—something that was true very widely indeed—"they kept and fattened slaves for the butcher, just as we keep cattle and poultry."[33] Similar to the accounts given by Glave and others,[34] he states that most of these slaves came from the markets around the Lulonga River. According to Bentley, some people made a business out of purchasing them from intermediaries in order to "feed [them] up . . . until they were fat enough for the market, then butcher them, and sell the meat in small joints." Any flesh not sold during the same day or so "would be dried on a rack over a fire . . . until it could be kept for weeks, and sold at leisure."[35]

Once a little enslaved girl was offered to Musy and his companions. They were in an openly cannibalistic region where they saw "human meat" cooking in pots, and it is possible that the girl was offered to them after they had asked for provisions, as they usually did when arriving in a settlement. But though they assumed (not without reason, as we have seen) that enslaved children in this region were frequently used as a source of food, they did not buy her, "since her presence on board could cause inconvenience." After recording this decision in a diary-style letter, Musy added: "maybe at this hour she is being eaten. That is very likely." It is not clear whether he had a specific reason to suppose this—had he heard or seen something?—or whether he was just expressing a general fear.[36]

At the Lulonga and surrounding rivers, slaves could also meet a premature end. One night, while traveling along the Maringa River, a headstream of the Lulonga, Glave

> heard a woman's piercing shriek, followed by a stifled, gurgling moan; then boisterous laughter, when all again became silent. In the morning I was horrified to see a native offering for sale to my men a piece of human flesh, the skin of which bore the tribal tattoo mark of the Balolo. I afterward learned that the cry we had heard at night was from a female slave whose throat had been cut.[37]

When he returned to the same village ten days later, Glave learned that five more enslaved women had been killed and consumed in the meantime.[38] If this frequency was typical (which is unclear), it would mean that a slave was slaughtered about every second day in that village alone, her flesh then apparently sold to passing sailors and quite possibly to the villagers themselves. While traveling along the Lulonga, Roger Casement once witnessed this as well: "A woman was killed in the village I was passing through, and her head and other portions of her were brought and offered for sale to some of the crew of the steamer I was on."[39]

These independent reports indicate that scenes of this kind seem not to have been rare in this part of the country—apparently the demand for human flesh was high enough to sustain the deadly business model. That all the victims in these cases were women seem too striking for mere coincidence. We will return to this question when discussing the patriarchal aspects of Congolese cannibalism.

An even crueler practice, noted by various observers, is that slaves or captives were presented alive to potential purchasers who then could choose which parts of the body they would buy before the victim was slaughtered. Gero learned from his local informants that this custom had formerly existed among the Kunda, one of the Zande clans:

> Before giving the death blow to a prisoner, they would parade him around like a beast for sale; actually they used to sell the parts of his body to dif-

> ferent bidders, marking in succession, with white ochre or with ashes, what was desired and paid in advance, while the wretch was still alive. The hapless victim was in this way meeting those who would gather around to partake of his flesh. When every part and limb was properly marked and sold out, he was butchered to satisfy the buyers and provide them with their macabre fare.[40]

The same practice is also documented from other areas in the north and northeast of the Congo basin. Father Allaire, one of the French Catholic missionaries, saw slaves offered in this way during his travels along the Ubangi River:

> In the tribe he [Allaire] had just visited . . . the slaves for sale are led to the markets. Some are bought wholesale, and others in parts. Whoever cannot afford a whole specimen, buys only one member, the arm for example, on which he makes a longitudinal mark with a kind of white chalk; a second customer buys the other arm or leg, and puts his mark on it; others buy the head, hands, chest, etc. When all the members have been marked, the head of the unfortunate is cut off, and each of the buyers devours the piece that belongs to him on the spot.[41]

Emil Torday ascribes the same practice to the Budja (a Bangala subgroup) and related peoples living around the central Congo River:

> It often happens that the poor creature destined for the knife is exposed for sale in the market. He walks to and fro and epicures come to examine him. They describe the parts they prefer, one the arm, one the leg, breast, or head. The portions which are purchased are marked off with lines of coloured ochre. When the entire body is sold, the wretch is slain.[42]

Ward describes the procedure as well, adding that he knew it from "personal observation."[43] A further description, possibly based on Allaire's account, comes from the mission historian Renouard.[44]

The distribution of the flesh of still living victims did not always take place in the commercial context of a marketplace. Dr. Poutrin notes that the M'Baka people on the upper Ubangi ate both "the dead and the wounded" during times of war as well as "the prisoners, brought back to their opponent's village."[45] The latter

> are tied by the neck and wrists to a kind of yoke and exposed against the pole which stands in the middle of the place. The chief, then his warriors, designate on their bodies, by limiting them by red lines, the part they reserve for themselves. Then the man is immediately killed and dismembered.[46]

In this case, the flesh was not sold, but the victorious warriors marked the chosen body parts in the same fashion as described by other observers for cannibal slave markets.

Ward calls this treatment of still living slaves (or captives) "the most inhuman practice of all," and Augouard concludes his retelling of Allaire's observation with the rhetorical question: "Can you imagine anything more barbaric and coldly cruel?"[47] Understandable as these sentiments are, Nigel Davies comments that the practice reminds him of how "in India in pre-refrigeration days British families would join forces to buy a whole sheep and eat it the same day."[48] Indeed it seems plausible that the practice was motivated by practical concerns rather than deliberately cruelty: once a large animal (including the human kind) had been slaughtered, the flesh had to be distributed quickly or it would spoil. Human flesh not eaten immediately was often smoked for later consumption,[49] but people certainly preferred fresh meat to smoked.

However, together with the cruel custom of breaking people's arms and legs and letting them soak in a river for days—which was apparently motivated by culinary considerations—this practice clearly shows that slaves and captives were considered of no concern: their fate, their suffering and humiliation simply did not matter.

The Price of Slaves and of Human Flesh

If human flesh had to be purchased, was it a rare and expensive luxury? Or was it priced similar to the meat of edible animals? Information from the cannibal regions of the Congo basin is relatively sparse, but the information that can be found points to regional differences that need to be explained.

As already noted, John Weeks writes that slaves were relatively expensive among the Bangala: for the price of one man, one could buy about seven goats, and this "prohibitive price" prevented them from "gratify[ing] their desire for human flesh very often."[50] Women were even more expensive in this area and therefore rarely eaten—a point to which we will return later.

Farther south, slaves seem to have been considerably cheaper. In Luebo, a town in the Kasai region, Samuel Lapsley once asked a Mr. Engeringh, a white settler, how the latter got "wives" for his native workers. Engeringh answered that he bought enslaved women from the Zappo Zaps, the Songye fighters known and feared for their involvement in the slave trade.[51] A woman, he explained, could be bought for just two pieces of handkerchief, while male slaves were more expensive, costing "three pieces, or four if he is plenty large. If there is as much to eat on a man as on three goats, he brings the price of three goats, that is, three handkerchiefs."[52]

Engeringh added that, while the Zappo Zaps themselves engaged in cannibalism, they spared most of the slaves they bought or captured in order to resell them eastward. Ultimately most of these slaves were purchased by cannibals who lived around the Sankuru River (where Hinde was stationed)—the people living in this area were Songye, just like the Zappo Zaps themselves. "And as the point of view of the final purchaser determines the price, and the consumers are cannibals, the price of a man is generally determined by the amount of meat on him."[53]

The goats domesticated in the Congo basin were dwarf goats, as Harry Johnston points out.[54] The breed commonly found in West and Central Africa reaches an adult weight of eighteen to twenty-five kilograms.[55] That a man could weigh as much as three or four of these goats is therefore not unrealistic.

According to Engeringh, the Kuba people, who live between Luebo and the Sankuru, did not eat people, but some of them had no scruples to act as intermediaries in this murderous trade.[56] Around the Kwilu River, a tributary of the Kasai farther in the west, similar interactions between cannibal buyers and non-cannibal sellers or traders seem to have taken place. The anthropologists Emil Torday and T. A. Joyce claim that the people living around this river "buy many slaves . . . for eating" from neighboring communities that did not practice cannibalism.[57]

The anthropologist Melville Hilton-Simpson (1881–1938) writes that, among the Songye people, the price of a male slave rarely exceeded the price of five goats—somewhat, but not much higher than the price quoted by Lapsley, especially considering that Hilton-Simpson mentions only the usual maximum, not the average price. The price of a woman bought as a "wife" varied between the equivalents of 2.5 to 7.5 goats, likely depending on characteristics such as youth and beauty.[58] At the lower end, this price range is close to Engeringh's statement that he only had to pay the equivalent of two goats for an enslaved "wife" meant for his own workers.

If Engeringh is right, buyers in the Kasai region were very pragmatic—they bought both slaves and goats for consumption, paying for the "amount of meat," but without seeing a reason to pay a premium for human flesh. This corresponds to Frobenius's observation that the Songye considered its taste as "very pleasant [and] similar to pork"[59]—it seems they were happy to get tasty meat from whatever mammals were available, as long as prices were comparable. Hilton-Simpson's higher price suggests that human flesh might actually have been somewhat more expensive than that of goats, but not by a huge amount. The Bangala were more enthused, praising human flesh as "better than any other meat."[60] Here the flesh of slaves seems to have been about twice as expensive as that of goats, according to the price quoted by Weeks.[61] Still a low price for a human life.

That slaves could be fairly cheap is confirmed by Ward, who notes—without revealing which specific region he had in mind—that "two ordinary women may be purchased for the price of one pig."[62] Obviously, he does not talk about modern, systematically fattened pigs which might reach a weight of two hundred kilograms or more. Red river hogs—a species that is widespread in the Congo basin—weigh between 45 and 115 kilograms when fully grown.[63] Two women will have easily reached, if not surpassed, that weight—indicating that, if they were purchased for consumption, their flesh was hardly more expensive than that of a pig.

But as Hilton-Simpson, Weeks, and other sources indicate, the prices of women tended to vary more than those of men and could be considerably higher. Throughout Central Africa, there was usually a higher demand for female than for male slaves because of their gender and sexuality—a point to which we will return later. On the other hand, the demand for slaves that were too young or too old to make useful workers or beautiful "wives" was very low or even absent—outside the cannibal regions at least. François Coulbois, a missionary purchasing and liberating slaves around Lake Tanganyika (east of the Congo basin) in the 1880s notes the typical prices of slaves as follows: healthy adult males cost a hundred francs; twelve-year-old children about fifty. Younger children cost fifteen to twenty-five francs, while tiny four- or five-year-old ones could be had for just five francs. Toddlers and old people were not even offered for sale; there was no market for them.[64]

No cannibalism has been documented for this region (to my knowledge), but if any cannibals had strayed into the markets visited by Coulbois, they would have considered the prices charged for young children very attractive: twenty children aged four to five could be purchased for the price of a single adult man, while their combined weight, and hence the "amount of meat" on their bones, might have been five times as much.[65]

Since the non-cannibal demand for young children was so low, their risk of ending under the butcher's knife must have been even higher than that of adult slaves in regions where slave eating was accepted—as the many sources who mention children as victims indeed seem to indicate. In Luebo, Lapsley was once offered a six-year-old girl in return for a goat—the weight of both might have been about the same.[66] Farther east, in Maniema, James Jameson purchased a ten-year-old girl for just half the price he had recorded for a goat. Even if merely the "amount of meat" is considered, this price seems very low—but the deal was arranged by an Arab-Swahili merchant who might well have been able to negotiate considerably better prices than Jameson, an inexperienced foreigner, could himself have done.[67]

One of the French missionaries working in the Ubangi region once exchanged an empty bottle for "a four-year-old child [who], sick and frighteningly thin, was worthless from a nutritional point of view," as the mission historian Jehan de Witte comments.[68] In a region where glass was a rare foreign import, an empty glass bottle may actually have had more value than the missionaries realized. Still, there can be no doubt that the lives of young children were cheap at that time and that those who preferred eating a child over eating a goat were not ruined by doing so.

The discussion so far has referred to the prices of living slaves. Very little pricing information is available regarding the flesh of slaughtered human beings that was sometimes offered for sale around the Ubangi, the Lulonga, and possibly other rivers. Prices are mentioned, however, in two letters by Augouard written from the Ubangi area. In one he states that "the people . . . offered us a human thigh or arm for ten or fifteen sous," in another he notes: "they sell an arm or a leg for a value of one franc" (that is, twenty sous). In an earlier letter he had mentioned that the price of a chicken was six to seven sous.[69] While the data is too sparse to allow a robust judgment, these statements suggest that the prices of human flesh and chicken meat may have been roughly similar.[70] This would fit the largely pragmatic attitudes documented from at least parts of this area, where slaves were simply called "meat" and where people failed to see an essential difference between the consumption of fowls, goats, and human beings.[71]

To summarize, it seems that the prices of human flesh and animal meat were generally comparable, typically varying from the same price to about twice as expensive for the human variety. How does this fit with our earlier observation that human flesh was considered a proper dish for feasts and might have increased the prestige of those who could provide? Actually, these observations are not as contradictory as it might appear from the viewpoint of a society where many people eat meat products on a daily basis, more or less. But to understand this better we will further investigate, in the next section, how often and under which circumstances human flesh was eaten.

Famine Food or Occasional Diversion?

Several sources consider Congolese cannibalism as motivated, at least in part, by hunger. Referring to the Ubangi region, Renouard argues that "the cannibalistic peoples are not agricultural. Thus famine would be the order of the day if, to prevent it, they did not keep stocks of children for fattening and of slaves destined for slaughter."[72] Josef Fräßle considers "essential destitution" (German: *Lebensnot*) one of the reasons for the cannibalism practiced by the Turumbu;[73] Auguste Chevalier thinks that the Banda and the Mandja (two ethnic groups in today's Central African Republic) practiced cannibalism out of necessity and destitution.[74]

It is well known that, in times of famine, desperate people will turn to human flesh if all other sources of food are exhausted—sometimes even killing for the purpose.[75] And it is plausible enough that within and around the Congo basin, cannibal activities might have increased during times of starvation. According to Gero, adult slaves who had not been eaten immediately after capture were generally safe among the Zande as long as times were good, but if provisions ran low in times of famine, some (or all) of them were slaughtered for food.[76] If this was not enough to ward off starvation, desperate husbands sometimes exchanged a wife "with the wife of another family. Both unfortunate women were destined to the same fate of being butchered and eaten up, each away from her former home." In this way, at least, "the woman slaughtered and consumed was not the family partner." He found recollections of such practices among various clans.[77] According to E. E. Evans-Pritchard, the victims of these exchanges made only "in exceptional circumstances of famine" were usually girl children ("daughters") rather than married women.[78]

Glave reports that the frequent raids against the Balolo people on the Maringa River led to a collapse of their provisioning systems and forced the survivors to consume the corpses of their dead: "Throughout the regions of the Malinga [Maringa] they become so brutalized by hunger that they eat their own dead, and the appearance of one of their villages always denotes abject misery and starvation."[79]

While famine could lead to cannibalism, such periods of extreme food scarcity were exceptional episodes, not characteristic for the whole of the Congo basin over long periods of time, and Glave's account is of an unusually gentle form of cannibalism, where dead bodies were eaten, but nobody was killed. Episodes of famine cannibalism reported from other regions are strictly limited in time—lasting from weeks to at most a few years. A whole population could not over longer periods sustain itself largely from human flesh because the number of victims would be so substantial that the population would literally eat itself out of existence.[80]

The sources we have reviewed indicate that cannibalism was practiced from time to time, often when there was reason for a feast, but that it was by no means a daily affair (with the possible exception of war campaigns). Some sources indicate that the inhabitants of a village might have been able to feast on human flesh a few times a year, others from the Ubangi area claim up to about two victims (possibly mostly children) per week, or a hundred per year.[81] One or two sources assert that kings or wealthy men might have been able to eat human flesh almost daily, but conceivably these are just exaggerated rumors—and even if true, they would only have applied to a tiny minority of people.[82] Had cannibalism been primarily a hunger phenomenon, we would expect a different pattern with human flesh being a regular constituent of lean meals held in dire times by people who would otherwise face starvation, but not eaten at all during better times. But this is not what we see from the Congo, where apparently it was rather a dish of choice for occasional lavish feasts.

Even the authors who consider Congolese cannibalism as driven by hunger tend to agree that this was not the only reason. Renouard notes that cannibalism was also practiced on the Ubangi because well-armed attackers found that they could capture people more easily than many animals, and adds that the flesh of children was preferred over that of elephants and other large animals because it was not only more tender, but also much quicker to cook.[83] Fräßle lists "palatal delight" (*Gaumenlust*) among the motives driving cannibal acts.[84] Chevalier notes that, among the Mandja, while young captives were kept or sold as slaves and slain enemies and adult prisoners were eaten, old captive women were considered useless for any purpose: they were killed immediately and their corpses discarded as too stringy.[85] This is not something one would expect if a lack of other food had really been the primary motive for their cannibalism.

While the consumption of slaves and captives thus cannot be explained as a hunger phenomenon, periods of famine and situations of temporary food scarcity during wartime might nevertheless have helped to establish the custom and make it socially acceptable. As we have already observed for New Zealand (Chapter 2), slave eating can hardly be understood without taking war cannibalism into account. In the Congo, slaves were more often and more widely traded than in New Zealand, but a large part of them were taken in wars or warlike raids. War cannibalism was more widespread, and it might well have been older than slave eating.[86] And in addition to a desire to humiliate the enemy,[87] the consumption of killed or captured foes was repeatedly motivated by convenience in a situation where food was otherwise hard to get.

Evans-Pritchard observes that Zande warriors seem to have considered human flesh a handy source of food, especially during war campaigns, when they "were often desperately hungry" and found it difficult to secure enough provisions. Though taste mattered as well: "I can add, having on a number of occasions discussed the matter with middle-aged and elderly Zande, that I have never heard any other reason given for devouring human flesh than either hunger, or more often, a taste for it."[88] Gero agrees, noting that war cannibalism was practiced, "we could almost say, for logistic reasons": after a battle, human flesh was readily available and would spoil if not used, while other food sources were less easy to secure or, if among the "spoils," could be taken home for future consumption.[89]

Convenience was also given as a reason for war cannibalism in West Africa. In Liberia, the American journalist William Seabrook talked with an old fighter from the Krahn people, who explained: "Perhaps there are sheep and goats and chickens in the conquered village, perhaps not, but why slay them when there is already slain provision of good meat? Is it reasonable to let it spoil and wastefully kill other which is no better?"[90] And A. O. Arua (born ca. 1927), "a very well informed local historian" from southeastern Nigeria, remembered in 1973 that in former times "the human flesh [of enemies] was eaten" because "feeding in the battle field was difficult" and provisions were always scarce.[91]

While it seems clear that Congolese cannibalism in general cannot be explained as a hunger phenomenon, hunger—in times of famine or during war campaigns—might thus certainly have helped to establish the practice. People who had become used to eating human flesh in such circumstances might well have decided to continue the practice in better times, provided that convenient victims—such as captured enemies, kidnapped outsiders, or slaves not urgently needed for other purposes—were available. That war cannibalism was associated with a sense of accomplishment and superiority—in order to eat your enemies, you had to defeat them first—may well have shaped the festive mood of elation that people still seem to have felt when eating slaves.

A Certain Scarcity of Meat

We have seen above that human flesh does not seem to have been an ultimate luxury good whose price exceeded that of animal meat by a huge margin. But this certainly does not mean that it was just a daily, ordinary dish. Rather, meat of any kind may have been a rare and highly valued delicacy. Several sources suggest that human flesh was appreciated as an occasional diversion in a diet that might otherwise have been somewhat monotonous and largely devoid of meat.

Gero notes that Zande, the largest of the languages spoken among the Zande people, had two negatively connoted words that might be translated as "cannibal": *rîaboro* (someone who eats people) and *barîkangba* (someone who eats corpses). These terms were used for acts considered abominable, such as the snatching of corpses from funerals. English has a few terms for cannibals ("cannibal," "man-eater," "anthropophagus"), all of which have negative connotations as well (only very bad, or maybe extremely desperate people will become cannibals). But in the Zande language, according to Gero, there was also a third term without negative overtones, used for cannibalistic acts that were considered socially acceptable, such as the consumption of enemies and strangers. Surprisingly enough, it was simply *rîkawa* (someone who eats meat).[92]

Gero's informants explained that the Zande were limited to a mostly vegetarian diet in times of peace. Domesticated animals could not be eaten on a regular basis, because there were too few of them. Hunting game was only possible during some parts of the year, and even during these times, hunters would often return unsuccessfully (if they had success, they most often caught monkeys, small antelopes, wild cats, and rodents). Capturing and butchering the occasional passing stranger as well as eating persons killed or captured in war and (among a few clans) the corpses of deceased community members thus became a way of making an otherwise monotonous, largely vegetarian and often scarce diet more varied and plentiful. Human flesh, though by no means the only meat eaten, thus became to be considered the prototypical "meat," and "meat eating" and "cannibalism" (in a nonpejorative sense) became synonymous.[93]

Gero points out that two Zande clans that had been particularly cannibalistic—the Abarambu-Adhuga and the Apambia—had owned no domestic animals except dogs (which were sometimes eaten), speculating that this might have increased their propensity for human-based dishes. The Amadi, another cannibal clan, raised goats in addition to dogs. They, too, enjoyed human flesh, but seemed less "voracious," often selling the flesh and fat of enemies and murdered strangers to the Abarambu-Adhuga and other neighboring peoples instead of eating it themselves.[94]

In other Congolese regions, the situation might have been similar. About one of the peoples on the Ubangi River once known as "Bondjos," Dr. Poutrin writes: "the scarcity of the game, the monotony and poverty of the vegetable food easily explain the avidity of the M'Baka for all that is human flesh."[95] Jean Dybowski agrees:

> Cannibalism, however repugnant it may be, becomes more explainable . . . if one considers that all these people, very hungry for meat, have no domestic cattle. They are reduced, at most, to a few small goats and dogs that they eat, but no oxen, sheep or pigs, and there is no doubt that, from the day we import cattle and they will find fresh meat on a regular basis, they will no longer fight each other in order to get it.[96]

Several Europeans complained that the (nonhuman) meat commonly eaten in the Congo basin was not particularly flavorful: "The principal domestic meat supply to be had on the Congo is fowl. . . . For table use he is not a success; no amount of fine cooking will change his tasteless nature," notes Glave.[97] Ward laments about a "meagre diet—sometimes so meagre that it can scarcely be termed monotonous."[98] In a similar tone, Melville Hilton-Simpson complains about "districts where game is so scarce that one has little or no break in the monotony of meals off skinny chickens and insipid goats' meat."[99]

Some of the animals eaten most frequently in modern society were largely unknown in the Congo basin: cattle was almost completely absent from the forest regions of the basin; small pigs were domesticated in some western and southwestern regions, but this was probably largely outside of the central, northern, and eastern regions where cannibalism was common. Chickens and dwarf goats were often domesticated for consumption; sheep were also widespread but not as commonly consumed. Dogs were kept as "an auxiliary in hunting," but in some regions also fattened as "an article of diet."[100]

Coquilhat doubts that cannibalism among the Bangala could have been motivated by hunger since vegetables and fish were plentiful in the area. But he admits that "chickens, geese, goats and sheep are not numerous," a fact he explains by "the carelessness of the native for breeding and the absence of pastures."[101] An oral account from northeastern Nigeria provides an alternative explanation for why domestic animals were rare, one that might equally apply to those parts of the Congo basin where warfare and slave raids were common: "when we ran away if there was war, the animals would make a noise and reveal where you and your family were hiding."[102] That meat in general was a rare "luxury," eaten only at "occasional feasts" among the wealthy and largely out of reach for the poor, has also been observed by missionaries and anthropologists writing about southern Nigeria[103]—a region where slaves were sometimes consumed as well.[104]

Another factor that made the keeping of domesticated animals difficult was the tsetse fly. Gaetano Casati might have been the first European who noticed this, observing that "cattle cannot be successfully reared by the Mambettu [Mangbetu] on account of a fly called *tsetse,* the stings of which cause death."[105] Trypanosomiasis, a parasitic disease transmitted by this fly, can reduce the growth, strength, and milk productivity of domesticated animals, and often sooner or later causes the death of the infected animals. Among the affected species are cattle and pigs—besides poultry, the two most important meat providers in the modern world—small ruminants (sheep and goats), as well as camels and horses.[106] Tsetse flies can be found in large areas of Central and West Africa—including all the regions where cannibalism was common.[107]

Several observers state that the Congolese peoples exploited food—including meat—from a variety of sources. Coquilhat writes: "the natives also eat the flesh of rats, mice, snakes, wild pigs, hippopotami, crocodiles, turtles, antelopes, iguanas, ducks, guinea fowl, ravens, bats, snails, civets, leopards, buffaloes, elephants and insects."[108] Harry Johnston notes that, while "fish are . . . the main staple of food amongst the Congo peoples," frogs and insects were also eaten by many peoples. In some areas, people ate "almost every form of animal food they can procure, including human flesh, grasshoppers, crickets, termites, frogs, owls, hawks, vultures, snakes, and certain kinds of clay." Rats, lizards, crocodiles, gorillas, and leopards were also eaten in at least some parts of the Congo basin.[109] Torday reports from the Kwilu River that "animal food is not limited to goats, pigs, and other domestic small fry, for, frogs excepted, everything helps to make a stew, from ants and grasshoppers upwards to man."[110]

This, however, does not mean that people had plenty. Rather it indicates that protein, especially animal protein, was sufficiently hard to come by that people tended to exploit almost any source at their disposal—sometimes including the human kind. Referring to the area around Luebo, William Sheppard writes:

> The people were not wasteful! Every dead sheep, goat, hog, duck or chicken was eaten. Dead elephants have been found in the forest and over ripe, the pieces gotten together in baskets, carried to the town, cooked and eaten. We saw men put out rapidly in their canoes after a large dead floating fish.[111]

The limited availability and—according to some observers—mediocre quality of other meats eaten throughout the Congo probably helps to explain why human flesh became popular. Faced with a scarcity of animal protein, people were apparently willing to extend the realm of the "edible" farther than elsewhere.

There is, however, an opposing viewpoint. While observing that animals of nearly any kind were eaten around the Kwilu, Torday also states that in this region,

> any amount of chickens could be purchased at threepence apiece, goats and pigs were frequently refused when the top price asked was two shillings. As for native food, enormous quantities of cassava, sweet potatoes, yams, bananas, beans . . . , plantains, maize, &c., are exported, the people not being able to consume all that they produce.[112]

He wonders—without venturing an explanation of his own—how to "explain the fact that it is precisely in this country that cannibalism is most rife," with slaves being deliberately murdered for consumption by those who could afford to do so.[113] He adds that "cannibalism is much less frequent" farther south in a "sandy bush country" that sustained much fewer domesticated animals and less agriculture than found around the Kwilu.[114]

It is probably necessary to distinguish here between the original emergence of cannibalism and its continued practice. On the one hand, the limited availability of animals, or even food in general, likely helped to stretch the concept of "edibility" until it could include the flesh of one's fellow-humans—though only some of them, as community members were very rarely eaten and never killed for this purpose (with the exception, in some communities, of convicted criminals or low-status persons in times of dire famine). On the other hand, with the exception of mutual practices such as the exchange of dead bodies for consumption—which will be covered later[115]—cannibalism required either a warlike attitude or a certain wealth. Poor people were unable to purchase either animals or slaves for consumption, hence it is not so surprising that in the southern "poor country" mentioned by Torday,[116] cannibalism was rare—as was, quite likely, meat eating in general.

But in the wealthier region around the Kwilu, food was apparently so plentiful that some of it was exported—a surplus that allowed chiefs and wealthy men to acquire slaves, whether for consumption or for other purposes. In a similar vein, as we have seen, "edible" slaves on the Ubangi River were often exchanged for ivory which was subsequently exported. A scarcity of meat might have helped to make cannibalism acceptable, but a certain wealth was required to continue the practice even in times of peace.

But is it then not illogical that the practice flourished around the Kwilu River, where meat was (according to Torday) by no means rare? Not necessarily—for one thing, that provisioning was not easy during war campaigns was likely true of this region just as well as of others, with fighters being unable to carry large supplies with them and unwilling to needlessly waste spoils that could also be taken home for future consumption. Alternatively or additionally, it is possible that the acceptance of cannibalism spread from nearby regions where animal food was less widely available.

Notes

1. Augouard, *28 années au Congo*, 1:426.
2. See Chapter 6, this volume.
3. See Chapter 4, this volume.
4. Augouard, *28 années au Congo*, 1:426.
5. Ibid., 2:184.
6. Glave, "Slave Trade," 832.
7. Poutrin, "Notes ethnographiques," 53.
8. Gero, *Cannibalism in Zandeland*, 137; Jewsiewicki and Mumbanza mwa Bawele, "Social Context of Slavery," 75–76.
9. Speke, *Journal*, 103.
10. d'Uzès, *Le voyage*, 156; Casement, *Correspondence and Report*, 40.
11. See Chapter 4, this volume.
12. Bergemann, *Die Verbreitung der Anthropophagie*, 41.
13. Witte, *Monseigneur Prosper Philippe Augouard*, 101.
14. Renouard, *L'Ouest Africain*, 297, 298 (quotes).
15. Hinde, *Fall*, 62.
16. Frobenius in Volhard, *Kannibalismus*, 116.
17. Lapsley, *Life and Letters*, 221.
18. See Chapter 6, this volume.
19. Fräßle, *Meiner Urwaldneger Denken*, 28.
20. Ibid., 68.
21. See Chapter 6, this volume.
22. Ward, *Voice from the Congo*, 315.
23. Ibid., 313.
24. Hinde, *Fall*, 54.
25. Renouard, *L'Ouest Africain*, 135.
26. Coquilhat, *Sur le Haut-Congo*, 270; see Chapter 6, this volume.
27. Roget quoted in Chapaux, *Le Congo*, 543–44.
28. Quoted ibid., 544.
29. Quoted ibid., 543.
30. Augouard, *28 années au Congo*, 1:470, 480.
31. Musy, "Correspondance," 27:456.
32. Gero, *Cannibalism in Zandeland*, 58, 68. For foreigner poaching, see Chapter 12, this volume.
33. W. Bentley, *Pioneering on the Congo*, 211.
34. See Chapter 4, this volume.
35. W. Bentley, *Pioneering on the Congo*, 211.
36. Musy, "Correspondance," 28:67.
37. Glave, *In Savage Africa*, 198.
38. Ibid.

39. Casement, *Correspondence and Report*, 44.
40. Gero, *Cannibalism in Zandeland*, 90.
41. Augouard, *28 années au Congo*, 2:101.
42. Quoted in Johnston, *George Grenfell*, 1:403.
43. Ward, *Voice from the Congo*, 312.
44. Renouard, *L'Ouest Africain*, 135.
45. Poutrin, "Notes ethnographiques," 52.
46. Ibid.
47. Ward, *Voice from the Congo*, 312; Augouard, *28 années au Congo*, 2:101.
48. Davies, *Human Sacrifice*, 157.
49. W. Bentley, *Pioneering on the Congo*, 211; Hinde, *Fall,* 53, 175; Johnston, *George Grenfell*, 1:401–2; Poutrin, "Notes ethnographiques," 53; Schweinfurth, *Heart of Africa*, 93.
50. Weeks, "Anthropological Notes," 121; see Chapter 6, this volume.
51. For more on the Zappo Zaps, see Chapter 5, this volume.
52. Quoted in Lapsley, *Life and Letters*, 175.
53. Quoted ibid.
54. Johnston, *George Grenfell*, 2:616–17.
55. R. Wilson, *Small Ruminant Production*, 106–10.
56. Lapsley, *Life and Letters*, 175.
57. Torday and Joyce, "On the Ethnology," 134, 143 (quote).
58. Hilton-Simpson, *Land and Peoples*, 37.
59. Frobenius in Volhard, *Kannibalismus*, 117; see Chapter 6, this volume.
60. Weeks, "Anthropological Notes," 121; see Chapter 6, this volume.
61. This estimate is based on the fact that, according to Engeringh, an adult man might have provided about three or four times as much flesh as the dwarf goats commonly found in the Congo basin.
62. Ward, *Voice from the Congo*, 293.
63. Kingdon, *Kingdon Field Guide*, 479.
64. Coulbois, *Dix Années au Tanganyka*, 112.
65. Family Practice Notebook, "Weight Measurement in Children," last modified 22 February 2015, http://www.fpnotebook.com/Endo/Exam/WghtMsrmntInChldrn.htm.
66. Sheppard, *Presbyterian Pioneers,* 66. Instead of giving a goat, Lapsley paid for the girl with "some foreign cloth" of unspecified value (ibid.); see Chapter 4, this volume.
67. See Chapter 9, this volume.
68. Witte, *Monseigneur Prosper Philippe Augouard*, 111.
69. Augouard, *28 années au Congo*, 1:293, 470, 480; see also the section, "Human Flesh as a Commodity."
70. In a study that gained him the Ig Nobel Prize for odd scientific research, James Cole calculated the nutritional value of the edible parts of an adult male body. According to his results, the weight of the edible parts of a (male adult) thigh is about 5.1 kg, of an arm (upper arm and forearm) 3.5 kg, of a whole leg (thigh and calf) 6.9 kg (Cole, "Assessing the Calorific Significance," 3). While most of the chickens eaten in the modern world are slaughtered before being fully grown, an adult chicken provides about 1.6–2.7 kg of edible meat (Steven Jerkins, answer to "What's the Average Weight of a Whole Chicken?" *Quora*, 13 July 2018, accessed 21 October 2020,

https://www.quora.com/Whats-the-average-weight-of-a-whole-chicken). Based on the midpoints of Augouard's price ranges, the price per kilogram would have been 2.5 sous for a human thigh (12.5 sous for 5.1 kg), 4.3 sous for an arm (15 sous for 3.5 kg), 2.9 sous for a leg (20 sous for 6.9 kg), and 3.0 sous for a chicken (6.5 sous for ca. 2.15 kg).

71. See Chapter 6, this volume.
72. Renouard, *L'Ouest Africain*, 98.
73. Fräßle, *Meiner Urwaldneger Denken*, 28.
74. Chevalier, *Mission Chari–Lac Tchad*, 99, 112.
75. For some sources covering famine cannibalism, see Chapter 1, note 16, this volume.
76. Gero, *Cannibalism in Zandeland*, 39, 79.
77. Ibid., 69, 86 (quotes), 123.
78. Evans-Pritchard, "Zande Cannibalism," 251.
79. Glave, *In Savage Africa*, 197.
80. James Cole calculated that the nutritional value of the edible parts of an adult male body is about 126,000 calories (Cole, "Assessing the Calorific Significance," 3). Considering that the average weight of a woman compared to a man is about 86 percent, eating both men and women should provide about 117,000 calories per dead adult body (James Roland, "What's the Average Weight for Men?" *Healthline*, 7 March 2019, accessed 21 October 2020, https://www.healthline.com/health/mens-health/average-weight-for-men). To maintain current body weights, women require at least 2,000 calories daily, men at least 2,400—otherwise they will lose weight, and, if this continues for too long, ultimately die of starvation (Karen Gardner, "Minimum Amount of Calories Needed Per Day to Survive," *Livestrong.com*, 7 August 2019, accessed 21 October 2020, https://www.livestrong.com/article/310517-minimum-amount-of-calories-needed-per-day-to-survive/).

    Generally, people in famine periods seem to turn towards human flesh only if all other sources of food are completely (or nearly so) exhausted, but let us assume that there are still some other food sources and only half the required food energy has to come from human flesh—or 1100 calories per day, averaged over men and women. To get that much food energy from human flesh over the course of one year, a village of one hundred adults (we ignore children for these calculations) would have to slaughter and eat 343 adult victims—about one per day! Hence, less than a quarter of an original population of 443 adults would survive the year (and that ignores the problem of how the victims are fed before they are killed). At this level of shrinkage, only three people out of an original population of ten million would be alive after ten years.
81. See Chapter 6, this volume.
82. See also Chapter 5, this volume.
83. Renouard, *L'Ouest Africain*, 132.
84. Fräßle, *Meiner Urwaldneger Denken*, 28.
85. Chevalier, *Mission Chari–Lac Tchad*, 112–14; see also Chapter 4, this volume.
86. See Chapter 4, this volume.
87. See Chapter 6, this volume.
88. Evans-Pritchard, "Zande Cannibalism," 255.
89. Gero, *Cannibalism in Zandeland*, 85.
90. Quoted in Seabrook, *Jungle Ways*, 166.
91. Isichei, *Igbo Worlds*, 128, 130.

92. Gero, *Cannibalism in Zandeland*, 133–34.
93. Ibid., 134–35.
94. Ibid., 58, 60, 71, 82.
95. Poutrin, "Notes ethnographiques," 53.
96. Dybowski, *Le Congo méconnu*, 171.
97. Glave, *In Savage Africa*, 64.
98. Ward, *Voice from the Congo,* 228.
99. Hilton-Simpson, *Land and Peoples*, 290.
100. Johnston, *George Grenfell*, 2:614 (quotes), 616, 620.
101. Coquilhat, *Sur le Haut-Congo*, 273.
102. Nwachukwa Onyeokoro quoted in Isichei, *Igbo Worlds*, 84.
103. Basden, *Among the Ibos,* 139; Talbot, *Peoples of Southern Nigeria*, 3:827.
104. See Chapter 4, note 50, this volume.
105. Casati, *Ten Years in Equatoria*, 160.
106. Iowa State University, Center for Food Security and Public Health, "African Animal Trypanosomiasis," last modified October 2018, http://www.cfsph.iastate.edu/Factsheets/pdfs/trypanosomiasis_african.pdf.
107. Leak, *Tsetse Biology*, 82, figure 7.1.
108. Coquilhat, *Sur le Haut-Congo*, 273.
109. Johnston, *George Grenfell*, 2:613–15.
110. Torday, *Camp and Tramp*, 81.
111. Sheppard, *Presbyterian Pioneers*, 73.
112. Torday, *Camp and Tramp*, 67–68.
113. Ibid., 68.
114. Ibid., 120.
115. See Chapter 13, this volume.
116. Torday, *Camp and Tramp*, 120.

CHAPTER 8
EXPLOITATION AND PATRIARCHY IN THE CONGO

Slave eating is just a particularly grim aspect of the exploitation of enslaved persons in general. In the Congo basin, living slaves were exploited just as in other societies that accepted slavery—though additionally, and in contrast to most other societies, their dead bodies were also considered a useful resource. In this chapter we will explore the interconnections between the ways in which living and dead slaves could be exploited in societies where masters were free to use their slaves in any way they liked—including as a source of food. Moreover, cannibalism is closely connected with patriarchal social structures, in the Congo as well as elsewhere. These interconnections are the second topic of this chapter.

Slaves as "Dual-Use Goods"

As already mentioned, slaves who permanently lived with this status had been rare in Central Africa before the mid-nineteenth century. Captured women and children were sometimes incorporated into the community of their captors, while other captives were killed (and often eaten) or sold to be eaten elsewhere or to be exploited as slaves on the west coast or across the Atlantic. But slaves were rarely kept alive for long and employed as laborers. This changed, however, when the Congo basin became a regular supply zone for the transatlantic and the Arab slave trade. Now warfare and slave raids became much more common and some of the peoples living in the area got used to exploiting captives or traded persons as slaves of their own.[1]

John Weeks estimates that, while he lived among the Bangala on the central Congo River, about a quarter of the population were slaves. Some were children born with this status, others had been captured in wars or sold into servitude because of crimes or unpaid debts. Slaves were sometimes butchered for feasts, but most slaves were made to work for purposes such as farming, clearing bushes, paddling canoes, or building houses.[2]

There is a certain tension between cannibalism and the exploitation of forced labor—when all captives are eaten, none can be employed as slave workers, and vice versa. This is, however, not an absolute contradiction. If there are enough captives, some can be kept as slaves, while others are eaten. And even those slaves used for work or sexual pleasure can be slaughtered and eaten if their owners consider them no longer useful, if they want to teach other slaves a lesson, or if they decide that a meal of delicious human flesh has become more important than a slave's potential future services.

In the Bangala area, it seems that slaves who had been incorporated into a community as laborers were generally safe as long as they performed to their owner's satisfaction, but this could quickly change if they did not. Ward tells that, in the late 1880s, the local agent of a trading company had rented an enslaved boy from a village chief. When the agent complained that the boy was unreliable and did not always show up as expected, calling him "a lazy fellow and not worth much,"[3] the boy's owner reacted in an unexpected way:

> A day or two later the chief told the trader, with evident satisfaction, that the boy would not trouble him again, for that he had killed him with a thrust of his spear; and the white man's horror was increased when, on the following day, the chief's son, a youngster of sixteen or seventeen years of age, came swaggering into the station with spear and shield, and nonchalantly remarked that—
>
> "That slave boy was very good eating—he was nice and fat."[4]

The "white man's horror" is especially understandable considering that his own complaint had led to the boy's death! According to Ward, the case was no exception: "if a slave . . . became 'uppish' and discontented with his walk in life, the remedy was simple. . . . The pot became his destination, and he soon ceased to afford even a topic for conversation."[5] Among the Bankutu people, who live farther south, in the eastern Kasai region, the anthropologist Melville Hilton-Simpson recorded a similar reaction: "a lazy slave is often sold as food."[6]

In these cases, it seems that laziness and a general dissatisfaction of the owner with a slave's performance could be enough to get a slave murdered and eaten. Among the Mangbetu and Zande in the northeast (and possibly elsewhere as well), slaves could suffer the same punishment if they tried to run away or otherwise misbehaved. Gaetano Casati saw how the leg of an enslaved woman who had visited friends without her master's permission was served at the court of the Mangbetu king.[7] Among some Zande clans, slaves who tried to run away were likewise punished with death and consumption, according to Gero.[8]

We have seen in earlier chapters that the consumption of slaves in New Zealand was often justified as a measure of punishing them for misbehavior, while in the Bismarck Archipelago such a justification was absent. In the Congo, while not unheard of, this justification was relatively rare. Many sources indicate that slaves were purchased for outright consumption without any need to justify such acts; however, in several regions—at least those mentioned so far in this section—slaves employed in a community as workers seem to have been relatively secure as long as they performed as expected. Knowing that disappointing their owners could lead to them being killed and eaten, or sold to others who might use them as food, likely had a strongly disciplinary effect on the slave population. This effect might well have motivated owners to occasionally sacrifice slaves for such purposes as a warning to others—in addition to other motives, such as the prestige that could be gained by regaling one's friends and followers with human flesh.

But in some regions at least, even slaves who had lived for some time in their owner's households or communities could fall victim to cannibalism, without such acts being motivated by misbehavior on their part. Disasi Makulo remembers that "two slaves were seized" in order to be butchered for his welcome feast, where they would have been served together with goats and dogs. These slaves had already been around, probably employed by the village or some wealthy villager for useful work—but at that moment, being able to feast on the "delicious flesh of man" was considered more important than the work they might have accomplished otherwise.[9] There is no indication that their planned slaughter was motivated by any misbehavior on their part, though it is quite possible that slaves considered lazy or unreliable were preferred for such festive occasions.

Another case where a slave singled out for consumption had already lived in their owner's household is reported by Guy Burrows. While employed as a Free State official in Riba-Riba (today Lokandu), a town in the Maniema region in the east of the country, he saw "a small native boy weeping bitterly," while lingering near his house, but not daring to approach the white man directly. When an annoyed Burrows finally asked what was wrong, he got the reply: "My master is going to kill me." It turned out that a group of enslaved women owned by the boy's master had been accused of witchcraft after the brother of a local chief had developed a large ulcer on the leg. Suspected of having caused the illness, they were subjected to a trial by poison that killed seven of them—according to local legal tradition, a confirmation of their guilt.[10]

But the ill man's powerful brother was not yet satisfied. He urged Munyumbi, the boy's master, to organize a banquet for himself, his brother, and their "cronies," in order to compensate them for the ill man's suffering and to "appease the evil spirit." Possibly fearing that he might otherwise be implicated in the crime supposedly committed by his slaves,[11] Munyumbi gave in and selected the young enslaved boy as the "pièce de résistance"—apparently, a proper banquet would have been incomplete without human flesh. When the boy got wind of the plan, he ran away to the government post, hoping for salvation.[12] Burrows arrested Munyumbi and the "fetish-doctor" who had performed the deadly poison ordeal and confronted them with the boy's statement. "They not only admitted their guilt, but apparently failed to see anything heinous in their offence."[13]

According to Leo Frobenius, a slave's fate was sometimes preordained among the Songye people in the Kasai region. When he explored this region in a research expedition in 1904–6, he heard that it was not rare for whole villages to jointly acquire a slave (by purchase or through kidnapping) for the express purpose of exploiting first their labor and then their meat. The victims had to work under the supervision of the village chief until the time had come to slaughter them; in the last weeks before that happened, they were fed particularly well to make them fat. On a day determined suitable by an oracle, the slave was taken outside the village and there murdered and dismembered by a few strong young men. The flesh was then distributed among all the families of the village. All edible parts were consumed, except for the penises of male victims (male scrota and female genitals, on the other hand, were considered particularly tasty because of their high fat content).[14]

Female slaves and captives were often exploited sexually as well. This did not mean, however, that their lives were secure, as Frobenius found out during the same expedition. Three of the Songye men accompanying him as porters had started to quarrel about their wages. When he inquired what was wrong, he was told that one of them had once caught a "skinny woman" during a raid whom he had kept for "fattening up." Later he went away to earn money, leaving the woman in the care of the two other men. They took a liking to her (who by then had become quite chubby) and impregnated her (they both considered themselves fathers of her child).[15]

Sometime after the birth of the child, the two "fathers" went on a journey. They took the woman with them and ate her on the way—it is not clear if they had deliberately taken her along as "provisions" or if they decided to kill and eat her after some kind of quarrel. They had left the baby with the woman's original owner, who made up for the loss by killing and eating it—evidently feeling that the men who had consumed his slave owed him some human flesh in return. But he did not consider the baby sufficient compensation, instead complaining that the two men still owed him payment for eating his slave (who, after all, had provided much more meat). The two fathers, in turn, asked to be paid for the child they had sired and which, as they argued, had therefore been their rightful property.[16] None of the men seems to have shown any particular feelings of mourning, not even the fathers who had lost their child.

Gender and Age of the Victims, and the Influence of Prices on Cannibal Choices

This last case leads us to the question of how strongly and in which ways Congolese cannibalism was influenced by patriarchal patterns. The stereotypical view of a patriarchal society in which cannibalism was practiced would be

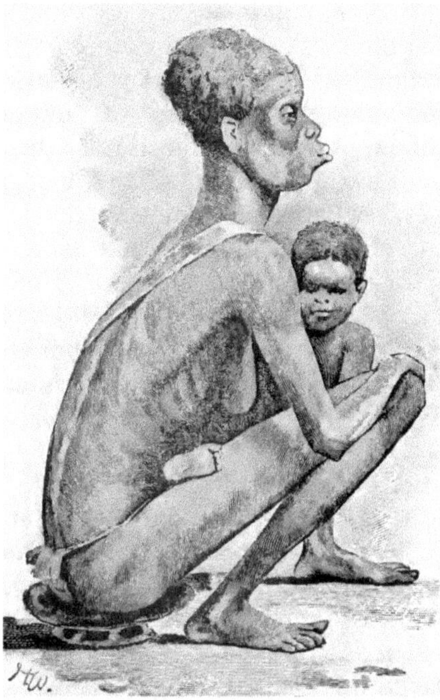

Figure 8.1. An enslaved woman from the Aruwimi region with her baby. From Herbert Ward's *Five Years with the Congo Cannibals* (London: Chatto & Windus, 1891), 160.

that men were the primary perpetrators, while women and children were the primary victims—forced to serve and service the men, and, at the men's whim, killed and eaten. This case fits the stereotype perfectly, but how representative was it?

There can be little doubt that many of the Congo's societies were indeed highly patriarchal. Elizabeth Isichei remarks that throughout large parts of Africa, "women bore the heavier work load, [while] older men controlled the lion's share of power and resources."[17] Harry Johnston adds that in the Congo basin, even free women were considered little more than "chattels," rarely allowed to hold property of their own and passed on to other men after the death of their husbands.[18] Confirming this, a young boy told the German missionary Josef Fräßle that his father's heir had sold his mother into slavery after his father's death, leaving the children to care for themselves.[19] When a man married a free woman, he had to pay a bride price which usually went to her father or uncle; men could also buy enslaved women and keep them as wives. In both cases, marriage was a financial transaction and even free women had hardly a say in the matter.[20] Girls were often married at the age of nine or ten[21] or even earlier.[22]

Men were thus clearly dominant in at least the typical Congolese societies, but does this mean that their risk of falling victim to cannibalism was lower? Not necessarily—throughout Africa, there was usually a higher demand for female slaves than for men, "both because of their sexuality (their value in reproduction and their use as sex objects) and because their economic productivity could be utilized without entailing the degree of physical rebelliousness of male slaves," as Patrick Manning explains.[23] This higher demand meant that women and girls were often sold at higher prices, making them less attractive targets for people eaters—at least, if the latter just preferred to get their "meat" at a reasonable price. Ward, who was too Victorian to talk about sex, expresses this as follows: "a greater number of men than women fall victims to cannibalism, the reason being that women who are still young are esteemed as being of greater value by reason of their utility in growing and cooking food."[24]

The same observation was made by other Europeans who visited the Congo. Camille-Aimé Coquilhat writes about the Bangala: "It is very rare that women are eaten; their commercial value is too great."[25] Weeks confirms this, noting that the price of enslaved women was usually about four times that of men, "on account of their farm work, and child-bearing capacity."[26] The Swedish explorer Theodor Westmark states that, because of their higher "intrinsic value," enslaved women in this region usually "escape . . . the human sacrifices made solely for the purpose of obtaining human flesh to eat."[27]

The situation on the upper Ubangi River seems to have been similar, according to Jean Dybowski, who writes that the "Bondjos" mostly bought male slaves from neighboring peoples willing to supply them, because "women, being apparently of superior value," were typically sold to non-cannibal buyers ready to pay more.[28] Several travelers visiting the Ruki (on the other side of the Congo River) found that the inhabitants of this area were very willing to exchange women against men—with the stated intent of eating the latter. The German officer Curt von François writes that, while traveling along this river in the early 1880s, his party was "offered women in exchange for men they intended to slaughter."[29] Especially a "fat" man, the interpreter of the group, attracted the attention of would-be buyers: "Today, a few brazen young men had pinched him again in his arm, pointing to their stomachs and voicing 'Niama! niama!' meaning: Meat! meat!" On the same river, George Grenfell was offered "a fine-looking woman as a wife in exchange for a plump boatman whom they wanted to eat!"[30]

In the latter case, the locals were apparently willing to exchange one woman against one man, indicating that in this area women were not generally more expensive than men. While François concluded from these offers that only men were slaughtered in this area, there are no strong indications that this was indeed the case. Both sources note that the people eaters did not just look for any man, but especially for those who were "fat" or "plump"—from their viewpoint, the attractive feature of such men might simply have been that they had "more meat" on their bones than a typical woman.

In other regions, it seems that the demand for women was likewise comparable to that for men. In the Kasai area, if the settler Engeringh is right, "the price of" not just "a man," but also a woman, was "generally determined by the amount of meat on him"—and women were therefore cheaper than men.[31] It is very possible that this applies only to "ordinary women," as Ward calls them, while those who were particularly attractive still fetched higher prices, rendering them a bad deal for price-aware cannibals. Hilton-Simpson notes, as we have seen, that the prices of women sold in this area varied considerably, ranging from cheaper to considerably more expensive than the typical male slave.[32]

Even in regions where the general demand for enslaved women was high, premium prices were probably paid only for teenagers and young women of "prime age," while younger and older slaves were still at risk of becoming food. Emil Torday notes this explicitly for the region around Basoko, where the Aruwimi River joins the Congo: while both male and female victims could be killed for "feasts," the latter were "usually . . . young girls or elderly matrons who have ceased child-bearing."[33] Several sources from the Ubangi region also indicate that girl children were eaten in this area—in contrast to women of child-bearing age who apparently had a good chance of being spared.[34] Among the Zande, as Georg Schweinfurth writes, captured young women "were destined for their houses"—likely to be exploited as consorts and servants, "the middle-aged" had to work in the fields, but "the eldest" went into the "caldrons."[35] Young children were also commonly eaten, as Schweinfurth and several other observers note, with no indications that those of either gender were spared.[36]

Rather than causing more women to be eaten than men, the patriarchal structure of Congolese societies thus seems to have had the opposite effect (at least in some regions): young and attractive women were commonly bought for sexual exploitation, and those who were healthy and not too old were bought as servants and field workers because they were supposedly easier and less risky to exploit than men. In many cases it seems that the people eaters were willing to buy those for whom such competing demand was absent or reduced: old women, young girls, and men of any age.

On the other hand, the higher prices often charged for attractive young women might have turned them into favorite targets of those for whom cannibalism was a mode of "conspicuous consumption."[37] Butchering an attractive woman for food was a sure way of wasting her beauty, but this might have driven some wealthy or powerful men to single out such victims just to show that they could afford to do so rather than having to resort to cheaper victims. James Jameson heard from a group of Bangala people that "one of their chiefs, who was very rich, is now quite poor from buying nice, fat, young women to eat."[38] In this case he could not afford it in the end, but it seems he had tried. Coquilhat's, Weeks's, and Westmark's statements that women were rarely eaten among the Bangala indicate that such a behavior was by no means typical, but this does not mean that it did not occur.

Other observations, especially from the Ubangi region, also suggest that women could be preferred eating. Frobenius claims that a powerful Gbaya leader liked to keep nubile, "buxom" girls in his possession, but not, he writes with some astonishment, "to spend sultry nights with her, but to fatten her, making her plump, and then to butcher and roast her," subsequently regaling his followers with her flesh. Grenfell adds that some of the peoples on the upper Ubangi once summarized (like the Gbaya) under the generic "Bondjo" label, "preferred the flesh of women and infants," while on the lower Ubangi, "women are . . . valued greatly as the material of the banquet."[39] Among the Nzakara, who live around a northern tributary of this river, and in the northeastern Tshopo province, the flesh of women and children was likewise praised as tastier than that of men.[40]

Ward notes that, while in most regions more men were eaten than women because of the latter's "greater value," the proportion was "reversed" around the Aruwimi River, which flows through the Tshopo province—he does not offer an explanation for why this was so.[41]

Apparently, the patriarchal structures of Congolese societies could have a double effect on cannibalism: in many regions, there was a higher demand for woman who could be used as sex objects, wives, or servants, and who were considered less risky to control and exploit than adult men. This motivated people eaters to turn to other, more affordable victims—except in cases where they deliberately choose such expensive victims to make it clear that they could afford to do so. Both these reactions seem to have occurred, with the pragmatic choice more frequent than the prestige-driven one—hence the statements of various observers that more men than women were consumed.

There are two further complications: one is that women were not always higher priced than men. In the Kasai region, as we have seen, the prices of "ordinary women" (Ward) seem to have been lower than those of men, though some—possibly the most beautiful ones, or those considered most likely to bear healthy children—were more valuable. This might have been due to an oversupply of slaves that drove prices drown. In some other regions, the situation might have been similar, but since pricing information on slaves is generally sparse, it is hard to tell where and exactly why this was the case.

The other complication is that in slave raids as well as in war campaigns against enemies, men were often killed outright, either because there was a lower demand for them as slaves, or because they were considered too dangerous to keep alive, or both.[42] This seems to have been the case especially in the eastern regions of the Congo basin from which slaves were commonly exported into the Arab world, since there, just as in Africa itself, there was a considerably higher demand for female than for male slaves, with purchased women and girls commonly being made into "wives, concubines, and servants."[43] In such cases, men killed or captured in raids were often eaten immediately,[44] while those kept or sold as slaves were usually women, girls, and young boys.

This suggests that, if people in these regions wanted to buy a slave for a "feast," they had to take a victim from one of these latter groups, since men were not regularly offered on the slave markets. This might explain Ward's observation that more women than men were eaten around the Aruwimi River, and it might explain why, whenever specific details of slaves used or intended for consumption around this river and from the Maniema region (both in the east of the country) are given, the victims seem to have been women or children.[45]

A curious contrast is notable in reports from the Ruki and the Lulonga, two left-bank Congo tributaries whose mouths are only about sixty kilometers apart. François and Grenfell both encountered male slaves about to be slaughtered on the Ruki,[46] while the flesh of enslaved women was offered to the crews of Glave's and Casement's steamers on the Lulonga and its headstreams, with Glave learning that six women had been consumed in the course of ten days in one village alone.[47] Was this just by chance or did it reflect real differences in the preference for or treatment of victims?

Around the Ruki, as we have seen, people were quite willing to exchange enslaved women against men, as long as the latter were "fat" or "plump." This seems to reflect a pragmatic attitude where people mostly cared for the "amount of meat" on the bones of their victims. Why then the apparent preference for women on the other river? It is conceivable that the difference was just by chance, but Glave's account of six women (and no man) being murdered in order to sell their flesh in what seems to have been a more or less regular business operation seems too conspicuous to attribute to mere chance. Casement reports a similar case of commercial cannibalism, where the flesh of a newly killed woman was offered for sale. Maybe those who engaged in this deadly business preferred female victims because they considered them easier to subdue and less likely to make trouble? Or maybe people in this region were willing to pay a premium for women's flesh, which was apparently regarded in several regions as better than that of men?

While this cannot be answered with certainty, it is clear that, in general, Congolese cannibalism was shaped by both patriarchal attitudes and economic considerations in complex ways. Men were, as we will see, indeed often the primary eaters of human flesh, but the eaten could be women, men, and children alike. Young enslaved children in the cannibal regions were in the unfortunate situation that they were in high demand for the table—with their flesh often regarded as better than that of adults, or at least of adult men—and in low demand for anything else.[48] Young women, on the other hand, were in demand as sex objects, future mothers, and servants, and that increased their chances of surviving. But, of course, it did by no means secure it—enslaved women were eaten too, especially, it seems, when an oversupply of slaves drove prices down or when men chose to display their wealth by deliberately purchasing young women for consumption.

Captured men were likewise eaten when they were considered too dangerous to keep alive or when there was little demand for their labor power. Though the perpetrators were often men, their "male solidarity" did not extend to enemies or outsiders. Men, women, and children could all be eaten alike when they were available. But it seems that men were nowhere the food of choice—when the cannibals expressed a preference, it was usually for the flesh of women, children, or both, just as one might expect of patriarchal societies. In addition to the statements we have already heard in this regard, there is Gero's observation that, among the cannibalistic Zande clans, women were considered "choice food, their flesh being more tender and containing more fats." And an Amadi informant told him that children had in former times been particularly sought after because of their "very delicate meat"; members of the Adhuga clan supposedly shared this preference.[49]

Gero even claims that in the Apambia clan, a spinach-like plant prepared with "fat from a woman's breast" had been considered the "national dish." In earlier times, warfare and raids had provided victims for this dish. During colonial times, when open warfare was no longer possible, the human ingredient had to be acquired by stalking and killing women and girls from foreign clans in the forest. From his local informants, Gero heard that in the early 1930s this dish was still occasionally prepared in its original form, though not as often as it had been formerly, because this mode of securing victims was risky and most Apambia had already given up on cannibalism. When visiting a mission station in the region in 1934, Gero asked the local teacher for the "national dish." Visibly shocked, the teacher replied: "Have we then to kill a girl?" Gero, who had assumed that by then the dish was commonly prepared with vegetal fat, hastily explained that he would be happy to go for a vegetarian variant.[50]

How often this dish had actually been eaten in former times is unclear—after all, the sources indicate that captive women of "prime age" were more often enslaved than eaten among the Zande, and when it came to breast fat, neither little girls nor old women will have been ideal victims. But the choice of a distinctly female body part as main ingredient of a prized dish points to a very patriarchal worldview in which women could be used by men in any way that pleased them.

The Gender of the Cannibals

The Congolese people eaters were often—though by no means always—men. In this section we will explore more closely what the available sources have to say on this topic, and how it relates to patriarchal social structures in general.

When looking at the sources, it becomes quickly clear that there is some disagreement between different observers about whether or not women and children were allowed to join in the consumption of human flesh, with several sources explicitly noting that customs varied between regions. David Livingstone writes that women did not eat human flesh in the Maniema region; Johnston notes the same for the lower Ubangi region.[51] Augouard confirms that some of the ethnic groups in the latter region excluded women and children from eating human flesh, but he adds that no such restriction existed among the "Bondjos," who lived farther upriver. There women did not only join their husbands in cannibal meals, they also "display[ed] remarkable skill in disarticulating limbs or carving up a corpse."[52] Among several Zande clans, such as the Babangbing, Babukur, and Bahum, everybody, "men and women, boys and girls alike," participated in meals of human flesh, as Gero learned from his informants.[53] Among the Mangbetu, Schweinfurth saw a group of women dress a human body for consumption, but it is not clear whether they were allowed to share in the upcoming meal.[54]

Auguste Chevalier and John Weeks likewise note that customs varied from region to region.[55] The British missionary and explorer Albert Lloyd states that among the Bangwa people on the upper Aruwimi River, women ate human flesh, but sitting "in a separate group by themselves" rather than commingling with the men.[56] This, however, might well have applied for all meals rather than just cannibalistic ones. According to Johnston, there was a widespread custom of men and boys eating "by themselves. Even in the great feasts there is to a certain extent a separation of the sexes." He explains this as "partly [due to] the tabu placed on the unfortunate women in respect of articles of food, to the advantage of the male sex."[57]

Other observers reveal that, when human flesh was forbidden to women, other meats were often forbidden to them as well. Torday writes that, around the Kwilu River, "human flesh is, of course, a special delicacy, and its use is forbidden to women, though they do not disdain to indulge secretly." They were likewise forbidden to eat the meat of goats, birds, and wild animals, with just "two exceptions—the antelope and a small rat."[58] The sole purpose of these restrictions, according to Torday, was to ensure "that there may be a larger supply for the men."[59] He investigated several cases in which a person (a slave or captive?) had been murdered and eaten, finding in all cases "that every male in the village had shared in the feast on the remains, the children being given the bones to gnaw."[60]

In this region, at least, there seem to have been no special taboos that restricted the consumption of human flesh to adult men. Children (maybe just boys?) were allowed to have some of it, though only little bits remaining on the bones discarded by the men. Women did not hesitate to "indulge" if given the opportunity, but could do so only rarely and in secret, because the men preferred to keep the bulk not just of human flesh, but indeed of nearly any meat, for themselves.

Carol J. Adams notes that throughout patriarchal societies—including our own—meat eating is often predominately "a male activity associated with virility," associated with "the assumption that *men need meat,* have the right to meat," and that in cases "when the meat supply is limited, men will receive" all or most of it.[61] Restrictions that forbade women to eat chicken or other (nonhuman) meat products also existed elsewhere in the Congo[62] as well as in other African regions.[63] It seems that the Congolese cannibals were not so different from men in other patriarchal societies in this regard: they preferred to keep the best for themselves, at least if supplies were scarce.

Though, as we have seen, there were regions where women were allowed to taste human dishes. While the evidence is inconclusive, this does not necessarily point to full gender equity between male and female people eaters in these areas. Even in male-dominated societies men will have been more inclined to share if they had plenty, and it is quite possible that the differing customs noted by observers depended more on the amount of meat available at any given time than on strict and unbending rules.

Wife Eating

In and around the Congo basin, those deliberately killed for eating were usually outsiders of some kind or other—usually enemies, slaves, or kidnapped strangers. In some areas, those considered guilty of some serious act of wrongdoing could be punished by death and subsequent consumption—acts of punitive cannibalism have been documented for the Nzakara,[64] the Bangala,[65] the Kasai region,[66] the Mangbetu,[67] and the Zande.[68] Criminals, however, might well have been considered some kind of outsiders too, who in consequence of their (suspected) act no longer deserved to be treated as community members.

Married women were no outsiders, but in the Congo's patriarchal societies they did not always enjoy the full protection due to community members. Free wives usually came from other communities (marriage was exogamous) and their husbands paid a bride price (also known as bridewealth) to their families. Enslaved wives were purchased like any other slave, but, at least after they had become mothers, they were usually safe from being arbitrarily resold.[69]

In the modern viewpoint, people are thought to have fundamental rights—such as, most essentially, the right to life—independently of their connections. But in Central Africa, as Bogumil Jewsiewicki and Mumbanza mwa Bawele point out, a person's rights depended on their ties to a community. If people were killed or otherwise harmed, it was up to their kin or their community to revenge them. This gave them protection as long as people who felt responsible lived nearby. Slaves were people who had no known kin and hence no protection—therefore their masters could treat them in any way they liked, including killing them for food. A free wife, on the other hand, could not be arbitrarily killed or severely hurt as long as her kin lived in a nearby community, since they would feel obliged to revenge her if necessary.[70]

Weeks writes that, among the Bangala, a free wife was sometimes "thrash[ed] unmercifully" if she had offended her husband—this might not have pleased her relatives, but they tolerated it as long as nothing worse happened. Slave wives, on the other hand, were occasionally killed by their husbands due to "a whim or in a fit of temper"; afterwards, the latter would "fling the corpse into the river, or invite their neighbours to feast with them on the body."[71]

One Bangala chief became known among Europeans for having eaten seven of his wives. It was Mongonga, the chief who utterly failed to grasp the European aversion of his consumption of slaves.[72] Coquilhat, the Belgian officer who had observed his slave-eating feast and tried in vain to convince him of the wrongness of his ways, noted in his diary: "When, two years ago, one of Mongonga's wives gave birth to a malformed child, he decapitated and ate her."[73]

Theodor Westmark describes this as a habit rather than an exception:

> A notable Bangalla called Mongonga had ten wives. The man's passion for human flesh was so great that, in order to satisfy this filthy taste, he did not hesitate, in various circumstances, to accuse seven of these unfortunates of imaginary crimes, for which he had them killed and then he ate them. One of these unfortunates was executed on the evening of the day on which she had brought a child into the world.[74]

The women's "crimes" were certainly "imaginary" according to European legal standards. But as Coquilhat notes, the unfortunate woman killed just after childbirth had produced a "malformed" baby, which in the eyes of her husband might well have indicated a failure as a mother. What (if anything) the other wives had done to provoke his wrath is not mentioned in any of the sources. However, according to William Bentley, who had also met the chief, "there had [in all cases] been some breach of morals, or in some way he had been offended; so, he had made a family feast of the delinquent, *pour encourager les autres!*" Though the man had "eaten at least seven of his wives," Bentley found him "smiling, amiable, mild-looking," rather than the monster he might have expected.[75]

It is unclear whether Mongonga's eaten wives had all been slaves or whether he had dared to subject free women to this treatment. Bentley writes that "he had somewhat beggared himself in consequence" of his wife eating,[76] but since a price had to be paid for free women (bride price) as well as for slaves, this does not tell us much. If some of the victims had been free, they might have lost the contact to their kin; Jewsiewicki and Mumbanza mwa Bawele note that, when that happened (usually because the relatives had moved away or died in an attack), a woman "became in effect a slave to her husband" who could now treat her as it pleased him without having to fear revenge.[77] It is also conceivable that the wives' relatives knew of his acts but did not dare to get revenge because Mongonga was too powerful.

Cases of wife eating have also been reported from other regions. When visiting the "Bondjos" in 1889, the French explorer and colonialist Maurice Musy found their women to be "very beautiful," but he also heard that they did not live long if they used their beauty in ways that displeased their husbands: "the husbands are extremely jealous and cut off their heads and then eat them at the slightest infraction."[78] In the case of adultery, not even a woman's relatives might have been able (or willing) to protect her from the wrath of her husband.

The tension of men's notions of absolute power over their wives and the general obligation to protect one's own kin is observed by Gero. He notes that among some Zande clans, such as the Babukur and Apambia, wives were occasionally killed and eaten if they "insulted their husbands, or showed laziness in work." But if the clan of a killed woman noticed what had happened, they would try to get revenge and kill the murderous husband or some other member of his clan. The murder and consumption of free women therefore generally took place only in secret.[79]

Notes

1. Jewsiewicki and Mumbanza mwa Bawele, "Social Context of Slavery," 73, 75; see also Chapter 4, this volume.
2. Weeks, "Anthropological Notes," 427–29.
3. Ward, *Five Years*, 133.
4. Ibid., 133–34.
5. Ward, *Five Years*, 132–33.
6. Hilton-Simpson, *Land and Peoples*, 148.
7. Casati, *Ten Years in Equatoria*, 119; see Chapter 5, this volume, for more details.
8. Gero, *Cannibalism in Zandeland*, 39.
9. Makulo, *La vie*, 57–58; see also Chapter 6, this volume.
10. Burrows and Canisius, *Curse of Central Africa*, 206–8.
11. "A master was responsible for the actions of his slaves," writes Weeks ("Anthropological Notes," 429). While he refers to the Bangala, legal notions in other parts of the Congo basin were probably similar.
12. Burrows and Canisius, *Curse of Central Africa*, 208.
13. Ibid., 209.
14. Frobenius in Volhard, *Kannibalismus*, 116–17.
15. Ibid., 115.
16. Ibid., 115–16.
17. Isichei, *History*, 81.
18. Johnston, *George Grenfell*, 2:697.
19. Fräßle, *Meiner Urwaldneger Denken*, 81–82. For the boy's story, see Chapter 12, this volume.
20. Lovejoy, *Transformations of Slavery*, 14.

21. Ward, *Voice from the Congo*, 281.
22. Lapsley, *Life and Letters*, 183.
23. Manning, *Slavery and African Life*, 22.
24. Ward, *Voice from the Congo*, 312.
25. Coquilhat, *Sur le Haut-Congo*, 274n1.
26. Weeks, "Anthropological Notes," 420.
27. Westmark, "Chez les Bangallas," 435.
28. Dybowski, *La route du Tchad*, 137.
29. François, *Die Erforschung des Tschuapa*, 116.
30. Johnston, *George Grenfell*, 1:141.
31. Quoted in Lapsley, *Life and Letters*, 175; see also Chapter 7, this volume.
32. Ward, *Voice from the Congo*, 293; Hilton-Simpson, *Land and Peoples*, 37; see also Chapter 7, this volume.
33. Cited in Johnston, *George Grenfell*, 1:404.
34. Augouard, *28 années au Congo*, 1:426, 2:70, 278–79; Musy, "Correspondance," 28:67.
35. Schweinfurth, *Heart of Africa*, 222.
36. See Chapter 5, this volume.
37. See Chapter 6, this volume.
38. Jameson, *Story*, 31.
39. Frobenius, *Und Afrika sprach*, 189; Johnston, *George Grenfell*, 1:402.
40. See Chapter 4, this volume.
41. Ward, *Voice from the Congo*, 312.
42. Brode, *Tippoo Tib*, 92; Gero, *Cannibalism in Zandeland*, 39, 79; Johnston, *George Grenfell*, 2:775.
43. Lovejoy, *Transformations of Slavery*, 34; Shillington, *Encyclopedia*, 225–26, 1383 (quote).
44. See references in note 42, this chapter.
45. Chapaux, *Le Congo*, 543–44; Makulo, *La vie*, 72; Burrows and Canisius, *Curse of Central Africa*, 206–9; Jameson, *Story*, 290–91.
46. François, *Die Erforschung des Tschuapa*, 119–20; Johnston, *George Grenfell*, 1:140; see also Chapter 4, this volume.
47. Glave, *In Savage Africa*, 198; Casement, *Correspondence and Report*, 44; see also Chapter 7, this volume.
48. See the main text of this chapter, as well as Chapters 4 and 7 in this volume.
49. Gero, *Cannibalism in Zandeland*, 40, 55, 67.
50. Ibid., 79, 82, 121.
51. Livingstone, *Last Journals*, 98; Johnston, *George Grenfell*, 1:402.
52. Augouard, *28 années au Congo*, 2:582–83.
53. Gero, *Cannibalism in Zandeland*, 38.
54. Schweinfurth, *Heart of Africa*, 93.
55. Chevalier, *Mission Chari–Lac Tchad*, 100; Weeks, "Anthropological Notes," 457.
56. Lloyd, *In Dwarf Land*, 296.
57. Johnston, *George Grenfell*, 2:631.
58. Torday, *Camp and Tramp*, 81.
59. Ibid., 84.
60. Ibid., 177.
61. Adams, *Sexual Politics of Meat*, 4 (emphasis in original), 27.
62. Johnston, *George Grenfell*, 2:614.

63. Adams, *Sexual Politics of Meat*, 50.
64. Chevalier, *Mission Chari-Lac Tchad*, 232; Mecklenburg, *From the Congo,* 1:200.
65. Weeks, "Anthropological Notes," 121; Westmark, "Chez les Bangallas," 431.
66. Hinde, *Fall*, 89; Wissmann, *My Second Journey*, 303–4.
67. Junker, *Travels*, 248–49.
68. Evans-Pritchard, "Zande Cannibalism," 251; Gero, *Cannibalism in Zandeland*, 39–40, 50, 66, 77, 111, 114; Junker, *Travels*, 148.
69. Shillington, *Encyclopedia*, 1389.
70. Jewsiewicki and Mumbanza mwa Bawele, "Social Context of Slavery," 74.
71. Weeks, *Among Congo Cannibals*, 78.
72. See Chapter 6, this volume.
73. Coquilhat, *Sur le Haut-Congo*, 274n1.
74. Westmark, "Chez les Bangallas," 435.
75. W. Bentley, *Pioneering on the Congo*, 177, 213.
76. Ibid., 177.
77. Jewsiewicki and Mumbanza mwa Bawele, "Social Context of Slavery," 74.
78. Musy, "Correspondance," 28:131.
79. Gero, *Cannibalism in Zandeland*, 40 (quote), 78.

CHAPTER 9
THE JAMESON AFFAIR

In the usual Western ways of looking at cannibalism, the cannibals are always "the others"—far remote from *us*, the civilized folk, who would never engage in, or get in any way involved with, such terrible practices. We have already seen that the reality in the Congo basin, as well as elsewhere, was much more complex. Some Europeans, whether working for the Congo Free State or for private companies, did not hesitate to collaborate with cannibals and sometimes deliberately provided them with victims for consumption. Except for William Seabrook,[1] there is no evidence that they deliberately sought to consume human flesh themselves (though, of course, an absence of evidence is not evidence of absence). Still, the borders between the cannibalistic "others" and the non-cannibalistic "us" were not drawn as clearly as Europeans liked to imagine—especially at a time when "the white man's burden" to spread a supposedly superior civilization was a right and privilege that allowed for exploitation and subjugation of everyone else.

In the late nineteenth century, much of the evidence pointing towards deliberate cooperation between supposedly civilized Westerners and supposedly primitive cannibals was either unknown or ignored. An exception, however, was an event that would soon be called "the horrible Jameson affair."[2] James Jameson, a wealthy Scot from the family of whiskey producers with the same name, had been one of the Europeans who accompanied Henry Morton Stanley during his last expedition through Africa and who had effectively been abandoned by Stanley in the eastern Congo basin to form part of his "rear guard."[3] During that time, Jameson had—whether wittingly or not—paid for a young enslaved girl who was then handed over to cannibals for consumption, while he witnessed everything and made drawings of the proceedings. Accusations that he had deliberately arranged the deadly episode sent shock waves through the British and American press in 1890.

Since the case is well documented and has attracted a considerable amount of discussion and controversy, at that time as well as later, it is worth analyzing in detail, to understand what happened there and why the episode attracted so much media attention in the first place. From the discussion of this specific event, we will subsequently turn towards broader reflections regarding Western influences on cannibalistic "others."

The Evidence

Because Jameson died of a severe fever in August 1888, a few months after the incident, he was unable to defend himself against the charges. In his diary, published posthumously by his wife and brother,[4] he describes the episode as something that took him by surprise and happened against his will.

After several months of being stuck with Stanley's "rear guard," Jameson traveled to Kasongo (a town in the Maniema region) for a personal meeting with Tippu Tip, the powerful Swahilo-Arab merchant and slaver. The rear guard was waiting for a large number of porters which Tippu Tip had promised to provide. The goal of Jameson's trip was to convince Tippu Tip to finally fulfill his promise after a long series of delays and postponements. The journey was indeed a partial success—on his way back he was accompanied by Tippu Tip and four hundred of the promised porters. They rested for a day and a half in Riba-Riba (today known as Lokandu), a small town on the Lualaba River (the largest headstream of the Congo). A few years later, while employed in the same town, Guy Burrows would—according to his own account—save a young enslaved boy from being killed for a cannibal feast.[5] Jameson's story is very different.

On 11 May 1888, as he subsequently recorded in his diary, he "went over to the old chief's house to have a talk with him, when presently a band, consisting of four drummers, arrived with three pedestal-shaped side-drums, and one wedge-shaped chondo." The diary entry continues with a detailed description of an artful and acrobatic dance performed by more than a dozen male and female dancers in the "reception house" of the chief.[6] The drummers and dancers, explained the chief, belonged to a people called "Wacusu,"[7] and

> Tippu-Tib, who came in before it was over, told me that they usually kill several people, and have a grand feast, for the Wacusu are terrible cannibals. He then told me, amongst other stories, that long ago, when fighting near Maléla, they killed a great many of the enemy. The natives who were with him were cannibals, and not a body could be found next morning. (He tells me that two men will easily eat one man in a night.) He sent for water in the night to wash his hands and to drink, the water there being in a well. When it was brought, he could not make out why it stuck to his hands, and was so oily and bad to drink. Next day he and several Arabs went up to see what was the matter with the water, and there they saw a most horrible sight. The top of the water was all covered with a thick layer of yellow fat, which was running over the side, and he found out that his

Figure 9.1. James Jameson. From Henry M. Stanley's *In Darkest Africa; Or, the Quest, Rescue and Retreat of Emin, Governor of Equatoria*, vol. 1 (New York: Charles Scribner's Sons, 1890), 501.

natives had taken all the human meat to the well to wash it before eating. At the next place he camped by a stream, and made the natives camp below him. I told him that people at home generally believed that these were only "travellers' tales," as they are called in our country, or, other words, lies. He then said something to an Arab called Ali, seated next him, who turned round to me and said, "Give me a bit of cloth, and see." I sent my boy for six handkerchiefs, thinking it was all a joke, and that they were not in earnest, but presently a man appeared, leading a young girl of about ten years old at the hand, and I then witnessed the most horribly sickening sight I am ever likely to see in my life. He plunged a knife quickly into her breast twice, and she fell on her face, turning over on her side. Three men then ran forward, and began to cut up the body of the girl; finally her head was cut off, and not a particle remained, each man taking his piece away down to the river to wash it. The most extraordinary thing was that the girl never uttered a sound, nor struggled, until she fell. Until the last moment, I could not believe that they were in earnest. I have heard many stories of this kind since I have been in this country, but never could believe them, and I never would have been such a beast as to witness this, but I could not bring myself to believe that it was anything save a ruse to get money out of me, until the last moment.

> The girl was a slave captured from a village close to this town, and the cannibals were Wacusu slaves, and natives of this place, called Mculusi. When I went home I tried to make some small sketches of the scene while still fresh in my memory, not that it is ever likely to fade from it. No one here seemed to be in the least astonished at it.[8]

A contrasting account, documented in the London *Times*, comes from Assan Farran, a Syrian whom Jameson had hired as interpreter and later dismissed:[9]

> We are enabled to publish to-day the full text of Assad Farran's affidavit, sworn in Mr. Stanley's presence at Villa Victoria, Cairo on March 4, 1890. . . . We reproduce it without any attempt to remedy its imperfections of grammar and expression:—
>
> . . . The object of the following pages is to give an account of what had transpired during our stay at Yambuya Camp . . . , although when I was in London I was obliged to make a contradiction of this account for certain reasons, and especially because it was not desirable by the Committee that I should give any information about the expedition. . . .
>
> After staying 14 days at Cosongo, we returned to Yambuya with Tipoo Tib and the 400 men. We passed Nianguy, and from thence to Riba Riba. . . . Mr. Jameson went to the chief's house, Mahomed Ben Chamese, to visit him; there he saw Tippoo Tib and Muni Somoai, the chief leader of the 400 men, and many others present. After talking on different matters through Selim Masoudi, Tippoo Tib's interpreter, Mr. Jameson said that he was very anxious to see a man killed and eaten by cannibals, because, he said, "in England we hear much about cannibals who eat people, but, being myself in the place, I should like to see it done." This was interpreted by Selim Masoudi to Tippoo Tib and the other chiefs, whereupon, after consulting each other, told Mr. Jameson that if he wants to see a thing like this, he should buy a slave, and which he can present to the cannibals and they will eat him before him. Mr. Jameson then asked how much is the price of a slave there. They told him half a pice [*sic*] of handkerchiefs (six single pieces). He then told them that he will pay that price and went to his house where he lodged and brought half a pice and came back; this was handed to a man who went away and in a few minutes came back leading a girl of about ten years old.
>
> This girl was led by the orders of Tippoo Tib and the other chiefs, at the request of Mr. Jameson, to the native huts to be eaten. Mr. Jameson and myself, Selim Masoudi and Farhani, Jameson's servant, presented to him by Tippoo Tib, and many others, followed. On reaching the native huts, the girl, which was led by the man who brought her, was presented to the cannibals, and a man told them that "this is a present from the white man, he wants to see how you do with her when you eat her." The girl

> was taken and tied by the hand to a tree; about five of the natives were sharpening their knives; then a man came and stabbed her with a knife twice in the belly, the girl did not scream, but knew what was going on; she was looking right and left as if looking for help, and when she was stabbed she fell down dead. The natives then came and began cutting her in pieces, one was cutting the leg, another the arm, another the head and breast, and another took inner parts of the belly. After the meat was divided some took it to the river to wash it, others went straight to their huts. During this time Mr. Jameson had his book and pencil in hand, and was making rough sketches of the scene. After this was over we also went back; I went to the chief's house, and Mr. Jameson went in his house. On my return to Mr. Jameson, he had his sketches already finished, painted with water colours. They are six small sketches neatly done, the first when the girl was led by the man, the second when she was tied to the tree and stabbed in the belly, the blood gushing out, another when she was cut in pieces, the fourth a man carrying a leg in one hand and the knife in the other, the fifth a man with a native axe and the head and the breast, and the last a man with the inward parts of the belly. Mr. Jameson, when he finished those sketches, took them to the chief's house and showed them to all the people there, with many other sketches that he did.[10]

At the beginning of his affidavit, Farran admits that earlier he had given a contradictory account. A letter published in the *Times* a few days later reveals more details. It was written by the Secretary of the Emin Pasha Relief Committee, P. L. M'Dermott, who declared that in September 1888 Assad Farran had made a "recantation" of his earlier accusations. M'Dermott and another witness had been present during Farran's statement, and M'Dermott assured that "nothing was either given or promised to Farran to induce him to make the statement, which was voluntary on his part."[11] The letter ends with a written reproduction of Farran's testimony:

> Mr. Jameson was second in command in the camp. He was fond of sketching, and of collecting birds, plants, and other things of the kind. On one occasion Mr. Jameson sketched some things he saw the cannibals doing in getting the body of a girl, whom they had killed, ready to be cooked. They were cutting her up when Mr. Jameson saw them. Such sights could be seen by any one about the villages, as they were quite common. He had seen them do these things himself. They (Mr. Jameson and Farran) were then stopping two or three days at a village called Riba-Riba, on the way between Yambuya and Kasongo. Mr. Jameson gave the chief, Mohamed bin Hamis, six handkerchiefs as a present. He did not buy a girl to be killed, and he did not see her killed; he happened to see the cannibals carving parts of her body, and made a sketch of what he had seen. He (Assad Farran) knew the way they would kill her, by tying her to a

> tree and striking her twice in the belly with a knife; he had seen it done. He admitted that when coming down the country he had bad feelings towards Major Barttelot and Mr. Jameson, and said more than he would have said if his feelings were not hostile. What he had now said was what the story of Mr. Jameson buying a girl rested upon. He was very sorry and troubled when he learned the manner in which the story had been sent to England.[12]

One day earlier, the *Times* had printed another accusatory statement sent by Stanley—this time from "Saleh Ben Osman, his Zanzibari servant." However, this statement can hardly be taken seriously, since it not only contradicts the account given by Farran, Stanley's other witness, but it is also contradictory in itself. Saleh, who readily admits that he was not an eyewitness, but that he merely retold "what he learned concerning these events from Zanzibaris, Arabs, Manyuemas, and Soudanese, who witnessed the different events enumerated," describes the incident as follows:

> Mr. Jameson gave the man Hamadi some cloth to buy a young slave. Presently Hamadi came back, bringing a young girl, which he had bought. Mr. Jameson then ordered him to hand her over to the natives, and to tell them to kill, cook, and eat her. The Zanzibaris flatly refused to do this, and expressed their disgust by going away. Mr. Jameson himself took the girl by the wrist and handed her over to the savage executioners. She was then stabbed with a knife. While the body was still quivering, the natives cut off the flesh from the bones, and having toasted it on sticks over a fire, they ate it. During the whole of this ghastly performance Jameson sat and made sketches. He was accompanied by Mafelia, his boy, Hamadi, and the Zanzibaris.[13]

According to Farran, the man who had brought the girl also handed her to the cannibals, while Saleh has Jameson do so personally. Saleh also contradicts himself by first stating that the "Zanzibaris . . . expressed their disgust by going away," but later, when Jameson made sketches of the girl's body being dismembered and "toasted," they were supposedly present again.

Both Jameson's diary and Farran confirm that Jameson had traveled from Yambuya, where the rear guard had its camp, to Kasongo, about seven hundred kilometers further south. He had met Tippu Tip there and they were already on their way back when the incident happened. But according to Saleh, "Mr. Jameson was visiting Stanley Falls for the purpose of urging Tippoo Tib to provide the carriers which he had promised."[14] In Saleh's version, Tippu Tip was absent from the scene and Jameson was still on his way to Stanley Falls (today Boyoma Falls) to meet him there. But Stanley Falls is between Riba-Riba and Yambuya, so in that case it is entirely unclear why Jameson should have turned up in Riba-Riba at all! All in all, it seems pretty clear that Saleh's account is just distorted and exaggerated hearsay.

Understanding the Jameson Affair

Stanley's other witness is a different matter: Assan Farran clearly knew a lot, as the many agreements between his statement and Jameson's diary show. (And he could not have based his account on Jameson's, as the diary had not been published when Farran's statement appeared in the press.) Both agree that Jameson gave six handkerchiefs to pay for the unfortunate girl—though Jameson claims he did not realize this until it was too late. Both agree that Jameson and various other persons were present while she was killed (by stabbing her twice) and dismembered. Both agree that the proceedings started at the house of the local chief; according to Farran, they later returned to it, while according to Jameson they never left it. And both agree that Jameson made sketches showing the girl's cruel end, though there is disagreement about whether he started drawing them while the events unfolded or only later.

The price of six handkerchiefs for a girl might seem very low, though the anthropologist Greg Laden argues that "they would have actually been fairly valuable," as European cloth was a rare and precious imported good.[15] Generally it seems that slaves, or at least female children, could be bought cheaply—two American missionaries purchased a young enslaved girl from the Zappo Zaps for the equivalent of seventy-five cents.[16]

A month before the murderous incident, Jameson had made a note on local prices: "The money chiefly used here is ribas, small pieces of native grass-cloth. Fifty of these native cloths can be bought for six handkerchiefs; for one cloth you may buy twenty-five pieces of dried manioc, or fourteen plantains; for twelve pieces, one fowl; for one hundred, a goat."[17]

Jameson paid six handkerchiefs for the enslaved girl, half of the price he quotes for a goat. Other sources indicate that the prices of goats and enslaved children could be comparable, and that even adult women sometimes cost no more than two goats.[18] The girl's price—on which both witnesses agree—thus fits other pricing information available from the region.

What makes Farran a doubtful witness is that he changed his story twice. First, he had apparently said that Jameson had deliberately instigated the murder in order to witness cannibalism. He must have said this shortly after the event took place. In early August 1888, two weeks before his death, Jameson worried about "foul reports being spread by Assad Farran."[19]

Apparently Farran's accusation also reached the British Emin Pasha Relief Committee that had financed Stanley's expedition. In late September 1888, two committee members questioned Farran in London. There he revoked his story, instead stating that he had spread it only because of his "bad feelings" against Jameson (who had dismissed him) and claiming that the girl had already been dead when Jameson arrived on the scene. This, however, cannot be true, as Jameson himself admits to having seen the girl's death.

One and a half years later in Cairo, Farran changed his story again, swearing in Stanley's presence that his original accusations against Jameson were true. He gave no comprehensible reason why he had told something else in

London, just referring vaguely to "certain reasons, and especially because it was not desirable by the Committee that I should give any information about the expedition." But since nobody except two committee members had been present, why should they have minded Farran telling them what had really occurred?

All in all, it seems that Farran must have been somewhat opportunistic, telling people what he thought they preferred to hear. The committee hardly would have liked seeing a member of their expedition guilty of murder. While Stanley later was clearly collecting accusatory evidence, as his publication of the two (contradictory) statements shows—Farran was willing to supply it.

When writing his own account of the expedition, *In Darkest Africa*, Stanley had known of at least rumors of the affair. He mentions that "human limbs are said to be found in cooking-pots, sketches by an amateur artist are reported to have been made of whole families indulging in cannibal repasts." However, these and other rumors spread about the expedition are dismissed by him as "calumnious fables" and "a vast crop of lying."[20]

After the book's publication, the European and American press started to discuss the sad fate and more than dubious behavior of the rear guard, which had been effectively abandoned by Stanley and had to stay in Yambuya—an unhealthy place in the upper Congo—for almost a year while waiting for additional porters. During that time, more than eighty persons died from illness or maybe hunger.[21] And since the locals refused to sell them food (probably because they associated with the Swahilo-Arabs who continually made slaving expeditions against surrounding villages), the members of the rear guard repeatedly captured native women to ransom them for food, threatening to otherwise kill them.[22] Stanley, as leader of the expedition, was ultimately responsible for the situation. He reacted to the public discussion by publishing the most serious accusations against Edmund Barttelot and Jameson, two of the Europeans leading the rear guard. Both men had conveniently died in the Congo and so could not defend themselves against the charges. It is not far-fetched to consider Stanley's behavior an attempt to divert the attention of the public from the question of his own responsibility.

Of course this does not prove that the charges are wrong, but it suggests caution in regard to Stanley and his wavering witness, Farran. What made Farran change his mind twice? Is it possible that he was unsure about what to say since he did not know exactly what had really happened? Farran's and Jameson's account agree that it was one of Tippu Tip's men who took the initiative by arranging the purchase of the enslaved girl and collecting six handkerchiefs from Jameson to pay for her (though Jameson claims he did not know what the currency would be used for). It is possible that Farran had not actually witnessed this interaction, or had not heard the dialogue, and later drew his own conclusion. Jameson's account of the sequence of events preceding the fatal request for handkerchiefs has a ring of truth to it. It seems unlikely that he would have invented the dance performance and

Tippu Tip's story—both relayed in detail—merely to cover his tracks. But for anybody who later heard what had happened, and that Jameson had given six handkerchiefs to pay for the cannibalized child, the conclusion that he had deliberately triggered the whole incident must have seemed plausible.

Moreover, Jameson's retelling of Tippu Tip's anecdote is quite similar to the version the latter told to his biographer, Heinrich Brode.[23] Hence it is highly plausible that Jameson, like Brode, did indeed hear of Tippu Tip's halfhearted (and unsuccessful) attempt to stop the cannibalism of his allies from the famous slaver himself. Among other similarities, Jameson attributes to Tippu Tip the statement that "two men will easily eat one man in a night" which also appears in Brode's account. This may well be an exaggeration, but it is certainly an exaggeration made by Tippu Tip himself.

To Stanley's accusations against Jameson, Tippu Tip later reacted with outright denial:

> The story is a lie. I was not there, but neither saw nor heard anything of it till to-day among you. That he—Jameson—could do such a thing is absolutely impossible. Or do you think that I would tolerate such a thing? But I have never seen a European or any other being that could lie like [Stanley].[24]

This triple denial (I was not there, I would not have tolerated it, Jameson would never have done such a thing) may well be a case of "the lady doth protest too much." Jameson's own diary leaves no doubt that the deadly incident did take place and that Tippu Tip was present; moreover, the latter's "I would [not] tolerate such a thing" is somewhat at odds with his description of the large-scale cannibalism he tolerated among his allies. On the other hand, the similarity of the account of these events given in Tippu Tip's biography (published long after Jameson's death) and the tale attributed to Tippu Tip by Jameson makes the latter sound more credible than Farran, at least regarding the first part of the fateful evening.

If Farran had not personally witnessed the cannibal scene or at least its preliminaries, it is understandable that he, upon cross-examination by the Committee members in London, withdrew his story. Unsure about what really had happened, he went as far as saying that Jameson had not witnessed the murder—though actually, only he (Farran) might have been absent. Later, when Stanley encouraged him to provide testimony against Jameson, he let himself be persuaded to return to his original account, which (though based on guesswork or hearsay) must still have sounded pretty plausible to him.

Aside from the question of whether Jameson had deliberately requested to "see a man killed and eaten by cannibals," Farran's and Jameson's versions also differ in regard to the place where the girl was killed. Both agree that the incident started in the house of the local chief, but Farran claims that she was taken outside and tied to a tree, while Jameson states that she was brought into the house and then killed almost immediately, leaving him no time to intercede before it was too late. Both sides have a potential motive for lying: Jameson to make himself appear innocent and taken by surprise, Farran to make Jameson appear guilty and so get revenge for his dismissal. The third possibility is, again, that Farran had only heard about the event and probably seen the sketches, but that he had not been an eyewitness and so did not know what exactly had happened. According to his London statement, he had indeed seen how a girl (or maybe some other slave) had been tied to a tree before being butchered for food, but it had happened some other time, not when Jameson was present.

Evidence that Jameson's version might be closer to the truth comes from William Bonny, a former British sergeant who was one of the other European members of the rear guard. Jameson had shown him his sketches after his return to Yambuya. After the controversy about Jameson's behavior had reached the European press, Bonny made the following statement:

> Mr. Jameson showed me the sketches and described the scene in detail. I cannot now describe each of the six sketches; but they begin with the picture of the girl being brought down tied by one hand to the native, who holds in his right hand the fatal knife. He is then represented thrusting the knife into the girl, while the blood is seen spurting out. Then there is the scene of the carving up of the girl limb by limb, and of the natives scrambling for the pieces and running away to cook them, and the final sketch represents the feast. These sketches are now, or were until very recently, in the hands of Mrs. Jameson.[25]

Bonny does not say what exactly Jameson told him—it seems likely that he told the events as he had recorded them in his diary. It is hard to imagine that he would have admitted buying the girl in order to have her murdered, and Bonny certainly does not claim he did so. After Bonny heard Farran's version he seems to have believed it. Nevertheless, Bonny's own description of what he had seen in the sketches better fits the account given by Jameson.

According to Jameson, "presently a man appeared, leading a young girl of about ten years old at the hand, and . . . then . . . he plunged a knife quickly into her breast." This corresponds almost exactly to the contents of the first two sketches as remembered by Bonny. In Farran's account, the second sketch shows how "she was tied to the tree and stabbed in the belly." But there is no tree in the sketches seen by Bonny, nor in Jameson's diary. Bonny's description also reveals that Jameson seems to have witnessed the fatal proceedings until their very end, also observing "the feast" where the cooked remains of the girl were consumed—a detail mentioned neither by Jameson nor Farran.

In all, it sounds likely that Farran either was not an eyewitness and just reported what he thought to be true, or else that he might have deliberately modified his account of the events to make Jameson appear guilty of premeditated incitement to murder. But though Jameson probably was not as guilty as Farran suggests, neither can he have been as innocent as he himself pretends. Though he might have mentioned that Europeans at home tended to dismiss reports of cannibalism as "travellers' tales," he himself knew better, as his diary shows. Shortly after his arrival in the Congo basin, he met a group of Bangala people who told him that they consumed all their enemies as well as purchased slaves. And the Swahilo-Arab leader Selim bin Mohammed explained to him that "all the natives from Bangala up to the Falls, both on the Congo and on all its tributaries, are cannibals."[26]

Both these statements he wrote down without expressing any incredulity. And just a few weeks before the deadly incident, he recorded that he had personally witnessed traces of a cannibal meal: "One day, as I passed through a native village from which the people had just run away, I picked up a thigh-bone freshly cooked and picked. The natives who live inland eat any of the natives from the river whom they can catch, and *vice versâ.*"[27]

Jameson's companion, Ward, had seen human flesh being roasted and had been invited to eat it.[28] Probably they had talked about these events during their time with the rear guard. All in all, it is clear that Jameson knew well enough that cannibalism was more than just a myth. It therefore seems hardly credible that the idea that he might be about to witness a cannibal act never occurred to him, even after being told quite explicitly, "Give me a bit of cloth, and see [cannibalism]." And it seems pretty clear that mere passive watching is not the right course of action if a man appears with a knife and a bound young girl! Yet that is exactly what Jameson did, according to his own account. Even if events proceeded quickly, he must have had some time in which he could have tried to intervene and save the girl, but he did nothing of the kind.

Another dubious point in Jameson's account is the payment he made. If Ali had merely asked for "a bit of cloth," why did he decide to give exactly six handkerchiefs, which apparently were quite valuable? It seems clear that Jameson is deliberately vague here—he must have been told the exact amount to give, like Farran asserts. The actual dialogue between the Scot and the Swahilo-Arab might have gone along the following lines:

> Jameson: "I have often heard of these things, but still cannot quite believe they really happen. I've never seen it myself, and back in Europe they think it's all travelers' lies."
>
> Ali: "The only reason you aren't seeing cannibalism right now is that those men are poor and have no human flesh at their disposal. Gift them a slave and you'll see it here and now."
>
> Jameson (upset): "I don't have a slave I would give up to cannibals!"
>
> Ali: "Give me six handkerchiefs and I'll handle the rest."

At which point Jameson, half thinking it a joke but also curious what might happen, sent for the handkerchiefs. Once the enslaved child was brought in, he must have realized that it probably was not a joke. Still, he apparently decided not to intervene but rather to coolly observe and document the series of events his action had triggered. Events that started with a living girl—a girl he had bought—and ended with her cooked flesh being consumed by a group of cannibals.

Jameson may not be quite as guilty as charged by Farran and Stanley, but guilty he was.

Notes

1. See Chapter 6, this volume.
2. "The Horrible Jameson Affair: Assad Farran Tells His Story of the Cannibalism," *New York Times*, 14 November 1890: 2.
3. See Chapter 5, this volume.
4. Jameson, *Story*.
5. See Chapter 8, this volume.
6. Jameson, *Story*, 289.
7. The "Wacusu" lived in another part of the Maniema region, as Jameson explains elsewhere (ibid., 242–43).
8. Ibid., 290–91.
9. Ibid., 262, 356.
10. "Stanley's Rear Column," *Times* (London), 14 November 1890: 9–10.
11. "To the Editor of the Times," *Times* (London), 18 November 1890: 10.
12. Ibid.
13. "Stanley's Rear Column," *Times* (London), 17 November. 1890: 9–10.
14. Ibid.
15. Greg Laden, "On Cannibalism and Jameson," *Greg Laden's Blog*, 17 February 2015, accessed 21 October 2020, http://gregladen.com/blog/2015/02/17/on-cannibalism-and-jameson/.
16. Edgerton, *Troubled Heart of Africa*, 119.
17. Jameson, *Story*, 252.
18. See Chapter 7, this volume.
19. Jameson, *Story*, 356.
20. Stanley, *In Darkest Africa*, 511.
21. Jameson, *Story*, 304.
22. Ibid., 83–90, 135, 139.
23. Brode, *Tippoo Tib*, 91–92; see the quote from Brode's book in Chapter 5 of this volume.
24. Quoted ibid., 235.
25. "Stanley's Rear Column," *Times* (London), 10 November 1890: 9.
26. Jameson, *Story*, 31, 151.
27. Ibid., 263 (italics in original).
28. See Chapters 5 and 6, this volume.

CHAPTER 10
THE QUESTION OF EUROPEAN INFLUENCES AND THE OBEYESEKERE CONJECTURE

The Jameson affair may be a good starting point for pondering European influences on cannibalism more generally. There can be no doubt that it was Jameson's presence that triggered the consumption of the young girl on that fateful evening—even in his own account, it was his dialogue with Tippu Tip and his men that set the event in motion. What would otherwise have become of the girl is impossible to say—maybe she would have been sold to another group of cannibals, or maybe she would have been sold for another purpose and lived for decades longer. But she would likely not have died that very night. Thus, there can be no doubt that in this case the European influence on the cannibal meal was strong, even though (for all we know) Jameson himself did not eat human flesh on that or any other occasion. He was no cannibal, but he certainly facilitated cannibalism.

On the one hand, Jameson's case is unusual because it seems to be the only documented case in Africa of a European getting himself involved in an act of people eating—of murder for meat—apparently just out of curiosity. A similar case that happened elsewhere—in the Bismarck Archipelago—is the confession of the German travel writer Stefan von Kotze that he deliberately got himself invited to a cannibal banquet and financially supported the purchase of an enslaved woman who was slaughtered for the occasion.[1] While Kotze went even further than Jameson, who apparently never expressed any desire to eat human flesh himself, his case seems to have been more or less ignored by the German press—in notable contrast to the reception of the "horrible Jameson affair."

The novelty value of Jameson's behavior was likely influenced by several factors: he was a member of a wealthy and well-known family owning one of the largest whiskey producers in the world; the act had taken place while he was a member of the latest (and last) expedition of the famous Henry Morton Stanley; and—maybe most importantly—it was Stanley himself who publicized the charges against Jameson, apparently to distract from his own shortfalls. While all these factors made the Jameson affair impossible to ignore, it seems that in other cases newspapers and maybe the general public in Western countries were not particularly keen to discuss connections between their own citizens and cannibalistic acts. The cannibals were "the others," safely isolated from one's own lives and from "civilized men," and people certainly preferred to ignore any hints that suggested otherwise.

The Obeyesekere Conjecture

While Westerners at that time preferred to downplay or disregard any connections between their countries and compatriots and cannibal acts elsewhere, Gananath Obeyesekere, in his influential book *Cannibal Talk* (2005), takes the opposite viewpoint. For him, socially accepted cannibalism was generally rare and usually tied to sacred religious circumstances of human sacrifices—until European explorers and invaders appeared, unsettling and disrupting traditional social structures and leading, in some areas, to the spread of cannibalistic practices far beyond their sacred origins.

Obeyesekere's work is limited to the "South Seas," referring in particular to New Zealand and Fiji. It it nevertheless worthwhile to consider whether his conjecture likewise applies to Central Africa, since—as we have seen—there is ample evidence of the interconnections between external influences, such as the international slave trade, and cannibal practices. One might ask especially whether slave eating had emerged only as a by-product of the international slave trade, or whether it had already existed at the time when the Congo basin had not yet come under pressure as a "catchment area" for both the western (transatlantic) and eastern (Arab) slave trade.

First, however, a few words about Obeyesekere's book are necessary. While he shows strong sympathies for the denialist camp, writing "I share Arens's view that cannibalism must be seen as a European projection of the Other," he also realizes that the evidence for cannibal practices is far too strong for the thesis that *all* of it is mere fabrication or falsehood to be seriously defensible. He thus grants "that anthropophagy existed in several human societies, for the most part as kind of sacrament associated with human sacrifice."[2]

He suggests to use the latter term, "anthropophagy," for "the actual consumption of human flesh," and "cannibalism" for accounts and discourses on such practices that express "essentially a fantasy that the Other is going to eat us" and that may lack or distort an actual factual basis.[3] In normal usage, both these terms are synonymous, as long as human eaters are concerned. Obeyesekere's suggestion to always use the longer term for the actual practice thus seems needlessly cumbersome and is not one I have followed—he himself observes that he found it impossible to consistently do so, noting instead that "I shall sometimes use and sometimes blur" the proposed distinction.[4]

Leaving aside these terminological differences, Obeyesekere accepts that famine cannibalism and antisocial cannibalism sometimes did or do occur as practices that were not generally accepted by the society in which they took place.[5] He also accepts funerary cannibalism—the nonviolent consumption of deceased persons as a funerary rite—and sacrificial cannibalism, describing the latter as a "phenomenon . . . associated with a widely dispersed and variable institution shared by both savagism and civilization, namely, human sacrifice."[6] He is, however, very skeptical about any other cannibal (or anthropophagous) practices, considering accounts of such practices as either fabrications or as traces of new developments that emerged only in "reaction to the European presence."[7] Rather than merely observing and reporting practices that had gone unreported previously, European visitors to New Zealand or other regions thus actually brought them about, he suggests.

Obeyesekere's reading of cannibalism is thus very postmodernist in nature: the observed phenomenon, he claims, is a result of observers starting to appear and to observe; it does not exist (more or less) independently of them. When it comes to evidence, however, his case is very weak. In the absence of clear indications to the contrary, it seems reasonable to assume that people do not radically and quickly change their behavior and way of life just because a few external visitors show up. If and when such change occurs, however, one would expect it to leave clearly detectable traces—say in differences in the descriptions left by earlier and later visitors, or in oral accounts of those who lived through the change or heard about it from their ancestors. But Obeyesekere does not have any such evidence revealing that or explaining why "conspicuous anthropophagy"—as he calls it—emerged in New Zealand and Fiji as a result of Europeans settling in these regions.

When it comes to New Zealand, he argues, convincingly enough, that "the British presence not only escalated tribal wars, but the availability of guns in combination with new political alliances to capture the European trade escalated that killing to a degree unprecedented in traditional Maori warfare." This is plausible and well-supported by evidence. He further argues that "the sheer availability of corpses of enemies contributed further toward a more general, nonritualized anthropophagy."[8] This too is plausible and in agreement with the sources: because more killed or captured enemies were available, more were eaten. This, however, is merely a quantitative change, while Obeyesekere would have to demonstrative a qualitative change, since he claims that enemies were not eaten at all before Europeans showed up—or if they were, it was only in the sacred context of a human sacrifice, in which the consumption of an enemy's body was largely "symbolic."[9]

But if cannibalism was formerly limited to the symbolically charged consumption of just small body parts of maybe one or two particularly hated enemy chiefs, it is hard to see why the "sheer availability" of additional corpses would have turned this sacred, symbolic act into the large-scale eating of whole human bodies documented for later times. Moreover, Obeyesekere's conjecture that such a change took place is only possible because he chooses to disregard numerous oral accounts of Maori sources indicating that large-scale enemy eating had already occurred before any Europeans showed up. He does this by claiming that such sources were mere parody and satire, ironically playing with European expectations of Maori cannibalism.

He compares these accounts with the famous satire, *A Modest Proposal for Preventing the Children of Poor People from Being a Burthen to Their Parents or Country*, published in 1729 by the Irish writer Jonathan Swift (1667–1745), the author of *Gulliver's Travels.* Such Maori accounts, Obeyesekere suggests, should not be taken as truthful accounts of actual practices any more than Swift's ironical "proposal" to solve the problems of poverty and overpopulation in Ireland by encouraging poor people to sell their young children to high-class taverns and the families of wealthy gentleman as food.[10]

There are several problems with Obeyesekere's comparison. Swift wrote for an Irish and British public that knew the context of his writing and easily understood the satire as such—he would hardly have made similar suggestions if asked by a clueless foreigner about local habits. Moreover, his text was, of course, not the only information available on Irish eating habits; anyone comparing his "proposal" with other documents would quickly have realized that he could not have meant it seriously. In New Zealand, on the other land, various sources all agree that practices such as war cannibalism and slave eating did occur and were socially accepted, at least in certain northern regions. And finally, Swift could only write his satire because human flesh was not actually eaten in Ireland; had cannibalism been an established practice, only not in the specific form he suggests, his text would have lost its clearly ironical intent and might have been perceived as a more or less well thought out suggestion to extend the practice.

But cannibalism did exist as an accepted practice in New Zealand, both before and after the appearance of Europeans—even Obeyesekere accepts as much. His suggestion to disregard as mere satire and parody the Maori accounts that he dislikes (because they contradict his thesis that cannibalism had traditionally been limited to the strictly ceremonial context of human sacrifice) is thus unconvincing. Of course, some accounts may be exaggerated or otherwise contain false information, but a summary dismissal as suggested by Obeyesekere is not acceptable.

Regarding New Zealand, Obeyesekere's arguments are convincing insofar as they suggest that the appearance of Europeans and the better weapons they supplied did lead to a quantitative change in cannibalism: for some time, warfare became more widespread and more deadly; accordingly, the number of consumed enemies increased as well. However, his claim that "battlefield cannibalism" itself had been unknown in earlier times and only emerged as "a new tradition" in result of these changes,[11] is unconvincing and contradicted by the available evidence. When it comes to Fiji, his case becomes even weaker, since here he cannot even show convincingly that the European presence led to a quantitative change (let alone a qualitative one). He himself admits that, while his "hypothesis underlying Fijian anthropophagy is that both colonialism and the European intrusion had consequences similar to what happened in New Zealand, . . . I cannot document them adequately."[12]

Finding that two early accounts of Fijian cannibalism are largely in agreement with each other, he concludes—without any supporting evidence—that one of them must have copied the other and then dismisses the latter, claiming that the author "seems to have invented much"—again without any internal or external evidence supporting this statement. About the alternative—taking "the cannibal descriptions . . . at face value"—he states: "I find it hard to accept that in 1808–09 . . . mass anthropophagy virtually without ritual or decorum was established [in Fiji] and that women were permitted to cut up corpses and eat of the flesh of victims."[13] In other words, he dismisses these accounts because their contents would force him to adjust his worldview, something he is unwilling to do. This, of course, is not a serious way to do research.

How Well Does the Conjecture Fit the Evidence from Africa?

When it comes to Central Africa, the case for some version of Obeyesekere's conjecture may be stronger than in the countries he explored himself. What was the role of external influences in shaping "conspicuous" cannibal practices such as the consumption of enemies and slaves? The inhabitants of New Zealand and Fiji first came into contact with the Western world when European ships reached their shores. In the case of the Congo basin, the situation was different. Europeans reached the inner parts of this region only in the 1870s, but already in the first half of the century the western parts of the basin had been affected by the transatlantic slave trade.[14]

The thesis that it was only the arrival of Western explorers and settlers from the 1870s that brought about "conspicuous" cannibalism would be the most literal translation of Obeyesekere's conjecture in regard to the Congo. However, this thesis does not seem at all plausible. Even very early settlers such as Camille-Aimé Coquilhat—one of the first white men to arrive in the Bangala area—found that captives and slaves were eaten as a matter of course. More plausible, however, is the notion that the international slave trade might have been the original cause of cannibal practices—or, at least, of the specific consumption of slaves which has been the topic of the preceding chapters.

This trade, in the Congo basin, came in two varieties: from the western parts of the basin, slaves were originally exported to the Americas; later, when the transatlantic trade had been effectively abolished, they were still sent to the African west coast and the islands in front of it for exploitation on the (often European-owned) plantations there. Slaves exported from the

Figure 10.1. Arab-Swahili slavers forcing a group of captives along. From Hermann von Wissmann's *My Second Journey through Equatorial Africa from the Congo to the Zambesi in the Years 1886 and 1887* (London: Chatto & Windus, 1891), opposite p. 244.

eastern regions were instead shipped to Zanzibar and other places on the east coast dominated by the Arab-Swahili culture, to North Africa, the Arab Peninsula, and India. This eastern slave trade continued, despite European protests, at least until the end of the nineteenth century.[15]

Since cannibalism and slave eating have been reported for both western and eastern regions, a potentially defensible variant of Obeyesekere's conjecture as applied to Central Africa might be that cannibalism in this region was a result of external (but not exclusively Western) influences—that it was the demand for slaves (and possibly ivory) in the West and in the Arab world that was the original cause of Central African cannibalism, or at least a factor that greatly contributed to its spread, despite the fact that the West and the Arab world both agreed in their judgment that cannibalism was unacceptable.

In its weaker form—that the external slave and ivory trade was a factor that helped to propagate cannibal practices—the plausibility of this thesis can hardly be denied. We have seen that slave raiding and cannibalism went hand in hand, with those considered unfit for use as slaves or too weak to move on killed and eaten by the raiders or sold to those who would eat them; persons killed in raids were often eaten as well. The slave trade led to a state of widespread warfare and frequent raiding to secure victims for sale; it led to increased violence and hostilities between peoples whose interactions might—conceivably—have been much more peaceful in the past. Referring to the area around the Aruwimi River, Ward observes that a state of permanent warfare prevailed:

> Each village is at strife with its neighbors. Every man fears all but the inhabitants of his own immediate vicinity; and should he be unfortunate enough to get caught by any of the neighboring tribes, he is killed and eaten, or perhaps sold to the Arabs, if his captors are on friendly terms with them.[16]

This situation, he adds, might well have been a result of the repeated raids of Swahilo-Arab slavers: "What the earlier state of this country might have been, before the Arab invasion in search of ivory and slaves increased its confusion, it is impossible now to say, for the first white men to reach the Basoko found that the Arabs had already marauded through these territories."[17]

Ward here puts the blame on the "Arabs," considering the "white men" as guiltless, which is not true, of course, when it comes to the regions of the Congo basin that are closer to the African west coast. Both slave raiding and cannibalism were common along parts of the Ubangi, the Lulonga, the main Congo River in the area where the Bangala and related peoples live, and around the Kasai and its tributaries—and from all these regions slaves were commonly exported towards the west coast, and in former times across the Atlantic. It is true that white traders rarely got their own hands dirty—they preferred to buy slaves from African middlemen rather than getting personally involved in the dangerous business of raiding and warfare. But since they, and those who ultimately bought the slaves, profited from this trade, they must also take the blame for all its aspects—the loss of liberty, the suffering, the destruction of communities, the many violent deaths, and the consumption of victims who had been killed or captured in slave raids or slavery-related warfare.

The same is true of the ivory trade, with ivory then being one of the most important export goods of the Congo, destined for the West, the Arab world, and India. Especially around the Ubangi River, as we have seen, the ivory trade and the cannibalization of slaves often went hand in hand, with ivory being sold by elephant hunters in return for slaves who were—in many cases—subsequently eaten. Except for the cases reported by John Weeks and Emil Torday, there is little evidence that the European traders who bought the ivory were directly involved in such deadly exchanges. Though, as noted earlier, the fact that European captains and traders often received frank and apparently serious offers of such exchanges leaves room for doubt—would not the inhabitants of the Ubangi riversides have ceased making such offers to Europeans if they had noticed that they were hardly ever accepted?[18] In any case, the European receivers of the ivory ultimately benefited from the bloody exchange. And again, there can be little doubt that the ivory trade lead to an increase in cannibalism in this region: had the elephant hunters not found buyers for their ivory, they would not have been able to purchase slaves for consumption (or at least not as often).

But what about the stronger version of the Obeyesekere conjecture? In its stronger version, this conjecture would assert that Congolese cannibalism evolved only in response to external influences—in this case, due to the international slave (and possibly ivory) trade. Or rather, that sacrificial cannibalism in contexts charged with a sacred meaning might already have existed earlier, but more "profane" practices such as the consumption of enemies and slaves did not. Because it deals with times for which no direct evidence from the Congo is available, this thesis is hard to evaluate. However, for it to be plausible it should be backed by some kind of positive evidence—say by oral accounts of people remembering that cannibal practices had been unknown when they were young or when their parents were young. The international slave trade reached the Congo basin only around the middle of the nineteenth century, so when Europeans started to arrive in the area several decades later one might expect that some of them would have heard and recorded such statements if such a change had indeed occurred recently. But, to my knowledge, this is not the case.

Instead, it seems rather that war cannibalism and slave eating were well established practices, with no hints that they were particularly new. Europeans found them practiced, to their astonishment, as something that was entirely natural and self-evident—not necessarily something one would expect had the practice been established only recently. Based on their analysis of oral records, Bogumil Jewsiewicki and Mumbanza mwa Bawele conclude that the consumption of enemies and captives went a long way back, and that the sale of persons—who thus effectively were slaves—was associated with cannibalism already before the region started to get involved in the international slave trade: "Because cannibalism was common, and slaves were purchased especially for such purposes, people assumed that slaves who were sold were probably sacrificed [for food]."[19]

Early Accounts of Slave Eating in Central and Western Africa

While most of the information on Congolese slave eating comes from the late nineteenth and early twentieth centuries, an earlier account indicates that slaves were eaten in this region already in the late sixteenth century. It was published in 1591 by the Italian Filippo Pigafetta (1533–1604) and is based on the memories of the Portuguese trader and explorer Duarte Lopez (1550–?), who had just spent five years in the coastal Kingdom of Kongo. Pigafetta mentions a people he calls Anzichi (or Anziques) who lived "on both sides" of the Congo River, farther upriver than the coastal kingdoms.[20] About them he writes:

Figure 10.2. Illustration to one of the earliest editions of Pigafetta's account: "They have shambles for human flesh as we have of animals." From Thomas H. Huxley, *Evidence as to Man's Place in Nature* (New York: D. Appelton, 1863), 69.

> They have shambles for human flesh as we have of animals, even eating the enemies they have killed in battle, and selling their slaves if they can get a good price for them; if not, they give them to the butcher, who cuts them in pieces, and then sells them to be roasted or boiled. It is a remarkable fact in the history of this people, that any who are tired of life, or wish to prove themselves brave and courageous, esteem it great honor to expose themselves to death by an act which shall show their contempt for life. Thus they offer themselves for slaughter, and as the faithful vassals of princes, wishing to do them service, not only give themselves to be eaten, but their slaves also, when fattened, are killed and eaten.[21]

According to Lopez, adds Pigafetta, "in consequence of this people being so cruel, they were not traded with, excepting in so far as they came to Congo"—that is, the Kingdom of Kongo. Apparently though there was by no means a trade boycott. Traders might have feared to visit the country of the Anzichi, but when they came, they were welcome. They sold, he adds, slaves from their own as well as neighboring peoples and also ivory and cloths; as payment they accepted salt, shell money, and "goods brought from Portugal, including silk, linen cloths, glass, and suchlike."[22]

Despite their cannibal customs, Lopez had a high opinion of the Anzichi, calling them "faithful, truthful, loyal, and simple" and believing that they might become good Christians if missionaries were sent to them.[23] It is not clear if he had any actual contact with them or if the information relayed by Pigafetta is mere hearsay. Some of it is certainly doubtful—the notion that people voluntarily gave their own lives to provide an ample meal for their "princes" is not confirmed by later sources and it is hard to believe that such acts, if they occurred at all, were more than rare exceptions. On the other hand, that enemies and slaves were killed and eaten and that slaves were sometimes deliberately fattened for this purpose is in agreement with many later sources reporting from the Congo basin. This makes it plausible that these practices did really exist already at that time among the Anzichi, whoever exactly they were—it seems unlikely that hearsay accounts would have falsely claimed something that later actually became true.

Pigafetta's account cannot be considered a refutation of the strong version of the Obeyesekere conjecture, since the Anzichi were already involved in the slave trade; they sold slaves in the Kingdom of Kongo, and from there, no doubt, many of these slaves were shipped to the Americas. Pigafetta explicitly mentions the connection between the slave trade and cannibal acts which we have also observed in later times; the Anzichi sold their slaves "if they can get a good price for them," while the unsalable ones were sent to the "butcher," who then sold their meat. From the owners' viewpoint, cannibalism here seems to have been mainly an alternative way of making money out of their slaves. This specific custom could have evolved only once the Anzichi got involved in the slave trade, which might well have happened as a result of the increasing demand for slaves which were sent across the Atlantic.

On the other hand, cannibal acts arguably cannot have evoked among these people the same kind of horror as they do in the West, otherwise this custom could hardly have evolved. If human flesh had already been eaten in certain contexts—say when enemies were killed in war—it is plausible that the custom could have spread from such beginnings. Human sacrifice, as Obeyesekere suggests, might conceivably have been another starting point of the practice, but Pigafetta does not mention any such practice and, in general, there are ample reports of war cannibalism from the Congo basin and nearby areas, but relatively few of human sacrifice associated with the consumption of the flesh of the victims. In the absence of evidence pointing in the opposite direction, I would therefore consider warfare a more plausible starting point for cannibal customs than human sacrifice.

Emil Torday and T. A. Joyce mention that Frobenius identifies the Anzichi with the Teke people who live around Stanley Pool (Pool Malebo), on the shores of which the capitals of the two Congo states, Kinshasa and Brazzaville, are situated today. They merely call this assessment "interesting" which seems to express some reservations.[24] From later times, there are (to my knowledge) no hints attributing slave eating to the inhabitants of this region and very few mentions of cannibalism in general. In the late nineteenth century, the area from which slave eating was reported started about five hundred kilometers upriver (northeast) around the confluence of the Ubangi into the Congo. Pigafetta leaves no doubt that the Anzichi lived around the Congo River but does not indicate from how far away they came. If they came from the regions for which slave eating has been documented in later times, they might conceivably have belonged to some of the ethnic groups which later became known as Bangala. In later times, the Bangala were known as diligent merchants who not rarely covered long distances while conducting their business, which fits quite well with the description given by Pigafetta.[25]

Pigafetta's account seems to be the first description of slave eating attributed to inhabitants of the Congo basin. Just like later sources, he does not describe the custom as something that was new—thus it seems quite possible that similar acts had already occurred in earlier centuries, but since the basin itself was not visited by people who wrote about it until the second half of the nineteenth century, we cannot be sure one way or the other. But the same custom has also been documented for Nigeria and some other West African regions[26]—and in this region, early accounts indicating that slaves were considered "good to eat" were written down by Arab historians and travelers centuries before Pigafetta's work.

Shihab al-Umari (1300–1349), a historian from Damascus, records what a friend of one of his informants told about his visit to an unidentified West African town. When the visitor "presented to the king of this place . . . a quantity of salt," he was given "two most comely slave girls" in return. A few days later he talked with the king who was surprised and maybe a bit offended when he heard (or saw) that the girls were still alive. "I sent those girls to you," he told his visitor, "so slaughter and eat them! Their flesh is the best thing we have to eat. For what reason have you not slaughtered them?" When the visitor replied, "This is not lawful for us," the king inquired which foods were allowed to him, and subsequently sent him cattle and sheep for consumption. The enslaved girls are not mentioned again.[27]

Considering that this is a third-hand account, it might be seriously distorted, but the anecdote is close enough to later accounts to assume that there may be some truth in it. This would make it is one of the earliest accounts of the slaughter of slaves for food. It also indicates that the practice might have been considered so self-evident that the king was surprised to hear that his visitor was *not* allowed to eat human flesh. And it reflects an attitude also recorded, in much later times, both in the Congo and in West Africa—that human flesh is “the best thing we have to eat.”[28]

Another early account of cannibalistic hospitality comes from the Moroccan explorer Ibn Battuta (1304–1368/1369). In this case, the situation was reversed: the donor of the human gift was not a cannibal, but the recipients were. In 1352, during the last of his extensive journeys, Ibn Battuta visited the Mali Empire, one of the largest African empires of its time. While its inhabitants were Muslims like Ibn Battuta, some of their customs were deeply foreign to him. He was shocked to note that there were friendships between married women and men who were not their husbands, and that husbands did not mind if their wives spent time with other men. Equally displeasing to him was that all unmarried girls and women, even the sultan’s daughters, as well as enslaved women of all ages, went around fully naked.[29] (Comments on the partial or total nudity of the inhabitants of tropical regions are also a recurrent feature of the later European travel literature.)

During his stay in the capital, a group of warriors “who eat human kind” came to visit the sultan, Suleyman.[30] Eager to please his visitors,

> The sultan did them honour and gave them a slave girl as part of his reception-gift. . . . They slaughtered her and ate her and smeared their faces and hands with her blood and came in gratitude to the sultan. I was informed that their custom whenever they come in deputation to him is to do that, and I was told . . . that they say that the tastiest part of women’s flesh is the palms and the breast.[31]

Though Ibn Battuta had earlier complained that the sultan was “a miserly king from whom no great donation is to be expected,”[32] he was apparently “generous” enough to donate a slave to his cannibal visitors every time they came to his court.

These fourteenth-century Arab sources indicate that cannibalism and the eating of slaves were apparently practiced in certain West African regions long before the first Europeans arrived in these regions. Both sources mention the practice in the context of gift giving: living slaves were donated by kings and sultans to guests who then ate them, or who were supposed to do so. Just as we have observed of later times from the Congo,[33] it seems that this kind of flesh was considered appropriate for special festive occasions and was certainly not a daily fare. Ibn Battuta’s account also indicates that there was no absolute dividing line between those who practiced cannibalism and those who condemned the practice: Suleyman was a Muslim, and we may safely presume that he did not eat any human flesh himself—yet he apparently had no qualms about donating enslaved girls to visitors who would treat them as a source of food.

All in all, it seems pretty clear that the strong version of the Obeyesekere conjecture overestimates the influence of European contacts on other cultures.

Such contacts did not have the astonishing effect of turning non-cannibals into cannibals or turning cannibalism from a rare sacred ritual into a "conspicuous" and relatively profane practice. Practices such as war cannibalism likely reach back into times long preceding the first European contact. This also seems to be true of slave eating, at least in regard to West Africa. When it comes to the Congo basin, the verdict is not so clear, due to a lack of sources. There can be no doubt that the consumption of slaves and persons captured and killed in slave raids intensified as a result of the international slave trade. The trade in other export goods—ivory, in particular—further helped to enable such practices, in stark contrast to the contemporary European view of such trade as "legitimate" and harmless.

But, as Jewsiewicki and Mumbanza mwa Bawele observe, the sale of persons seems to have been associated with their subsequent consumption already at times and in places where the international slave trade had not yet left any notable effects. Cannibalism and slave eating were not independent of international trading networks and European influences, but neither were they simply their result and offspring.

The Slow Disappearance of Congolese Cannibalism

Considering that the international slave trade was clearly related to the more localized consumption of slaves, we might well ask about the effects of the abolition of the transatlantic slave trade and of slavery itself on Congolese customs. This is a sensitive issue since effects in the long term might have been quite different from those in the short term. In the long term, the logical consequence is clear: if there are no slaves, nobody can buy them for food. In the short term, however, very different effects may have resulted because a decreased demand for slaves exported into the Americas did not immediately lead to an equal reduction of slavery and slave raiding in the Congo or other regions which had become "supply areas" for this trade.

The transatlantic slave trade flourished until the middle of the nineteenth century, when abolitionist attempts to stop it finally started to pay off—although a certain amount of illegal smuggling of slaves from the Congo basin and other areas into, in particular, Cuba and Brazil, continued until the end of the century. Demand nevertheless dropped sharply, but the supply of newly captured slaves did not immediately shrink, because the "mechanisms for procuring slaves endured when the external demand ended," as Elizabeth Isichei notes.[34] As a result, the prices of slaves fell considerably, but the collapse of demand did not lead to an immediate collapse of supply.

Patrick Manning observes that "the economics of slave capture . . . are the economics of theft": the complete cost of "producing" and raising a person is borne by their family and finally the person themself, not by the raiders who take them captive. For raiders and warriors used to the capture and sale of slaves, it therefore made sense to continue this "business" even as the price of their "goods" fell, because their own "cost of production" was nearly zero. In other cases, previous war campaigns or slave raids had left a desire for revenge which in turn produced more captives, regardless of whether or not the latter still fetched a good price.[35]

Slaves were therefore still captured in wars and raids, but their prices were lower than before, and many slaves who would otherwise have been exported were now purchased by African buyers—often as laborers and servants, but also for more sinister purposes.[36] Isichei observes that the number of human sacrifices increased in parts of West Africa, because the fallen prices made the practice more affordable.[37] In the West African regions where cannibalism was unknown, there were sometimes "mass executions of male captives [since] even at very low prices, no buyers were to be found."[38] The local purchase of slaves also increased in the Ubangi area—where they were apparently not infrequently bought for food—according to the historian Robert W. Harms.[39] Edward Glave notes that, when he visited the area around the mouth of the Ubangi in 1890, the number of slaves sacrificed and often eaten was higher "than when Stanley first saw these people in 1877; the reason being . . . that contact with white men has made them richer, and has enabled them to obtain more slaves."[40]

There are thus two ways in which interactions with the West and changes in the Western mode of living and production might have led to a temporary increase in Central African cannibalism, in general agreement with Obeyesekere's thesis. On the one hand, slaves became cheaper and thus more affordable for purposes such as sacrifice and consumption. On the other hand, as highlighted by Glave, an increasing trade with Europeans brought more wealth into the area, which could, among other things, be spent on purchasing slaves. The well-documented direct exchange of ivory against "edible" slaves has been covered in earlier chapters, but even in cases where the connection between trade and subsequent cannibalism was less obvious, trade generated an income that could be used for arbitrary purchases.

While in the short run the abolition of slavery and the increasing contacts with Western traders might thus have led to an increase in cannibalism, the long-term effect was clearly very different. Today cannibalism has all but disappeared from the Congo basin, except possibly during times of violent conflicts. Various reports indicate that cannibal acts still took place during the Second Congo War that ravaged the country around the turn of the millennium (1998–2003),[41] and there are also reports of such acts committed during a later conflict in 2016/17.[42] But, while cannibalism might not yet be wholly a thing of the past, the practices covered in this book—slave eating, foreigner poaching, and commercial cannibalism—disappeared during the course of the twentieth century.

European observers in the early years of that century already noted that attitudes and behaviors had started to change. Weeks writes about the

Bangala: "In the early nineties there was no shame in admitting that they had eaten human flesh, but after a few years of teaching they were ashamed to confess to such a custom. Men whom I had seen eating human flesh later on denied ever having tasted it."[43]

Remembering how the flesh of slaughtered slaves had formerly been openly offered for sale, Roger Casement states that "sights of this description are to-day [1904] impossible in any part of the country," thanks to the efforts of the colonial government (which he otherwise severely criticizes for its exploitative treatment of the population). But he also notes that cannibalism was still practiced in some parts of the county—in particular around Lake Tumba, near the mouth of the Ubangi River—though "repressed and not so openly indulged in as formerly."[44]

Weeks explains the change as due to the missionaries' "teaching," while Casement explains it as due to the fear of the colonial government, which could and sometimes did prosecute those involved in murders and other acts that had become illegal under colonial law. Another factor that certainly contributed to the disappearance of slave eating was the suppression of slavery itself. Here too the Congo Free State, though officially outlawing slavery, was slow to take action. In 1902, slaves were still "almost daily . . . exposed for sale" in Luebo[45] (where Sheppard and Lapsley had been employed more than a decade earlier)—but in subsequent years, the trade in slaves had at least to move underground, if it did not disappear altogether.

In the Ubangi region—shared between the French Congo (which controlled the right riverbank) and the Congo Free State (which controlled the left), the open trade in captives or slaves purchased for consumption seems to have come to a stop in the 1890s or early 1900s. After visiting the French Congo in 1902–4, Auguste Chevalier calls the "Bondjos" still openly and "passionately cannibalistic," but adds that meals of human flesh had become less frequent than in the past, because raids on other villages had largely ceased "thanks to the surveillance of our administration."[46]

Here it seems that, at least on the French side, the state fairly effectively suppressed warfare and slave raids—and without such activities, no victims could be acquired for consumption. In the inner parts of the Free State, where state control was often weak or where the state had other priorities, the disappearance of cannibal customs seems to have been slower. Torday, who from 1900 to 1907 lived mostly in the Kasai region,[47] comments upon his time there:

> For a European who has neither the right nor the power to intervene, it is a most uncomfortable position to be obliged to witness, or at any rate know of the perpetration of acts of cannibalism in his immediate neighbourhood. But I hear that the Government is now proposing to establish several small posts with the express intention of putting down the practice.[48]

It is not quite clear to which year the "now" in this quote refers, as Torday had started to write the book immediately after his return, but only published it six years later.[49] In 1908, after the complaints about the abuses of Leopold's ultra-exploitative regime had become too large to ignore, the Belgian government annexed the country and turned it from the king's private dominion into a regular colony. But while this might have stopped Leopold's attempts of enriching himself at the cost of the Congolese, the new government does not seem to have taken its role as law enforcer very seriously, at least not everywhere.

After vising the Belgian Congo (as the country was now called) around 1920, the British traveler Frederick Migeod (1872–1952) wrote: "It seems that cannibalism is rank all up the Kasai and Sankuru rivers, and the State largely leaves it alone." He excused this, somewhat weakly, as possibly caused by the "difficulty . . . of obtaining evidence for a judicial trial, for in the absence of the body it is difficult to have proof of the murder."[50]

From a Portuguese trading agent working in the Ubangi area, he heard that the M'Baka people—formerly known under the generic "Bondjo" label—still loved to consume human flesh, killing slaves for this purpose whenever they could afford to do so. While adults were "dispatched with a lance," purchased children were supposedly disposed of more cruelly by submerging "the child's head . . . in a pot of boiling water until it is dead"—possibly a modification of the earlier practice of soaking intended victims in the river overnight. Afterwards "the body is cut up and cooked as ordinary meat." While the agent admitted that he had not seen this, he assured that "it was everywhere accepted as a fact."[51]

While the agent's account may be unreliable, it is remarkable that the Europeans in this area were apparently widely convinced not only that slaves were still commonly bought and sold but also that they could be murdered without the state taking a serious interest in the matter. It is a much more pessimistic judgment than Chevalier's assessment given nearly twenty years earlier, according to which the "Bondjo" were still "passionately cannibalistic" in theory and inclination, but mostly lacked suitable opportunities in practice. It is possible that the difference is due to the sides of the river they had visited—Migeod reporting from the side belonging to the Belgian Congo, whose government seems to have largely neglected to enforce its laws at least where native victims were concerned, while the French colonial government might well have taken its duties more seriously.

It even seems that the greater mobility of people that became possible, and sometimes necessary, under the colonial regimes, allowed cannibal customs to occasionally spread into regions where they had formerly been unknown. Migeod, who wrote shortly after World War I, opined that "during the War non-cannibal soldiers and carriers became associated with others who enjoyed human meat, and many are bound to have tried it from curiosity." He heard that "quite recently some human meat was bought and sold openly in the Kinshasa market, right in the middle of European life."[52] Kinshasa, which a few years later would become the capital of the Belgian Congo, is outside the regions from which cannibalism had been reported in earlier times.

Prosper Augouard heard of a similar incident that happened in 1917 near Brazzaville, then the capital of French Equatorial Africa and situated opposite Kinshasa on the other site of the Congo River. Two "Bondjos" had moved there in search of work—a remarkable feat, considering they came from the area around Bangui, situated a thousand kilometers northeast of Brazzaville. While fishing in the river, they saw

> Two harmless Batekes (people from this region) repair[ing] their nets on an island. In front of such defenseless victims, their instinct reappears. The Bondjos approach them amicably and suddenly strike them down unexpectedly, killing them, cutting them up and smoking them, then carrying them off to the village. They even have the audacity of selling pieces in the open market![53]

According to Augouard, the incident was only discovered because of a quarrel between one of the men and his wife. He beat her when she asked for money to buy clothes. "Furiously, the woman stealthily took a smoked arm out of the hut, the fingers still attached, and took this piece of evidence to the police commissioner. The two murderers were arrested."[54]

Such acts of kidnapping and killing unrelated others in order to eat them (or sell their flesh) fall under the general category I propose to call "foreigner poaching"—though in this case the attackers rather than the attacked were of a more or less foreign status, having only recently moved into the area. Reports of foreigner poaching from earlier times will be covered later,[55] but in the context of discussing the disappearance of cannibal customs it is noteworthy that such acts seem to have persisted at least as long, if not longer, than the consumption of slaves.

When the American traveler Hermann Norden visited the Kasai region in 1923, a *menagère* (black concubine of a white man) told him she was afraid to visit the next village, fearing she might be caught and eaten on the way. Such fears were apparently not groundless—a few months before his arrival, a "*menagère* had been eaten by the Badinga, a tribe notoriously cannibalistic." And while he stayed in the village, "another woman fell exhausted on the station verandah. Her chest had been pierced with an arrow, and she told us of an attack as she came through the forest. The man who walked with her had been killed and would be eaten."[56]

Norden talked with the son of a local chief who explained that "human meat tasted better than any other." Turning to an old Belgian who had translated Norden's question, the young man added: "Why do you ask me these things? You know that the flesh of a man tastes better than the flesh of a goat." The Belgian admitted that it was quite likely he had occasionally been served human flesh without knowing what he was eating.[57]

While traveling in the company of a Norwegian trader, Norden met a village chief whose people had once eaten one of the "soldiers" employed by the trader. But these old things were forgotten, the Norwegian explained, and now they were on very friendly terms.[58] While in the modern world, meeting one's end in order to serve as food for others might seem the ultimate horror, Norden found a quite different attitude in this area, where such occurrences were still sufficiently frequent to get used to: "I was to become accustomed to this casual mention of cannibalism. . . . No stress was put upon it, nor horror shown. This person had died of fever; that one had been eaten. It was all a matter of the way one's luck held."[59]

Lonely travelers were also still occasionally kidnapped and eaten in the 1920s by members of the Abarambu-Adhuga, one of the Zande clans in the northeast, according to Filiberto Gero's local informants. But by then, they added, such acts happened only in secrecy and were disapproved of by most.[60]

After the 1920s, there are no more reports that clearly refer to slave eating or foreigner poaching. It seems that these practices disappeared for good at about this time; or if they were still practiced, it was so rarely and so discreetly that they do not show up in the historical record. But acts of commercial cannibalism—the sale of human flesh—still took place several decades later. "In 1961 in Uganda," reports the anthropologist Robert Edgerton, "a man offered to sell me human fingers that had been smoked. When I declined in horror, he offered to return with a smoked slab of a young woman's buttocks, a truly 'choice cut,' as he put it."[61] Who the unfortunate young woman was and how her body ended up for sale is unclear.

Around the same time, human flesh might also have been available for purchase in war-torn parts of today's Congo-Kinshasa, which finally gained its independence from Belgium in 1960. Immediately after independence, two southern provinces—Katanga and South Kasai—declared their secession from the new state, encouraged by the Belgian government which thus hoped to regain effective control over at least part of its lost colony. The American journalist D'Lynn Waldron, who visited the country at the beginning of the five years of conflict and warfare that would follow, claims that unscrupulous "entrepreneurs" quickly discovered that the flesh of war victims could be sold with a profit. Supposedly the government reacted by passing "a law that no meat could be sold without some of the hide attached" in order to prove that it had come from an animal.[62] In this case it seems that the human flesh had not been openly sold as such, but presented as if it were of animal origin—a practice also reported from China during times of famine.[63]

Again, it it interesting that the geographical spread of reports of cannibalism from this time is wider than in earlier times. While Kinshasa and Brazzaville are to the west of the areas of the Congo basin from which cannibalism had once been commonly reported, Uganda is to the east. It seems that the movement of people had indeed caused cannibal practices to occasionally spread into areas where they had been unheard of before.

Another remarkable detail of Edgerton's account is that the seller apparently considered the demand for human flesh sufficiently large that he found it reasonable to approach random people on the street in the hope of making a sale (similar to what illegal drug dealers might do in certain areas). While Edgerton was horrified, it does not seem that such an attitude was already so widespread as to make that business model impossible or inadvisable. But this may have changed quickly in subsequent years, as there are no later reports of even a secret trade in human flesh.

How and Why Did Cannibalism End?

While cannibalism in the Congo did not disappear overnight—and reports of wartime cannibalism continue into the most recent times—it is nevertheless remarkable how much of a change took place within the course of just one or two generations. In the late nineteenth century, cannibalism—including the killing and consumption of captured enemies and slaves—was not only practiced widely in certain parts of the Congo basin, but it was also seen as a natural act and an expression of wealth and power. It was not considered shameful or morally reprehensible.

In the 1920s, just a few decades later, slaves and poached foreigners were still eaten in a few regions, but such acts were apparently much rarer than in earlier times, and when they happened, they happened in secret. Among the Zande, according to Gero's observations, most people now disapproved of such acts, although a few active cannibals still remained. Another generation later, in the 1960s, it seems that there was still a discreet underground market in human flesh, but in subsequent years, all traces of commercial cannibalism disappeared as well.

How had such a big change in attitudes and behaviors come about so quickly? Was it mostly the fear of legal repression that caused people to change their ways? Did cannibalism disappear (for the most part) due to a lack of victims? Or did people's attitudes and values themselves change in a way that made such an eating style unattractive even outside of such external factors?

Arguably, the disappearance of cannibalism might have been driven by all these factors, but it will require further research to understand which of them was most important. I am not aware of clear statements indicating that cannibalism in the Congo was abolished out of a fear of legal prosecution, but such statements were recorded in other parts of the world.

Traveling through Liberia in the 1920s, the British writer Lady Dorothy Mills (1889–1959) met men who told her that they had eaten the flesh of enemies and poached foreigners until a few years prior, when the state had started to seriously prosecute such acts. She notes that they "spoke of the present prohibition with regret and utterly without shame or real consciousness of wrongdoing, as one speaks of the 'drink' prohibition of the United States."[64] In New Britain, as already quoted, the missionary Matthäus Rascher heard from people that they had had to abandon cannibalism, to their regret, because of "the fear of the [colonial] judge and the difficulty of getting human flesh without attracting attention."[65] Similar declarations have been made elsewhere.

There can be little doubt that law enforcement, if it effectively prosecuted either the consumption of human flesh itself or acts that usually preceded it—such as murders, kidnappings, and the slave trade—was a deterrent that contributed to the disappearance of cannibalism. This also means that it is pretty clear that the neglectful attitude of the Congo Free State—and to a certain degree apparently also of its successor, the Belgian Congo—to effectively prosecute crimes against native victims allowed cannibalism to flourish longer and take more victims than it would have if these colonial regimes had taken their role as law enforcers more seriously.

However, the emergence of states in a region that can well be considered as "stateless" in earlier times had an effect beyond the simple enforcement of laws. Cannibalism depends on access to victims, and the new regimes made such access more difficult or impossible. G. Renouard writes that "cannibalism is not possible without slavery," since no "free man" would voluntarily give himself up to be killed and eaten.[66] This is of course not generally true, as victims for cannibal meals were also secured through other means such as warfare, kidnapping, or criminal conviction—depending on local customs and circumstances. But in a country where slavery does not exist, where people can travel freely over longer distances without fear of being kidnapped and killed, and where no one is sentenced to death (or those sentenced to death are not eaten)—in such a country cannibalism becomes effectively impossible due to a lack of victims.

That is true at least when it comes to people eating, the consumption of deliberately killed persons—the consumption of the corpses of those who had died a natural or accidental death would conceivably still be possible. But it seems that corpse eating (to be discussed in Chapter 13) was never very widespread in the Congo basin and that it disappeared even earlier than other cannibal practices. By making local warfare impossible, by ensuring that travelers could move safely and that people were no longer bought and sold as slaves, the colonial regimes—however ineffectual or exploitative they might otherwise have been—removed the soil in which cannibalism could flourish.

But finally, if people had just been *compelled* to abandon cannibalism, we might expect that they would have strongly objected to such a change being forced upon them. But no open resistance is known, and while people might have quietly complained about the abandonment of old customs, all in all they seem to have accepted it without a fuss.

Analyzing the situation in one of the Solomon Islands, Martin Zelenietz concludes that there the practice of headhunting and the cannibal feasts accompanying it disappeared not so much out of legal repression—though that played a role as well—but because of changes in customs which meant that they ceased to fulfill their earlier functions. Headhunting raids had helped to build alliances and to "maintain and increase political prestige and power." When the situation changed and access to European trade goods became an important indicator of power and success, raids became a hindrance, because the fear of counter raids and the general high degree of violence made such access more difficult. Consequently, they were abandoned.[67]

Something similar might have happened in the Congo. Slave eating in particular and cannibalism in general had been highly social affairs. Leaders and wealthy men regaled their followers with human flesh to show their power, wealth, and generosity; whole villages as well as members of neighboring communities joined in cannibal feasts to celebrate important occasions. People eating had served to increase prestige and social cohesion. But once the newly powerful and influential—colonial rulers, missionaries, foreign traders—made it clear that they considered cannibalism an abominable crime, it could no longer effectively do so. People might have continued their human-flesh feasts for a while in secret, but a feast that must remain hidden for fear of prosecution is hardly an impressive sign of power and status, and secret events could hardly involve whole communities and neighbors, like earlier feasts had.

Moreover, it seems quite likely that the younger generation, raised in missionary schools or otherwise under the influence of Western values, started to regard the customs of their elders as gross and unacceptable, just like Disasi Makulo did. And ways of signaling status and power likely changed as well under the influence of capitalism, with cars or other expensive import goods replacing earlier markers of prestige such as regaling one's followers. Ultimately, cheap and easy access to a variety of animal meats and other new foodstuffs might have made human flesh lose much of its appeal as a rare delicacy.

Though revenge- and hate-driven war cannibalism might still occasionally be practiced, peacetime cannibalism in the Congo disappeared over the course of just one or two generations and with very little protest and resistance. While further research is needed to understand this process in detail, it seems plausible that cannibalism ended not just because of legal repression, but because it went out of fashion.

Notes

1. See Chapter 3, this volume.
2. Obeyesekere, *Cannibal Talk*, 2. For "Arens's view," see the Conclusion of this book.
3. Ibid., 14.
4. Ibid., 15.
5. Ibid., 15–16; see Chapter 1 in this volume for the taxonomy of cannibal practices used here.

6. Ibid., 15 (quote), 16.
7. Ibid., 73.
8. Ibid., 58–59.
9. Ibid., 107.
10. Ibid., 92–106.
11. Ibid., 133–36.
12. Ibid., 191.
13. Ibid., 190.
14. See Chapter 4, this volume.
15. See Chapters 4 and 5 in this volume for more details and sources.
16. Ward, *Five Years*, 160.
17. Ibid., 159.
18. See Chapter 4, this volume.
19. Jewsiewicki and Mumbanza mwa Bawele, "Social Context of Slavery," 73, 75 (quote).
20. Pigafetta, *Report*, 25, 75 (quote).
21. Ibid., 28.
22. Ibid.
23. Ibid., 27 (quote), 28.
24. Torday and Joyce, "On the Ethnology," 135.
25. Van Reybrouck, *Congo*, 215; see also Chapter 6, this volume.
26. See Chapter 4, note 50, this volume.
27. Quoted in Levtzion and Hopkins, *Corpus*, 273.
28. See Chapter 6, this volume.
29. Levtzion and Hopkins, *Corpus*, 285, 296.
30. Ibid., 298.
31. Ibid.
32. Ibid., 289.
33. See Chapter 6, this volume.
34. Slade, *King Leopold's Congo*, 18; Isichei, *History*, 404.
35. Manning, *Slavery and African Life*, 34.
36. Lovejoy, *Transformations of Slavery*, 139.
37. Isichei, *History*, 365–66.
38. Manning, *Slavery and African Life*, 109.
39. Harms, *River of Wealth*, 31. While Harms admits that "there was some cannibalism in the area" and that slaves were sometimes purchased for consumption, he thinks that European observers tended to exaggerate the significance of cannibalism in the Ubangi slave trade, pointing out that slaves were also purchased for other purposes such as "paddling trade canoes, fishing, or serving as soldiers" (ibid.). Glave and other observers, however, had already granted as much, though they believed the number of slaves bought for non-cannibal purposes to be small (Glave, "Slave Trade," 833).
40. Glave, "Slave Trade," 836.
41. Human Rights Watch, *Curse of Gold*, 45; Human Rights Watch, *Ituri*, 43; MRG and RAPY, "Erasing the Board," 12–13; "UN Condemns DR Congo Cannibalism," *BBC News*, 15 January 2003, http://news.bbc.co.uk/2/hi/africa/2661365.stm; "MONUC Confirms Cannibalism in Mambasa, Mangina," *The New Humanitarian*,

15 January 2003, https://www.thenewhumanitarian.org/news/2003/01/15/monuc-confirms-cannibalism-mambasa-mangina; "Death in the Congo," *Telegraph*, 30 May 2003, http://www.telegraph.co.uk/news/worldnews/africaandindianocean/democraticrepublicofcongo/1431506/Death-in-the-Congo-a-mother-watches-as-machete-militiamen-murder-her-little-girls.html; "The Truth Behind the Cannibals of Congo," *Independent*, 26 March 2004, https://www.independent.co.uk/news/world/africa/the-truth-behind-the-cannibals-of-congo-5355387.html; "UN Reports Atrocities in Congo," *Guardian*, 17 March 2005, http://www.theguardian.com/world/2005/mar/17/congo.sarahleft; "Cannibalism in DR Congo: Zainabo's Agony," *ReliefWeb*, 19 March 2005, http://reliefweb.int/report/democratic-republic-congo/cannibalism-dr-congo-zainabos-agony. All websites in this note were accessed 15 September 2020.
42. United Nations Human Rights Council, *Rapport détaillé*, §§ 62, 304–5, 415.
43. Weeks, "Anthropological Notes," 122.
44. Casement, *Correspondence and Report*, 30, 44.
45. William Morrison quoted in Benedetto, *Presbyterian Reformers*, 141.
46. Chevalier, *Mission Chari–Lac Tchad*, 89.
47. Torday, *Camp and Tramp*, 17.
48. Ibid., 68–69.
49. Ibid., 17.
50. Migeod, *Across Equatorial Africa*, 346.
51. Ibid., 152–53, 154 (quotes).
52. Ibid., 347.
53. Quoted in Witte, *Monseigneur Prosper Philippe Augouard*, 95.
54. Quoted ibid.
55. See Chapter 12, this volume.
56. Norden, *Fresh Tracks*, 275–77.
57. Ibid., 277.
58. Ibid., 201.
59. Ibid., 201–2.
60. Gero, *Cannibalism in Zandeland*, 72.
61. Edgerton, *Troubled Heart of Africa*, 255.
62. D'Lynn Waldron, "Tribal War in Luluabourg, Belgian Congo," 1960, accessed 18 September 2020, http://www.dlwaldron.com/Luluabourg.html.
63. See Chapter 14, this volume.
64. Mills, *Through Liberia*, 120.
65. Rascher, *Baining,* 301; see Chapter 3, this volume.
66. Renouard, *L'Ouest Africain*, 132.
67. Zelenietz, "End of Headhunting," 92–93, 100 (quote), 104.

CHAPTER 11
FOREIGNER POACHING IN NEW GUINEA AND THE BISMARCK ARCHIPELAGO

In cases of socially accepted violent cannibalism—people eating—the victims were nearly always outsiders of one kind or another—enemies, slaves, or foreigners. This is hardly surprising, since a society whose members randomly killed and ate each other would certainly not be stable—in fact, it would not be a society at all. In the preceding chapters, we have focused on slavery-related cannibal acts—acts whose victims were slaves or persons killed or captured in slave raids. Now we will turn to victims who were also considered outsiders, but of a different kind: unrelated and unwanted foreigners.

While xenophobia—fear or hatred of foreigners—is a widespread and well-known phenomenon, the connection between xenophobia and cannibalism has rarely been mentioned and never been systematically studied, to my knowledge. And yet there were regions where unwanted foreigners could be entrapped or hunted down and turned into food. The victims were usually lone individuals or small groups of people who had left the safety of their own community and could be captured or killed with limited risk to the attackers. I will use the term *foreigner poaching* for this mode of acquiring victims since it resembles the hunting or entrapping of wild animals. Such acts are documented in certain islands and groups of islands in the southern Pacific Ocean as well as in several regions in central and western Africa.

In this chapter, we will investigate reports of such practices in the Bismarck Archipelago (which was already a topic of Chapter 3) and the neighboring larger island of New Guinea. The next chapter will extend the discussion to Fiji and—once more—to the Congo basin as well as some other Central African regions. This selection is not arbitrary but rather depends on the wealth of source materials which exist for these regions. Similar practices could also be found in some other regions and sources referring to other regions will sometimes be mentioned in passing or in endnotes. But the most plentiful and reliable sources are available for the regions selected as the main areas of investigation.

New Guinea

It seems that in all regions where foreigners were "poached" and eaten, enemies killed in warfare could be eaten as well (the inverse is not true).[1] But it would be premature to conclude that both these acts took place for the same reasons. The British ethnologist Charles Gabriel Seligman (1873–1940) observes that the Wagawaga language spoken in southeastern New Guinea has two different terms for victims of cannibalism. Those killed and "eaten in revenge for a comrade who had been eaten by a hostile community were called *maia* or *maiha.*" The killing and consumption of enemies was part of a potentially endless cycle of revenge—if members of one's community had died in an attack, it was necessary to kill and consume at least the same number of persons from the responsible community to make up for it.[2]

Anyone killed and eaten for other reasons was called *idaïdaga*, a term "meaning a debt or an unpaid score that is not going to be paid," used for "strangers and castaways [who] were invariably killed and eaten, and the same fate often befell straying bushmen, as here reprisals would not as a rule be feared." The term was also employed for murdered "members of weak distant communities who were so unlikely to take vengeance that none was feared." Killing such persons did not require a specific explanation or justification—"the desire for a favourite food" was considered sufficient reason.[3] Seligman notes that those who "talked freely" about the subject agreed that human flesh had a "more delicate flavour" than pork, "as well as the further advantage . . . that it never produces any painful feeling of satiety or induces vomiting."[4]

Regarding the Orokaiva people in eastern New Guinea, the Australian anthropologist Francis E. Williams (1893–1943) likewise notes that revenge killings of enemies were distinguished from the simple entrapment of foreigners. If a member of one's own group had died violently, it was necessary to kill someone belonging to the slayer's group to get revenge. A simple exchange of a life for a life was sufficient—there was no need to specifically target the responsible person. Foreigners from unknown groups were regarded with "suspicion," if not outright "hostility; a complete stranger wandering alone would be regarded both as potential enemy and good meat." One was not bound by promises given to foreigners—successfully entrapping them through false promises was considered an accomplishment, not something to be ashamed of.[5]

Within one's own group, on the other hand, a very different ethics applied: here gift-giving, generosity, and mutual help were widespread and expected.[6] The consumption of foreigners does not seem to have had a religious or spiritual meaning; instead, as Williams comments: "The reason for cannibalism itself has been given by natives as the simple desire for good food."[7]

A similar distinction between acts of cannibalism motivated by revenge and those that did not need a particular justification seems to have existed in the western part of New Guinea.[8] In the mid-1960s, the anthropologist Klaus-Friedrich Koch did field research in the central highlands of this region, among people whose first contact with the outside world had been the establishment of a Christian mission station a few years earlier.[9] He collected accounts of various cases of revenge-driven cannibalism involving members of communities hostile to each other.[10] But revenge was not always necessary. Around 1925, his informants remembered, a man had convinced a girl from a distant village to "elope" with him. Later, possibly after the man had lost interest, "the girl was killed, cooked, and eaten. Since no hostilities existed between the two regions, her slaying was without cause, and not 'for an eye'—an act of revenge."[11]

While such acts seem to have been relatively rare in the area, cannibal killings for which no revenge motive is known still occasionally occurred even after Koch had left the region. During his stay, he had made a trip to some previously uncontacted "Jalé villages in the Seng Valley south of the Central Range." While he managed to establish friendly relations with the villagers, two years later they "killed and ate two white missionaries traveling through their valley."[12] It is unclear whether the missionaries had somehow offended the villagers or whether they were treated as any foreigner not considered a friend might be treated.

Among the cases of foreigner poaching described by Seligman is the oral account of a woman named Laido, near whose village in southeastern New Guinea four people—two men and two women—had been shipwrecked. Four men from the village approached them, killing them with tomahawks and a spear, as Laido saw herself. Then "the people made a big fire and scorched the bodies on it, and then they cut pieces off with knives, and put these pieces into pots and cooked them, and when they were cooked the people, and there were many, sat down and ate of the flesh." In precolonial times, "this was the custom of my country," she explained.[13]

In addition to castaways, those who had temporarily left the safety of their community to fish or otherwise gather food were at risk of themselves being captured and used for food. The British colonial officer Wilfred N. Beaver, who spent twenty-seven years in southeastern New Guinea, saw "many hundreds of skulls" in communal longhouses in the delta of the Purari River, all coming from "slain enemies or strangers." The latter, he notes, were usually random victims encountered "while fishing or hunting." When he came into the area, cannibalism was still practiced openly, though it was by no means a daily affair, as suitable victims could only be captured from time to time—but whenever that happened, their flesh was "highly appreciated."[14] Cases of fishers and food gatherers—often women and children—being captured and eaten have also been reported from other island groups in the southern Pacific, especially the Loyalty Islands[15] (today part of New Caledonia) and the Marquesas Islands[16] (today part of French Polynesia).

Runaway carriers from the gold fields in eastern New Guinea also frequently fell victim to cannibal attacks, as both the British resident magistrate Charles Arthur Whitmore Monckton (1873–1936) and the British traveler H. Wilfrid Walker remark. Walker, who visited various South Pacific islands in the early twentieth century, claims that "these carriers"—who had often been recruited by cunning or outright force—"are constantly running away," but "never" make it to the coast, "being always killed and eaten on the way."[17]

Monckton writes that carriers deserting from the gold fields on the Mambare River "were continually being caught and eaten by the tribes along the coast" and that, in particular, a people he calls Mokoru who lived northwest of Cape Nelson had "captured and [eaten] a number of runaway Mambare carriers." When Monckton threatened the Mokoru with punitive action, "they calmly told me that they would do the same to the police, if I interfered with them, but added, that I myself was so repulsively coloured that they would not dream of eating me, but would feed me to the pigs instead." Sometime later, he claims, "the Arifamu, to the south, ate some carriers and snapped up one of my constabulary," who managed to escape.[18]

Undeterred by the threats, Monckton launched an attack against the Mokoru that ended with the surrender of their chief, Paitoto. The latter "later turned out to be an excellent man" and Monckton appointed him "Government chief and village constable." After the surrender, Monckton seized one of the chief's pots for cooking. Later Paitoto told him: "That was the pot in which my wife had made a stew of carriers' hands."[19] Carriers were also occasionally eaten by Monckton's own allies, as he mentions elsewhere.[20]

Another time, Monckton was asked for help by the inhabitants of Collingwood Bay (near the eastern end of New Guinea). They urged him to stop the attacks of the neighboring Doriri people who repeatedly sent "very small parties, which ceaselessly snapped up and killed men, women, and children." In a punitive expedition, Monckton's men came across four Doriri fighters, two of whom were killed, while the other two were arrested. When he interrogated them, they told him that "their food supplies were none too good. They really made their expeditions to Collingwood Bay in order to hunt game and make sago, and the killing of the people there was only a supplementary diversion, though of course the bodies of the slain gave them an agreeable change of diet."[21]

Monckton's own carriers, who had suffered under Doriri attacks, would have liked to consume the vanquished enemies. They argued that, if they were "allowed to eat any future Doriri killed . . . it would not only be a great satisfaction to them but also a considerable saving to the stores of the expedition. 'Really' they urged, 'there was no sense in wasting good meat on account of a foolish prejudice.'" Monckton was not moved by their arguments, instead threatening them with a severe beating.[22]

The Bismarck Archipelago

In the Bismarck Archipelago, a group of dozens of smaller islands situated to the northeast of New Guinea, travel by sea is even more important than on the huge island. From around 1884 to 1919, both northeastern New Guinea and the archipelago were claimed by Germany as a colony. Heinrich Schnee, the

Deputy Governor of German New Guinea from 1898 to 1900, lists six cases, with more than thirty victims, of castaways being killed and eaten in New Britain and New Ireland (the two largest islands of the archipelago) between 1896 and 1899. Usually, these cases only came to the attention of the colonial government because some of the castaways managed to escape and report what had happened—the actual figure might therefore have been considerably higher.[23]

During a punitive expedition which followed one of these incidents, Schnee observed that human bodies were not only eaten but also traded. Several of the eleven victims of the attack had been sold by their killers to inhabitants of surrounding settlements. Schnee notes that the price charged for a corpse was the same as for a fully-grown pig; corpses and pigs were also carried (by tying them to poles) and cooked (by roasting large pieces between hot stones) in the same manner. In one of the villages that had purchased a body, Schnee saw a human shoulder blade and other body parts which had been roasted in this way and were still wrapped in leaves when he reached the fireplace. The flesh, he observed, looked and smelled similar to veal.[24] While Schnee was shocked, the native policemen in his company clearly were not. When he queried them, they told him that in their home villages human flesh was prepared in the same manner, so they were accustomed to the sight.[25]

Albert Hahl, the last governor of German New Guinea, writes that another case of castaways being consumed took place around 1901 not far from Herbertshöhe (today Kokopo), the colonial capital in the east of New Britain. Two survivors arrived in the capital and complained that their companions had been "killed and devoured." Hahl was particularly disappointed because "this crime was committed so to speak at the very threshold of headquarters and by people who we believed had already been won over to peaceful ways."[26] In another case investigated by Hahl, a group of canoeists had been butchered and eaten after accidentally landing in the wrong spot.[27]

Sometimes castaways were kept alive until a suitable time to consume them arrived. During one of his journeys to the Bismarck Archipelago, the Australian government agent Douglas Rannie was approached by a man looking notably different from the other islanders, who asked to be hired as a sailor. He explained that he came from the Ontong Java Atoll, a group of islands located seven hundred kilometers to the east.[28]

> He and five others had been blown away from his island in a gale of wind. After several days at sea they were seen and picked up by the Caen islanders [the island where Rannie met him], in a very emaciated condition. They were well treated by their hosts; but as they improved in condition, his mates had been one by one killed and eaten. As he saw nothing in store for himself but a similar fate, his joy was unbounded when he found a chance of escape in our arrival.[29]

Rannie also describes three other cases of foreigner poaching, unrelated to shipwrecks, which took place in the Bismarck Archipelago, the Solomon Islands, and Vanuatu.[30]

The English Methodist missionary and ethnographer George Brown (1835–1917) heard of another case of a castaway kept alive for consumption which had occurred in New Britain. He was told that, some time ago, a local chief had rescued a man spotted adrift in his canoe. He treated the man well until his health had been restored and he had gained some weight. Then he took the castaway to a dance. Since the latter knew that dancing was usually followed by a feast, he asked whether they had a pig to eat. "'Oh no,' they replied, 'there is no pig, but we are going to eat you after the dance.' And they did so that same day!" His informant, notes Brown, treated this incident as a "quite ordinary occurrence," reporting it in passing "without any feeling of reprobation."[31] Castaways, and outsiders in general, had no rights, and treating them in such a way was apparently considered entirely appropriate.

On another occasion, Brown himself witnessed the preparation of a cannibal meal. During his first visit to a certain village in New Britain, "they were cooking a man a few yards distant from the place where I was sitting."[32] He does not say who the victim was.

As in New Guinea, castaways were not the only persons at risk. It rather seems that in some parts of the archipelago, any lone individual or small group of people not tied by friendly relations to the locals could fall victim to a cannibal killing. The German missionary Gerhard Peekel (1876–1949), who worked in New Ireland in the early twentieth century, records that, in addition to enemies killed in battle, "people were also often slain with or without reason, and then appeared on the banquet table as a welcome roast." In his book on the island, he lists more than twenty cases of people who had been killed and consumed during the living memory of various inhabitants of Namatanai, one of the largest settlements. While all the victims came from the same island, they were inevitably eaten in a settlement different from the one where they had lived, likely after having ventured too far from home.[33] One of Peekel's own pupils told that he had attended a human flesh meal around the year 1900, but he did not eat the flesh since he had been too young; a pupil of another missionary admitted having participated in another meal, but assured that he had only consumed a tiny piece.[34]

It seems that every foreigner from an unknown region was considered a potential enemy. The German anthropologist Simon Haberberger heard this when he interviewed, in 2002, an inhabitant of the Baining Mountains in the interior of the Gazelle Peninsula (northeastern New Britain), whose father had known men who once practiced cannibalism. The victims, said the fifty-eight-year-old informant, had been enemies or "foreigners who passed through the Baining area and were considered enemies for this reason alone." Their flesh was said to taste similar to that of tree-kangaroos. No specific spiritual or magical meaning was attributed to the consumption of human flesh, it was simply considered good food.[35]

In other cases, it seems that people belonging to hostile communities were deliberately kidnapped and then eaten. In 1885, F. T. Goedicke, a young German settler living in the Gazelle Peninsula, convinced the young men of a nearby village to let him spend a few nights in the big longhouse "where the unmarried men of the village lived at night." Usually, these houses were off-limits to outsiders, but Goedicke won them over with a gift of tobacco. His first night in the longhouse was uneventful, but during the second, a group of young men carried a young woman into the house, ignoring her struggling and screaming. They told him that they had "stalked, and stolen [her] from an enemy village"—as no revenge motive is mentioned and the communities, though hostile to each other, do not seem to have been openly at war, this case may fall between war cannibalism and foreigner poaching.[36]

"With some ceremony, but with beastliness indescribable, the woman was then taken in turn by all the men" and afterwards killed. "With considerable expertness, the body was divided into small pieces. The fires had meantime been built up; the men, singly or in small groups, squatted around and roasted the bits allotted to them, and thus made their supper." Goedicke himself was "offered some of the toasted flesh." He was so traumatized by the events of the night that he soon after left New Britain, never to return. But he recorded the incident in his diary, where the historian Robert W. Robson found it.[37]

Motives

The accounts we have encountered point to several interrelated explanations driving cannibal acts: foreigners could be eaten because it seemed safe to do so (revenge was unlikely); since one did not know their motives, it was safer to treat them as "potential enemies" and get rid of them before they could do harm; and their flesh was considered "a favourite food" and "an agreeable change of diet."

The latter motive is confirmed by various other sources. Sir Hubert Murray (1861–1940) led the colonial government of Papua (the southeastern, formerly British part of New Guinea which in 1905 had been transferred to the Australian government) from 1908 until his death. Since he also served as a judge, he was repeatedly involved in cases of alleged murder and cannibalism. A man who confessed to having "killed and eaten a woman" who, as he explained, had tried to steal from his garden, was acquitted by Murray—it seems he considered the deed justifiable because the woman had first transgressed against the man's property. Another time he acted as an interpreter in the case of "a man . . . charged with having killed and eaten a baby"—he does not report the outcome of the case.[38] Regarding the motives of the cannibals, he writes that they "generally give as their usual reason for eating human flesh the simple fact that they like it. . . . [M]ost seem to consider it superior to other flesh."[39]

Both in New Guinea and in Fiji, Wilfrid Walker met self-admitted former cannibals who assured him that "human flesh . . . was far better than pig."[40] Among those who said so was Walker's Papuan "boy," who freely admitted that "he had often eaten human meat." Skeptical that those times were really over, Walker adds: "I had good reason for suspecting the young rascal of having partaken of human meat since he had been my servant."[41] Statements praising human flesh as particularly tasty have also been recorded from Vanuatu[42] and the Loyalty Islands.[43]

Some foreigners were seen not so much as potential enemies but as unwanted competitors—this too might have been a reason to "poach" them. In 1878, George Brown heard from "an old fellow called Kail, one of whose accomplishments was that of cutting up the bodies of men or pigs before or after the operation of cooking them," that several native Christian teachers, including a man named Sailasa, had been murdered and eaten in the interior of New Britain. Knowing that they had indeed recently started a journey inland, Brown "felt a great sinking of heart." The next day, a man who had hoped to meet Sailasa confirmed the report. As Brown reconstructed the case, Taleli, the chief responsible for the deed, had feared losing his trade monopoly if the missionaries started sending their own men into the interior. Moreover, the attack on the unarmed teachers was "profitable to the assailants, as they would be able to sell portions of the dead bodies to surrounding villages for native money."[44]

The incident is also described by the British captain and geographer Wilfred Powell, who writes the chief's name as "Tarlily."[45] He too notes that "the bodies of these four poor men were then sold in pieces to the inhabitants of all villages anxious to buy them."[46] That human flesh was considered a salable item in the Bismarck Archipelago (and in some other regions) is a point to which we will return later.[47] Further accounts of foreigner poaching in the Bismarck Archipelago come from the Danish explorer and anthropologist Richard Parkinson and the German traveler Joachim von Pfeil.[48] These will be discussed in more detail later, because they likewise mention the sale of the victim's flesh.

Patriarchal Patterns: Men Keeping the Best for Themselves, Breasts Preferred

We have already noted earlier that cannibalism often had a distinctly patriarchal form, with men being the primary perpetrators and beneficiaries of such acts, and women and children possibly at a higher risk of falling victim to them, at least in certain situations. When it came to foreigner poaching, it seems that the age and gender of the victims did not matter much—anyone could potentially be eaten. There is a certain disagreement between the sources whether men and women were both allowed to eat human flesh or whether it was restricted to men. Simon Haberberger heard from an informant that men, women, and children had been equally consumed, but the eaters of human flesh had usually been men; only occasionally had one of them shared some slices with his wife or children.[49]

Joachim von Pfeil likewise notes that any foreigner, whether "adult or elderly man, woman, boy or girl," was considered a suitable victim, as long as they could be killed without undue risk. He agrees that woman were generally excluded from eating human flesh: "Women have to prepare the meat, but are not allowed to join the meal; they are only entitled to lick the leaves soaked in juice" in which the flesh had been roasted.[50] Richard Parkinson, on the other hand, notes that "men, women and children" joined in the consumption of human bodies.[51] He need not be wrong, as it is quite possible that customs differed between regions. Moreover, the remark of Haberberger's informant that men sometimes, at their discretion, shared some of the meat with their wives and children, and Pfeil's statement that women were allowed to "lick the leaves" indicate that there was no strict taboo against women eating human flesh—it rather seems that, in general, men preferred to keep the best for themselves.

While these accounts refer to the Bismarck Archipelago, the situation in neighboring New Guinea might have been somewhat different. According to Charles Gabriel Seligman, this kind of flesh was generally eaten by men and women alike, but not by children below puberty.[52]

Another indication of the patriarchal nature of cannibal acts is that women's breasts are often mentioned as one of the, if not *the* preferred part of the edible human body. Seligman writes that "the best pieces were the tongue, hands, feet and mammae; the brain, broken up and extracted through the foramen magnum of the boiled skull, was considered a special delicacy."[53] According to Wilfred Beaver, "the arms, legs and the breasts of women are esteemed the best portions, but the whole body is eaten roasted with sago."[54]

While these accounts refer to New Guinea, Parkinson claims that, among the people he met in the Bismarck Archipelago, "flanks, fingers, brain and, in the case of female carcasses, the breasts, are considered the best pieces."[55] Haberberger's informant, on the other hand, does not mention breasts—according to him, heart, liver, and brain had been the favored parts.[56] Clearly, such lists should not be overrated. There is a huge amount of variety between the lists given by various authors and the stated preferences might, at least to some degree, have been individual rather than collective—arguably, they may depend strongly on the taste of the informants rather than truly expressing widespread attitudes. Nonetheless it is remarkable that breasts, together with the brain, show up in three of these four lists—arguably this might mean that both were really among the preferred body parts in this region.

A decided preference for female breasts has also been recorded from Vanuatu (formerly New Hebrides), farther in the southeast. According to the British anthropologists A. Bernard Deacon and Camilla H. Wedgwood, "women were specially fattened for eating, the breasts being the great delicacy."[57] Female victims may have been in particular demand for lavish "feasts for the chiefs and warriors," where, as the missionary William Gill claims, "a body of a female usually formed the principal part of the repast."[58] In a similar vein, the Swiss ethnologist Felix Speiser (1880–1949) writes about one of the islands belonging to Vanuatu: "In Tanna women were killed on the conclusion of treaties and eaten in a common meal."[59]

Speiser states that "the breasts of women and the genitals of men, [as well as the] palms of hands and soles of feet were the most coveted morsels." While thus also noting a preference for male genitals not recorded in other sources, he adds that, "particularly among the old men, it is a special pleasure to eat female victims and young girls most of all. . . . A chief in Aoba [Ambae Island], according to fairly reliable sources, had a young girl killed every few days but is said to have eaten only her breasts."[60] If this is more than just a rumor, it does not necessarily mean that the rest of the victim's body was discarded—rather it may have been eaten by the chief's followers. Likewise reporting from Vanuatu, the French marine officers A. Hagen and A. Pineau note that the breasts of young women, as well as the heads of all victims, were generally reserved for chiefs, while the limbs were distributed among their helpers; the trunk, however, was often thrown to "the dogs and pigs."[61]

When it came to being eaters rather than being eaten, Speiser states: "In principle women were debarred from the consumption of human flesh, just as they were forbidden other good food."[62] Similar to the Bismarck Archipelago, it seems that men preferred to reserve "good food" for themselves, while women (and possibly boys as well) had to make do with more modest meals.

But why the preference for female breasts? Was this an alternative way of men taking control of women's sexuality, by destroying and consuming it (and them) rather than subjugating it to their wills? This may be an explanation—indeed, Speiser notes that "the old men's craving for human flesh seems to me to be rooted in sadistic perversion."[63] An alternative explanation was recorded by the American anthropologist Michael Krieger, who visited Melanesia in the 1980s. In Malaita (one of the Solomon Islands, situated between the Bismarck Archipelago and Vanuatu), he met an old man who had eaten human flesh in his youth. The best parts, he remembered, were women's breasts because of the "amount of fat" they contained. "Because of the very low fat content of their diet, any fat is considered a great delicacy."[64]

The sources leave little doubt that men were the primary eaters of human flesh in the regions explored in this chapter—but what about the victims? Were women and children more or less likely to fall victim to foreigner poaching than men? Here the situation is less clear. On the one hand, several sources indicate that fishers and food gatherers, who were generally unarmed women or children, were at a high risk of falling victims to such acts. On the other hand, people who traveled far from their own communities, whether by canoe or on foot, were also at risk, and such long-distance travelers might have been men more often than women. Despite the noted preference for women's bodies and breasts, the cannibals seem to have been quite willing to take victims of whatever gender and age they could get.

Foreign-Born Children and Women as Victims

While travelers were at risk regardless of their gender, the patriarchal character of at least some of the societies investigated here also shows itself in the uncertain status granted to foreign-born women and children. Such women and children were sometimes incorporated into communities—but without completely losing their status as outsiders whose lives could be sacrificed under certain circumstances.

Francis Williams notes that, among the Orokaiva (in eastern New Guinea), captives taken in warfare were usually killed to prevent a possible escape, and then eaten. "Desirable women," however, were often spared and forced to marry one of the warriors; "little children" were sometimes spared as well and adopted into someone's family. While adopted children were safe from being eaten within the village which had taken them, their bodies could still be used for political purposes. If a village received a pig from another village and the inhabitants were unwilling to give up one of their own pigs in return, a child captured years earlier might be killed and the body, tied to a pole, sent back as a counter-gift.[65] A child born to community members would certainly not have been treated in such a manner, but the status of foreign-born children seems to have been so low that their lives were sometimes considered less valuable than those of pigs.

Charles Monckton reports a seemingly similar case that took place in southeastern New Guinea. When a chief and village constable whom Monckton knew well held a feast for some guests, he ordered a woman who was "staying" in the village to bring her ten-year-old son to him; he then murdered the child before the mother's eyes and had his flesh served to his guests, together with "plenty of pig, dog, and fish." While the status of the mother and child is not quite clear, it seems they did not permanently live in the village and no husband or family ties are mentioned—in the chief's eyes, that seems to have made the boy an expendable outsider. When Monckton heard of the incident, he had the culprit arrested and later executed.[66]

A desire for revenge could also lead to foreign-born children being killed and consumed. In the 1970s, the anthropologist Don Gardner undertook fieldwork among the Mianmin (or Mian people) in central New Guinea. Gardner collected several eyewitness accounts of an event that had taken place about twenty years earlier. A group of travelers had rested in an abandoned garden when a "strong gust of wind blew down a gigantic tree," killing three people immediately and hurting another man, the leader of the group, so bad that he later died of his wounds. The people somehow decided that their hostile neighbors, the Atbalmin, had in some way "precipitated" the accident. When Betenab, the uncle of a boy who had died in the accident, heard this, he shot and killed a young girl who had not quite reached marriageable age. "Betenab's anger was such that he butchered and cooked the girl, then shared her flesh with the rest of the village." The girl had been abducted from the Atbalmin as a young child and Betenab had raised her as his daughter. But the desire to get revenge for the supposed crime was evidently stronger than whatever family feelings he might have had.[67]

Like Williams notes regarding the Orokaiva, Gardner heard that the Mianmin had generally killed any enemy men they could lay hands on, while women were abducted and distributed by the warriors among themselves. Women who were crippled or otherwise considered undesirable, however, were killed and eaten. Children were sometimes adopted into the families of the victors; if girls, they were married off to one of the men in the village at a later date.[68]

Gardner also heard of a case where a local leader was "mourning the death of his child. In his sorrow he decided to kill Sunagei," a woman who had been abducted in an earlier raid. She was killed with arrows, then her body was cut up and eaten in what seems to have been a mourning ritual.[69] Though the abducted women and children were not formally slaves, it seems they were far from being accepted as full community members, and their lives remained at the mercy of the local men.

The status of married women could be uncertain as well. In New Guinea and the neighboring islands, wives usually came from outside their husband's clan and moved into the latter's village when entering the marriage.[70] If their husbands died and they had no living descendants, this left them in a precarious position—without strong ties in the community, they were essentially outsiders and could be treated as such. In 1907, the German district judge Benno Scholz reported that a widow had recently been murdered and eaten in Nissan, an island situated east of New Ireland.[71]

A detailed account was published by the Austrian anthropologist Richard Thurnwald (1869–1954), who accompanied Scholz on the punitive expedition that followed the incident. He states that the victim, whose name was Henot, had been born in Buka Island (60 kilometers southeast of Nissan). Three months after the death of her husband, a chief named Salin took her into his house; she became his sexual consort and ran his household. But since Salin had earlier promised to deliver human flesh to Somsom, another chief, the two men agreed that the widow would be "fattened" to fulfill the promise. About half a year later, Somsom hired a man named Mogan to kill and dismember Henot with Salin's consent. For these services, Somsom gave him a pig, a knife, and various arrows and arm rings. Somsom then sold several body parts in return for arm rings or arrows. Most parts, however, were given away as a compensation for earlier gifts of human flesh or in return for a promise of reciprocating in the same way sometime in the future—a mutual gift exchange at the cost of the victims.[72]

The relationship between Salin and Somsom was also shaped by such deadly gift giving. Thurnwald states that Salin had to hand the widow over in return for another woman he had received from Somsom. The latter in turn had already started to fatten a woman whom he had planned to give to Salin for consumption one month later—Thurnwald learned the names of all three victims. But cannibalism also had a commercial side: not only had Somsom sold several body parts of the murdered woman, but Thurnwald claims that in earlier times Nissan islanders had frequently sold both women and pigs to the inhabitants of neighboring Buka Island, knowing full well that the latter would eat them. The victims were either captives or women who had no one who might revenge them—because they lacked a protector, being eaten or sold for food was not an unusual end for a widow.[73]

Ninety-six years later Haberberger visited Nissan and talked with seven locals (aged from thirty-six to about eighty) who still remembered the case. One of them told him that Henat (the woman's actual name which had been misspelled by the Europeans) had been raped before her death. Another interviewee stated that his great-grandfather had received and eaten the right leg; his young son (the interviewee's grandfather) had also shared in the meal. The interviewees were unaware of any magical associations of cannibalism. They had heard that it had been practiced "because of the flesh," and, when enemies were eaten, to prove one's own superiority. They also knew that Henat's death had been the last case of cannibalism on the island; the strong reaction of the colonial government—which had sentenced several men to prison—convinced people that they had to give up the practice. Two big men ("chiefs" in older Western sources) reached an agreement that henceforth pork should be consumed instead of human flesh—up to that time, pigs had been eaten rarely and only on special occasions.[74]

Haberberger points out that the consumption of social outsiders shows the importance of groups and proper group membership. Henat had been accepted as a community member while her husband was alive; after his death, her status became uncertain. Individuals had no rights of their own; if the group to which they were attached decided they were disposable, their fate was sealed.[75]

The German traveler Friedrich Burger, who visited the Bismarck Archipelago in 1911/12, reports a similar case that had taken place a short time earlier on an island he calls "St. John"—which might have later changed its name, as today no island with this name can be found in the archipelago. As Burger tells it, a widow named Karas had no living relatives; a chief had taken her in and, after using her to satisfy his "lust," he "fattened her up like you fatten a pig." Then she was killed with a club, dismembered, "roasted on hot stones," and eaten by a group of chiefs. According to tradition, each of the invitees was supposed to compensate the host by inviting him at a future date to a similar feast. Widows were usually chosen as victims because they had no relatives who would feel obliged to revenge them.[76]

Another widow was singled out by one of the participants as material for the next feast. But when she grasped what was about to happen, she fled into the house of a white trader who informed the colonial authorities. The German government then sent a punitive expedition and arrested the chiefs who had joined in the cannibal meal.[77] It is not inconceivable that Burger's description actually refers to the case investigated by Scholz and Thurnwald, but the widows' names are clearly different and "St. John," whatever island it might have been, seems to be distinct from Nissan, which had its name already at that time. Thus, it seems more likely that his account refers to another instance of the same deadly tradition.

Even the lives of married women were not safe if their husbands lost interest or decided that they deserved punishment. A. Kleintitschen, one of the German Catholic missionaries employed in New Britain, knew a chief who had bought a young girl and made her his fifth wife, but she was unhappy and repeatedly ran back to her family. Finally, writes Kleintitschen, the old man "lost his patience": he killed and ate her.[78]

In what may be a reference to the same or a different case, Karl Lüders, the author of a small book published around 1890 in Germany states that "a chief in Blanche Bay [on the Gazelle Peninsula in New Britain] slaughtered and consumed his wife at a feast." He adds that such acts occurred from time to time since "the husband has the right of life and death over the wife" and if a man had "bought a woman who cannot feel at home in her new home, does not want to work, and repeatedly arouses [his] wrath," she was occasionally sentenced to death. He notes that the feasts that followed such acts were the only cases of cannibalism where the victim had lived in the same village as those who ate her—otherwise only enemies and foreigners were consumed.[79]

A German botanist, Kleinschmidt, who had settled in the Gazelle Peninsula some time before the region became a German colony, claims to have twice been invited to feasts where human flesh was consumed. At one, a young woman was served as the main course—he was told that she had been the inviting chief's ninth wife, but "because she had been afraid and had cried he had become angry and killed her." At the other feast he attended, the victim was a captured enemy: "a man and his wife from enemy territory had been captured. The man was promptly killed but the wife was added to the chief's harem and at their wedding feast had helped to eat her late husband."[80] This corresponds to the observations of Williams and Gardner that captured women (and children) had a better chance of being spared and incorporated in the community. But as the cases of the eaten widows and wives show, such an incorporation was not necessarily permanent, and the lives of former outsiders were never completely safe.

That wives could be killed and eaten has also been reported from Fiji[81] and from the Congo.[82] Just as in the Congo, it seems plausible that a husband's "right of life and death over the wife" (Lüders) was checked by the risk that her relatives might avenge her if they learned of her death. In the Congo, it therefore seems that, in particular, enslaved women made into wives and women whose relatives had died were in danger of falling victim to their husband's whim. In the Bismarck Archipelago, though both Kleintitschen and Lüders state that the eaten wives had been "bought," this does not necessarily mean that they had been slaves—rather it might refer to the custom of men paying a bride price (bridewealth) to the relatives of their future wife. Kleintitschen specifically mentions that the family of the sacrificed girl had lived nearby and that she had repeatedly run back to them. Maybe, as Lüders suggests, the status even of a freeborn woman was so low that her husband had the right to dispose of her as he wished without giving her family a right to revenge; or maybe the responsible chief did consider himself so powerful that he did not have to fear revenge.

Is it just by chance that all the cases of foreign-born children being eaten are from New Guinea, while all reports of wives and widows meeting the same fate are from the Bismarck Archipelago? Alternatively, this may be due to subtle differences in local customs. In New Guinea, except for the case reported by Monckton (where the situation is unclear) the sacrificed children and women had been kidnapped from hostile groups; they were still vaguely associated with the groups from which they came and could be killed as an act of revenge against these groups. It also seems that their lives had very little value for the group in which they lived; they could be killed in mourning or even, as Williams has it, when a community needed to make a present and did not want to sacrifice a pig.

In the Bismarck Archipelago—or maybe only in New Britain, as all cases of wife eating come from that island—on the other hand, it seems that even wives born in friendly communities were at the mercy of their husbands, and that butchering them was an accepted (though rare) alternative to getting a divorce. The fate of widows on Nissan (and possibly elsewhere) is again a somewhat different issue; the lack of living relatives seems to be the main point here. Women usually came from other communities, whether friendly or hostile; if they had lost their husband and had no other strong ties in the community, they could be treated once again as outsiders.

In any case, it is noticeable that the status of women and children oscillated in these patriarchal societies in a way that the status of men did not: they could be integrated into communities, but they could also easily be ejected from them if circumstances changed, with deadly consequences. The status of men was more clear-cut: if they belonged to the local community or to friendly communities, they were usually safe from harm; if not, they were typically treated not just as outsiders but as potential enemies. Men from unknown or hostile communities were often killed and eaten quickly;

castaways were sometimes kept alive for some time until meeting the same end, but it seems they were never integrated into a community in the way women and children could be.

White People Rarely Eaten

While the status of women and children who had been married or adopted into neighboring communities was uncertain, white people who came into the region from Europe or the Americas were doubtless foreigners. And occasionally, at least in New Guinea proper, they were treated like any foreigner might be treated—hunted down, killed, and consumed if they were unable to defend themselves. Haberberger documents the case of John Werner, a German American prospector who in 1913 was killed and eaten in the interior of New Guinea. Haberberger found no indications that Werner could have acted in a manner that provoked hostilities; if anything, he seems to have been too sweet-natured and credulous. Nor does revenge seem a plausible reason for his death since he was likely the first European the villagers who killed him had ever met.[83]

Also in New Guinea, two white miners, Campion and King, were entrapped and carried off to a village, "where they were both roasted alive over a slow fire" and then eaten, according to Walker. The colonial government subsequently arrested several persons who confessed to having participated in these acts.[84] The cruel treatment might have been due to culinary reasons, as Walker explains elsewhere: "The Papuans, as a rule, do not torture their prisoners for the mere idea of torture, though they have often been known to roast a man alive, for the reason that the meat is supposed to taste better thus. This they also do to pigs, and I myself, on this very expedition, caught some of our carriers making preparations to roast a pig alive, and just stopped them in time."[85]

While these reports show that Westerners were not exempt from being eaten, such cases were rare. In particular it seems that white-skinned individuals were never eaten in the Bismarck Archipelago and the neighboring North Solomon Islands[86]—or at least no cases where this happened are on record. This caught the attention of Heinrich Schnee, the Deputy Governor of German New Guinea, who notes that in all cases of murder investigated by him, the corpses of white victims were thrown into the sea, while those of "colored" people were consumed.[87]

Schnee claims to have encountered this unequal treatment of corpses in at least five cases, several of which he describes in his book. In 1898, a ship returning contract workers to Bougainville (the largest of the North Solomon Islands) was raided by a group of men who had come on board under the pretense of trade. They killed the white captain and one "boy" belonging to his native crew, taking the other three "boys" captive—all the "boys" were from neighboring Buka Island. The captain's corpse was thrown into the sea, but the dead "boy" was sent to a friendly "tribe" for consumption. The captives were taken along for later consumption, but they managed to escape and were picked up by a ship.[88]

Another time, two white traders and three of their native employees were attacked and killed on Pak (one of the Admiralty Islands in the north of the Bismarck Archipelago). Two other employees, from New Ireland, were on a fishing trip during the attack—they saw what happened but could not help. The corpses of the killed traders were thrown into the sea, while those of the native workers were eaten. Part of the bounty were several rifles which the attackers subsequently used in various raids against neighboring peoples who were only armed with spears. While the victims of these raids were eaten, the two New Irelanders were spared because they had agreed to show the raiders how to use the rifles. Three years later they were picked up by a passing ship and reported what had happened.[89] In a third incident reported by Schnee, a trading ship was attacked on Manus, the largest of the Admiralty Islands. Captain and second mate—both white—were killed and thrown overboard, while several native crew members were killed and consumed; the rest were taken captive.[90]

Robert Robson also observes that cannibals in New Britain hesitated to eat Europeans, asserting that "white-skinned meat was ill-flavoured." Robson describes the case of a cutter belonging to the trading company of the American-Samoan businesswoman Emma Forsayth (1850–1913). In October 1880, this cutter landed near a village to collect a load of copra (dried coconut kernels). Though supposedly promised, the load was not ready, and a dispute over who was responsible turned into a deadly conflict. Four members of the cutter's crew were killed—three Europeans and a Buka Islander. Fearing vengeance, the villagers fled into the hills, taking the latter's body with them for eating, but throwing the dead Europeans into the sea. Forsayth's request to send a punitive expedition in response was turned down by the commander of a British warship who considered the Europeans responsible for the fight.[91]

Kleintitschen notes that it is doubtful whether Europeans were ever eaten in New Britain. While he does not venture an explanation of why this was so, he rejects as "fairy tale" the notion spread by some that they were considered "too salty," pointing out that salt was a sought-after delicacy.[92] Also fitting the pattern that white people could be killed but were not eaten is the end of Kleintitschen's colleague Matthäus Rascher. In August 1904, Rascher and nine other missionaries (five of them nuns) were murdered by a group of local men. The historian Paul Steffen concludes that Rascher had been over-ambitious. He had urged the people to quickly and radically change their customs, relentlessly attacking traditional religious beliefs and social structures. Finally, some of the affected decided to turn against the mission in a hopeless attempt to preserve their traditional way of life.[93]

Three or four orphan boys raised by the mission, aged from approximately three to fourteen years, were murdered as well. Several witnesses later reported that their bodies were consumed during a feast held on the mission premises to celebrate the victory over the missionaries.[94] Once more the bodies of native victims were eaten, while those of white people were not.

In Vanuatu too, "whites are very seldom eaten," as Felix Speiser observed. He was sceptical of local explanations that they "taste bad," instead vaguely explaining this restraint as "probably [due to] religious motives."[95] Schnee conjectures that the locals ascribed strong magical powers to white people because of their superior weapons and technology and might therefore have feared that such powerful magicians would, even after their death, harm those who dared to touch their bodies.[96] However, considering that the same white people were apparently unhesitatingly killed if the local situation allowed it, this hypothesis is hardly convincing.

In New Guinea, Monckton was once threatened by a group of cannibals who told him that he "was so repulsively coloured that they would not dream of eating me, but would feed me to the pigs instead."[97] In various Asian and American cultures, as well as large parts of Africa, the color white is associated with death, mourning, and illness.[98] If such associations existed in the Bismarck Archipelago and possibly other parts of Melanesia as well, it might have been the reason why people shied away from eating white persons—eating those who looked ill or more or less like walking dead must have seemed a dangerous and unhealthy proposition.

Elsewhere in the South Pacific Ocean, cases of foreigners being poached and eaten have been reported from Australia,[99] Vanuatu[100] and the neighboring Loyalty Islands,[101] as well as from the Marquesas Islands.[102] Context and motivations of such acts in these regions seem to be similar to those we have investigated in this chapter. More interesting, however, is the situation in Fiji, which reveals a distinctly different context of cannibal kidnappings. This will be the first topic of the next chapter, before we then turn to a different continent altogether.

Notes

1. On war cannibalism in the areas in the Pacific Ocean from which foreigner poaching has been reported, see Bride, *Letters from Victorian Pioneers*, 111n2, 222, 273; Howitt, *Native Tribes*, 752, 755 (both Australia); Pfeil, *Studien und Beobachtungen*, 131–32, 288; Schnee, *Bilder aus der Südsee*, 335–39 (both Bismarck Archipelago); Tautain, "Sur l'anthropophagie," 449–51 (Marquesas Islands); Garnier, *Voyage*, 146–47, 156–57, 192 (New Caledonia); Beaver, *Unexplored New Guinea*, 220, 223–24; Brown, *Pioneer-Missionary and Explorer*, 207–10 (both New Guinea); Fox, "Big Nambas Custom Texts" (Vanuatu); on Fiji, see note 1 in Chapter 12, this volume.

   For a list of sources covering war cannibalism in the Congo basin, see Chapter 4, note 39, this volume. On West Africa, see Seabrook, *Jungle Ways*, 164–66; Volz, *Reise*, 102–3 (both Liberia); Basden, *Among the Ibos*, 38–39, 105; Burns, *History of Nigeria*, 164–66; Isichei, *Igbo Worlds*, 128, 130, 261; Meek, *Northern Tribes of*

Nigeria, 54–56; Talbot, *Peoples of Southern Nigeria*, 1:343, 3:826–29, 841, 850 (all Nigeria).

2. Seligmann, *Melanesians*, 553. In this book, the author's name is spelled with a double *nn*, while elsewhere the spelling *Seligman* is used.
3. Ibid., 559, 569.
4. Ibid., 552–53.
5. F. Williams, *Orokaiva Society*, 312.
6. Ibid., 316–18.
7. Ibid., 171.
8. Which today belongs to Indonesia, while the eastern half of New Guinea and the Bismarck Archipelago are parts of Papua New Guinea.
9. Koch, *War and Peace*, 3, 13.
10. Ibid., 80–81, 151–57, 208–9, 219–24.
11. Ibid., 207.
12. Ibid., 16.
13. Seligmann, *Melanesians*, 548, 549 (quotes).
14. Beaver, *Unexplored New Guinea*, 249.
15. Andrew Cheyne (1817–1866), the British captain of a trading ship who in the 1840s traveled extensively through the South Pacific, notes that "small parties will waylay others, murder defenceless men, women, or children when fishing, and carry their bodies home to feast on" (Cheyne, *Description*, 17).
16. Stevenson, *In the South Seas*, chapter 12; Tautain, "Sur l'anthropophagie," 445, 449–51.
17. Walker, *Wanderings*, 146.
18. Monckton, *Some Experiences*, 182, 192.
19. Ibid.
20. Ibid., 290.
21. Ibid., 176, 218, 221.
22. Ibid., 221.
23. Schnee, *Bilder aus der Südsee*, 237–38, 338–39.
24. Ibid., 245, 341, 343. This observation is in agreement with the statements of William Seabrook, who voluntarily became a cannibal (corpse eater) out of curiosity (see Chapter 6, this volume).
25. Ibid., 343.
26. Hahl, *Governor*, 87.
27. Kleintitschen, *Die Küstenbewohner*, 311.
28. Rannie, *My Adventures*, 50–51.
29. Ibid., 51.
30. Ibid., 221 (Vanuatu), 271 (Bismarck), 306 (Solomon).
31. Brown, *Pioneer-Missionary and Explorer*, 201.
32. Ibid., 172.
33. Peekel, *Religion und Zauberei*, 20 (quote), 21–22.
34. Ibid., 22–23.
35. Haberberger, *Kolonialismus und Kannibalismus*, 54, 55 (quote).
36. Robson, *Queen Emma*, 147.
37. Ibid., 147–48.
38. Murray, *Papua*, 232–33.
39. Ibid., 218.

40. Walker, *Wanderings*, 45.
41. Ibid., 145.
42. See quotes in Chapter 13, this volume.
43. In Maré, the second largest of these islands, Ta'unga (ca. 1818–1898), a Christian mission teacher from the Cook Islands, once met a priestess who, together "with a few sacred friends," was given the hands of killed enemies for consumption. When he expressed his disapproval, she told him: "Oh, there is no food so sweet and savoury as that of human flesh; oh! If you did but taste it! There is nothing equal to it" (quoted in Crocombe and Crocombe, *Works of Ta'unga*, 95).
44. Brown, *Pioneer-Missionary and Explorer*, 252–53, 256, 316.
45. Powell, *Wanderings*, 118–22.
46. Ibid., 121.
47. See Chapter 13, this volume.
48. Parkinson, *Im Bismarck-Archipel*, 121–22; Pfeil, *Studien und Beobachtungen*, 76, 131.
49. Haberberger, *Kolonialismus und Kannibalismus*, 55.
50. Pfeil, *Studien und Beobachtungen*, 131.
51. Parkinson, *Im Bismarck-Archipel*, 121.
52. Seligmann, *Melanesians*, 552.
53. Ibid.
54. Beaver, *Unexplored New Guinea*, 225.
55. Parkinson, *Im Bismarck-Archipel*, 121.
56. Haberberger, *Kolonialismus und Kannibalismus*, 55.
57. Deacon and Wedgwood, "Notes on Some Islands," 496.
58. Gill, *Gems*, 123.
59. Speiser, *Ethnology of Vanuatu*, 214.
60. Ibid., 217.
61. Hagen and Pineau, "Les Nouvelles Hébrides," 327–28.
62. Speiser, *Ethnology of Vanuatu*, 217.
63. Ibid., 121.
64. Krieger, *Conversations*, 187.
65. F. Williams, *Orokaiva Society*, 172. Williams's work is based on field research done from 1923 to 1925. It seems unlikely that such practices still occurred at that time, but his informants apparently remembered how things had been in former times.
66. Monckton, *Some Experiences*, 322 (quotes), 323.
67. D. Gardner, "Anthropophagy," 34–35.
68. Ibid., 32, 34.
69. Ibid., 32.
70. Encyclopedia Britannica, "Papua New Guinea: Daily Life and Social Customs," last modified 9 May 2019, https://www.britannica.com/place/Papua-New-Guinea/Daily-life-and-social-customs.
71. Scholz, "Kannibalismus im Bismarck-Archipel."
72. Thurnwald, "Nachrichten aus Nissan," 107–8. Scholz gives fewer details and writes "Somson" instead of "Somsom," otherwise both accounts are in agreement (Scholz, "Kannibalismus im Bismarck-Archipel," 804–5, 809–10).
73. Thurnwald, "Nachrichten aus Nissan," 107–9.
74. Haberberger, *Kolonialismus und Kannibalismus*, 84–86.
75. Ibid., 88.

76. Burger, *Unter den Kannibalen*, 168 (quotes), 169.
77. Ibid., 169.
78. Kleintitschen, *Die Küstenbewohner*, 202.
79. Lüders, *Der Bismarck-Archipel*, 15–16.
80. Robson, *Queen Emma*, 106.
81. The Methodist missionary Walter Lawry describes the case of a woman who was killed, roasted, and partially eaten after she had (accidentally?) "offended [her husband] in the preparation of some food" (Lawry, *Friendly and Feejee Islands*, 94).
82. See Chapter 8, this volume.
83. Haberberger, *Kolonialismus und Kannibalismus*, 112–17.
84. Walker, *Wanderings*, 140 (quote), 141.
85. Ibid., 129.
86. Both of which then belonged to German New Guinea, while today they form the Islands Region of Papua New Guinea.
87. Schnee, *Bilder aus der Südsee*, 344–45.
88. Ibid., 127–28.
89. Ibid., 166–67.
90. Ibid., 186–87.
91. Robson, *Queen Emma*, 97, 109.
92. Kleintitschen, *Die Küstenbewohner*, 328.
93. Steffen, "Die katholischen Missionen," 355–57.
94. Rascher, *Baining*, 431.
95. Speiser, *Ethnology of Vanuatu*, 216.
96. Schnee, *Bilder aus der Südsee*, 347–48.
97. Monckton, *Some Experiences*, 182; for context, see the first section of this chapter.
98. Vanka, *International Color Guide*, 9, 15, 17, 21, 25; Van Reybrouck, *Congo*, 46.
99. Bates, *Passing*, chapter 11; Bride, *Letters from Victorian Pioneers*, 4; Lumholtz, *Among Cannibals*, 72, 176, 271, 274; Oberländer, "Die Eingeborenen," 239; Christie Palmerston, "The Diary of a Northern Pioneer," *Queensland Figaro*, 12 March 1887: 433, https://trove.nla.gov.au/newspaper/article/84120232.
100. Gill, *Gems*, 78, 89, 94, 122–23, 227; Hagen and Pineau, "Les Nouvelles Hébrides," 326–27; Prout, *Memoirs*, 388–89, 393–94; Speiser, *Ethnology of Vanuatu*, 216, 218; Speiser, *Südsee, Urwald, Kannibalen*, 51, 55, 58; see also the section "Patriarchal Patterns" in this chapter.
101. See notes 15 and 43 in this chapter.
102. See note 16 in this chapter.

CHAPTER 12
FOREIGNER POACHING IN FIJI AND CENTRAL AFRICA

Fiji: Cannibalistic Feasting and Christian Abolitionism

Like the Bismarck Archipelago, Fiji is an archipelago of numerous islands situated in Melanesia. In certain parts of this archipelago, cannibalism was widespread not only in warfare[1] but also, among those who could afford it, in times of peace, with kidnapped foreigners frequently mentioned as victims. It would be wrong, however, to consider the cannibal customs of both these regions as largely identical. In New Guinea and the Bismarck Archipelago, the capture and consumption of foreigners seems to have been motivated largely by convenience and a desire to get rid of potential enemies—in Fiji, on the other hand, prestige might have been the most important factor.

John Elphinstone Erskine (1806–1887), a British admiral who in 1849 visited the region on a private trip, tells that a few weeks before his visit, "400 men, women, and children [known] as the Butoni, had arrived" in Bau Island from neighboring Viti Levu, the largest island in the archipelago. They brought a large amount of tribute with them—at that time, Bau, though a small island, was the main power in the region and able to extract tribute from most of the inhabitants of Viti Levu and other nearby islands.[2] To furnish "the best" for the "first breakfast" of the visitors, "a tributary town on Viti Levu" was obliged "to provide one or two human bodies." Accordingly, "two poor wretches were entrapped on a small island" and delivered to Bau, "where they were slaughtered and eaten."[3]

But this was not enough—while the visitors stayed, they had to be regaled. For another "breakfast" (Erskine does not say whether it was held the next day or later) the chiefs of a recently subjugated city in Rewa (a region in the southeast of Viti Levu) were therefore asked to supply human bodies. After they failed expectations by delivering "one man only," one of the chiefs of Bau—"Navindi, the . . . chief of the fishermen, whose duty it is more particularly to procure human flesh"—decided to take over. But his first attempt at ambushing a few people in Viti Levu failed, and the Bauans started to fear

Map 12.1. Fiji, with islands and regions mentioned in the text shown. By the author, based on a map from FreeVectorMaps.com (https://freevectormaps.com/fiji/FJ-EPS-02-0001).

that they might be forced to "have recourse to their own resources; that is, to slaughter some of their own slaves to furnish the Butoni banquet, a sacrifice of course to be avoided if possible."[4]

But this fear was groundless, since a second ambush, laid in the mangroves near a village on the main island, where "the women are accustomed to come to the coast to pick shell-fish for food," turned out a full success. Navindi's men captured fourteen women, while one or two others were "clubbed to death" trying to escape. "One man, attempting to save either his wife or daughter," was captured as well. Soon after, a chief who had converted to Christianity informed the mission station on neighboring Viwa (another small island north of Bau) of what had happened. The missionaries were on a trip to another island, but their wives, "Mrs. Lyth and Mrs. Calvert," decided to try and save the lives of the captives. Together with the Christian chief, they went by canoe to Bau. Upon their arrival, they heard "the shrieks of two women then being slaughtered for the day's entertainment"—a remark that suggests that about two of the captives might have been killed every day (or every few days) to provide meat for the visitors.[5]

Undeterred, the three hurried to "the house of old Tanoa," the principal chief. The Christian chief appealed to Tanoa after gifting the latter two whale's teeth—"a necessary offering on preferring a petition to a chief." After consulting with Navindi, Tanoa decided: "Those who are dead, are dead; those who are alive shall live." But the majority of the captives was dead. Of the fifteen ambushed (one of them a man), "ten had been killed and eaten, one had died of her wounds," and one girl had been claimed as a slave by the principal wife of Tanoa's son Thakombau. Three others remained, who were handed over to the petitioners and taken to the mission station.[6]

Erskine, who heard of these events from the missionaries, adds that their account was "corroborated by the testimony of many of the white residents here."[7] James Calvert (1813–1892), the husband of one of the heroines, left a shorter account of the incident. His version is written in a more dramatic language, and he claims that one additional captive was saved; otherwise, both accounts are quite similar.[8] Calvert also reports a similar, smaller case that took place in Rewa: "A party who went in search of a victim to feast the people employed in building the King's house, killed a Christian woman while out fishing." Hearing what had happened, the local missionary hurried to the landing place where the canoe of the killers had just arrived and "pushing his way through the crowd who exulted at the prize, found the body lying naked in the bottom of the canoe." With the king's permission, the missionary claimed the body and took it to the mission station for a Christian burial.[9]

Calvert's colleague and coauthor Thomas Williams (1815–1891) adds that cases of persons being kidnapped "on purpose to be eaten" were not rare, which he saw as proof that "this flesh is in high repute." He writes that "one of the last bodies which I saw offered to a Chief was thus obtained [through kidnapping] for the special entertainment of the distinguished visitor," and that, in cases which had a happier end, he had "conversed with those who had escaped, severely wounded, from an attempt to steal them, as a supply for a forthcoming feast."[10]

David Cargill (1809–1843), another Wesleyan missionary who arrived in Fiji in the 1830s, also observed that victims for cannibal feasts were frequently kidnapped. "The natives . . . kidnap men, women and children to glut their appetite for human flesh," he wrote in his diary.[11]

The reports of kings and chiefs (terms often used interchangeably in the sources) in which they agree, under pressure from Christian missionaries, to free prisoners or at least give up dead bodies for burial indicate a society torn between different value systems. In the Christian understanding, cannibalism was wrong and evil, but traditionally, serving human flesh to one's guests and helpers (such as the builders working for the king) had been a matter of prestige for those powerful enough to do so.

In Bau and a few other regions, cannibal meals were apparently held fairly frequently before the missionaries managed to discourage the practice. Mary Davis Wallis, the wife of an American captain who accompanied her husband on his extensive journeys during the 1840s,[12] heard from a man who had spent two years on the island "that dead bodies were brought to Bau as often as twice, and sometimes three times in a week"; once divided and cooked, they were distributed for consumption. "If they had more than could be devoured in Bau, portions were sent to other towns."[13]

Cannibal practices were so common that even the missionaries, though trying to abolish them, could not help getting used to them: "Cannibalism soon lost its dreadful novelty, and began to be regarded as a matter of course," Calvert remembers.[14] Even missionaries and other travelers who visited Bau for just a short time saw how cooked human bodies were taken out of earth ovens or how human body parts were prepared for consumption: "Two human bodies were in the ovens" when Mr. Cross, another Wesleyan missionary, arrived in Bau in 1838.[15] Three years later, his colleague Thomas J. Jaggar noted briefly in his diary: "Visited Bau—whilst there a man been roasted."[16] And a man who made just a few short visits to the island wrote that on his "first visit, I saw them opening an oven, and taking a cooked human body out of it; second visit, limbs of a body preparing for being baked."[17]

In Rewa, such sights were common as well. Calvert claims that "bodies were frequently brought to Rewa for cannibal purposes, where, just opposite the Mission premises, they were dragged, washed, and abused with every obscene indignity, and then cut up or torn to pieces and cooked."[18] As Wallis had noted as well, bodies were exchanged as gifts between the principal islands and regions. In May 1841, "there arrived [in Rewa] the bodies of twenty persons who had been entrapped and killed by the young Chief of Viwa, and by Thakombau," the son of Bau's paramount chief.[19] Jaggar notes as well that people were kidnapped and killed for this purpose.[20]

Prestige and Human Tributes in Fiji

While there can be little doubt that cannibal meals were quite common in Bau and Rewa, it would be wrong to consider these two places as typical for Fiji as a whole. Bau was the dominant power in the archipelago, and the paramount chief of Rewa was the leader of the Burebasaga Confederacy, the largest alliance of Fijian rulers.[21] The leading chiefs of these regions were the most powerful men in the whole archipelago—and the regular feasts and gifts of human flesh were an expression of that power. They could order people in other regions to be kidnapped with impunity and they could request the chiefs of lesser regions to provide some people for consumption. In other regions, human flesh was eaten as well, at least during wartime—but a more or less regular access to human flesh even outside of warfare was likely the privilege of the most powerful few, as well as of allies, subordinates, and friends with whom they decided to share it.

Those unable to capture outsiders from neighboring communities might have been forced to give up some of their own community members if human tributes were expected. "More than one white man has seen the canoe of Tanoa, after a condescending visit to Ovolau, returning to Bau, with the bodies of infants, offerings from the people of Levuka, ostentatiously hanging at the yard-arms," writes Erskine.[22] Ovalau is another island near the east coast of Viti Levu (and Levuka its largest settlement)—much larger than Bau, but its inhabitants apparently considered it wise (or necessary) to contribute human "offerings" for the ovens of the more powerful neighbor.

To understand the "yard-arms" one must know that Fijian canoes—also known as *drua*—were much larger than the vessels typically called canoes today. They could be more than thirty meters long and they often had two parallel hulls (like a catamaran), a mast, and a large triangular sail.[23] That children were hung from the mastheads or other exposed parts of the rigging has also been reported for canoes returning from successful war campaigns—in such cases (maybe not in the case of offerings) it seems that the victims were usually still alive at the start of the trip. In November 1839, Cargill saw a large number of ships delivering war captives to Rewa: "About 30 *living* children were hoisted up to the mastheads as flags of triumph. The motion of the canoes while sailing soon killed the helpless creatures and silenced their piercing cries." Their bodies, as well as those of supposedly more than two hundred other captives, were subsequently "roasted and eaten."[24]

Thomas Williams likewise notes that "children have been hung by their feet from the mast-head of a canoe, to be dashed to death, as the rollings of the vessel swung them heavily against the mast."[25] Thomas Jaggar describes the same cruel custom.[26] According to the English-Australian missionary and ethnologist Lorimer Fison (1832–1907), the children exposed and killed in this manner were mocked as "birds of the sail."[27]

Erskine notes that the "ostentatious" shipment of human offerings from Ovolau to Bau was just one instance of a tradition in which "children [were] offered by the people of their own tribe to propitiate a powerful chief," who used them to furnish a "banquet." Since no one who had any choice in the matter would have given up their own children, it is certainly no accident that he writes "tribe" rather than "their own family"—orphans and young members of poor or unpopular families likely stood the highest risk of losing their lives at such occasions.[28]

In other cases, those who were given away for consumption had reached adulthood or at least adolescence. Williams writes that "young women have been placed alive beside a pile of wood given by the Kandavuans to the Chiefs of Rewa. I knew also of a man being taken alive to a Chief on Vanua Levu, and given him to eat."[29] (Vanua Levu is the second largest island of the archipelago, while Kadavu—sometimes spelled Kandavu—is the fourth largest one.) John Jackson, an Englishman who spent several years in Fiji and was later hired by Erskine as an interpreter,[30] once secured himself a "wife" by liberating a young woman who would otherwise have been given away together with a heap of provisions—of which, he suspected, she was meant to be a part:

> We all went out to look at the provisions collected in a heap, which were raw, and to my surprise I saw a young virgin sitting on the top of the yams, oiled all over, her skin decorated . . . with leaves. . . . It struck me instantly what she was intended for, because I had been told that when they give the provisions away raw to any great personage the animals are always given away alive to correspond; and having already had proofs of their notorious cannibalism, I was quite certain she was to be cooked with the yams. . . . I began therefore to upbraid them in a very abusive manner . . . and swore the first that offered to butcher the woman I would shoot.[31]

He then turned to Bonavidongo, the chief with whom he was traveling, and complained "that I had been so long with him, and had not been offered a wife, and that it was more than I could stand to see him eating nice young women who were so desirable in my eyes alive, and if he did not save the girl's life I would leave him altogether." When the locals merely laughed at him, he became so "exasperated" that he "rushed up the yam heap and laid hold of the girl by the hand and hauled her down, and then led her up to a tree, sticking my back against it, and cocked my musket . . . , swearing I would shoot the first one that came towards me." Still laughing, they said "they were sorry to see me put myself in such a rage, adding, 'Watima, watima' (she is your wife, she is your wife)."[32]

This happened in Natewa Bay, a large bay on Vanua Levu. Whether or not the "virgin" would really have been eaten (considering the accounts by Williams and others, it does not seem implausible), she knew what was expected of her in her new role: "She remained with me all the time I stayed in Nateva, and proved very faithful and grateful for my saving her life."[33] Once Jackson left Natewa Bay, it seems he left her behind.

In this case and in the cases mentioned by Williams it is unclear whether the victims were kidnapped foreigners, captured enemies, or community members of those who handed them over—but, in any case they were human tributes or gifts (the distinction might have been rather subtle) given to the powerful.

But why did the powerful like to regale their followers and guests with human flesh? Two reasons are mentioned in the sources: on the one hand, meat in general was a rare luxury—and human flesh was considered even tastier than other kinds of meat; on the other hand, being eaten was seen as deeply humiliating—a sign of inferiority. Being able to eat others, or having human bodies at one's disposal, might in turn have been a sign of superiority and power.

Figure 12.1. Thakombau, the paramount chief of Bau. From Thomas Williams and James Calvert's *Fiji and the Fijians* (New York: D. Appleton, 1860), frontispiece.

The first motive came up when Erskine invited Thakombau (the chief's son and later paramount chief of Bau) on board his ship. He used the opportunity to harshly criticize the local cannibal customs in a speech translated by Calvert. While Thakombau listened politely, at some point he murmured some angry words which Calvert later translated as: "it was all very well for us who had plenty of beef . . . to remonstrate, but they had no beef but men."[34] Calvert himself quotes the remark as follows: "You foreigners have salt beef to eat when you sail about; we have no beef, and therefore make use of human flesh."[35]

Erskine notes that edible animals were rare on the archipelago and that people were limited to a largely vegetarian diet, except "at feasts and on great occasions."[36] Fison adds that "the common people rarely taste flesh meat of any kind, but live almost entirely on a vegetable diet." Pigs, the only edible mammals (besides people), were "reserved almost exclusively for the chiefs and their favoured henchmen." He concludes that "the Scarcity of Animal Food" might well have been "the primary cause of cannibalism."[37]

But the preference for human flesh was not merely due to a lack of alternatives—several sources indicate that, from a culinary viewpoint, pigs were considered inferior to people. The Methodist missionary Walter Lawry (1793–1859), who visited Fiji in 1847, calls it "remarkable" that many Fijians told him "that the flesh of human beings is really very good, and they like it"—clearly preferring it to pork even when both were available, as he notes elsewhere.[38] In the early twentieth century, Wilfrid Walker met three Fijian men who frankly told him that they had eaten human flesh and remembered it as "far better than pig."[39] A few decades earlier, Alfred St. Johnston, another British traveler, had noted: "So delicious was human flesh considered, that the highest praise that they could give to other food was to say, 'It is as good as *bakolo.*'"[40]

Bokola (or *bakola, bakolo*) was the term used for "a dead body which is to be eaten" and for the flesh of such a body. Calling a living person *bokola* or suggesting that one of their ancestors had ended as an "inmate of the oven," were deeply offensive insults, as Fison notes.[41] The term *bokola* has survived as an insult even in contemporary Fiji, though cannibal practices have long ceased.[42] An analogous insult was used in the Duke of York Islands (part of the Bismarck Archipelago), according to George Brown: "Their language contains separate words for a corpse (*minat*), and for a body to be eaten (*wirua*). One of the most abusive words which can be used is to designate a man by the latter term."[43]

Being eaten meant that you had lost out, that others had overpowered you and were able to exploit and destroy you for their own purposes; it was not only a terrible end, but also humiliating for the victim and their relatives and descendants. Having human bodies at one's disposal—whether by subduing and killing enemies and strangers or by forcing others to offer you human tributes—was a very visible way of demonstrating one's superiority. The historians Korn, Radice, and Hawes observe that "the supply of bakola to a town was, in a sense, the *raison d'être* of a chief"—an undeniable proof that the community was stronger and more powerful than those around it.[44]

Maybe to show off further and leave no doubt about who was for dinner, bodies were sometimes roasted whole and decorated in a way that made them seem almost alive—according to Fison, such bodies were called "trussed frogs":

> The limbs having been arranged in the posture which it is intended they shall assume, banana leaves are wrapped round them to prevent the flesh falling off in the possible event of over-baking, and the whole body is carefully bound with the *walai* [a tough runner used as string or rope], so that the desired posture may be preserved. A hole of sufficient size is then dug in the earth, and filled with dry wood, which is set on fire. When it is well kindled, a number of stones, about the size of a man's fist, are thrown into it; and when the firewood is burnt down to a mass of glowing embers, some of the heated stones are lifted nimbly by tongs made of bent withes, and thrust within the dead man's body. The fire in the hole is then raked level and covered with large leaves, on which the body is carefully laid: the hot stones are arranged around and over it; it is covered with banana leaves, and then the dug out earth is shovelled back upon it and heaped above it. Presently the mound swells and rises; little cracks appear, whence issue jets of steam diffusing a savoury odour; and in due time, of which the Fijians are excellent judges, the culinary process is complete. The earth is then cautiously removed, the body lifted out, its wrappings taken off, its face painted, a wig or a turban placed upon its

head, and there we have a 'trussed frog' in all its unspeakable hideousness, staring at us with wide open, prominent, lack-lustre eyes. There is no burning or roasting: the body is cooked in its own steam, and the features are so little disturbed by the process that the dead man can almost always be recognised by those who knew him when he was alive."[45]

Several accounts claim that victims were sometimes still alive when they were put into an earth oven[46]—it is unclear whether this was deliberate torture or whether (like apparently in parts of New Guinea)[47] it was motivated by a belief that it would improve the taste of the flesh.

While many of those killed and subsequently eaten in war campaigns were male warriors, Erskine notes that the victims of kidnapping were "generally females"[48]—maybe because they regularly had to leave the security of their villages to gather food. Lawry states that "one way of obtaining food is to lie in ambush, and seize upon females, as they return with water, or from bathing." He adds that groups of fishers were also frequently attacked, clubbed to death, and eaten[49]—while he does not mention the gender of these fishers, notes from elsewhere[50] indicate that they might often have been women. When people were given as more or less voluntary "offerings," it seems that the victims were usually children or young women. They might have been considered the least important members of the community—those the male decision makers were most willing to give up, if a human victim was required of them.

Culinary preferences might have played a role as well: the men "interview[ed]" by Walker assured him "that women and children tasted best"; Erskine observes that "the flesh of women [is] considered more tender than that of men" and other missionaries and travelers agree.[51] Such preferences, however, where relative rather than absolute. Remembering that "I have seen the grey-headed and children of both sexes devoted to the oven," Williams concludes: "Cannibalism does not confine its selection to one sex, or a particular age."[52]

Because of the high prestige and supposedly superior taste of human flesh, many members of less powerful communities likely craved to eat it as well, but for them, opportunities to do so will have been rare. One occasional opportunity in coastal communities were foreign castaways who shipwrecked at their shores. Like in New Guinea and the Bismarck Archipelago[53] and in other Melanesian regions such as Vanuatu,[54] it seems that castaways were killed and eaten almost as a matter of course.[55] Mary Davis Wallis notes about a specific case:

> They were not enemies, but such is their custom. If the canoe had arrived in safety, the lives of the visitors would have been spared, and they would have welcomed them; but when a canoe is cast away, the natives say that it is sent them by their gods, and as they are fond of something to relish their vegetables once in awhile, the flesh does not come amiss.[56]

It also seems that foreigners who had voluntarily come into a community but were not accepted by the locals could be treated as a source of meat. The Wesleyan missionary Joseph Waterhouse (1828–1881) tells that a woman had run away to a different town after a quarrel with her husband. The friends of her husband asked that she be sent back, strengthening their request by giving a whale's tooth. "The townspeople then assembled and deliberated on the case, and decided that they would *not* send her home, but *kill her for their Sunday's meat!* Whereon they put her to death, cooked her body, and ate it the following day, which was the Sabbath."[57] Apparently the missionary was especially annoyed because he got the impression that the people had mixed their cannibal customs with the Christian tradition of a Sunday roast. Teaching new values was not always easy.

Central Africa

Travelers and foreigners were also at risk of being "poached" and eaten in certain parts of central and western Africa. The following account will focus on central Africa—especially, but not only, the Congo basin, from which a large part of the reports of foreigner poaching in Africa originates.

Camille-Aimé Coquilhat, the founder of Bangala Station, heard that cannibal meals had been quite common in the area before the arrival of the Europeans. While slaves could be killed for consumption, many of the victims were captured enemies or foreigners. In June 1885, two young Bangala soldiers told him that, before his arrival, "it was rare that they spent eight days without attacking either some village or some passing canoes to procure human flesh."[58]

Similar practices are reported from the Ubangi River. Herbert Ward writes that "every village seems to be continually at war with its neighbors." While villages were fortified and secured by "stockades of sharpened poles," individuals or small groups who approached the river were in constant danger of being snatched by warriors "prowling about in their large war-canoes, making excursions to parts known to be frequented by small bands of hunters and fishermen, who are easily vanquished, bound, and, in due course, killed and eaten."[59] Edward Glave likewise states that fishers surprised by warriors from neighboring communities were often "spear[ed]" and "devour[ed]."[60]

According to Maurice Musy, such attacks on people with a foreign and potentially enemy background were a kind of low-intensity warfare. He observes that, while open attacks on hostile villages were relatively rare, the usual style of warfare was "to steal a few isolated men" belonging to enemy communities "and eat them."[61]

Farther east, near the Mongala River, Guy Burrows met a chief who boasted that he and his family had eaten dozens of captives belonging to "tribes of the interior." Some of the eaten, he explained when questioned, had been individuals spotted alone "in the neighbouring bush," while others had been captured in raids on enemies' villages made when the latter "were attacking some other tribe," leaving mostly women, children, and old men behind as easy targets.[62]

It seems that any foreigner was a legitimate target, as all were considered potentially hostile. Burrows observes that, while cannibalism was officially condemned by the colonial government, it was secretly considered quite useful because it discouraged native soldiers from deserting. He notes that soldiers were deliberately stationed far away from their villages, "and the bush is no place for a stranger in tropical Africa. It would merely mean that sooner or later they would be killed by some village, and a grand feast would follow." Women captured in punitive expeditions and forced to work on Free State plantations had to stay for the same reason: "If they attempted to wander home there would be an end to them, for they would sooner or later be killed in the bush and eaten by one or other of the cannibal tribes through whose district they would have to pass."[63]

Occasionally soldiers nevertheless tried their luck, but at least sometimes the outcome was as predicted. Referring to people who live on the northern shore of the Congo River, Ward writes that "it was these populous tribes that caught the Houssas last year, who deserted [Captain] Deane. . . . They ate five and sold four back to the State."[64] Soldiers employed by the French Congo did not necessarily fare better. In a letter written in late 1889, Musy reports that five men had deserted from a colonial post near the Ubangi River. After about a week, three of them had voluntarily returned to the post; a fourth had been captured and returned by the inhabitants of a friendly village. "The fifth [however] was eaten by the natives who took him."[65]

The same fate expected some of the soldiers and porters fleeing from Henry Morton Stanley's last expedition. While forced to stay behind in a village on the Aruwimi River as a member of the so-called rear guard,[66] Ward met Nasaro bin Sef, a Swahilo-Arab slave and ivory trader. The latter gave him "a Remington rifle . . . found by his men in a native house when raiding a village" for slaves. Ward suspects that the weapon "must have belonged to a deserter" from Stanley's part of the expedition, explaining that "the natives . . . confess having captured and eaten five of seven [deserters] who were trying to get down the river in canoes."[67]

Three months later, in June 1888, the rear guard had started to move, attempting to catch up with Stanley. Now several of their own soldiers tried to escape, with a predictable outcome recorded by Ward's companion James Jameson, the antihero of the "horrible Jameson affair"[68]: "The natives tell Muni Somai that some of them belonging to another village have caught and eaten three of the deserters."[69]

There was, it seems, no clear distinction between the kidnapping and consumption of isolated individuals belonging to hostile groups and attacks against unknown foreigners from farther away, as any foreigner was considered a potential enemy. This corresponds to reports from the Bismarck Archipelago, which document similar attitudes, but it contrasts with the situation in New Guinea, where at least the same number of enemies had to be eaten in revenge for slayed community members, while foreigners from unknown or weak groups could be used as food without fear of reprisals.[70]

A similar lack of such a distinction has also been reported for the Fang (or Fan) people who live west of the Congo basin, near the Crystal Mountains (today shared between Equatorial Guinea and Gabon). Albert Bennett, a missionary and medical doctor, found that the Fang still practiced cannibalism when he worked in the area in the late 1890s. He notes that enemies killed in war as well as "members of other tribes waylaid and killed while journeying in the bush" were among the victims. There was no strict separation between these two methods of procuring victims, as any outsider was treated as an enemy. Women belonging to enemy populations were shot and killed on sight when encountered outside the safety of their own towns. "It is always *safe* to shoot a woman because she cannot shoot back," a Fang man told him with satisfaction. In a village, Bennett saw a captive teenage boy who, as he later learned, had been killed and eaten shortly after his visit.[71]

About twenty years earlier, Oskar Lenz (1848–1925) had visited the area on behalf of the *Deutsche Gesellschaft zur Erforschung Äquatorial-Afrikas* (German Association for the Exploration of Equatorial Africa). During his stay, he saved a man who had been attacked by a group of Fang:

> Suddenly we heard a human sound on the left river bank. Carefully we approached and discovered a Galloa man with numerous gunshot wounds in a completely helpless condition. He was unable to move ahead and would certainly have died quickly if we had not found him. We took him in our boat and learned from him that he had been traveling towards the Apinshi together with a compatriot. But their small canoe was attacked by three Fans. They killed his colleague and took the body with them to eat. He had managed to swim to the shore, but their shots had hurt him so severely that he could not get up any more.[72]

It seems that the attacked men were random victims, as no specific enmity between Fang and Galloa has been reported.

Around the Kasai River, insufficiently armed foreigners were considered fair game as well. The Free State captain Sidney Hinde tells of an incident where several dozen prisoners of war had escaped. He asked the chief of the local Songye people (Basongo) to find and return them, but got the reply "that, with the exception of one prisoner, they had all been eaten." The survivor, who was promptly sent back to Hinde, turned out to be "a little boy-servant of mine who had been persuaded to run away by some of the deserters." The boy said that "by a lucky chance . . . he had found a friend in the village" and had therefore been spared. But he had witnessed what had happened to the other fugitives and "his descriptions of what he had seen at the time were quite sickening." As compensation for the eaten runaways, the chief sent Hinde "thirty-seven slaves."[73] Apparently, he had concluded that they had been Hinde's slaves and that he had to make up for their loss.

That people could be "poached" and eaten in this region is confirmed by Melville Hilton-Simpson, who claims that the Bankutu people (who live east of the Songye) "actually stalk and shoot men for food as other natives hunt animals, and this despite the fact that their country teems with game."[74]

David Livingstone was one of the first Europeans to set foot into the Congo basin. In 1870, sometime after his arrival in the Maniema region, he heard of several people who had been killed and eaten upon venturing too far from home:

> It transpired that Kandahara, brother of old Moenékuss, whose village is near this, killed three women and a child, and that a trading man came over from Kasangangayé, and was murdered too, for no reason but to eat his body. . . . The people over a hill N.N.E. of this killed a person out hoeing; if a cultivator is alone, he is almost sure of being slain.[75]

The original version from Livingstone's handwritten journal leaves no doubt that the women and the child were likewise killed for consumption: "It transpired from Monanyembo's statements that old Kandawara—in addition to the trader from Kasangangazi—killed three women and a child for no other reason than to eat the bodies."[76]

The original journal also reports cases of cannibalism motivated by revenge and of slave eating that are not mentioned in the printed edition compiled after Livingstone's death:

> A very fine fair woman far gone in pregnancy was killed close to our camp by the sons of Moenekuss because she belonged to a chief who killed their elder brother. Her blood stained all the path—and her body was hid in the forest for a feast. Another slave was killed and dismembered for the same purpose.[77]

A few months later, Livingstone heard of another cannibal killing: "Moenembegg, the most intelligent of the two sons of Moenékuss . . . told us that a man was killed and eaten a few miles from this yesterday: hunger was the reason assigned." Livingstone, who had earlier noted that "the soil is excessively rich, and the people, although isolated by old feuds that are never settled, cultivate largely," found this motive unconvincing. Instead, he comments: "The love of high meat is the only reason I know for their cannibalism."[78]

Similar practices existed among several Zande clans in the northeast of the Congo basin. Filiberto Gero learned from an Amadi informant that his people once liked to capture and eat members of the neighboring Babukur clan. Others of Gero's informants agreed, remembering that members of several clans—Amadi, Adhuga, and Apambia—used to kill and eat unprotected strangers they spotted outside of settlements.[79] They told him that the victims were often women and children from neighboring groups who had ventured too far from home while gathering firewood or fetching drinking water—such victims were targeted not only because they were easier to overpower than adult men, but also for culinary reasons.[80] Spotted strangers were killed by shooting them with poisoned arrows or smashing their heads with a club. In colonial times, when cannibalism could no longer be practiced openly, those who caught a human victim spent days in the forest while consuming the flesh; the victim's fat was taken home in a pot to be used as a cooking ingredient and dressing.[81]

The German explorer Adolf Friedrich, Duke of Mecklenburg, and the English anthropologist E. E. Evans-Pritchard likewise observed that outsiders belonging to foreign tribes or clans were sometimes killed and consumed among the Zande. Adolf Friedrich states that, when he visited the area around 1910, human flesh was still a "favourite food" among the Apambia and that "any member of another tribe who ventured too near their mountainous dwellings fell a victim to cannibalism."[82] According to Evans-Pritchard, most of those eaten among the Zande had been killed enemies and convicted criminals, but from time to time "a fat Buguru, a member of a neighbouring and subject foreign people and a man more or less without the law, was slain and eaten."[83]

A rare survivor's account has been recorded by the missionary Josef Fräßle, who was stationed near Basoko, where the Aruwimi joins the Congo. One day, Fräßle spotted a young boy running out of the forest towards the mission station, his skin bloody from the thorns of the jungle, his body covered in dirt. The boy, who might have been about seven, begged for protection. "Sir, down there in the woods, far behind the last huts," he exclaimed, "there they're eating my brother Kitibo. . . . They have slaughtered him like an antelope; they have cut his throat and put him on the fire, and now they're eating him."[84]

Asked to tell his story, the boy said that he and his twin brother had been orphans living near the other shore of the Congo River.[85] After their father had died of an illness eight months earlier, their mother had been sold into slavery by his heir. The boys, forced to take care of themselves, often went into the forest to collect food. While capturing crabs, they were surprised by eight men from Basoko who seized them, tied their hands behind their backs and took them to their canoe on the Congo. They traveled downriver for some time, later steering into a side arm (possibly the Aruwimi). When night fell, they tied their young captives to two trees and kindled a large fire.[86]

> Then they came to us and inspected us. . . . "This one," they said at last, "we'll take first; he has more fat than his brother." They untied my Kitibo

> and dragged him towards the fireplace. Both of us cried and screamed; my brother struggled with all his strength. But what can a child do against big men, and the forest has no ears for the voice of a child. Sir, they threw my brother to the ground, I saw it and I screamed, and all eight of them crouched around him, fixing his hands and feet, and then they cut his throat. I heard my Kitibo, my dear brother, groan, groan like a dying antelope. His groans became slower and weaker, and then he was dead. My brother was dead. My soul broke in pain! They carved him up and put his flesh into their pots. "This one we'll eat here," they said, "and the other one we'll smoke afterwards."[87]

Animated by a desperate fear, the boy managed to bring one of the lianas with which he was bound to his mouth and ultimately bit through it. He slipped away while the men were busy cooking his brother. After running for hours through the forest, he finally reached the safety of the mission.[88] If the boy's account is accurate, the children had been caught near their own village by a group of men who lived more than a day's journey away. Why the kidnappers ended up in their proximity is not known—they might have stalked their village in a revenge mission, they might have been deliberately "hunting" for people, or they might have been travelers looking for provisions and deciding that the children would do.

From Nigeria, an oral account likewise indicates that, at the end of the nineteenth century, children spotted outside alone were at risk of "being kidnapped and either killed and eaten or sold away [as slaves] or sacrificed to one god or the other"; travelers faced the same risk.[89] Several other accounts also report that foreigners and lonely individuals belonging to hostile communities were often kidnapped and slaughtered for food.[90] Cases of foreigner poaching in the nineteenth and early twentieth centuries are also documented for an area ranging approximately from western Ivory Coast to Sierra Leone.[91]

On the Origins of Foreigner Poaching

The oldest known source mentioning foreigner poaching in Africa likewise refers not to central, but to western Africa. The Andalusian historian Al-Bakri (ca. 1014–1094) mentions a "kingdom called Damdam, the people of which eat anyone who falls into their hands." The *Akhbar al-zaman,* a collection of facts and anecdotes about the known world written around the start of the eleventh century in Egypt, also mentions this kingdom, simply stating that its inhabitants "eat men." Both these Arab sources locate the kingdom on the western bank of the Niger River, somewhere downriver of Kawkaw (an old name for Gao in today's Mali).[92] These early accounts do not necessarily mean that foreigner poaching in West Africa is older than in Central Africa. Rather, Arab travelers at that time occasionally reached Western, but not Central African regions. Much time would pass until Europeans would reach either region.

Neither for Africa nor for Melanesia is there direct evidence revealing how and why the practice of capturing and consuming foreigners emerged—all accounts refer to the custom as already well-established, if not under siege and disappearing. As pointed out earlier, the practice only seems to have existed in areas where war cannibalism occurred as well, indicating that it might have been a descendant of the latter practice. Indeed, the boundaries between war cannibalism and foreigner poaching are blurred because a state of hostility between neighboring peoples usually prevailed in the regions from which such practices have been reported; killing and eating members of hostile groups might thus have been a part of ongoing low-intensity war campaigns, as Musy concluded.[93]

In regions where any unknown foreigner might potentially have meant trouble—conceivably, they might have been spies for groups who planned an attack or raid—it also seems to have been quite common to treat such foreigners as potential enemies. This might explain why in regions where war cannibalism was already common, foreigners from unknown groups were subjected to the same treatment as killed or captured enemies.

Nevertheless, while suspicions of foreigners as potential enemies might have helped to establish such practices, the practice sometimes spread beyond such origins. The killing and consumption of castaways, reported from various Melanesian islands, was hardly due to a fear of what these shipwrecked foreigners might bring—rather, they seem to have been considered suitable victims because they had been cut off from their home communities and their consumption was unlikely to trigger revenge. Such acts seem to have been driven by convenience and tradition, not by fear and certainly not by hatred.

This corresponds with Charles Gabriel Seligman's observation that in New Guinea revenge-driven cannibalism was clearly distinguished from "unpaid score[s]": the killing and consumption of castaways and strangers from faraway or weak communities whose deaths were considered unlikely to trigger a revenge. Such killings, he notes, did not have to be motivated—since they were unlikely to hurt the community, "the desire for a favourite food" was considered sufficient explanation. The lives of strangers did not matter; therefore their death was not considered a matter of moral concern.[94]

The British writer Lady Dorothy Mills observed a similar attitude when traveling through Liberia in the 1920s. She learned that both war cannibalism and foreigner poaching had been common until four or five years earlier: "The victims were generally prisoners taken in the innumerable little internecine wars, or unwary travellers, generally of another tribe." Twice she met Kpelle men who freely "admitted having eaten human flesh" and who "spoke of the present prohibition with regret and utterly without shame or real consciousness of wrongdoing"[95] People knew that it was now forbidden to kill and eat enemies and foreigners, but at least for some of them this was merely a rule imposed from above—morally, the fate of strangers was not a concern, and overpowering and killing enemies or (possibly armed) travelers might even have been a proud accomplishment.

The fate of foreign-born women and children in New Guinea and the Bismarck Archipelago[96] indicates that the circle of persons who mattered was very limited. Even those who had lived in a community for years could be exploited as a source of meat if convenience, a desire for revenge, or the need for a precious gift made it opportune to do so. Only those born into a community, it seems, were truly safe.

How well does the Obeyesekere conjecture—that cannibalism, except possibly as practiced in the context of religious sacrificial ceremonies, emerged only as a result of interactions with Westerners—fit the evidence of foreigner poaching? Quite badly, one must say. Since most of the evidence was indeed recorded by Westerners, our insight into earlier times remains very limited. However, none of the sources gives any indication that the practice was of recent origin; and oral statements such as recorded by Seligman and Coquilhat suggest that foreigner poaching was practiced at least in some areas before interactions with Europeans intensified. That foreigner poaching in West Africa is mentioned in an Arab source from the eleventh century—centuries before Europeans started to trade with these regions—is also hard to reconcile with the Obeyesekere conjecture. Moreover, there is little or no evidence that foreigner poaching was related to or associated with religious ceremonies—indeed, both Seligman and Simon Haberberger explicitly note that the practice did not have any magical or spiritual meaning.[97]

Notes

1. On war cannibalism in Fiji, see Erskine, *Journal*, 192, 197, 257–60, 272, 284, 290–92, 321, 390–91, 436–38, 446–47; Jaggar, *Unto the Perfect Day*, 1, 27, 37, 43, 52, 57, 59, 70, 74–76, 87, 89, 110–11; Korn, Radice, and Hawes, *Cannibal*, chapter 4; Lockerby, *Journal*, 42–45, 57–59, 108, 171–74, 195–97, 210; Wallis, *Life in Feejee* (numerous references); T. Williams and Calvert, *Fiji* (numerous references).
2. Erskine, *Journal*, 180.
3. Ibid., 181.
4. Ibid., 181–82.
5. Ibid., 182–83.
6. Ibid., 183.
7. Ibid., 180.
8. T. Williams and Calvert, *Fiji*, 436–38. Calvert writes that "Thakombau's chief wife and Ngavindi's wife had already secured the life and liberty of two of the victims," implying that they might have done so because of the influence of the mission (ibid., 438). In Erskine's version, Thakombau's principal wife claimed one of the captives as a slave, while the wife of Navindi (Ngavindi) is not mentioned at all. In Calvert's account, the role of the Christian chief is downplayed and the wives

personally "raised their voices higher to plead for their dark sisters' lives"—though how "old King Tanoa" could have understood them is not said. Calvert writes that, after Tanoa had decided to show mercy, it turned out that "five still lived," giving the impression that they had been saved by his wife and Mrs. Lyth (ibid., 437). But a close reading makes it clear that the two women supposedly saved by the intervention of the chief's wives are counted among the five survivors, hence both accounts agree that only three were saved thanks to the European women's plea.

9. Ibid., 346.
10. Ibid., 165. Both authors were Wesleyan missionaries; the first part of the book (up to page 209) was written by Williams, the second part by Calvert.
11. Quoted in Hogg, *Cannibalism*, 25.
12. Narrative Press, "Book Detail: *Life in Feejee: Five Years among the Cannibals*," accessed 2 July 2020, https://narrativepress.com/product/life-in-feejee-five-years-among-the-cannibals/.
13. Wallis, *Life in Feejee*, 290.
14. T. Williams and Calvert, *Fiji*, 235.
15. Ibid., 230.
16. Jaggar, *Unto the Perfect Day*, 76.
17. Quoted in T. Williams and Calvert, *Fiji*, 167.
18. Ibid., 345–46.
19. Ibid., 341.
20. Jaggar, *Unto the Perfect Day*, 91.
21. Ross Nepia Himona, "Strategic Marriages," *Te Karere Ipurangi—Maori News Online: Fiji Coup Supplement*, 2 August 2000, accessed 2 July 2020, https://maorinews.com/karere/fiji/stratmarr.htm. On Bau, see the beginning of this chapter.
22. Erskine, *Journal*, 261.
23. Museum of New Zealand, "Drua—Double Hulled Voyaging Canoe of Fiji," accessed 2 July 2020, https://collections.tepapa.govt.nz/topic/2356.
24. Quoted in Hogg, *Cannibalism*, 28 (emphasis in original).
25. T. Williams and Calvert, *Fiji*, 41.
26. Jaggar, *Unto the Perfect Day*, 37.
27. Fison, *Tales from Old Fiji*, xvii.
28. Erskine, *Journal*, 261.
29. T. Williams and Calvert, *Fiji*, 165.
30. Erskine, *Journal*, 411.
31. Quoted ibid., 435.
32. Quoted ibid.
33. Quoted ibid., 436.
34. Erskine, *Journal*, 188–89.
35. T. Williams and Calvert, *Fiji*, 441.
36. "They have no cattle in this island; but pigs are plentiful, although they seem not to be used as daily articles of food, but only at feasts and on great occasions. . . . They have also poultry; but the principal articles of food are bread-fruit, taro, and bananas . . . , and yams in the season" (Erskine, *Journal,* 59).
37. Fison, *Tales from Old Fiji*, xl.
38. Lawry, *Friendly and Feejee Islands*, 91 (quotes), 207.
39. Walker, *Wanderings*, 45.

40. St. Johnston, *Camping among Cannibals*, 229.
41. Fison, *Tales from Old Fiji*, xxxv–xxxvi.
42. "Asia-Pacific Fijians find Chutney in Bad Taste," *BBC News*, 13 December 1998, accessed 2 July 2020, http://news.bbc.co.uk/2/hi/asia-pacific/233880.stm.
43. Brown, *Melanesians and Polynesians*, 146.
44. Korn, Radice, and Hawes, *Cannibal*, 69.
45. Fison, *Tales from Old Fiji*, 164–65. Other descriptions of the same process can be found in Hogg, *Cannibalism*, 25 (quoting Cargill); Lawry, *Friendly and Feejee Islands*, 94; and St. Johnston, *Camping among Cannibals*, 227–28.
46. Hogg, *Cannibalism*, 25 (quoting Cargill); St. Johnston, *Camping among Cannibals*, 228.
47. See Chapter 11, this volume.
48. Erskine, *Journal*, 261.
49. Lawry, *Friendly and Feejee Islands*, 88, 89 (quote).
50. For example, Stevenson, *In the South Seas*, chapter 12.
51. Walker, *Wanderings*, 45; Erskine, *Journal*, 262. "The flesh of women is preferred to that of men" (Cargill quoted in Hogg, *Cannibalism*, 25). "The flesh of women is [considered] rather better than the flesh of men; and when the Chief wants something very delicate, or in case many bodies are before him, a child is roasted for his repast" (Lawry, *Friendly and Feejee Islands*, 91). "Women were considered better for cooking than men, and the thighs and arms the best portions" (St. Johnston, *Camping among Cannibals*, 229).
52. T. Williams and Calvert, *Fiji*, 165.
53. See Chapter 11, this volume.
54. Gill, *Gems*, 78, 122–23.
55. Brown, *Melanesians and Polynesians*, 147; Lawry, *Friendly and Feejee Islands*, 91, 255; Wallis, *Life in Feejee*, 44–47, 287, 317–18; T. Williams and Calvert, *Fiji*, 165 ("fourteen or sixteen persons, who lost their canoe at sea, were cooked and eaten" in a single incident), 215, 240.
56. Wallis, *Life in Feejee*, 287–88.
57. Quoted in T. Williams and Calvert, *Fiji*, 486 (emphasis in original).
58. Coquilhat, *Sur le Haut-Congo*, 347.
59. Ward, *Five Years*, 120.
60. Glave, *In Savage Africa*, 212.
61. Musy, "Correspondance," 28:379.
62. Burrows and Canisius, *Curse of Central Africa*, 213.
63. Ibid., 24, 38.
64. Ward, *My Life*, 98. Captain Deane was an officer of the Free State army with whom Ward had traveled before (Ward, *Voice from the Congo*, 76).
65. Musy, "Correspondance," 28:380.
66. See Chapter 5, this volume.
67. Ward, *My Life*, 84.
68. See Chapter 9, this volume.
69. Jameson, *Story*, 318.
70. See Chapter 11, this volume.
71. Bennett, "Ethnographical Notes," 84, 93 (emphasis in original).
72. Lenz, *Skizzen aus Westafrika*, 99–100.
73. Hinde, *Fall*, 64–65.

74. Hilton-Simpson, *Land and Peoples*, 148.
75. Livingstone, *Last Journals*, 48.
76. Livingstone, "Unyanyembe Journal."
77. Ibid.
78. Livingstone, *Last Journals*, 33–34, 92.
79. Gero, *Cannibalism in Zandeland*, 53–55, 69, 77.
80. Ibid., 80; see also Chapter 8, this volume.
81. Ibid., 121–22.
82. Mecklenburg, *From the Congo*, 230.
83. Evans-Pritchard, "Zande Cannibalism," 251.
84. Fräßle, *Meiner Urwaldneger Denken*, 79–80, 81 (quote).
85. Actually, he calls the river "Lulalaba" (ibid., 81). The Lualaba is the largest headstream of the Congo. In modern usage, the name Congo is already used from Kisangani, a town situated about two hundred kilometers upstream (southeast) of Basoko.
86. Ibid., 81–82.
87. Quoted ibid., 82–83.
88. Ibid., 83.
89. Isichei, *Igbo Worlds*, 111.
90. Basden, *Among the Ibos*, 38, 146, 175; Burns, *History of Nigeria*, 200, 216; Meek, *Northern Tribes of Nigeria*, 54; Talbot, *Peoples of Southern Nigeria*, 3:849.
91. Kalous, *Cannibals and Tongo Players*, 95–96; Mills, *Through Liberia*, 113, 120; Seabrook, *Jungle Ways*, 144–45; Volz, *Reise*, 101–2, 104.
92. Levtzion and Hopkins, *Corpus*, 33–34, 36–37, 86, 450.
93. Musy, "Correspondance," 28:379; see previous section, "Central Africa."
94. Seligmann, *Melanesians*, 559, 569; see also Chapter 11, this volume.
95. Mills, *Through Liberia*, 113, 120; see also Chapter 10, this volume.
96. See Chapter 11, this volume.
97. Seligmann, *Melanesians*, 552; Haberberger, *Kolonialismus und Kannibalismus*, 55.

CHAPTER 13
THE TRADE IN HUMAN FLESH AND IN "EDIBLE" CORPSES

When human flesh is eaten, there is always the possibility that it had been traded or exchanged in some way before this happens. We have already seen that in some regions, especially the Congo basin, enslaved persons were frequently purchased and then used for consumption. While such acts of slave eating have a commercial side—without a trade in slaves, they could not take place—they are not the focus of this chapter. In such cases, the buyers are cannibals, but have no commercial interest, and the sellers might pretend that they do not know or care about the subsequent cannibalism—from their viewpoint, what the buyers do with the merchandise is not their affair. Clearly, such a separation of concerns between slavers interested only in making money and cannibal buyers interested only in the "edibility" of their slaves is not really possible. As has been argued earlier, a cannibal demand for slaves leads to changes in the patterns of demand and the prices paid for slaves, turning slaves that might otherwise have been unsalable—such as very young children—into a sought-after commodity and shaping prices until in some regions the "amount of meat" on a slave's bones determined their price.[1]

However, while slave eating and commerce are invariably interconnected, there are also other ways in which commercial interests and cannibalism might interact. One is the sale of the flesh of human beings who have already been butchered—something that has been reported from parts of the Congo basin[2] and, as we will see, also from some other regions. In such cases, the sellers themselves—who may or may not be cannibals—perform the bloody work of turning a living human being into pieces of edible matter rather than leaving this job to their cannibal buyers. Another is the sale of dead bodies to those who are known to eat them. While in some places and times, corpses may be sought after for other purposes—say for performing autopsies or for extracting organs—in general, a dead body has no commercial value. In cases where this is different, the acts of the sellers—who give away a body in return for payment or some other kind of compensation—and the uses to which the buyers want to put the body are thus again connected.

The cases covered in this chapter are limited to two regions: parts of central and western Africa and of Melanesia. Similar acts were not necessarily unknown in other parts of the world, but they do not seem to have been as widespread elsewhere as in the regions covered here.

Related to trade, though clearly not the same, is the giving of gifts with the expectancy of a suitable counter-gift at some later point in the future. In contrast to trade, where an interaction essentially ends once merchandise and payment have changed hands, gift giving is a way of building long-term relations, because each act of giving creates some kind of obligation of giving something back at a future date, with the return gift then again creating a new obligation for the recipient.[3] In contrast to such gifts between equals, gifts can also be a more or less concealed form of tribute, with the givers knowing that if they do not hand over what is expected of them, trouble may result. Cases of the giving of human flesh and bodies intended for consumption as gifts or tribute are also covered in this chapter, in so far as they come from regions for which a commercial trade in such goods has been reported as well.

Corpse Exchange in Central Africa

As noted earlier,[4] *people eating* (the deliberate killing of people and their subsequent consumption) can be distinguished from *corpse eating* (the consumption of corpses of people who died of unrelated reasons). Both slave eating and foreigner poaching, our topics so far, were usually instances of the violent practice of people eating—cannibalized slaves, persons captured in slave raids, and foreigners very rarely died a natural death.

Corpse eating, by comparison, is a more benign form of cannibalism where certain people who have died of natural or accidental reasons are eaten, but the cannibal act is not preceded by deliberate murder. As concluded in Chapter 1, we have to further differentiate between *funerary cannibalism* and the usage of corpses as food (*corpse food*). While both are nonviolent, the consumption of the dead as a funerary rite is a way of honoring dead people whom one had known and loved (however strange and off-putting the practice might seem to us).[5] I propose to use the term *corpse food,* on the other hand, for cases where there is neither a positive nor a particularly negative attitude of the eaters to the eaten—where the latter are considered neither honored friends nor hated enemies, but simply edible matter.

When corpses are considered edible, they might also become items of trade. They can be sold to people who will eat them, or different communities can exchange their dead so that people do not have to eat the bodies of individuals they have known. The French American zoologist and anthropologist Paul

Belloni Du Chaillu (1831–1903) found such a practice among the Fang people in Western Central Africa, who also practiced foreigner poaching.[6] Shortly after his arrival in a Fang village in September 1856, he observed that "some Fans brought in a dead body which they had bought in a neighbouring town, and which was now to be divided. I could see that the man had died of some disease."[7]

Du Chaillu, who already a few days earlier, just after his arrival in the village, had seen parts of a dead human body that had just been divided for consumption,[8] writes that he was surprised. Not, he explains, by the cannibalism as such, but by the fact that "the bodies of persons who have died of sickness" were eaten—"a form of cannibalism of which I had never heard among any people." When he inquired about the practice, the Fang he spoke to answered "without embarrassment,"[9] telling him that

> they constantly buy the dead of the Osheba tribe, who, in return, buy theirs. They also buy the dead of other families in their own tribes, and, besides this, get the bodies of a great many slaves from the Mbichos and Mbondemos, for which they readily give ivory, at the rate of a small tusk for a body.[10]

A small tusk for a slave is an exchange ratio also documented from the Ubangi region farther in the east, where living slaves were expected as payment.[11] The Fang, on the other hand, paid for the corpses of those who had already died. Considering that the price of a corpse seems to have been similar to that of a living slave, it is not inconceivable that the sellers might have killed an otherwise hard-to-sell slave in order to sell the body, indicating that (nondeadly) corpse food and (deadly) people eating are not always easy to distinguish. But in contrast to "some of the Middle Congo tribes," the Fang did not purchase living slaves for fattening and subsequent consumption, as Mary Kingsley (1862–1900) notes with a certain approval.[12] Kingsley, who visited them in the 1890s, was an English writer and one of the first European women to travel through Central Africa on her own.

"Prisoners taken in war," however, were killed and eaten, according to Du Chaillu.[13] The German explorer Oskar Lenz likewise observes that they "kill and eat all their prisoners of war, while other tribes . . . sell them as slaves."[14] Kidnapped foreigners met the same fate, as we have already seen.[15]

The villagers whom Du Chaillu met not only bought corpses from others, they also sold their own. After a hunter had been accidentally killed by an elephant, Du Chaillu learned that "the body of the poor fellow who was killed to-day is, I am told, to be sent to another Fan village, to be sold and eaten. This seems the proper and usual end of the Fans."[16] Persons belonging to the same village were not eaten by their relatives or neighbors, but they could be sold or exchanged against the edible bodies of foreigners. Kingsley points this out as well—in reply to distorted rumors of the local customs, she writes: "He [the Fang] is always very much abused for eating his relations, but he really does not do this. He will [merely] eat his next door neighbour's relations and sell his own deceased to his next door neighbour in return."[17]

After he had stayed in the Fang village for some time, Du Chaillu visited a nearby Osheba village and observed that "a large part of their intercourse with the Fan village consists in the interchange of dead bodies, and I saw as many human bones lying about the Osheba village as among the Fans."[18] The consumption of traded bodies was indeed a mutual affair.

Du Chaillu, who was probably the first Westerner to visit the region, encountered people who saw no reason to hide their practice or to regard it as strange or shameful. But this changed quickly once he and later visitors started to express their disapproval. When Lenz arrived in the area—about twenty years later—corpse eating seems to have still been practiced, but people had become unwilling to admit it: "From all sides I was assured that Fan families exchange their dead in order to eat them! I repeatedly interrogated Fan people about this, but they did not give me a definite answer and generally reacted with discomfort when I mentioned human flesh."[19] Another two decades later, Kingsley observed that, while the Fang people she spoke to did not hesitate to praise human flesh as "good to eat, very good, and he wishes you would try it," they also tended to deny all personal involvement in cannibal practices.[20]

While the Fang live west of the Congo basin, similar customs have been been reported from several regions in the north of the basin. While stationed near the Mongala River, a northern tributary of the Congo, Guy Burrows noted that

> Among the riverside tribes . . . regular rules of etiquette concerning the disposal of their dead friends exist. If in two villages, say a quarter of a mile away from each other, any member of one community dies, the body is promptly placed in a canoe and taken to the other village, where it is handed over to supply a banquet for the chief and his friends. The compliment, of course, is returned when a member of the other village likewise fulfils the debt of nature.[21]

Among the Fang and neighboring peoples, dead bodies were items of trade—they were bought and sold, according to Du Chaillu and Kingsley. Around the Mongala the corpse exchange seems to have been rather an issue of mutuality: no price was charged for a corpse, but villages participating in such exchanges could expect that their own gifts of dead bodies would in turn be rewarded with a counter-gift of the same kind. Such a mutual gift exchange makes sense considering that relatives or community members were widely considered as "inedible," but that the members of communities that participated in such exchanges apparently had no qualms about eating dead foreigners, even if they had been members of friendly groups. In such cases, cannibalism was driven neither by hatred (as war cannibalism might be) nor by love and respect (as funerary cannibalism usually is)—rather, unrelated dead bodies seem to have been regarded more or less as a convenient source of nutrition.

Farther east, Filiberto Gero heard from his local informants that in former times corpses had been exchanged among several Zande clans. Both the Babukur and the Amadi had eaten almost all dead corpses, except for those suffering from skin diseases. The latter also spared the bodies of distinct elders, war leaders, and young children, while the former knew no such restriction. Among both groups, family members were not eaten but donated to a neighboring family; the latter would reciprocate the favor once one of their members died. Occasionally the corpse of a relative was sold instead of being given away—but the exchange of corpses as gifts on the basis of mutuality seems to have been the typical mode of exchange.[22]

Two other clans, the Apambia and the Bahum, also regularly exchanged their dead bodies on the basis of mutuality. Members of several other clans occasionally joined in similar exchanges by buying or selling dead bodies intended for consumption—in these latter cases, an explicit price had to be negotiated since no future counter-gift could be expected. In all cases, the persons whose bodies were sold or given away had died of natural or accidental reasons; no clan member was ever killed to sell their dead body. According to Gero's informants, these practices faded once the different clans became united under the leadership of the Avongara clan. While this clan (grudgingly) accepted certain cannibal practices such as the consumption of enemies, it was strictly opposed to corpse eating. In later times, corpses of clan members could still be exchanged for consumption in times of famine, but otherwise they were buried.[23]

Georg Schweinfurth, who visited some Zande clans around 1870, heard that the body of a "lone and solitary individual" who died without relatives was usually eaten. He does not say whether such corpses were exchanged or sold, but from his description it is clear that people would not have eaten their own relatives—indeed, anyone who had relatives who took care of their body was buried instead of becoming food. Thus, it seems that at that time the switch from corpse exchange to burial, described by Gero's informants, was well underway; people had started to object to the consumption of their own relatives and friends even by unrelated others. Schweinfurth thoughtfully comments that European customs in his time were not necessarily more dignified, consigning the corpses of those who died lonely and poor "to the knife of the anatomist."[24]

In some areas, the bodies of persons executed as punishment for a crime could be sold for consumption. Among the Fang, notes Du Chaillu, anyone suspected of witchcraft was killed. The body was then sold as food, as all corpses were. He suspects that the fact that "the dead body has its commercial value" increased the inclination of chiefs to pronounce the death penalty even in cases where clemency might have been called for—another case where the boundary between corpse eating and people eating became blurred.[25]

A trade in dead bodies intended for consumption might also have existed in some other parts of the Congo basin. Livingstone, the first European to venture into the Maniema region in the east, accompanying a group of Swahilo-Arab slave traders, heard from his companions that, a few years earlier, "dead slaves were openly purchased from them" for consumption—and, though condemning the habit, they were apparently quite willing to sell. Writing in early 1871, Livingstone adds that, though it "is still common to devour the dead," the open trade in dead bodies had ceased in this region under the influence of the Arabs.[26]

It seems, however, that dead criminals could still occasionally be sold for cannibal purposes. In February 1890, writes George Grenfell, a woman considered guilty of "some misdemeanour" was executed in the proximity of Basoko. Her body was sold as "meat" to a neighboring community, "for the price of a couple of [enslaved] boys."[27]

In other cases, people considered guilty of a crime were sold alive in the knowledge that the buyers would kill them for food. Gero notes this regarding the Avongara, the ruling Zande clan. While they did not practice cannibalism and discouraged the practice among other Zande clans, they were quite willing to sell "condemned men and women to be eaten [to] the cannibals who lived on the Uele river." In return they received the "poison for their oracles" used to test the guilt of people accused of a crime.[28] This was not a case of corpse eating, but rather a boundary case between punitive cannibalism (people being killed and eaten as punishment) and slave eating—from the Avongara perspective, the sold had been convicted to death, while from the buyers' perspective they were slaves whom they could utilize in their preferred manner.

The most characteristic form of corpse food, however, was usually devoid of violence—it was to exchange the corpses of those who had died of a natural or accidental death in the knowledge that the recipients would eat them, in return for some kind of payment or a future counter-gift in kind. Among the Fang, around the Mongala River, and possibly in other regions as well, people apparently had a quite pragmatic attitude regarding the fate of their dead bodies: they knew that they would likely be eaten and did not mind, instead maybe even considering this a "proper and usual end," as Du Chaillu speculates. Still, they considered the consumption of relatives and community members as taboo and did not practice it as a honorable funeral rite, which would otherwise have led to the more widespread practice of funerary cannibalism. Under these circumstances, the exchange of corpses, on the basis of mutuality or for payment, made sense.

In general, though, it seems that these circumstances were not often fulfilled. In Central Africa, corpse exchange seems to have been much rarer than certain other cannibal practices such as war cannibalism and slave eating.

Outside of Central Africa, I am unaware of any reports of similar practices—they might well have existed in some regions, but it seems they were not widespread. While generally nonviolent, this practice could still lead to an increase of violence, as we have seen: when dead bodies had a price, the propensity of rulers to impose the death penalty might have increased, and slave traders might have murdered some of their slaves if they found that they could sell their dead bodies with a profit.

Sale of Human Flesh on the African West Coast

While the corpse exchange was largely a nonviolent affair, this cannot be said of the sale of human flesh in general. People do not generally eat carrion—when we eat the meat of animals, these animals, in nearly all cases, have been deliberately killed for consumption. Human flesh does not seem to be an exception in this regard—when it appeared on marketplaces or was otherwise offered for sale, as it sometimes was in certain regions, it usually came from persons who had been murdered a short time earlier. A partial exception was the sale of human flesh during times of famine—from many severe famines it has been reported that the flesh of corpses started to appear on the markets, often in addition to the flesh of people who had been kidnapped and killed.[29] But outside of famines, when cannibalism was a socially accepted practice, the sale of human flesh nearly always seems to have been preceded by an act of deadly violence.

We have already seen that in parts of the Congo basin, slaves were murdered on what seems to have been a more or less regular basis in order to sell their flesh.[30] But the sale of human flesh is also documented for certain regions on the African west coast, outside of the Congo basin. The Hungarian adventurer László Magyar (1818–1864) spent the last seventeen years of his life in the central and northern parts of today's Angola, west of the basin. He claims that, in several regions inhabited by the Ambundu people, who live around the Cuanza River, "human flesh is publicly offered for sale, but only to locals." He asserts to have "repeatedly seen" how people were butchered for food; the victims were usually "people who are ill or old as well as robbers, children, and slaves." Old people, he notes elsewhere, were "slaughtered when they became ill" (and were probably considered dying), while the cannibalized children had been "rob[bed] from their neighbors."[31]

These "neighbors" certainly did not live next door—Magyar likely refers to raids against neighboring peoples, which were, as he notes, quite common. He explains that there was always a "pretext" for opening hostilities; usually a claim that the targeted people had caused some bad event (drought or illness) through magical means. The main purpose of these expeditions, which often involved thousands of warriors, was the acquisition of cattle and slaves. After a raid, "the captives who are able to work are . . . dragged away as slaves," while "the elderly and children" were killed outright—or taken home in order to later sell their flesh. When Magyar was in the area, the transatlantic slave trade had already largely collapsed, but he explains that the Ambundu were a trading people and slaves had been their most important export good until shortly before his arrival.[32] Here, too, the international slave trade and local cannibalism had been intertwined, with captives considered unfit for sale ending up at the meat markets instead.

Other peoples were more peaceful and rarely engaged in raids—but this does not necessarily mean that they were opposed to buying and selling human flesh. The Ambuim, who live southwest of the Ambundu, are described by Magyar as diligent farmers and traders. He adds: "It is regrettable that these peaceful people likewise consume human flesh, even selling it publicly."[33] He does not say how they got victims for slaughter, but it seems plausible that slaves or captives were purchased from neighboring, more warlike peoples. Possible providers, in addition to the Ambundu, might have been the Selles people, who live south of the Ambuim. According to Magyar, they frequently attacked neighboring settlements, killing some of the inhabitants and enslaving the rest. Captives not sold were often eaten, with Magyar claiming that cannibalism was "so widespread among them that there is rarely an entertainment during which they do not consume one human being or several."[34]

I am not aware of other witnesses confirming Magyar's reports from Angola, which means that some doubt regarding their reliability must remain. Magyar himself states that the cannibal customs he wrote about were generally hidden from Europeans; this is plausible insofar as he was married to a daughter of a local ruler, which certainly gave him opportunity to see and hear about things that were inaccessible to others. Historians such as Joseph C. Miller tend to treat his accounts as generally reliably.[35]

Much farther north, in some parts of Nigeria, human flesh might also have been a marketable item. The Anglo-Irish explorer and colonialist Thomas J. Hutchinson (1820–1885) claims that "during the year 1859 human flesh was exposed for sale, as butcher's meat, in the market at Duketown, Old Kalabar."[36] According to E. Deas, a Presbyterian missionary, "cannibal markets" could be found "in many parts of Nigeria."[37]

An earlier and more detailed account comes from neighboring Benin in the early eighteenth century. In 1727, the English captain and trader William Snelgrave arrived in the former Kingdom of Whydah which had just been conquered by the neighboring Kingdom of Dahomey (both situated in today's Benin). There he met a ship surgeon from an Italian galley, Robert More, who told him that "he saw many strange things, especially human Flesh sold publickly in the great Marketplace" of Savi, the capital of the conquered kingdom. Snelgrave comments that he had not personally seen this since he had not visited the market, but that More was "a person of great Integrity." He adds that "there were many old and maimed Captives brought from Tuffoe [possibly referring to neighboring Togo] which no Europeans would have bought." These otherwise unsalable slaves, he concludes, were purchased cheaply by local butchers who made money from selling their flesh.[38]

While Snelgrave himself did not see this, he witnessed a sacrificial ceremony in which a large number of prisoners—men, women, and children—were publicly executed to celebrate the victory. The next morning, their dead bodies had disappeared, and his interpreter told him that they had been distributed "amongst the People who had eat[en] them."[39]

Both Magyar's and Snelgrave's accounts correspond with at least the weaker version of the Obeyesekere conjecture, according to which cannibal practices were tied to Western influences. Both suggest that slaves unsuitable for export were at risk of supplying the meat markets instead. In Nigeria, insofar as the short mentions of cannibal meat markets are more than just rumors, a similar connection might have existed.

Sale of Human Flesh in Melanesia

The reports from central and western Africa discussed in the preceding section and in earlier chapters indicate that the cannibalistic trade in human flesh was closely associated with slavery and the trade in living human bodies. Whether alive or (recently) deceased, the bodies of slaves could be valuable commodities. From parts of Melanesia, a trade in "edible" human bodies and body parts has been reported as well. In this region, however, this trade was related to warfare and to the kidnapping and consumption of unwanted foreigners, not to the trade in living human beings. This difference was likely due to the fact that the region never came under pressure as a supply area for the slave trade—in marked contrast to central and western Africa—and that slavery as an established institution seems to have been largely unknown outside of the Gazelle Peninsula.[40]

We have already encountered accounts reporting that the bodies of killed castaways and foreigners could be sold to neighboring villages for consumption—Heinrich Schnee, George Brown, and Wilfred Powell tell of such cases that occurred in New Britain, the largest island of the Bismarck Archipelago.[41] Other sources make it clear that such acts were not just exceptions, but seem to have been a fairly well-established custom. The Danish explorer and anthropologist Richard Parkinson (1844–1909) spent more than thirty years in the southern Pacific. While confirming that human flesh was eaten in the Bismarck Archipelago, he rejects the "very erroneous view" that it was a daily nourishment. Rather, he notes, the consumption of a human body was a rare event, and since the flesh was divided among many eaters, each of them received only a small piece.[42]

After a person from an "enemy district" had been killed, the killer brought the body home in order to sell the meat. A large drum was beaten to call the inhabitants of the village together; once enough people had gathered, the body was dismembered and the pieces sold in return for *diwarra* (or *dewarra*), a locally used shell money. According to Parkinson, the total gain from selling a body was usually about fifty to eighty fathoms of diwarra. He adds that he would have liked to see the division of a corpse but was repeatedly prevented from doing so. On several occasions, however, he saw pieces of roasted human flesh.[43]

The German count Joachim von Pfeil (1857–1924), who visited the Bismarck Archipelago in the 1880s, gives a similar account of the dismemberment and sale of killed foreigners. He explains that he did not see this, but that his description is based on the reports of participants. He comments that killing someone "who does not belong to the tribe is not regarded murder, but a meritorious act, because it reduces the number of enemies—and everyone who does not belong to the tribe is an enemy." That such acts also entailed "a tasty meal" for those buying the meat and "a treasure of diwarra" for the killer were seen as additional advantages, but not as primary motives of such killings.[44] According to Pfeil, there was thus no distinction made between the killing of enemies and of foreigners, since anyone who was not a friend or community member was treated as an enemy.

The anthropologist Douglas L. Oliver notes that, in New Britain's Gazelle Peninsula, human flesh was one of very few items—along with weapons—that was only traded by men, while trade was otherwise a women's business. Usually, the flesh came from enemies killed in war.[45]

But such acts were not limited to New Britain. In the late 1870s, George Brown wrote approvingly about a chief who lived in neighboring New Ireland and had recently converted to Christianity: "Some few weeks ago the bushmen were fighting, and one man was killed. They brought the body a long distance to Le Bera, fully expecting that he would buy it as he used to do; but he positively refused to do so, telling them . . . that he had given up cannibalism."[46]

Documentation of another case, which had taken place in the Duke of York Islands, a group of smaller islands situated between New Britain and New Ireland, was found by the German anthropologist Simon Haberberger in the archives of the English Wesleyan Mission. In the early 1880s, members of the mission working in these islands discovered to their dismay that a group of locals they considered friends and who they thought had converted to Christian values had recently eaten a human leg. They were told that several persons from another island had been killed in an attack; one of the corpses was brought to the main Duke of York Island, where it was dismembered and the body parts were sold for consumption. It turned out that, while cannibalism was no longer practiced openly because the mission's attitude was known, people still considered it wasteful to refrain from eating killed enemies (or foreigners). Therefore, instead of abandoning the practice as the missionaries wished, they had tried to hide it from them—unsuccessfully in this case.[47]

Additional reports of the sale of the flesh of captured enemies and entrapped foreigners in the Bismarck Archipelago come from the German Catholic missionaries A. Kleintitschen and Josef Winthuis.[48]

Other sources indicate that the practice also existed in the Solomon Islands, a group of islands situated not far from the archipelago in a southeastern direction. In 1872, Edwin Redlich, the captain of a British schooner, spent some weeks in Makira, one of these islands. Upon temporarily leaving the island for a rabbit hunting trip on another island, he and his companions "met with several large war-canoes, and pulling alongside one of them, found it to contain a dead body, dressed and cooked whole." Mr. Perry, a white settler who lived in Makira, "took it quite coolly, as an every-day occurrence," explaining "that he had seen as many as twenty bodies lying on the beach, dressed and cooked." There were also "two prisoners" in the canoe, "a boy about 14, and a girl 13 years of age. Intending to save their lives, I [Redlich] offered to buy them, but without avail." Returning from his hunt, Redlich learned that the canoe crew had left Makira after selling "half of the body" and "both the prisoners."[49]

That human bodies were sometimes cooked whole is not implausible. Pfeil writes that meat—whether animal or human—was roasted in an earth oven after wrapping it in banana leaves. He notes that, if one was patient, this cooking method was suitable even for large chunks and he "had seen a whole pig being roasted this way."[50] That human flesh was cooked in this manner is also documented by Parkinson.[51] While both refer to the Bismarck Archipelago, cooking methods in the nearby Solomon Islands will have been similar. In general, it seems to have been usual to divide the bodies of larger animals or people into smaller chunks, but if Perry's observation is correct, customs on Makira might have been different.

The sale of whole human bodies for consumption was still practiced decades later, according to the missionary Florence Coombe (1870–1933). "After a battle we find dead bodies hawked up and down the coast in canoes for sale," she writes about Makira, adding that both there and in neighboring Malaita Island human flesh was apparently eaten "for pleasure."[52]

According to these reports, the human flesh offered for sale in the Bismarck Archipelago often came from "poached" foreigners and occasionally from enemies killed in war, while in the Solomon Islands it predominantly came from the latter group of victims. Generally, foreigner poaching seems to have been rarer in the Solomon Islands than in the Bismarck Archipelago and in the other regions covered in the previous chapters on that custom. In both cases it is notable that the sale of human flesh was a side aspect of activities that were not driven by commercial considerations. Enemies were killed in war and foreigners were killed as unwanted intruders and potential enemies; the subsequent sale of their flesh was seen as a suitable opportunity to make money, but it was not the main motive driving these killings. This contrasts with the situation in Africa, where the sale of the flesh of murdered human beings was generally tied to the slave trade—the trade in living humans. Reports from the Congo and some other central and western African regions also tell of slaves who were killed in order to sell their flesh—a commercialization of cannibal customs that seems to have been unknown in Melanesia.

While enemies and foreigners were killed before being sold, it seems that those considered guilty of a crime could sometimes be sold alive for consumption. In the late 1880s, the British naturalist Charles Morris Woodford (1852–1927) arrived in a village in the New Georgia Islands, a group of islands in the west of the Solomon Islands. He heard that recently the local chief had fallen ill, and the "wise-man" had identified a woman who was suspected of having bewitched him. Under torture the woman confessed and produced an object which she had supposedly used to bewitch the man. The chief quickly recovered (Woodford suspects that he had merely been "sulky") and the alleged witch was "sold to the natives of a neighbouring island" who killed and ate her a short time later.[53] This is the same practice of selling convicted persons so that they may be eaten by others we have already encountered among some Zande groups in Central Africa.[54]

In the Bismarck Archipelago and the Solomon Islands, the demand for human flesh seems to have largely followed the supply—people were willing to buy such flesh when it appeared on the market because someone had killed a foreigner or enemy. In Vanuatu, another cluster of islands situated southeast of the Solomon Islands, on the other hand, the desire to have human flesh for feasts seems to have driven an occasional trade in people who were then killed for consumption.

The British anthropologist A. Bernard Deacon (1903–1927) did field research in Malakula, the second largest of these islands, from 1926 to his premature death of malaria. He notes that "it is said to have been common in days gone by to buy, or obtain in some other way, a human victim for an important *Nimangki* celebration"—a celebration held when a man acquired a new rank. Usually, one participant would buy a human victim—always an outsider from another clan—announcing beforehand that he would do so and killing the victim shortly before the feast. Deacon heard that having a human victim was not an "essential part of the ceremonial," but that the flesh was "regarded . . . as a tasty contribution to the feast."[55]

Coombe writes that most of the victims eaten in Vanuatu were killed enemies or criminals executed because of severe crimes (such as stealing a man's pig or wife), but occasionally "a man [was] killed simply to serve as a *chef d'œuvre* at a feast." When she arrived in the area, cannibalism was no longer practiced openly—the last such case she knew of took place in 1897, when "a man was added to fifty pigs for a feast that signified a chief's rise in rank."[56]

Out of view of the colonial government and prying missionaries, however, such feasts continued for longer. During a journey made shortly before World War I, the Swiss ethnologist Felix Speiser visited a village in Malakula where a "big dance feast" was about to be held. A few hours before the feast, he asked one of the participants how many pigs would be killed for the occasion. "'Oh,' he said, 'that doesn't matter now, we have a human being. Yesterday we killed him in the bush, and tonight we'll eat him.' He says it with the calmest face in the world, as if he was talking about the weather."[57]

Speiser observes that "no great feast where pigs are sacrificed is held to be complete if at the same time a human being is not eaten; this is not a matter of mere epicureanism but based rather on the notion that only the slain man fully consecrates the feast." While at least one human victim was considered necessary to make a feast a success, "human bodies were prepared for eating in much the same way as pigs." Occasionally "special ceremonies" accompanied the sacrifice of a human victim; "in most cases, however, there was no special ado." Pigs and human beings were usually slaughtered together in the same manner and cooked in the same ovens. Speiser notes that cannibalism seems to have been "purely culinary in nature," lacking an observable ritual or spiritual side.[58] Repeatedly he heard that "human flesh is particularly tasty; it is said to be much better than pork and more tender."[59] The abovementioned participant of a cannibalistic dance feast enthused about its "incomparable tenderness, whiteness and tastiness."[60]

Speiser writes that by securing victims for feasts, whether through kidnapping or purchase, ambitious men could increase "the influence they wield." The victims always came from other regions, since "for a fellow villager to be eaten brings the greatest shame on the whole village, perhaps simply because the personality of the dead person is completely destroyed in this way and therefore cannot even exist as an ancestral spirit."[61] Being thus able to destroy others and render their flesh into a tasty dish for oneself and one's followers was a sign of power and prestige.

Melanesia: Foreigner Involvement in Commercial Cannibalism

Several sources indicate that human flesh was offered for sale not only to inhabitants of nearby villages or to friendly "chiefs," but also to missionaries and sailors. In 1882, the German branch of the Catholic Missionaries of the Sacred Heart of Jesus set up its first mission station in New Britain. Father Fromm, one of the missionaries, writes that "boiled human flesh" was repeatedly offered to them for sale. "One day, in a farmhouse, a fellow brother noticed a boy who had been hanged and was in his final throes. People laughed, ranted and enjoyed his death struggle." When the missionary returned to the house in the evening, a basket claimed to be filled with pork was offered to him for sale. "When he opened the basket, however, he was horrified to see the whole arm and shoulder piece of the boy, cooked and wrapped in leaves."[62]

About the same time, the Australian government agent Douglas Rannie visited neighboring New Ireland. Upon seeing his ship, the locals "brought down quite a quantity of the flesh of a young woman whom they had just cooked. In offering parts for sale, they said that if we white men did not like to eat it possibly some of our native boatmen would enjoy it."[63] It seems they had already realized that Europeans tended not to eat human flesh—but not yet fully that they were usually strictly opposed to the idea of treating human bodies as edible matter.

In these cases, is it not clear who the victims were and why they had to die. (The "young woman" might conceivably have died a natural death, but it does not seem likely, as no cases of corpse food have been reported from this region.) Most likely they were foreigners, possibly from enemy groups, who had strayed too far from home; it is also conceivable that they were slaves or victims deliberately purchased for consumption.[64]

Among the evidence of human flesh sales discovered by Haberberger in mission archives is an account of a young mission teacher to whom several pieces of this flesh had been offered. It is notable that not only cannibalism but also the open offering of human flesh continued quite long into colonial times: the attempted sale took place in New Britain around 1900, at a time when the archipelago had already been a German colony for about fifteen years.[65]

In the 1890s, the French count Rodolphe Festetics de Tolna (1865–1933?) spent years traveling through Melanesia on his own yacht. While on Manus Island in the north of the Bismarck Archipelago, they were approached by a group of traders "from a nearby island who . . . brought us in their canoes a lot of things to trade, including [human] arms, legs and even whole bodies."[66] Sometime earlier on Bougainville, one of the North Solomon Islands, the locals who came on board had not only brought (non-cannibalistic) goods to sell, but they also "offered to buy" the young child of a crew member, indicating that the seriously ill boy—who died of meningitis a few weeks later—would make "a delicate morsel at their next cannibalistic banquet."[67]

While Festetics did not yield to the suggestion, Speiser writes that several credible reports indicate that white "sandalwood dealers sold human beings from other islands" to the inhabitants of Erromango, one of the larger islands of Vanuatu. While the dealers received sandalwood in return, the sold persons were subsequently consumed.[68]

The New Zealand missionary Edward Reeves, who spent many years on various islands in the southern Pacific, writes that several captains who had acquired their ships during the gold rushes in New Zealand in the 1860s, subsequently engaged in an illegal slave trade that sometimes catered to cannibal needs. "Native men and women, bought at auction or from the chiefs" in Tonga or Fiji, or in other cases simply kidnapped "from some lonely island," were sold at other islands, either "into slavery" or "to the cannibal for his gruesome feasts." He claims that several "successful captain[s] and crew[s]," who acquired a small fortune in this odious manner, later "retire[d] with a competency into honourable private life in England, or settle[d] as leading citizens in Fiji or Honolulu."[69]

Reeves does not state how he knew of these cases, and it is possible that he reproduces just baseless rumors, but jointly his and Speiser's statements suggest that in the southern Pacific, just as in Central Africa, white people sometimes sold slaves to those who would eat them, thus facilitating cannibalism, likely without being cannibals themselves.

Europeans were very rarely killed and eaten in Melanesia, as has already been discussed.[70] Non-white members of their crews, on the other hand, were at risk of falling victim to cannibalism, and some of them ended up supplying the local meat markets. The French marine officers A. Hagen and A. Pineau report that in March 1887 three Indigenous crew members of a French ship choose to spend some time on Malo Island (in western Vanuatu) in order to visit a friend. The captain asked a Mr. de L— to take care of them until the return of his ship. But on the island two of the men, who had been born in Pentecost Island (farther in the east), where shot and wounded. "They were not killed on the spot, but they were seized, their arms and legs tied."[71]

The "two half-dead men" were transported to Aore (Aura), a smaller island next to Malo, and there sold for "twenty pigs." Hearing what had happened, Mr. de L— immediately inquired into which village they had been sold, but he came too late. Upon reaching the village, he "surprised [the buyers] while they ate one of the two bodies"; already on his way he had encountered a man "carrying a thigh of one of the victims." The villagers threatened to shoot Mr. de L— if he reported the case, but apparently he was not deterred.[72]

Various members of the largely native crew of Edwin Redlich's schooner also became the objects of a cannibalistic commercial transaction. After leaving Makira, the schooner sailed towards the Bismarck Archipelago. In the Admiralty Islands, a group of islands in the northwest of this archipelago, Redlich sent out two "large boats, with eighteen men all told, for a three weeks' cruize [*sic*]." When they had not returned after four weeks, however, he started to worry. A local ruler (*rajah*) agreed to supply dozens of men and several boats for a search mission. After some time, two of the boats returned with three captives, who confessed to having participated in an expedition of about forty-five men who attacked and killed the sailors while they camped on a shore. "The savages took all the bodies up the River Crabara. There they cut off their heads, kept them for trophies, and sold the bodies to a neighbouring tribe, who had cooked and eaten them."[73]

Cannibalistic Gift Giving in Melanesia

Human bodies and body parts were not only sold, they were also considered suitable gifts, as a variety of reports indicates. When Festetics de Tolna visited Manus Island, in addition to the commercial offerings of human flesh and bodies, he received offerings of the same kind with no price attached. A local ruler came to welcome the foreign guests, bringing "not only . . . yams, taros

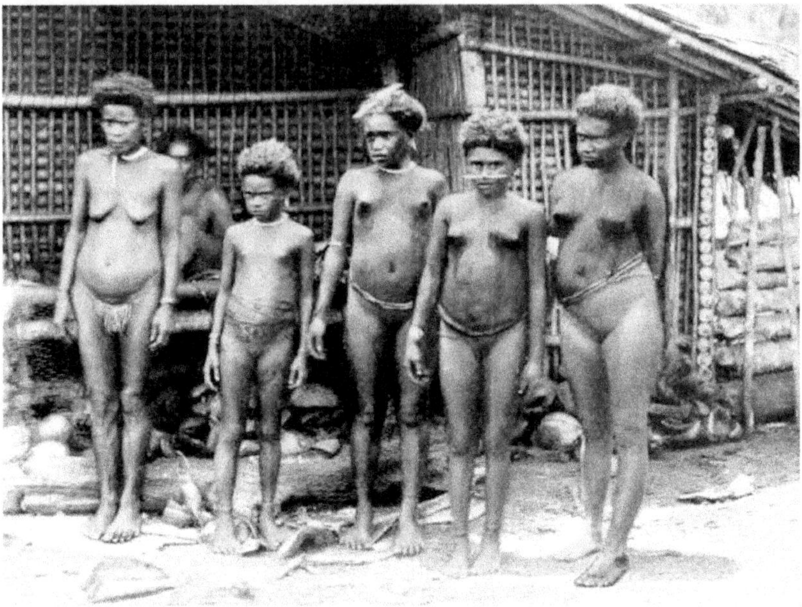

Figure 13.1. Photograph entitled "Slave girls being fattened for the cannibal feast" from Festetics de Tolna's *Chez les cannibales: Huit ans de croisière dans l'Océan Pacifique à bord du yacht "le Tolna"* (Paris: Plon-Nourrit, 1903), 308. If Festetics's account is correct, these girls were slaughtered later the same day for a feast held in his honor.

and obsidian; he also honored me with human limbs, a particularly honorable gift by which he showed that I was with him in a relationship of power to power."[74]

Fearing to offend the "king," Festetics not only purported to gladly accept these "gloomy consignments" but also reciprocated with some gifts of his own (of which kind he does not say). He ordered a Fijian sailor who supposedly "as a former savage had less horror than the other sailors of those bloody slices . . . to remove the flesh and to dry the bones in the sun to preserve them." But the seemingly friendly acceptance of the gifts seems to have convinced the generous ruler that Festetics and his crew were cannibals, and so he was motivated to repeat his gifts until the Europeans had collected "so many severed limbs that our steerage resembled a lecture hall of anatomy."[75]

Festetics, it might be mentioned in passing, had indeed eaten human flesh on at least one occasion, as he admits elsewhere in his works. He had already come at least close to cannibalism during a day trip into the interior of Espiritu Santo, the largest island of Vanuatu. He and his two companions had neglected to take any provisions. When they reached a village, they were attracted by a "tempting scent" coming out of an earth oven. They were assured that the oven contained "yams and pig," but when they unwrapped several of the bundles taken out of the oven, they found not only " yams and taros" but also a still clearly identifiable "human foot" and other human body parts.[76]

Festetics, who was quite hungry, admits that he "felt more disappointment than horror" at this discovery. He decided that he and his companions would eat of the yams and taros, leaving the flesh to their hosts. They ate with good appetite, though realizing that it was "a human sauce that glazed the yams, and the jelly that filled the taros had the same origin." The villagers joined in the meal and, while Festetics saw them eat pieces of meat of clearly human origin, he found them to be very friendly and hospitable. "In a short time we were the best friends in the world," he concludes.[77]

While this might be a borderline case, he clearly became a cannibal when visiting Roviana (Rubiana), one of the Solomon Islands. "The savages had gathered in considerable numbers and held a cannibal banquet in our honor. They made us eat with them." Festetics, who "found them looking a little worrying," considered it unwise to ignore the invitation.[78] And it seems this was not even the only cannibal meal held in his honor. In a village in Malaita, the young chief who showed him around, proudly

> showed me, locked up in a house, a group of young girls who had been caught on another island and who were kept and fattened for the next cannibal feast. It had just been decided that this feast would take place the same day on the occasion of our presence in Malaita. The girls were no doubt aware that their last hour was soon to come. . . . They seemed to accept the situation with great resignation.[79]

Festetics then immediately jumps away from the scene—if he made any attempt to save the unfortunate girls, he does not say so.

The British captain and geographer Wilfred Powell took a much stronger stance when it came to turning down cannibal offerings. At the beginning of the three years he spent in New Britain in the late 1870s, he acquired land from a local chief in order to build a house. "When everything was finished, we had a big feast and a dance by way of house-warming." Tor-Rarrabay, the chief who had given the land, "asked me if he should provide a human body for the feast"—apparently a well-meant offer, but decidedly rejected by Powell.[80] Soon after, he heard that Tor-Rarrabay's fighters had won a battle, "obtain[ing] two bodies, which of course were eaten." Powell told the chief that he found such small-scale battles quite ridiculous, boasting instead "about the white men's fighting; upon which he asked me what was done with all the bodies[;] when I told him they were buried, he turned away, evidently in disgust at such a waste."[81]

Again, as in the case of the Duke of York Islanders we have encountered earlier,[82] it is notable that the non-consumption of killed enemies was considered wasteful—human flesh was a resource too valuable to let spoil. Though not all flesh, as dead community members were not eaten, with the exception of (foreign-born) widows without strong ties into the community, who could be deliberately murdered for a cycle of cannibalistic gift giving that continuously created new obligations and hence required new victims, as we have seen.[83]

In parts of neighboring New Guinea, the status of foreign-born children was equally precarious, with some of them ending up as gifts sent for consumption to friendly villages.[84] That human flesh was regarded as a suitable present in parts of this island also came to the attention to the Scottish missionary James Chalmers (1841–1901) when his wife was given "a piece of a human breast, wrapped in leaves, and carried in a basket" from a well-meaning donor who seems to have sincerely believed that she would appreciate it for her kitchen.[85]

An exchange of human body parts as gifts for consumption has also been reported from Vanuatu. Several sources indicate that the corpses exchanged in this way were often "produced" in warfare. Referring to Ambae Island in the north of this archipelago, Speiser writes that "the corpses [of enemies killed in war] were sent to all the villages in the neighbourhood, where a dance was performed round them before they were eaten. Or if there was a surplus, the corpses were cut into pieces and portions were sent to villages with which friendship existed."[86]

The Scot John G. Paton (1824–1907) spent a large part of his adult life in Vanuatu as a Protestant missionary. In his autobiography he writes that in 1861, a few years after his arrival in Tanna Island (in the south), a war broke out on the island—driven by "old bitter grievances," but also by the question of whether the missionaries should be allowed to stay or whether they should be killed or driven away.[87] The conflict continued for months, with periods of largely passive hostility interrupted by occasional outbreaks of deadly fighting: "As many as ten men, they said, were sometimes killed in one day and feasted on by the warriors."[88] While the fighters were men, anyone unable to flee could fall victim to such attacks: "all the sick, the feeble, and the children who fell into their hands were reported to us to be murdered, cooked, and eaten," writes Paton about an attack on a friendly village.[89]

Repeatedly chiefs involved in these fights alluded to the custom of sending body parts of killed enemies to friendly villages for consumption,[90] and indeed it seems that such a behavior was expected. After a fight in which a hostile "district" had been "burned with fire," Paton heard Nowar, the local chief and his protector, complain: "When so many children are being killed, why do they not send one for food to me and my family? They are as tender and good as the young fowls!"[91]

In 1934/35, the British anthropologist Tom Harrisson (1911–1976) spent about a year in the north of Malakula (one of the largest islands of Vanuatu), living among several native peoples.[92] He notes that small acts of warfare and war cannibalism still took place at that time. Usually, a random individual from a hostile village was ambushed and killed; if possible, the body was then taken home, "cut into large pieces, wrapped in leaves and put to cook in a native oven." The body was then eaten by all the men in the village, except for those parts that were sent elsewhere: "Bodies are always divided and sent out to other villages on all cannibal occasions. The recipient of a portion has, of course, to reciprocate it in due course or lose face; this is the cause of many apparently pointless wars; it has also caused the sudden murder of unsuspecting whites."[93]

Such gifts were a means of establishing mutual friendship and support—if you engaged with others in processes of mutual gift exchange, you could feel reasonably safe that they would not suddenly turn against you and attack you. But gifts had to be reciprocated or the mutual trust would suffer, and the other party would feel exploited.

There is also a nonmutual form of gift giving in which the given object (or person) might be more properly regarded as a tribute, given to a superior power in order to ensure them of one's loyalty and goodwill. In Fiji, east of Vanuatu, we have already encountered the practice of giving human tributes—often children or young women—to powerful rulers who then ate them or distributed their flesh among their followers.[94]

Several sources indicate that similar practices existed in Vanuatu. Speiser writes that when a group of villages desired to make peace with a stronger opponent, they had to "surrender . . . human beings or pigs" to the victorious side. Living people given as tributes were often killed and eaten, while in other cases they were kept alive and "assimilated into the social unit" that took them—but the donors had no control over their future fate. Dead bodies were also accepted as tributes: "If there was no desire to sacrifice a fellow villager, there remained the possibility of killing someone in a third village and handing him over to the adversary as an atonement"—but in such cases there was the danger of triggering a new conflict with the "third village" and starting a new cycle of warfare and deadly revenge.[95]

The Irish naval officer and ethnographer Boyle T. Somerville (1863–1936) records a specific instance of this custom. A missionary employed in Uripiv (a small island next to Malekula) told him of "a vendetta between two villages which had been closed" by the weaker party "sending . . . a small boy as sacrifice" and peace offering; the boy was subsequently butchered and eaten. More usual, he adds, was the "payment of pigs" in such cases.[96]

In some regions powerful men seem to have been able to request human offerings even in times of peace. Speiser writes that in Ambrym, an island situated east of Malekula, "a man of high rank demanded in turn from one or the other village in his domain a human being for roasting—a demand which no one dared to refused. Children or well-nourished youths had to be delivered to him, bound to poles like pigs."[97] The Presbyterian missionary Robert Lamb reports this as well, based on the firsthand account of a missionary who worked on that island.[98] We may assume that most of the victims had been captured or maybe purchased elsewhere, with people giving up their own children only if they really had no other choice.

Gift giving was a way to assure mutually friendly relations (if symmetrical) or to confirm a hierarchy of power and superiority (if not). But why had human flesh and bodies become suitable gifts? The sources indicate that cannibalism was often a side effect of war and of acts possibly considered self-defense: vanquishing one's enemies and getting rid of potentially dangerous strangers produced dead bodies, and not to utilize these dead bodies would have been wasteful. Because enemies or strangers had to be overpowered first, access to human flesh also became a sign of power: in order to be able to consume others, you had to be stronger and more successful than they.

Festetics de Tolna, who not only had participated in at least two cannibal meals (see above), but who had also seen the consumption of human flesh at several other occasions,[99] comments that cannibalism was driven not only by the "need to vary the animal food in a country where no other edible mammal than the pig is known," but that "it is also a symbol. It is a sign of victory."[100] Moreover, whether because of this association with victory or for other reasons, human flesh was considered "particularly tasty" and "much better than pork," as Speiser and other observers noted.[101] These factors likely contributed to make human flesh not just one gift among many, but a particularly prized one.

Concluding Remarks

To return to the commercial aspects of cannibal practices in Melanesia and Africa, it is notable that such practices differed considerably from our modern notions of trade and commerce. In the modern world, meat production is a large-scale and highly industrialized process. Even in preindustrial societies, when meat appeared on the markets, it usually came from deliberately bred domesticated animals, much rarer from hunted animals, and hardly ever from carrion (dead animals not deliberately killed for consumption). But people, as far as we know, have never been deliberately bred for consumption. Nor were there "people hunters" who made a living by hunting or kidnapping and killing people in order to sell their flesh.

Commercial cannibal was shaped by the availability of victims—victims who, in contrast to animals, were not deliberately bred or systematically hunted. Depending on the local situation, captured enemies, kidnapped foreigners, convicted criminals, or otherwise hard-to-sell slaves could be slaughtered in order to sell their flesh. But since such victims could only be secured under certain circumstances and from time to time, nobody "made a living" just by selling human flesh. Therefore, the commercial trade in human flesh could exist only as a side activity connected to other practices such as warfare and slavery.

The regular exchange of corpses documented for parts of Central Africa likely was the most institutionalized practice investigated in this chapter, considering that in certain regions nearly every corpse seems to have been used for this purpose. In contrast to the sale of the flesh of enemies, victims of kidnapping, criminals, or slaves, this was (in general) a nondeadly practice. Often based on the notion of mutual gift exchange rather than money-based trade, it was also less commercial that many of the other practices examined in this chapter.

In Melanesia, on the other hand, a regular exchange of human flesh and corpses as gifts has also been documented, but here such flesh usually came from deliberately killed victims. While a gift exchange on the basis of mutuality is not a commercial transaction, it likewise creates an obligation in the recipient—who does not have to pay immediately but is expected to follow up later with a suitable counter-gift. In Melanesia, the cannibalistic gift exchange served to secure relationships of trust and friendship between influential men and maybe whole communities—at the cost of outsiders and weaker members of the society, such as captured strangers or foreign-born widows.

Notes

1. Lapsley, *Life and Letters*, 175; see Chapter 7, this volume.
2. See Chapter 7, this volume.
3. For a classical treatment, see Mauss, *Gift*.
4. See Chapter 1, this volume.
5. See, for example, Conklin, *Consuming Grief*.
6. See Chapter 12, this volume.
7. Du Chaillu, *Explorations & Adventures*, 88 (italics removed).
8. Ibid., 74.
9. Ibid, 88.
10. Ibid.
11. See Chapter 4, this volume.
12. Kingsley, *Travels*, 268, 269 (quote).
13. Du Chaillu, *Explorations & Adventures*, 96.
14. Lenz, *Skizzen aus Westafrika*, 84.
15. See Chapter 12, this volume.
16. Du Chaillu, *Explorations & Adventures*, 84 (italics removed).
17. Kingsley, *Travels*, 268.
18. Du Chaillu, *Explorations & Adventures*, 94–95.
19. Lenz, *Skizzen aus Westafrika*, 89.
20. Kingsley, *Travels*, 268.
21. Burrows and Canisius, *Curse of Central Africa*, 212.
22. Gero, *Cannibalism in Zandeland*, 40, 42, 56.
23. Ibid., 80, 111–12.
24. Schweinfurth, *Heart of Africa*, 18.

25. Du Chaillu, *Explorations & Adventures*, 96.
26. Livingstone, "Unyanyembe Journal."
27. Quoted in Johnston, *George Grenfell*, 1:402.
28. Gero, *Cannibalism in Zandeland*, 137.
29. Famine cannibalism is generally outside the scope of this book, but see Chapter 1, note 16 for some sources, as well as Chapter 14 in this volume.
30. See Chapter 7, this volume.
31. Magyar, *Reisen*, 126, 162.
32. Ibid., 125, 291–92 (quotes), 297.
33. Ibid., 380, 381 (quote).
34. Ibid., 373–74, 378 (quote).
35. See the mentions of Magyar's name in Miller, *Kings and Kinsmen*.
36. Hutchinson, *Ten Years Wanderings*, 61.
37. Hogg, *Cannibalism*, 93.
38. Snelgrave, *New Account*, 53 (italics omitted).
39. Ibid., 44, 51, 52 (quote).
40. See Chapter 3, this volume.
41. See Chapter 11, this volume.
42. Parkinson, *Im Bismarck-Archipel*, 121.
43. Ibid., 121–22.
44. Pfeil, *Studien und Beobachtungen*, 76, 131.
45. Oliver, *Oceania,* 526.
46. Brown, *Pioneer-Missionary and Explorer*, 233.
47. Haberberger, *Kolonialismus und Kannibalismus*, 78.
48. Kleintitschen, *Die Küstenbewohner*, 325–26; Winthuis, *Heidnische Greuel*, 41–43.
49. Redlich, "Notes," 31.
50. Pfeil, *Studien und Beobachtungen*, 39 (quote), 131.
51. Parkinson, *Im Bismarck-Archipel*, 121.
52. Coombe, *Islands of Enchantment*, 221.
53. Woodford, *Naturalist*, 150–51 (quotes), 152.
54. See Chapter 12, this volume.
55. Deacon, *Malekula*, 13, 228 (quotes).
56. Coombe, *Islands of Enchantment*, 9, 221.
57. Speiser, *Südsee, Urwald, Kannibalen*, 55, 58.
58. Speiser, *Ethnology of Vanuatu*, 216–18.
59. Ibid., 215.
60. Speiser, *Südsee, Urwald, Kannibalen*, 51.
61. Speiser, *Ethnology of Vanuatu*, 216.
62. Winthuis, *Heidnische Greuel*, 8.
63. Rannie, *My Adventures*, 276.
64. See Chapter 3, this volume, for accounts of slave eating in the Bismarck Archipelago.
65. Haberberger, *Kolonialismus und Kannibalismus*, 47.
66. Festetics de Tolna, *Vers l'écueil*, 145–46.
67. Ibid., 31, 40 (quotes), 104.
68. Speiser, *Ethnology of Vanuatu*, 219.
69. Reeves, *Brown Men and Women*, 2–3.
70. See Chapter 11, this volume.

71. Hagen and Pineau, "Les Nouvelles Hébrides," 326.
72. Ibid.
73. Redlich, "Notes," 34–35, 36 (quote). The three captives were subsequently executed (ibid., 36).
74. Festetics de Tolna, *Vers l'écueil*, 137.
75. Ibid.
76. Festetics de Tolna, *Chez les cannibales*, 251, 252 (quotes).
77. Ibid., 252–53.
78. Ibid., 324.
79. Ibid., 306–8.
80. Powell, *Wanderings*, 80 (italics removed).
81. Ibid., 82–83.
82. See the section "Sale of Human Flesh in Melanesia" in this chapter.
83. See Chapter 11, this volume.
84. See Chapter 11, this volume.
85. Lyne, *New Guinea*, 167. Chalmers told the newspaper correspondent Charles Lyne about this incident. Lyne's book also describes of a case of foreigner poaching that took place on a small island near New Guinea (ibid., 188–90).
86. Speiser, *Ethnology of Vanuatu*, 213.
87. Paton, *Missionary*, 304.
88. Ibid., 308.
89. Ibid., 321.
90. Ibid., 313, 315.
91. Ibid., 341.
92. Harrisson, *Savage Civilisation*, 7, 395–96.
93. Ibid., 403, 404 (quotes).
94. See Chapter 12, this volume.
95. Speiser, *Ethnology of Vanuatu*, 213–14.
96. Somerville, "Ethnological Notes," 383.
97. Speiser, *Ethnology of Vanuatu*, 218.
98. Lamb, *Saints and Savages*, 39.
99. Festetics de Tolna, *Chez les cannibales*, 237, 352–53, 355–56.
100. Ibid., 237.
101. Speiser, *Ethnology of Vanuatu*, 215; see the section "Sale of Human Flesh in Melanesia" in this chapter.

CHAPTER 14

FAMINE AND COMMERCIAL CANNIBALISM IN CHINA

The regions reviewed so far were usually highly decentralized; political units were small and fragmented (at least in precolonial times). China is very different. Chinese history consists of dynasties of kings and emperors that reach back more than three thousand years. While China was not always a single unified country during this time, many leaders ruled over large regions. Though this makes China, on the basis of our previous evidence, an untypical country for cannibalism, such episodes are well documented in the country's past. From ancient times to the twentieth century, human flesh was consumed—and sometimes sold—during times of famine and severe food scarcity. It also played a role in warfare, with some military leaders deliberately resorting to cannibalism to feed their troops. In a few cases, such practices seem to have developed into a custom, with human flesh being consumed even when there was no military reason to do so. Other motives, such as health concerns or revenge, could play a role as well.

The focus of this chapter and the next one will be commercial aspects of such practices and cases where the consumption of human flesh was seemingly motivated, at least to a certain degree, by culinary concerns. However, since the context and motives of cannibal acts were interconnected in complex ways, other aspects will be considered as well, since ignoring them could lead to a seriously distorted picture.

Famine and Commerce

Famine is a recurring topic throughout the thousands of years of written history recorded in China. Episodes of dire food scarcity were usually caused by either natural reasons—drought or natural disasters—or warfare. Repeatedly, when other sources of food were largely or fully exhausted, people resorted to the consumption of human flesh to avert starvation. Ample documentation on famines can be found in the dynastic histories, a collection of two dozen official history books compiled between the first century BCE and the early twentieth century CE by court historians. While largely silent on matters considered private, they contain dense, informative descriptions of political developments, war campaigns, and crisis situations affecting large parts of the population.

The sinologist Bengt Pettersson has found in them more than five hundred references to cannibalism describing more than three hundred different episodes where human bodies, or parts of them, were consumed. About half of the described episodes—170 in all—were motivated by food scarcity due to natural causes or warfare. The earliest episodes of hunger cannibalism reported in the official histories occurred around 140 BCE, the latest in the early twentieth century. Most of them took place in a densely settled, centrally located area that can be described as a triangle with Beijing, Shanghai, and Chengdu as its corners—not on the fringes of the empire, but in a region that was usually under tight imperial control.[1]

Sometimes famine cannibalism had a commercial side—human flesh was not only eaten by desperate people, but also sold and purchased; living people were bought in order to butcher and consume them. About a famine in the mid-sixth century, one of the dynastic histories writes that "everywhere, human flesh mixed with beef and horse meat was sold." Remarkable in this account is that human flesh appeared on the market even before other sources of meat were completely exhausted—in addition to mentioning beef and horse meat, the account also states that slaughtered cows and dogs were sold at very high prices.[2]

This was no exception. Describing a famine in the early tenth century, one of the official histories notes that "one *jin* of human flesh was valued at 100 *qian*," while those who bought dog meat had to pay five times as much.[3] And a survivor of a famine in the early twelfth century remembered that "the price of human meat was lower than that of dog meat or pork."[4] During famines, human flesh was eaten not by the wealthiest, but by those who could no longer afford other kinds of meat.

The poorest, on the other hand, probably had to do without meat altogether, or they had to sacrifice the life of one of their family members in order to get it. Over thousands of years, children—in patriarchal China, most of them girls[5]—were the victims of a practice known as "exchanging one's children and eating them." When threatened by starvation, poor parents gave a child to another family, receiving one of their children in return; each family then slaughtered the child they had been given. In this way, explains the British journalist Jasper Becker, they could "alleviate their hunger and . . . avoid consuming their own offspring."[6]

The oldest documented occurrence of this practice was in 593 BCE, when a city, Song, was besieged by the neighboring Chu people. The inhabitants sent a messenger to the Chu commander, telling him: "In the city we are exchanging our children and eating them, and splitting up their bones for fuel. Notwithstanding, if you require us to make a covenant with you under the walls, we will not do so." Realizing that the people in the city would never give up, the besiegers aborted their attempt to conquer the city and withdrew.[7] The exchange and consumption of children is also documented for various later sieges, both during the early "Warring States" period (ca. 475–221 BCE) as well as in later times, up to the twelfth century CE.[8]

Famines caused by drought or warfare led to the same reaction. During the early years of the Han dynasty (202 BCE–220 CE), the land was in turmoil and famine was widespread. Emperor Gaozu (256–195 BCE), the founder of the dynasty, reacted by allowing families to eat their own children or to exchange or sell them for cannibalistic purposes.[9] The exchange and subsequent consumption of children is also documented for later famines, including one in the year 400 CE.[10]

The same practice is mentioned in many accounts of the so-called Incredible Famine, a disaster that struck several northern provinces in the late 1870s. With an estimated death toll of nine to thirteen million people, it is considered the most lethal drought-related famine in Chinese history.[11] The deadly child exchange reappeared, for the last time, during the great famine in 1959–1961 caused by Mao's disastrously misdirected "Great Leap Forward." Decades later, Becker spoke with a famine survivor from the Anhui province in the east who "recalled that a traditional practice called *Yi zi er shi* ('Swop child, make food') was common."[12] This is the same phrase mentioned in many of the older documents, also translatable as "exchanging one's children and eating them."

Starving parents, the witness remembered, stopped giving food to one of their children—usually a girl, as boys were considered more valuable to continue the family line. Once the child was dead, her body was given to neighbors who in turn gave up one of their own children. (In older times, it seems that living children were exchanged and then killed by the recipient family. Maybe the new practice was perceived as safer, since there was no risk of anyone witnessing a murder and calling the police.) The dead body of the neighbors' child was used to make soup and nourish the family for some time. Sometimes up to seven women agreed to share their children in this manner, each giving up one child to save the rest of the family.[13]

The interviewee stated that "people accepted this as it was a kind of hunger culture" and did not criticize those who made such "swops," understanding that they were driven by desperation. He explained that people remembered this practice from severe famines of the 1930s where it had also occurred—he does not seem to have known that the practice was actually thousands of years older than that.[14]

In fact, the deadly child exchange was not limited to China but has also been reported from other parts of the world. On the "barren and rocky islands which form the windward [southeastern?] portion of the Fijian group," the

English-Australian missionary and ethnologist Lorimer Fison heard of an ancient practice known as *Veisaungone* or "child-barter." An old and "thoroughly trust-worthy man" stated that, when he was young, the older people often spoke of earlier bad times of famine, during which "children [were] commonly eaten until the hungry time was overpast." He explained: "Our fathers did not eat children of their own tribe. . . . People of other towns used to bring their boys and girls hither to us, and take away ours in exchange and this was called 'Veisaungone.'"[15] The Methodist missionary Walter Lawry also mentions this custom.[16]

The French explorer and captain Jules Dumont d'Urville (1790–1842) recorded recollections of the same practice in Mangareva, one of the islands of French Polynesia. In August 1838, he wrote: "It is even said that in a time of famine, parents went so far in forgetting their most natural feelings as to sacrifice their own children [for food]. But to avoid being reduced to eating them themselves, they were careful to exchange them between neighbors."[17]

And among the Zande in Central Africa, starving men sometimes exchanged either their daughters or their wives—sources differ—to be "butchered and eaten up," as already mentioned.[18] While mentions of this practice from elsewhere are not as frequent as those from China, it is remarkable that the same famine practice could be found throughout the world. Since it is very unlikely that such hunger customs in China, Polynesia, and Africa had somehow influenced each other, it seems that this approach to ensuring the survival of families at the cost of their weaker members—without, however, having to go as far as eating your own relatives—emerged spontaneously in various parts of the world. It is also notable, though not surprising, that in all these male-dominated societies it was children—girls more often than boys—or occasionally women who were sacrificed for food, never men.

A comment in one of the official histories also shows that being able to eat an unrelated child was considered a less appalling form of cannibalism than having to eat one's own. During the troubled times at the end of the Sui dynasty (581–618), notes the *Beishi*, things turned bad so quickly that people did not even have "time . . . to exchange the children before eating them."[19] Other sources confirm that having to eat one's own relatives was considered the worst calamity—something that only happened when people had run out of all other options. During a famine in 1622 (writes another of the histories), people proceeded from eating "the flesh of the dead" to eating "people . . . alive"—killing others to eat them. Ultimately, some became so desperate that "relatives ate each other."[20] Centuries later, Liu Xing, a survivor of the "Incredible Famine," described the same progression of events. After consuming everything else that was available, even tree bark and clay, people resorted to eating human flesh. First, they consumed the dead, he writes, then they killed and ate the living, including finally their own family members.[21]

These notes indicate that killing and eating strangers was seen as a less terrible choice than having to kill one's own children or relatives—people

Figure 14.1. Scenes of devastation during the "Incredible Famine," from the English translation of a Chinese booklet written to collect money for relief efforts. In the background, someone is eating bark from a tree. In the foreground, people are cutting flesh from a corpse for consumption. From Committee of the China Famine Relief Fund, ed., *The Famine in China: Illustrations by a Native Artist with a Translation of the Chinese Text*, translated by Ja[me]s Legge (London: C. Kegan Paul, 1878), 23.

never got used to the latter, but sometimes, it seems, to the former. Wang Xilun, a poet who engaged in relief work during the "Incredible Famine," later described "how children whose starving parents had abandoned them in ditches were slaughtered and eaten by other famine victims as though they were sheep or pigs," without the perpetrators showing any visible concern for the humanness of their victims. A booklet published during the disaster by a group of Chinese philanthropists collecting money for relief efforts complains that some had discovered that "killing people is as easy as killing pigs," leading to orphans and abandoned children being butchered without mercy "since meat has become more valuable than human life."[22] That children were kidnapped, killed, and consumed during the famine was also confirmed by various newspaper accounts published either during or after the famine as well as by several survivors, among them Liu Xing.[23]

While poor families had to exchange one of their children for one they could eat (if they did not want to become kidnappers), wealthier people could sometimes pay with money for a human life. The historians Korn, Radice, and Hawes point out that, in times of hardship, poor parents were often forced to bring one of their children to the market and sell them in order to allow the rest of the family to survive. What happened afterwards was left to the buyers. In normal times, most of the sold children will have faced a life of servitude and exploitation, but in times of famine, when servants were abundant but meat was scarce, their lives were sometimes brutally cut short.[24]

If sold to private buyers, parents might have had no idea what would happen to their children, but in some cases, there could be no doubt. Describing a siege in 883, one of the dynastic histories reports that husbands brought their wives and parents brought their children to butcher shops to sell them; those sold were "butchered like sheep and pigs."[25] In other cases, the sources do not clearly reveal the origin of the human flesh that appeared on the market[26]—much of it might have come from corpses, but in other cases it likely came from persons who had been either kidnapped or purchased.

Famine Culture: Corpses Eaten, Children Murdered

Generally, it seems that children and, to a lesser degree, women had the highest risk of falling victim to cannibalism. During a severe famine in 1647, "the strong killed hundreds of the young and weak" in order to eat or sell their flesh, notes the historian Key Ray Chong.[27] That the "weak" were kidnapped and eaten in times of food scarcity is also mentioned in several of the official histories.[28] Reports of the better documented large famines in the late nineteenth and the twentieth centuries indicate that a majority of those killed to be eaten were children, though kidnapped women and occasionally men were also among the victims.[29] During the Great Leap famine, one police officer wrote: "After investigation, we have found that reports of humans eating corpses, as well as killing and consuming children, are all true."[30]

Such acts were criminal, but it seems that the authorities often turned a blind eye when they took place in times of food scarcity. While the official histories never explicitly address the legality of eating or selling human flesh, they do not mention punishments for such acts occurring during times of hunger, with two halfhearted exceptions in the early thirteenth century. In the year 1223, those who had eaten human flesh during a severe famine were arrested; whether they were formally accused or convicted, is not said. About the same time, dismembering and cooking a man was pronounced "a crime against nature," but punished with a fine only.[31] No punishments for the sale of human flesh or of people destined for consumption are ever mentioned. Describing a famine in 1611, the *Mingshi*, the official history book later compiled about the era, writes apologetically: "People are selling their daughters and sons, and eating their wives and children. When driven towards dangers, what choices do they have?"[32]

The biologist and author Bill Schutt comments that the reactions of Chinese governments to famine cannibalism "varied from turning a blind eye to something close to official sanction."[33] Indeed, during another famine that occurred about ten years later, the army even officially took over the provisioning of the population with human flesh in several districts: "The troops of Yanfang and Yunqing openly butchered and sold people in a market where one *jin* of flesh could be exchanged for one *liang* of silver."[34] Army leaders also repeatedly relied on human flesh to feed their troops, as we will see later.

The ratio given in the previous quote allows comparing the prices charged during that famine with contemporary meat prices. Today silver can buy thirty-nine times its own mass (or weight) in beef,[35] while during the mentioned famine it could buy sixteen times its own mass in human flesh.[36] Assuming that silver is a reasonable baseline, human flesh was more expensive, but not as pricey as one might think.

Eyewitness accounts from the "Incredible Famine" indicate that, as in earlier famines, human flesh appeared on the markets, with the police seemingly doing little to stop or investigate such practices. Liu Xing writes that he saw with his "own eyes" not only how human flesh was eaten, but also how it was sold "at the market." While not openly labeled as such, its sale was an open secret, and buyers sometimes found human fingernails in the meat they had purchased.[37]

The already mentioned philanthropic booklet reproduced a letter written by a man from one of the famine provinces who had seen "a butcher's gate that displayed different kinds of human meat." Next to the meat, he spotted "a young woman . . . about to be cooked." Apparently not believing that the police would intervene in time, he instead "rushed home to get money with which to redeem her," but when he returned, she had already been butchered.[38] Such accounts were not exceptional: "The claim that human flesh was sold in shops and markets during the disaster appears in many famine texts" as well as in newspaper reports published during the famine.[39]

In 1912, the last emperor of the Qing dynasty (which had ruled since 1644) was forced to abdicate and China became a republic. But the times of hunger were not yet over. Several famines in the 1930s and 1940s led once again to cannibalism and the sale of human flesh not only in parts of the Republic of China,[40] but apparently also in Hong Kong and Macau, which were European colonies at that time. During the last years of World War II, Macau was overrun with refugees and food became quite scare. Meat was available in the local markets only from time to time, and while it was generally labeled as "pork," much of it was "suspected to be of human origin," as city dwellers subsequently remembered. A Portuguese woman later recalled how shocked she was when, during her visit to a market, she spotted, "in the bottom of a split-bamboo basket, the deboned face of a Chinese child," discreetly offered for sale "much like a pig face in any local wet market."[41]

The deadliest famine of all times (likely not only in Chinese, but in world history) devastated large parts of the country in 1959–1961 in the wake of Mao's "Great Leap Forward." Estimates for its death toll range from twenty to forty million, considerably higher than even for the "Incredible Famine."[42]

In Anhui, an eastern province which was hit particularly hard, an official report compiled in 1961 "identified nearly thirteen hundred" cases of cannibalism which had taken place in 1959 and 1960. A small percentage of these cases—thirty-six in all—"involved selling human flesh for profit," while in most cases the flesh was eaten by those who had killed a person or dismembered a corpse. If human flesh was sold, it was commonly labeled as pork. In one case, "a fifty-seven-year-old peasant killed a thirteen-year-old boy named Lianchen. After cooking and eating part of the boy's flesh, the man sold the remainder in the village as pork." In another case, a worker "dug up a corpse, ate part of it, and sold a kilo as pork."[43] The sale of human flesh is also documented in other provinces, such as Gansu in the northwest of the country. In 1961, a peasant bought a large piece of meat at a railway station, which turned out to be "from a human head, with a nose and ears" still attached.[44]

According to Jasper Becker, who in the 1990s collected oral accounts of the famine period, the two mentioned cases from Anhui might have been fairly typical. He found few reports of adults killed for meat, but many of murdered children. Desperate parents killed one or more of their children, subsequently either eating them themselves or exchanging them with other families in the ancient practice that has already been described. In other cases, children were kidnapped and butchered. While adults were rarely kidnapped or killed, the corpses of those who had starved or died a natural death were often partially or wholly consumed.[45]

Becker too found various reports and witnesses stating that human flesh was not only eaten, but also sold. Officials interviewed by him confirmed that cannibalism "was nothing exceptional" and had occurred "in every county and most villages" in some regions.[46] He also spoke with several people who "frankly admitted" having eaten human flesh during the famine. He observes that, "because there's not such a specific moral or religious taboo about this, they don't really feel particularly ashamed of it."[47]

From Famine to Preference?

Like Becker, Bengt Pettersson observes that a dedicated "famine culture" had evolved as a way of dealing with the high number of famines. People had learned how to behave in times of hunger to increase the food supply and ensure that at least some would survive. The knowledge that cannibalism could be resorted to as a measure of last resort was part of the famine culture, transported over millenniums by oral traditions and written sources. Pettersson notes that the dynastic histories "neither encouraged nor condemned" cannibal practices during times of food scarcity, rather accepting them "as a pitiable method of coping with a life-threatening situation."[48]

This silent acceptance also meant, however, that the particular injustices of the famine culture could not be addressed. During famines it seems that poor children, particularly girls, had the highest risk of falling victim to cannibalism, while wealthy men faced little personal risk and could still eat quite well. The famine culture might have ensured the survival of some at the cost of the lives of others, but the processes determining who would live and who had to die were grossly unbalanced.

It also seems that the consumption of human flesh during famines was not always driven by pure desperation, but that culinary choices could play a role as well. In the mid-1930s, the Sichuan province in the southwest was afflicted by several years of famine caused by natural calamities. According to records collected twenty-five years later (after the next big famine) by the People's Political Consultative Conference, a political advisory body, human

> flesh was bought in quarters, at prices that varied by a factor of one or two depending on whether it had been taken from a corpse or from a person killed for the purpose. In the east of Sichuan at the beginning of May 1936, the going rate was 500 copper pieces for a pound of flesh from a corpse and 1,220 copper pieces a pound if it was freshly killed.[49]

Flesh taken from a corpse would have been as suitable to face off starvation as that of a murder victim. Still, some buyers were willing to pay a considerable surcharge for the flesh of a "freshly killed" individual. Maybe they feared that the corpse of someone who had died of hunger or natural causes was infected with a disease, or that the flesh was close to going bad? This is conceivable, but is it enough to explain the price difference? Or were people willing to pay more because fresh flesh tasted better or because the victims of kidnapping and murder were, on average, younger than those who had died of natural reasons? If so, they were willing to put their culinary preferences over the lives of others.

While exact prices of human flesh are rarely recorded, during an earlier famine, in 1647, "man's meat was sold for seven ch'ien and woman's for eight ch'ien per chin."[50] Certainly, human flesh was equally nourishing regardless of whether it came from a male or female victim. It is therefore hard to explain this price difference except as due to a culinary preference.

Generally, the first half of the seventeenth century was a period of political unrest and economic instability. The Ming dynasty (1368–1644) was in decline and ultimately collapsed due to external attacks and internal difficulties. Famines became more frequent, in part due to economic and political troubles, but also because of an "unusually cold and dry weather that shortened the growing season"—part of a global period of cooling called the "little ice age."[51] The official histories recorded cannibalism for several of these famines. According to a folktale written down by the scholar Ji Yun (1724–1805), human flesh was also served in restaurants during this time of frequent famines. Innkeepers bought people (in the case of the folktale it was a young woman) and then washed and slaughtered them, and served their flesh to their customers, who generally seem to have known what was going on. Ji Yun treated the story as true—it was likely based on oral accounts he had received.[52]

Various tales and oral accounts circulating in later decades about the "Incredible Famine" of the late nineteenth century likewise claim that the flesh of kidnapped or purchased victims—usually "young women and children"—was served at inns "to undiscerning customers."[53] How much truth there is in such stories is difficult to determine. They may be more or less distorted depictions of actual practices, or they may be pure horror fantasies. But, in any case they are part of the oral record and, considering that cannibalism and the sale of human flesh are well documented for these times, it would be wrong to treat them as mere fanciful "fairytales." If human flesh was really served in restaurants, this would also hint at a certain preference—not particularly for human flesh, but certainly for flesh of any kind over a meatless diet. The patrons in these tales do not seem to have been threatened by immediate starvation, rather they were apparently willing to accept human-based dishes over having to forgo meat altogether.

Two other folktales taking place in the late Ming dynasty cover the sale of women by their own husbands to butchers and sellers of human meat—a practice that has indeed been documented for several famines.[54] They also claim that the sold women voluntarily sacrificed themselves in order to ensure the survival of their husbands and parents-in-law—something that may be doubted, though it certainly reflects the values of Chinese society, in which filial piety and a woman's devotion for her husband were among the highest virtues.

During an earlier famine, culinary choices also seem to have played a role. In 1125, a war broke out between the newly established Jin (or Jurchen) dynasty (1115–1234), which ruled the northeast of today's China, and the older Song dynasty (960–1279), which ruled the southeast. Due to severe attacks from the north, the Song rulers had to abandon their capital, Kaifeng, which was conquered by the northern forces in 1127. But the Jin troops did not stop there, even conquering two years later today's Hangzhou (750 kilometers farther southeast). Realizing that they "had advanced too far and too fast" and were unable to properly secure the territory they had conquered, the Jin army soon decided to abandon the city and withdraw to the north—but only after they had thoroughly "pillaged" the city.[55]

A few years later, the scholar Zhuang Chuo finished the *Jilebian*, a book in which he describes his memories of the time.[56] He writes that one year after the start of the war, a huge famine broke out in the regions which had been conquered and plundered by the northern soldiers. During the next six or seven years, people resorted to cannibalism and human flesh appeared on the marketplaces:

> Thieves and bandits, civil servants and soldiers, the entire population were eating each other. The price of human meat was lower than that of dog meat or pork. A fat, sturdy man was worth only 1500 coins. Human bodies were exposed to the sun in order to be processed into dried meat.[57]

Zhuang adds that when the Song troops returned to Hangzhou in 1133, after several years of chaos and lawlessness, they found that its inhabitants consumed human flesh—whether only by necessity or also by choice is not quite clear. In any case it seems that a culture had developed in which human flesh was sold almost openly, without any real attempt to hide its origin. While in other famines, this flesh was often mislabeled as "pork" or some other kind of animal meat, here it was known as "two-legged mutton"—a euphemism that hinted at its true origin in a not so subtle manner.[58]

Zhuang mentions several additional euphemisms which indicate that the buyers had become quite discriminating in regard to the origin of the meat they acquired, and the sellers readily told them (in a slightly veiled language) whether the victim had been young or old, female or male, chubby or skinny: "An old and skinny man was designated under the covert name . . . 'forcing the fire' (?); a fairly young woman was called . . . 'sheep with a hundred beauties'; a little child was named . . . 'tender including the bones' (?)."[59] Key Ray Chong interprets these names as indicating that "because of their superior tastiness children could be eaten whole, including their bones, when they were well-boiled," while "women's meat [was] more delicious than mutton" and "men's meat was . . . the least tasty of all human meat."[60] He also notes that "a suckling pig or a young ram" was often roasted or steamed whole (including the bones) after "remov[ing] the entrails, and fill[ing] the belly with dates"—the name used for young children might have suggested that they could be prepared in a similar manner.[61] Whatever the exact meaning of the used euphemisms, they leave little doubt that the flesh of little children and young woman was considered preferable to that of old men—and likely fetched a higher price. Such distinctions clearly went beyond the necessities of mere survival.

Notes

1. Pettersson, "Cannibalism," 85, 93, 180. Pettersson points out that the dynastic histories are generally judged to be very reliable. They may occasionally omit events for political reasons or simply because they were considered unimportant, but the information they provide tends to be accurate (ibid., 93–94).
2. Ibid., 88, quoting the *Weishu*. All works quoted by Pettersson are official (dynastic) histories, unless explicitly stated otherwise.
3. Ibid., 147, quoting the *Xin Wudaishi*. A *jin* (or *catty*) is a traditional unit of mass corresponding to about 605 grams.
4. Zhuang Chuo quoted in Rotours, "Quelques notes," 417. We will later return to Zhuang's account.
5. Becker, *Hungry Ghosts*, 137; Petrinovich, *Cannibal Within,* 185.
6. Becker, *Hungry Ghosts*, 211.
7. Pettersson, "Cannibalism," 82.
8. Ibid., 129, 142–43, 150.
9. Becker, *Hungry Ghosts*, 211; Korn, Radice, and Hawes, *Cannibal*, 90.
10. Pettersson, "Cannibalism," 137.
11. Edgerton-Tarpley, *Tears from Iron*, 1, 216.
12. Becker, *Hungry Ghosts*, 137.
13. Ibid.
14. Ibid., 138.
15. Fison, *Tales from Old Fiji*, xliii–xliv.
16. "It is even related, that, in times of scarcity, families will make an exchange of children for this horrid purpose [of eating them]" (Lawry, *Friendly and Feejee Islands*, 269).
17. Dumont d'Urville, *Voyage au pôle Sud*, 212.
18. Evans-Pritchard, "Zande Cannibalism," 251; Gero, *Cannibalism in Zandeland*, 69, 86 (quote), 123; see Chapter 7, this volume.
19. Pettersson, "Cannibalism," 140, quoting the *Beishi.*
20. Ibid., 156, quoting the *Mingshi.*
21. Edgerton-Tarpley, *Tears from Iron*, 49.
22. Quoted ibid., 77, 219.
23. Ibid., 211, 224.
24. Korn, Radice, and Hawes, *Cannibal*, 90.
25. Pettersson, "Cannibalism," 147, quoting the *Xin Wudaishi.*
26. Another famine for which this is documented in the official histories took place in 1457 (ibid., 154, quoting the *Mingshi*).
27. Chong, *Cannibalism in China*, 129.
28. Pettersson, "Cannibalism," 148, 153–154.
29. See, for example, Becker, *Hungry Ghosts*, 20–21, 137, 211–213; Bianco, *Peasants without the Party*, 153; Edgerton-Tarpley, *Tears from Iron*, 211–13, 217; Yang, *Tombstone*, chapters 3 and 8; Zhou, *Great Famine*, 62–70.
30. Quoted in Zhou, *Great Famine*, 68.
31. Pettersson, "Cannibalism," 149, 151 (quote).
32. Ibid., 156, quoting the *Mingshi.*
33. Schutt, *Eat Me*, 153.
34. Pettersson, "Cannibalism," 156, quoting the *Mingshi.*

35. In 2019, the average price of silver was US$16.19 per troy ounce (31.1 grams), while the average retail price of beef in the United States was $6.04 per pound (453.6 grams; Statista, "Average Comex Spot Price of Silver from 1975 to 2019," https://www.statista.com/statistics/253317/comex-spot-price-of-silver-since-1975/; National Chicken Council, "Wholesale and Retail Prices for Chicken, Beef, and Pork," https://www.nationalchickencouncil.org/about-the-industry/statistics/wholesale-and-retail-prices-for-chicken-beef-and-pork/. Both websites accessed 31 August 2020).
36. One *jin* comprises sixteen *liang*.
37. Edgerton-Tarpley, *Tears from Iron*, 211.
38. Ibid., 201.
39. Ibid., 212 (quote), 217.
40. Becker, *Hungry Ghosts*, 20–21, 138; Bianco, *Peasants without the Party*, 153.
41. Jason Wordie, "Cannibalism in Japanese-occupied Hong Kong—When Food Shortages Made Human Flesh the Only Option," *South China Morning Post Magazine*, 15 November 2019, accessed 28 August 2020, https://www.scmp.com/magazines/post-magazine/short-reads/article/3037647/cannibalism-japanese-occupied-hong-kong-when.
42. Becker, *Hungry Ghosts*, 95.
43. Yang, *Tombstone*, chapter 8.
44. Zhou, *Great Famine*, 61, quoting a police report.
45. Becker, *Hungry Ghosts*, 213.
46. Ibid., 212 (quotes), 213.
47. Ibid., 95–96.
48. Pettersson, "Cannibalism," 95.
49. Bianco, *Peasants without the Party*, 153.
50. Chong, *Cannibalism in China*, 129.
51. Spence, *Search*, 20 (quotes), 21.
52. Rotours, "Encore quelques notes," 26–27. Associations between the washing of people and their subsequent butchering have also been reported from elsewhere in the world. In the mid-nineteenth century, a Batak (from Sumatra) working in the neighboring Malay Peninsula, upon "seeing his master's child washed, made the following remark: 'In our country it would not be necessary to wash that child [who apparently looked quite clean]; he might be roasted at once'" (quoted in Yule, *Cathay*, 86n). This must have been a joke, as the servant certainly knew that "his master's child" was not about to be eaten, but it seems that he regarded the washing of a child as part of the preparations of a cannibal meal. As cannibalism was practiced in Sumatra (see Chapter 3, this volume), he might have heard about or even witnessed similar scenes at home.
53. Edgerton-Tarpley, *Tears from Iron*, 295n25.
54. Lu, *Accidental Incest*, 166–69.
55. Twitchett and Smith, *Sung Dynasty*, 28, 654, 655 (quotes).
56. The website *ChinaKnowledge* notes that Zhuang Chuo "migrated a lot around many regions of China and so experienced a lot of adventures and could see and hear much information that he decided to bring to paper." It considers his book "among the best . . . books including historiographic material" written about the era (ChinaKnowledge, "Chinese Literature: *Jilebian*, 'A Compilation of Chicken

Ribs,'" last modified 2 September 2013, http://www.chinaknowledge.de/Literature/Novels/jilebian.html).

57. Quoted in Rotours, "Quelques notes," 417.
58. Quoted ibid.
59. Quoted ibid. (question marks added by Rotours).
60. Chong, *Cannibalism in China*, 137.
61. Ibid., 150 (quotes), 152.

CHAPTER 15
WARFARE AND CULINARY CANNIBALISM IN CHINA

Cannibalism during Times of War

In times of war, cities under siege often suffered from a deliberately created famine situation—if an army could not conquer a city by military force, they tried to starve it out. In such situations, desperate inhabitants sometimes started to eat corpses and, if this was not sufficient, to kill and eat their own children or those they had exchanged with neighbors. Sometimes butchers purchased women and children sold by their own husbands and parents.[1]

The earliest accounts of the deadly practice known as "exchanging one's children and eating them" come from the philosopher Mencius (ca. 372–ca. 289 BCE) and the *Shiji* ("Records of the Grand Historian," finished around 94 BCE), the oldest of the dynastic histories. These accounts treat the consumption of children as a sign of determination rather than desperation: a city whose inhabitants were willing to sacrifice their own family members for food was essentially impossible to starve out.[2] About another siege that had been aborted after the inhabitants of the attacked city resorted to cannibalism, the *Shiji* notes approvingly: "When officers harbour no thoughts of rebellion although people are eaten and their bones burned, they can be called soldiers of Sun Bin's," a famous military strategist.[3]

In order to show that they did not just ask the population to make sacrifices they were not willing to make themselves, in a least three sieges between the second and thirteenth centuries military leaders supposedly ordered their own "favourite concubine" to be butchered to feed the hungry soldiers. The earliest recorded instance of this practice took place in 195 CE: "In the end, when there was nothing more to eat, [Hong] killed his favourite concubine and fed her to the soldiers. They all cried and lowered their heads in respect. Seventy to eighty men and women cuddled together and died [voluntarily sacrificing themselves for the famished soldiers?]. No one left or rebelled."[4]

In 1223, the leader's decision triggered a chain reaction of other officers trying to prove that they were no less loyal: "Within the walls provisions were exhausted. People ate each other. Heihan killed his favourite concubine and fed her to his officers. Officers then vied with each other to kill their own wives and children."[5]

Another account from the official histories shows with particular clarity the deadly logic with which those considered less essential for the war effort were sacrificed, and the hierarchies—in particular, of gender and age—that determined who had to die and who might live. In 757, writes the *Jiu Tangshu* (Old Book of Tang),

> Because Yi Ziqi's siege had lasted for a long time, food supplies within the walls were exhausted, children were being exchanged and eaten and their bones split for fuel. People had fear in their hearts and thought that there would be a mutiny. Because of this Xun fetched his concubine, killed her in front of the army and presented her to the soldiers saying: "Brothers, for the sake of your country you have defended this city with united efforts. . . . I am not able to cut my own flesh to feed you, but how can I take pity on this woman and just sit by and watch the dangers?" As tears rolled down their faces the soldiers were unable to eat. Xun forcefully ordered them to eat her. When the city's other women had perished, old men and small boys followed. Twenty to thirty thousand people were eaten. Still, at the bottom of their hearts, they remained loyal.[6]

The *Xin Tangshu* (New Book of Tang), which describes these events in a very similar manner, goes on to discuss their ethical implications:

> Critics have blamed Xun for eating humans and have ridiculed him for his win or die resistance. Myself, I look upon him humbly and in painful compassion. . . .
>
> If Xun in the beginning of his defence had already planned to eat people and lose a few hundred for the purpose of unification, I would still say that merits and faults cancel each other out and also ask whether it is not a question of eternal ideals.[7]

Maybe because of such an attitude which considered the fate of individuals as less important than military goals, war leaders occasionally seem to have been quite willing to utilize parts of their own population as food. During another siege in 908, "the daily killings to feed the soldiers" were handled by a specialized institution known as "slaughter service."[8]

Hostile captives or rebels were killed with even less hesitation to provide food for soldiers. In some cases, such acts were motivated by hunger: "In 22 A.D., during the reign of Wang Mang, 5000 soldiers in the western regions went hungry, but they survived on the flesh and blood of their prisoners of war."[9] A similar act was recorded sixteen centuries later, when the Ming dynasty (1368–1644) was about to collapse due to political chaos and famines.

Around 1640, "when the horses and mules in the camp were all gone, they killed rebels, took their corpses, divided them and ate them up."[10]

In other cases, it seems that hunger was not the only or primary reason, but that other motives such as convenience or a desire to humiliate the enemy played a role as well. During a conflict in 386, "Deng killed bandits in every battle and was famous for cooking and eating them. He said to his soldiers: 'If you fight at dawn, you can feast on flesh at dusk. Why worry about starving?' His men acted accordingly; ate the flesh of the dead and were always full, healthy and capable of fighting." In the same year, two other generals, Dou Chong and Li Bian, after defeating their enemies "slew 1800 people, butchered their bodies and ate them."[11] In this case, since the military conflict was already over, a desire to humiliate and completely annihilate the conquered foe might have been the main motive.

Occasionally captured enemies were sold prior to being eaten, adding a commercial aspect to the cannibal act. During the reign of Emperor Wu of Liang (464–549), the founder of a short-lived dynasty in southeastern China, "numerous prisoners of war were purchased and caged. Whenever there was a demand for meat, some of them were taken out, cut, broiled and consumed. Similarly, those disloyal to the throne were severely punished by having their tongues cut off, sold and cooked for consumption."[12] This account is somewhat mysterious, as it does not explain who purchased these prisoners and what exactly motivated the "demand for [their] meat."

Things turned particularly bad near the end of the ninth century, when the Tang dynasty (618–907) was challenged by large-scale rebellions. The *Jiu Wudaishi,* one of the official histories, notes that both rebels and government troops killed "common people . . . to supplement rations" and "used dismembered prisoners as an asset" when provisions ran low.[13] Sometimes these acts had a commercial side. Certain rebel leaders were supposedly willing to purchase kidnapped individuals "as food. One human fetched the price of several hundred thousand *qian.*"[14] One of the more successful warlords, Qin Zongquan (d. 889), who—ultimately without success—tried to take the imperial throne, seems to have been particularly ruthless in his reliance on cannibalism. According to one of the chronicles, his army routinely "captured the elderly and the young [and] slaughtered [them] like sheep." The human flesh not needed for the troops was sold on the market, thus helping to finance the rebellion.[15]

At this point it may well be asked how reliable these chronicles were—did they not just try to badmouth the rebels? While this is conceivable, it must be pointed out that the quoted chronicles were compiled during the subsequent Song dynasty, when the Tang dynasty, which suffered under these attacks, had already collapsed. They seem to show no particular sympathy for either side and observe that acts of cannibalism were committed by rebels and government troops alike. Moreover, the authors of one of these works, the *Xin Tangshu*, made the comment about cannibalism during sieges already cited above, indicating that they were not strictly opposed to even the deliberate killing of people for food as long as it served a legitimate military goal.

While it seems that cannibalism for military purposes was not strictly disapproved of, it could backfire if leaders got too ruthless. The same chronicles also report an earlier case of an initially successful warlord who apparently relied on human flesh to such a degree that the affected population ultimately turned against him. During the chaotic transition period from the Sui to the Tang dynasty, the soldiers of Zhu Can (d. 621), the leader of one of the factions competing for the throne, ran into difficulties securing provisions. When they "began to cook and eat infants," Zhu Can did not chastise or punish them, instead declaring: "Of all exquisite foods, does any surpass human flesh? As long as there are people in the other kingdoms what have I to worry about?" He told his men that "if they captured women and children they were all to be boiled and shared by the officers." Later he even ordered the inhabitants of the cities and villages under his control "to hand in their children to add to the soldiers' provisions." The people responded by rising in a revolt which contributed to his downfall.[16]

That cannibalism was seemingly not rare during the time of rebellions and chaos at the end of the Tang dynasty is confirmed by independent observers. The Arab-Persian author Abu Zayd al-Sirafi compiled a book from the reports of several Arab travelers who visited China in the late ninth century. After explaining that persons captured in war campaigns were often eaten, he adds: "cannibalism [is] permissible for them according to their legal code, for they trade in human flesh in their markets."[17]

During the Song dynasty (960–1279), no acts of cannibalism committed by government troops are known, but various cases of bandits and rebels kidnapping, killing, and eating people are documented in the dynastic histories.[18] One of the most famous early Chinese novels, *The Water Margin,* was written in the fourteen century (or possibly earlier) and based on folktales about Song Jiang, an outlaw whose gang surrendered to the Song government in 1121. The novel—which has also been translated under other titles, including *Outlaws of the Marsh* and *All Men Are Brothers*—gives the impression that the consumption of the flesh of kidnapped travelers was considered a pretty normal matter in the criminal underworld (celebrated as "gallant fraternity" in the book).

It repeatedly mentions inns in lonely places, run by bandits who engaged in the side business of kidnapping and killing travelers who appeared to be wealthy and then selling their flesh to other unsuspecting travelers. Some of the heroes of the book—all members of the "gallant fraternity"—almost suffer this fate, but inevitably the innkeepers discover in the last moment who they are and decide to spare them. The near-victims never particularly mind, but are happy to have survived and celebrate their newly sealed friendship with the criminal innkeepers.[19]

One innkeeper tells that they have clear rules about whom to spare: wandering monks because of their merit, singsong girls (singer-prostitutes) out of a fear that "if we kill one of them, word will get around, and they'll sing about it on the stage," and criminals condemned to exile because "there are many bold fellows among them."[20] People discovered sleeping in the streets, on the other hand, are considered suitable victims—when helpers of the same innkeeper spot a sleeping man, they comment, "The rascal is nice and fat" and announce him to the innkeeper as "a fine piece of merchandise."[21] Several other innkeepers have a "butchering shed" with a "skinning bench" behind their main house, used to dismember and process their human victims (and likely animals as well).[22]

On another occasion, a group of robbers captures a traveler and takes his goods. They decide to butcher their captive: "When [the big chieftain] sleeps off his drinks, we'll . . . give him a broth of the heart and liver of this ox to sober him up! And we'll all be able to eat fresh meat!" The chieftain approves and invites several other chiefs to join them for the upcoming meal, but—as usual—the captive is recognized just in time as a famous criminal and therefore spared. A big feast is given in his honor, for which "sheep and horses" are butchered—a hint that such acts were not motivated by a lack of meat.[23]

That such acts are described in a novel does not, of course, mean that they also occurred in real life—though the accounts of the official dynasties indicate that cannibalism among bandits and rebels was indeed not unheard of. And *The Water Margin* is not just any novel—its depiction of the outlawed, but "gallant" underworld held a considerable "romantic appeal to young men" for centuries after it was published; its heroes were seen as ideal "tough guy[s]" who preferred "personal honor and male comradeship" over the widespread "corruptions of local officials" and their "pursuit of material wealth."[24] That the honorable men depicted in the novel treat the consumption of travelers and kidnapped persons as a pretty normal part of their operations can thus be considered a hint that cannibalism was not seen as shocking as it was in the West—while there cannibals might have appeared as monsters, here they were heroes.

In the nineteenth century, human flesh again appeared on the marketplaces during times of rebellion, seemingly with the silent permission of the army. In 1850, a civil war erupted over attempts to establish a Christian fundamentalist state in the southeast of the country. This conflict—the Taiping Rebellion—lasted fifteen years and cost about thirty million human lives, making it the deadliest civil war in history.[25]

According to witnesses, "human flesh and organs were sold openly at the marketplace." A worker employed by a Shanghai trading firm later stated that he had purchased and "eaten the hearts of many Taiping prisoners" out of a belief—reportedly shared by many soldiers—that doing so was a way of strengthening one's courage. While assumptions about the beneficial consequences of eating human organs might have been one reason for such acts, a famine resulting from the devastation of warfare was another, since hungry parents once more murdered and ate their children and "many people were kidnapped and killed for food." Observers from the affected regions report that both "fresh" and "dried human meat" was offered for sale, usually labeled as "beef or mutton."[26]

Zeng Guofan (1811–1872), the leader of the imperial army which fought and ultimately suppressed the rebellion "confirmed in his diary that human meat was sold at the marketplace in Kiangsu Province." In one note he "complained about the high price of human meat, which had gone from 90 wen to 130 wen per chin"—a hint that he might have been among the buyers.[27]

Rebellions also repeatedly took place on the island of Taiwan (then known as Formosa), which from the late seventeenth century to 1895 was ruled by China. The Indigenous population was treated badly and reacted in a way described by a local proverb as "every three years an uprising; every five years a rebellion."[28] Describing the repression of a rebellion in 1891/92, the American consul James W. Davidson (1872–1933) writes:

> One horrible feature of the campaign against the savages was the sale by the Chinese in open market of savage flesh. Impossible as it may seem that a race with such high pretensions to civilization and religion should be guilty of such barbarity, yet such is the truth. After killing a savage, the ... body was then either divided among its captors and eaten, or sold to wealthy Chinese and even to high officials, who disposed of it in a like manner. The kidney, liver, heart, and soles of the feet were considered the most desirable portions, and were ordinarily cut up into very small pieces, boiled, and eaten somewhat in the form of soup.[29]

In 1891, he adds, "savage flesh was brought in—in baskets—... and sold like pork in the open markets of Tokoham [in the north of the island] before the eyes of all, foreigners included"; some of it was shipped to the neighboring mainland and sold there.[30] The open sale of human flesh during the rebellion is also confirmed by an article published in January 1896 in the *Hong Kong Daily Express.* There are no indications that these acts were due to food scarcity. Reviewing accounts from the time, the sinologist Robert des Rotours (1891–1980) concludes that the main motive seems to have been "contempt for an inferior race"—though hatred against those challenging the imperial rule certainly played a role as well.[31]

War and Culinary Cannibalism under Mongol Rule

In 1211, the Mongol Empire, founded a few years earlier by Genghis Khan (ca. 1162–1227), invaded China, attacking first the Jin dynasty in the north and later the Song dynasty in the south. The conquest of the whole country took decades, but in 1271, Kublai Khan (1215–1294), a successor of Genghis, declared himself emperor of China. The Yuan dynasty founded by him ruled

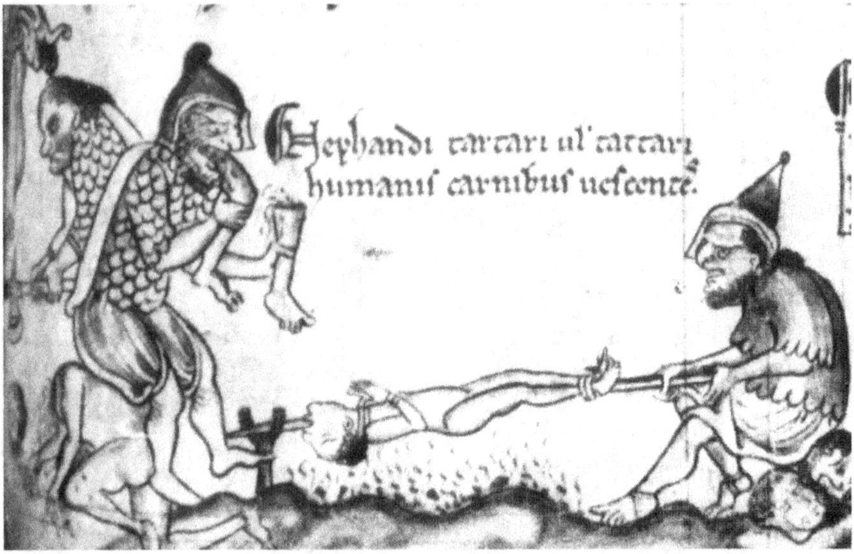

Figure 15.1. Illustration of Mongol cannibalism during the siege of Wiener Neustadt. From Matthew Paris's *Chronica Majora* (via Wikimedia Commons, https://commons.wikimedia.org/wiki/File:Tartar_cannibalism_illumination_Matthew_Paris_Chronica_Majora.jpg).

China for a century (until 1368), but the last decades of its existence were plagued by unrest and rebellions, until finally the Mongols were forced to retire.

After the collapse of the Mongol regime, Tao Zongyi, "an eminent scholar of the late Yuan period,"[32] wrote down his recollections of the period. He criticizes that, while in earlier times human flesh was sometimes eaten out of necessity, the soldiers deployed in the northern regions "enjoyed eating human flesh" and frequently sacrificed civilians for their culinary pleasure: "Young children were the most appreciated; women came next and men last." Some victims, he claims, were roasted whole in "large jars whose outside touched the fire," others were "placed on an iron grate to be roasted alive. . . . Sometimes, the victim was put inside a double bag . . . which was put into a large pot, in order to boil them alive." Corpses not needed for immediate consumption were "cut into pieces that were salted and dried. Sometimes, if it was a man, only his two thighs were chopped off, or if it was a woman, only her two breasts were chopped off."[33]

While the dynastic histories written during the Yuan period do not admit that human flesh was eaten for culinary reasons or that its preparation was accompanied by sadistic tortures, one of them seems to approve of the consumption of civilians as long as it serves the war effort. "Among the soldiers there were those who boiled and ate children, and, during the day, still fought bitter battles," notes the *Songshi* (written in the 1340s) about a war campaign against the collapsing Song dynasty in the 1270s.[34] A later chronicle, written a few years after the demise of the Yuan dynasty, dryly describes the strategy of the old regime in its attempt to fight the rebellions that had broken out during the last years of its rule: "the strong were ordered to enlist as soldiers and the weak were killed and eaten."[35] Those who opposed them, however, sometimes did no better: "Wherever they went they burnt and looted, and even ate the old and weak as food."[36]

Independently of the Chinese sources, European writers in the thirteenth century also noticed that Mongol fighters practiced cannibalism. During that century, the Mongol Empire grew at an enormous speed not only in the east, but also in the west. In 1241–1242, Mongol troops raided eastern and central Europe, coming as far as Austria before they chose to withdraw because of the death of their ruler, Ögedei Khan (ca. 1186–1241). Ivo of Narbonne was a Frenchman who at that time lived in Wiener Neustadt, a town south of Vienna which was attacked by the Mongols. While they withdrew without being able to conquer the fortified town, he later described in a letter that any "Christians in the adjoining province who . . . had been taken captive" were "without consideration of class, fortune, sex, or age . . . indiscriminately destroyed . . . by various forms of torture. The leaders, along with their dinner guests . . . fed on their corpses as though they were bread, leaving nothing for the vultures except bones."[37]

Any "old and deformed women they gave to the cannibals [a remark that implies that not all of the fighters ate human flesh] as food, as if it were a daily ration." "Beautiful women" and "virgins," on the other hand, were not eaten outright, but "raped until they died." Afterwards, "their breasts were cut off, which they kept for their leaders as delicacies, and they feasted on their virginal bodies in a more splendid manner."[38]

The observation that women's breasts were cut off as particular "delicacies" corresponds to Tao Zongyi's remark that they were sometimes the only part of a woman's body that was eaten. Both accounts indicate that the fighters showed a considerable degree of sadism, in particular in their treatment of female captives.

Simon of St. Quentin was a Dominican friar who visited the Mongol court in 1245 as a member of an embassy sent by the Pope in the hope of establishing better relationships between Europe and the expanding empire. While the mission was a diplomatic failure, St. Quentin was among the first Europeans to visit the central regions of the Mongol Empire and report what he had learned. He observes that the Mongols preferred to eat human flesh "roasted by fire rather than boiled." Regarding their motives he adds that it was eaten "sometimes out of necessity, sometimes out of pleasure, and sometimes in order to strike fear and terror in the people who will hear of it."[39]

The Italian merchant Marco Polo (1254–1324), who became famous for his travel report, spent more than fifteen years in China during the early years of the Yuan dynasty (from 1274 to about 1290). Referring to the inhabitants of the region around Hangzhou, he writes that "they eat . . . any kind of meat, including human flesh, which they devour with great relish. They will not touch someone who has died of natural causes, but if he has been stabbed to death or otherwise killed they eat him all up and consider it a great delicacy." He adds that soldiers, in particular, enjoyed to "drink [the] blood and eat [the] flesh" of those they had killed.[40] This is the same region from which cannibal customs, seemingly with a distinctly culinary side, had already been reported about 150 years earlier by the scholar Zhuang Chuo.[41] It is unclear whether this custom had persisted in the region or whether it had later been reintroduced by Mongol soldiers—but it is notable that cannibalism, practiced openly and with "relish," seems to have found a wider acceptance here than in other regions.

In 1368, the Mongols had to withdraw from most of China, but they managed to establish a successor dynasty, known as Northern Yuan, which ruled in Mongolia and northeastern China until the seventeenth century. In 1633, one year before this dynasty collapsed under internal rebellions and external attacks, the soldiers of its last ruler, Ligdan Khan (1588–1634), "killed and ate people" because "food supplies were exhausted." Soon, morale collapsed completely and "after continuous killings and lootings the troops dispersed in all directions."[42]

Culinary Cannibalism in Other Times

The dynastic histories reveal that human flesh was occasionally eaten by soldiers and rebels to celebrate a victory even when there was no food scarcity. In 868, after the conquest of Hao Prefecture (in today's Anhui province), "the many servants and concubines [belonging to the subjugated officials and soldiers] were all steamed and eaten by the rebels."[43] A similar victory feast, combining rape with cannibalism, had been held in 337, during a chaotic period later remembered as "Sixteen Kingdoms" (304–439): "All those who were beautiful of the Buddhist nuns within the palace were violated and killed. Their flesh was cooked and eaten together with beef and mutton."[44]

Another man who murdered beautiful women for culinary purposes was Shi Sui (d. 337), a son of Shi Hu (295–349), the emperor of Later Zhao, one of various short-lived kingdoms founded in northern China during that time. The emperor's biographer tells that for some of the feasts given by Shi Sui, one or more of his concubines were "beheaded [and] sent to the kitchen to be cooked." Their flesh was then served to the guests, while the "head was carefully cleaned [and] placed in plain view on the table or on the dish," supposedly in order to demonstrate that the victim had not been ugly. Often the human flesh was served together with beef or mutton and the young host challenged his guests to identify which was which.[45]

Neither the guests nor the emperor—who was later remembered as a "notoriously cruel and 'barbarous' ruler"—seem to have objected to these banquets. A few years after taking power, Shi Hu had his son executed—not, however, because of his treatment of women, but because he was suspected of having plotted against the father.[46]

Shi Sui was not the only man who occasionally regaled his guests with human flesh. A writer from the Tang dynasty remembers that a wealthy man used to organize lavish feasts attended by "hundreds of guests" during the final years of the preceding Sui dynasty (581–618). For one of his feasts, "ten chefs were put to work boiling [not only] pigs and sheep," but also "a pair of teenage twin brothers." The novelist and journalist Zheng Yi concludes from this report that "the rich competed in wealth, a sport that included competition over cannibalism." But the reaction of the guests renders this unlikely: apparently, they had not been told what they were eating, and when the "heads, hands, and feet" of the boiled children were presented after the meal, "everyone vomited."[47] Human flesh might have been eaten by some, but it was hardly a generally accepted food.

On the other hand, it is conceivable that the guests were shocked not so much by the serving of human flesh but by the realization that innocent children (slaves purchased by the wealthy host?) had been murdered to provide it. A folktale taking place during the same time treats the consumption of human body parts as a rather unremarkable occurrence. In this case, however, the involuntary provider is a man killed in an act of private revenge. In the tale, which describes the origins of the Tang dynasty, Li Shimin (598–649)—who would later become the second emperor of the new dynasty—meets another traveler in an inn. While they are drinking together, the traveler pulls a human heart and liver out of his bag, inviting Li Shimin to share them with him. He explains that they had belonged to "an ungrateful fellow on whom I have been keeping watch these ten years. Now I have caught him and worked off my resentment."[48]

While eating the organs and drinking wine, the two men talk of other things, as if nothing unusual is happening. Earlier they had already dined on mutton, so hunger or a lack of meat cannot be the reason for the meal, and the future emperor does not bother to ask who the eaten man was or how he had wronged his acquaintance.[49] The folktale, which was written down by Zhang Yue (667–730), leaves the impression that human flesh, when it happened to be at one's disposal, could be eaten more or less like any other, without anyone making a great deal of the matter.

A detail in two of the official histories written about the same time suggests that even the hunting of people for food might not have been considered as altogether reprehensible, provided the victims were seen as primitive foreigners. The *Liangshu* (Book of Liang), completed in 635, writes in its section of "barbarian" peoples that, about ten thousand *li* (ca. 5000 kilometers) southwest of Japan "live the ocean people. They are naked and ugly with black skin and white eyes. Their flesh is delicious. Some travellers shoot and eat them." The *Nanshi* (History of the Southern Dynasties), completed a few decades later, contains the same remark. Neither author expresses disapproval at the behavior of the "travellers" (whoever they were), and the statement "Their flesh is delicious" is recorded as an objective fact about the ocean people, as if it were enough to justify the killing of people who are otherwise merely characterized as naked, ugly, and black-skinned.[50]

The specified direction points approximately to the Malay Peninsula and Sumatra. On small islands and boats in that region live several peoples sometimes called "sea nomads," among them the *Orang Laut*, a group of Malay people whose name literally means "sea peoples"—quite similar to the term "ocean people" used in the quoted history books. Cannibalism has been documented for Sumatra[51] and some "sea nomads" might well have fallen victim to such acts.

One of the oldest surviving Chinese books, the *Guanzi*, also seems to show an ambivalent attitude towards cannibalism. The *Guanzi* has been traditionally attributed to Guan Zhong (d. 645 BCE), the chancellor of the early Chinese state of Qi, though actually at least large parts of it were written later.[52] According to an anecdote told by the *Guanzi* about its purported author, Guan Zhong recommended Duke Huan, the ruler of Qi, to banish his cook, Yi Ya. "When you [Duke Huan] said that the only thing you had never tasted was steamed child, he [Yi Ya] thereupon cooked up his son's head and presented it to you. It is human nature to love one's children. If he does not love his son, how can he have any love for you?"[53]

While the cook was condemned for killing his own son in order to please the duke, the latter's apparent curiosity about a "steamed child" is not criticized (at least not openly), and the whole incident seems to be treated rather as a gross violation of parental duties than as a breach of the rules of edibility.

The Tang dynasty was followed by a period of chaos and political division known as "Five Dynasties and Ten Kingdoms," which lasted throughout a large part of the tenth century. The official histories later written about the era deplore the fact that some powerful men who "liked eating human flesh" resorted to doubtful or clearly illegal means to acquire it. Around the year 930, a military leader "secretly caught people's babies for the purpose of eating them."[54] Thirty years later, "Chuyun released several tens of fat prisoners, and had his attendants eat them." Another fifteen years later, a local ruler "forced families . . . to give away their sons and daughters to his officials. If there was the slightest thing about their behaviour that he was not satisfied with he would kill and eat them, collect their bones and throw them away in the wild."[55]

A later account that indicates conflicting attitudes regarding the consumption of human flesh comes from the Jin dynasty (1115–1234). The Jin official Lieou K'i reports that, sometime during the period when the capital was in today's Beijing (1153–1214), a general invited several other generals and their wives to a feast, regaling them with "pork and bread rolls." When one of the women "told him that she usually did not eat pork," he "hurried his servants to change the meat." Later he asked her what kind of meat she had eaten. "Thanks to your favor, my share was changed to mutton which was excellent," she replied, but he corrected her: "You didn't [want to] eat pork but you have eaten human flesh. What do you think of that?" When she realized that she had involuntarily become a cannibal, the woman "was so appalled that she was sick for several days."[56]

The episode shows an ambivalent stance to the eating of human flesh. Many people—represented here by the woman—clearly disapproved of it; the general served the flesh to her out of spite since he was annoyed at her rejection of the offered food. On the other hand, portions of human flesh ready to be served were available in the general's house (or possibly on a nearby market), indicating that there were some who chose to eat it.

In the subsequent Yuan dynasty, cannibal acts with a notably culinary side were recorded among soldiers, as we have seen in the preceding section. Afterwards references to culinary cannibalism disappear from the historical records, at least as recorded by Chinese sources. Some later acts of war cannibalism, such as those recorded by James Davidson,[57] also seem to have a culinary aspect. While contempt and hatred for the vanquished certainly played a part here, that alone could hardly explain why their flesh was traded and seemingly eaten as a rare delicacy even among some of the wealthy, who were certainly not motivated by hunger.

Cannibalism for Medicinal Reasons or Out of Revenge

While the consumption of human flesh for culinary reasons was likely rejected by most, its usage for medicinal purposes seems to have been more widely accepted. The *Bencao Shiyi,* an influential collection of medical knowledge written in the early eight century, recommends it as a proven remedy against various severe diseases.[58] A monk who lived in Chang'an, then the capital of the Tang dynasty,[59] writes that the emperor Wuzong (814–846, ruled from 840) who had fallen seriously ill, "issued an edict ordering the provinces to submit the hearts and livers of fifteen-year-old boys and girls."[60] This medicine, however, did not save the emperor, who died half a year later.

Several centuries later, in the early thirteen century, a man was arrested in the Guangxi province in the south and charged with the murder of numerous boys and girls. According to an official report on the case written in 1218, the man, Lin Ts'ien-tche, suffered from an "incurable disease." He sought the advice of a Taoist monk who "taught him that by utilizing the flesh of a young boy or a little girl, the flesh and bones of men were strengthened." Accordingly, he hired several soldiers who "captured boys and girls between the ages of twelve and thirteen" and delivered them to his kitchen where their flesh was dried for consumption. As most of his victims were girls of low status ("young maidservants and concubines"), it seems that his deeds went unnoticed for quite a while. Ultimately, however, the many disappearances attracted the attention of the authorities; he had to flee and was subsequently arrested. Though several soldiers confessed to having kidnapped children for Lin's benefit, the latter ultimately got off with "a light sentence." The report listed complaints about that and urged the emperor to revise the verdict (with what outcome is not known).[61]

While cases of murder for medicine were certainly exceptional, the belief that eating human flesh was good for one's health also created a unique Chinese form of largely nondeadly cannibalism that persisted for more than a millennium. Driven by filial piety—the Confucian ideal that daughters and sons ought to do whatever they can to ensure the well-being of their parents and parents-in-law—young people more or less voluntarily maimed themselves, cutting a piece out of their body in order to feed it to an older relative who had fallen seriously ill. The earliest mention of this practice in the dynastic histories refers to the late seventh century:

> When his mother fell ill and a doctor said that consumption of human flesh would cure her disease, Youzhen cut a piece of flesh from his own thigh and presented it to her. His mother quickly recovered. An imperial edict said that a banner should be used to mark his door. . . . At the time he was considered a true gentleman.[62]

Bengt Pettersson's detailed work contains all descriptions of piety-related cannibalism from the official histories—more than 110 cases, spanning the whole period from the late seventh to the early twentieth century.[63] Newspaper reports indicate that the practice still occasionally occurred in the 1970s.[64] For a long time, the authorities approved of such acts as long as the donor voluntarily gave up a part of their body. Several accounts mention that the donor was rewarded; in one case, he was even invited to an audience with the emperor.[65]

In later centuries, the preferred body part changed. Instead of offering their thigh, donors now often cut into their abdomen and removed a part of their liver to be cooked for the recipient. This must have been a very painful procedure, and the donor did not always survive it. In 1728, a man died after removing parts of his liver to heal his mother. The emperor reacted by withdrawing his approval of the practice—it was not forbidden but should no longer be rewarded.[66] Though by then doctors had started to advise against such acts,[67] the practice nevertheless persisted.

The earliest reports refer to men who gave up a part of their body to heal their mother or father. The earliest case mentioning a female donor is from 1130—a woman cut a piece of flesh out of her arm and fed it to her sick mother-in-law who promptly recovered. From then on, cases involving female donors are as frequent as those involving male ones. But while men usually gave their flesh to help their own parents, women generally did so to heal their mothers-in-law or other relatives of their husbands.[68] This highlights the patriarchal nature of Chinese society. While filial piety was very important, a woman had to be loyal first and foremost to her husband's family, her own relatives took second place.

Some of the donors were very young—from the nineteenth century, several cases involving boys and girls between seven and twelve years old are documented.[69] Several accounts state that the self-sacrifice was in vain, and the ill person died nevertheless.[70]

While cases of self-mutilation were motivated by love and respect for one's elders—though certainly in combination with a considerable amount of social pressure—cannibalism could also be motivated by hatred and a desire for revenge. In the first millennium, official authorities sometimes ordered the killing and consumption of traitors or rebels in order to punish them. In 319, the general and warlord Shi Jilong (who would later take the name Shi Hu and become an emperor, as mentioned above) captured another general, Xu Kan, who had turned against him. Xu Kan was executed, then "cut . . . to pieces" and consumed by the "wives and children" of those who had fallen victim to his attack. In 403, ten supposed traitors "were cut to pieces alive and eaten by a group of officials."[71]

The earliest known account of China from the Arab world, assembled in 851/52 based on the reports of various travelers, notes that, when a local ruler had displeased the emperor, "they slay him and eat him. The Chinese eat the flesh of all who are killed by the sword." Abu Zayd al-Sirafi, writing a few decades later, confirms this, adding that whenever a criminal had been executed, "he is given over to those who will eat him."[72] Such practices were not always welcomed by the authorities: sometime during the Tang dynasty (618–907) a law was enacted that forbade the sale and consumption of the flesh of criminals—indicating that, until then at least, such acts had indeed occurred.[73]

Authorities often adopted a permissive stance when private persons took the law into their own hands, killing and mutilating those who had wronged their families. In 627, a young man killed an older man who twenty years earlier had murdered his father and escaped unpunished. After killing the killer, the young man "slit his stomach, grabbed his heart and liver and ate them on the spot." He was sentenced to death for murder, but when the emperor heard that he had acted to revenge his father's death, he was granted a full pardon.[74]

Several similar incidents are described in the dynastic histories. In all these cases, a man killed another who had wronged his father and subsequently ate some body parts (heart, ears, nose, or eyes) to complete the revenge. Usually, the attacker was pardoned since he acted out of revenge and filial piety.[75] Altogether, the official histories list about seventy cases of vengeance-related cannibalism committed either by officials or by private persons.[76] A majority of these cases occurred between 317 and 960, while a smaller number (about a quarter of the total) took place between 960 and 1911.[77]

In his discussion of the general treatment of cannibalism in the official histories, Pettersson observes that the descriptions of such acts do not serve the purpose of marking people as savage or barbarian—in clear contrast to European perceptions, where cannibalism and savagery are inevitably linked. While cases of famine cannibalism are seen as a lamentable necessity, a majority of the descriptions of the practice under other circumstances are even positive. Self-mutilations for medicinal cannibalism are described as laudable instances of filial piety; most descriptions of vengeance-related cannibalism consider the act as heroic, only a handful of accounts are of a derogatory nature.[78]

Nevertheless, cannibalism was never widespread—except possibly during certain famines and in times of war—due to a lack of victims. The corpses of those who had died of natural reasons were not eaten, except by desperate people during famines. In certain periods, the flesh of executed criminals or war victims seems to have been a salable commodity, but such supplies were clearly limited in peaceful times. In the first millennium, it seems that a few wealthy men ordered women or children (whom they might have purchased as concubines or servants) to be slaughtered for feasts, but such acts were certainly rare—they might have led to a murder investigation if those committing them had not been particularly influential or well connected. Only during bad times, when a region was ravaged by famine or warfare, could cannibal acts become more than rare exceptions. Soldiers and fighters, being used to death and caring little or nothing for those considered enemies, also seem to have been able and sometimes willing to commit atrocities against civilians, in particular under Mongol rule.

Notes

1. Pettersson, "Cannibalism," 82, 142–43, 147, 150; see Chapter 14, this volume.
2. Ibid., 82.
3. Quoted ibid., 83.
4. Ibid., 133, quoting the *Hou Hanshu*.
5. Ibid., 150, quoting the *Jinshi*.
6. Quoted ibid., 142.
7. Quoted ibid., 144.
8. Ibid., 148, quoting the *Xin Wudaishi*.
9. Chong, *Cannibalism in China*, 64.
10. Pettersson, "Cannibalism," 157, quoting the *Mingshi*.
11. Ibid., 136, quoting the *Jinshu*.
12. Chong, *Cannibalism in China*, 86–87, summarizing the *Liangshu*, another of the dynastic histories.
13. Quoted in Pettersson, "Cannibalism," 146.

14. Ibid., 145, quoting the *Xin Tangshu.*
15. Zheng, *Scarlet Memorial*, 145, quoting the *Zizhi Tongjian.* While the *Zizhi Tongjian*, written in the eleventh century, does not belong to the official dynastic histories, it is considered "an extraordinarily useful first reference for a quick and reliable coverage of events" (Wilkinson, *Chinese History*, 499).
16. Pettersson, "Cannibalism," 141, quoting the *Jiu Tangshu*; the *Xin Tangshu* contains a very similar account.
17. Kennedy and Toorawa, *Two Arabic Travel Books*, 71.
18. Pettersson, "Cannibalism," 149–51. The chronicles record such acts for the years 1118, 1125, 1130–1132, 1216, and 1232.
19. Shi and Luo, *Outlaws of the Marsh*, 1:266, 2:446–50, 495–96, 584–88, 640–41.
20. Quoted ibid., 2:450.
21. Quoted ibid., 495.
22. Ibid., 586, 640.
23. Ibid., 516–19.
24. Rowe, *China's Last Empire*, 177.
25. Ibid., 198.
26. Chong, *Cannibalism in China*, 106, 114.
27. Ibid., 129.
28. Kerr, *Formosa Betrayed*, 4.
29. Davidson, *Island of Formosa*, 254.
30. Ibid., 255.
31. Rotours, "Encore quelques notes," 36.
32. ChinaKnowledge, "Chinese Literature: *Chuogenglu*, 'Retirement to the Countryside,'" last modified 18 July 2010, http://www.chinaknowledge.de/Literature/Novels/chuogenglu.html. Tao Zongyi's work has been called "a very rich source for the political, social and cultural life under the Yuan dynasty" (ibid.).
33. Quoted in Rotours, "Encore quelques notes," 16–17.
34. Quoted in Pettersson, "Cannibalism," 149.
35. Ibid., 153, quoting the *Yuanshi.*
36. Ibid., 154, quoting the *Mingshi.* The quote refers to soldiers of Liu Futong (1321–1363), a leader of the Red Turban Rebellion (1351–1368) which ultimately terminated the Yuan dynasty.
37. Quoted in Andrea, *Medieval Record*, 338.
38. Quoted ibid., 338–39. There are some discussions regarding the authenticity and reliability of Ivo of Narbonne's letter. Peter Segl examines this question very thoroughly and concludes that the letter is almost certainly authentic and seems generally reliable, though it is possible that the descriptions of cannibalism and sexual cruelties were exaggerated or even fabricated by the letter writer or by Matthew Paris, the historian citing the letter (Segl, *Ketzer in Österreich*, 97–99, 108–11). Considering the fact that quite similar descriptions can be found in Chinese sources that were certainly created independently, I do not think it can be justified to wholly reject these passages while admitting the rest of the letter to be authentic.
39. Quoted in Guzman, "Reports of Mongol Cannibalism," 36. Guzman is skeptical regarding the accuracy of the European reports, claiming erroneously that "these Western texts are the only extant sources that repeatedly accuse the Mongols of eating human flesh. Chinese, Tibetan, and Muslim sources never do so" (ibid., 32).
40. Polo, *Travels*, 216. While there is some controversy about Polo's stay in China, with some claiming that his account may be based largely on secondhand information,

careful evaluations of his work come to the conclusion that "many of Marco Polo's descriptions are in excellent agreement with what is reported in Chinese sources" and that the most plausible explanation for the "many . . . amazingly correct and precise pieces of information to be found in [his] book" is that he did indeed visit China for an extensive period of time and reported generally reliably (Vogel, *Marco Polo*, 1, 39).

41. See Chapter 14, this volume.
42. Pettersson, "Cannibalism," 157, quoting the *Qingshi gao*.
43. Ibid., 163, quoting the *Jiu Tangshu*.
44. Ibid., quoting the *Jinshu*.
45. Rotours, "Quelques notes," 397–98.
46. Dien and Knapp, *Six Dynasties*, 130.
47. Zheng, *Scarlet Memorial*, 145.
48. Edwards, *Chinese Prose Literature*, 25, 39 (quotes).
49. Ibid., 39.
50. Quoted in Pettersson, "Cannibalism," 126.
51. See Chapter 3, this volume.
52. Rickett, *Guanzi*, 3, 8.
53. Quoted ibid., 428.
54. Pettersson, "Cannibalism," 164, quoting the *Xin Wudaishi*.
55. Ibid., 148 and 165, quoting the *Songshi*.
56. Quoted in Rotours, "Encore quelques notes," 22.
57. See the section "Cannibalism during Times of War" in this chapter.
58. Pettersson, "Cannibalism," 121.
59. Today Xi'an in central China.
60. Quoted in Rotours, "Encore quelques notes," 44.
61. Quoted ibid., 41, 42 (quotes).
62. Pettersson, "Cannibalism," 109, quoting the *Xin Tangshu*.
63. Ibid., 167–79.
64. Tannahill, *Flesh and Blood*, 152.
65. Pettersson, "Cannibalism," 112.
66. Ibid., 113–15.
67. The influential *Bencao Gangmu*, written by Li Shizhen in the late sixteenth century, disapproves of cutting one's thigh or liver, stating that "we got [our bodies] altogether from our parents, and so we have no right to maim or wound them" (quoted ibid., 122).
68. Ibid., 116–17.
69. Ibid., 116, 178–79.
70. Ibid., 172–73, 176, 179.
71. Ibid., 97 (quoting the *Jinshu*), 98 (quoting the *Weishu*).
72. Kennedy and Toorawa, *Two Arabic Travel Books*, 59, 73.
73. Pettersson, "Cannibalism," 111n155.
74. Ibid., 101, quoting the *Jiu Tangshu*.
75. Ibid., 101–2.
76. All of which can be found ibid., 159–67.
77. Ibid., 105.
78. Ibid., 180–81.

CONCLUSION

Edibility and Humanity

Violent cannibalism—the consumption of deliberately killed people—can be hard to stomach. Maybe this is why the practices discussed in this book have so far received little attention. It is much easier to imagine that such things have never taken place, or to shy away and pretend not to be interested, than trying to understand why and under what circumstances enslaved persons, foreigners, and other outsiders could become "edible," and how human flesh—in a literal rather than a metaphorical sense—could become an item of trade.

While I will not attempt to comprehensively summarize the tentative answers given to these questions in previous chapters, it may be noted that the question about the "why" has two parts: Why could people be killed? And why could the killed be eaten? One may also ask these questions in another way: Who could be killed? And, once killed, who could be eaten? When we are shocked by cannibalism, we are strictly speaking shocked by the answer to the second question: that people regarded certain killed others as edible. And yet, what should rather be shocking is not so much the "edibility," but the "killability" of others: that they could be killed, whether for food or for other reasons, without the perpetrators feeling bad about it (or at least not bad enough to refrain from such acts). Seen in this way, violent cannibalism becomes part of a much larger, more widespread, and more widely accepted set of deadly customs.

Cannibalism differs from the eating of animals not just in the choice of victims, but also in another crucial way: while animals are routinely bred for consumption (and have been for thousands of years), people never were, as far as we know. Sometimes children born to enslaved women were eaten,[1] but there are no indications that slaves were systematically encouraged or forced to "breed" just to produce "meat." Victims for consumption had to be caught or acquired in other ways.

Hunting and trapping are other means of acquiring animals—wild instead of domesticated ones—for consumption. Foreigner poaching may be considered related to this mode of acquiring victims—indeed it seems that in Fiji and parts of Central Africa, members of other (possibly, but not necessarily hostile) communities could be hunted down, killed, and eaten much like animals. But foreigner poaching was also related to more human ways of interactions: warfare, enmity, and the fear of intruders. Especially in New Guinea and the Bismarck Archipelago it seems that foreigners were often seen as intruders and potential spies and troublemakers: it was better to get rid of them before worse could result. The subsequent consumption of the troublemaker might have been more of an afterthought, an additional benefit rather than the main motive of such acts.

Slave eating may be even more shocking than foreigner poaching, since here the victims were so obviously "innocent" and unable to influence their own fate. Its connection to slavery is obvious, and if we keep in mind the separation between "killability" and "edibility," we may conclude that it is not so much the practice of slave eating but the formerly much more widespread institution of slavery that should be shocking. That enslavement led to mass death and that unsalable slaves were sometimes killed or left to die is well known—and yet, even such terrible facts seem easier to bear when the dead were subsequently buried, or even left to rot, than when they were used as food. Though, in general, even those who deliberately bought slaves for consumption treated them merely as slavery had conceptualized certain human beings to be treated: as things, as commodities, that could be used and abused by their owners as it pleased them.

While the modern rejection of cannibalism is universal, those who practiced it did not embrace it in a similarly comprehensive fashion: there was always a dividing line between those who could be killed and eaten, and those who could not. While the famous French anthropologist Claude Lévi-Strauss (1908–2009) notes that "no serious ethnologist disputes the reality of cannibalism," he calls it "an ethnocentric category: it exists only in the eyes of the societies that proscribe it."[2] While we all agree that nobody must be killed and eaten (though not everyone might agree that nobody must be killed), those who practiced cannibalism drew a different dividing line: some people were killable and edible, while others were not. They certainly had different words for the practices they considered acceptable and those they did not.

While this is not a linguistic study and further research will be needed to analyze the words used in different languages for various cannibal practices, their exact scope and their associations, Filiberto Gero's observation of different words—some clearly negative, some not—used for such practices in the Zande language is an example of such a distinction.[3] While in the modern word, eating a corpse would certainly be considered a lesser crime than deliberately killing someone, the Zande word for the snatching and secret consumption of a corpse was clearly negative, while the word used for the consumption of killed enemies or strangers had no negative associations.

Also relevant in this context is the question of how the cannibals saw their victims. Cannibalism, as used in this book, means "eating the flesh of one's own species,"[4] so if they did not recognize their victims as fellow humans, as members of the same species, they would not have been cannibals in their own understanding. Indeed, it is remarkable that in cultures where cannibalism is rejected, the humanness of the victims is stressed and any similarity to the eating of animals is downplayed, while among cannibals the opposite seems to be the case. In English it is even usual to talk about "human flesh" as opposed to "(animal) meat"—the term "human meat" is also used occasionally, but much rarer.

Cannibals, on the other hand, rarely stressed the humanness, or humanity, of their victims. In various Congolese languages, the words used for strangers or dead enemies were identical or very similar to those used for "meat" or "game," and in the Ubangi region it seems to have been quite usual to refer to slaves simply as "meat."[5] In Fiji and the Bismarck Archipelago, different words were used for "edible" bodies—those of enemies or foreigners—and the corpses of those who mattered. Using the latter as food was unimaginable and even joking about it was a grave offense.[6] In China, even in a time and place where cannibalism was more accepted than elsewhere, those engaging in such practices preferred to speak about "two-legged mutton" rather than explicitly mentioning the humanness of their victims.[7]

The last is arguably a euphemism, and in the Congo, human flesh seems to have been quite widely known as "the meat that talks,"[8] an expression that explicitly refers to a capability distinguishing people from animals. Nevertheless, the notion that cannibals did not see their victims as human—or at least, not as fully human—is widespread. Based on the terms used in Congolese languages, Kajsa Ekholm Friedman concludes that enemies and foreigners were seen as "game" rather than "real human beings."[9] Eli Sagan sees violent cannibalism as a prime example of "social aggression," stating that

> All societies that have practiced social aggression have done so by asserting, implicitly or explicitly, that certain groups of human beings are not human and are, therefore, legitimate objects of aggression. Such societies divide the human world into those who are human (we) and those who are subhuman (them).[10]

Korn, Radice, and Hawes assert that

> many "primitive" tribes considered people who were not members of their own particular tribe as not human. In fact, in the language of many of these tribes the word for their own particular tribe was synonymous with "man." So from their viewpoint it was not, strictly speaking, cannibalism if they ate the fallen warriors of an enemy tribe, because that enemy was not even "man."[11]

In a way, socially accepted cannibalism becomes easier to understand if you conclude that the cannibals saw their victims as nonhuman. In that case they agreed with us about the essential non-edibility of human beings—they just were under a misunderstanding about who was or was not a human.

The nonchalance visible in some of the sources about cannibal proceedings seems to confirm the viewpoint that the cannibals did not really see their victims as people. In the Congo, feasts for which slaves were slaughtered were apparently seen as joyful occasions—but how can that be when the death of a person—any person—is a tragedy? The notion that the cannibals failed to recognize the humanity of their victims offers a solution to this apparent paradox. But actually, the paradox exists only if one accepts Sagan's implicit assumption that "human beings" are never "legitimate objects of aggression." But the idea that *all* human beings matter, that all human life is sacred and must not be violated except for the most dire reasons has its own historical and cultural roots, like any idea.

If Sagan's assumption were correct, it would mean that in all the countless societies accepting slavery—doubtlessly an act of severe aggression against those kept in this status—slaves were seen as nonhuman or subhuman. Yet this is doubtful. In Ancient Greece, for example, Aristotle justified slavery by arguing that there were people whose characteristics made them fitter to be ruled than to rule, which made them "natural slaves."[12] While he saw these "natural slaves" as inferior to free people, there can be no doubt that he saw them as people too—only people fit to be ruled and ordered about. Others, such as the Stoics, saw slavery simply as a result of bad luck: you could be enslaved if you lived in a city that was conquered or traveled on a ship that was captured by pirates. Although they accepted that there were no innate differences between slaves and non-slaves, they did not reject slavery because of that: they could simply accept it as an existing institution, just as they could accept that some people were luckier than others.[13]

One can certainly say that those who ate slaves or "poached" foreigners did not consider their victims as "people who mattered"—otherwise they could not have murdered them as nonchalantly as they often did. But did they not see them as people at all? This is doubtful, especially because of different treatments granted to those who might otherwise have fallen to cannibalism. In the Congo, young enslaved women were often purchased as "wives," while little children, older women, or men faced a higher risk of becoming food. In New Guinea and elsewhere in the Pacific, captured women and children could be integrated into communities as wives or adopted children, or they could be eaten, depending on circumstances. Yet no doubt people did not see the spared women and children as belonging to a different "species" than those who were used for food, and you do not marry or adopt a pig.

The expressiveness of linguistic evidence is also limited, if one does not assume contradictions that did not necessarily exist. Even though "human being" and "animal" are used in contrast to each other in the daily language—human beings are not animals, and vice versa—biologically humans are mammals and hence animals too. In a similar manner, if foreigners were called "game" or slaves "meat," this does not necessarily mean that they were not also seen as people—only as people that could be treated like other game or butchered for meat. And if the word for one's own ethnic group is identical to the word used generally for "man" or "human being," this means that the group saw themselves as the prototypical humans—but not necessarily as the only ones. Other people might still have been people, though they presumably mattered less.

And finally, Carol J. Adams observes that a tendency to use euphemisms that hide the relation between a living creature and its eaten parts is typical for meat eating in general: "After death, cows become roast beef, steak, hamburger; pigs become pork, bacon, sausage."[14] This tendency may be more pronounced in English than in other languages,[15] but still it seems that a certain inclination not to be reminded of the origin of one's meat extends far beyond the cannibals.

The notion that humanity is a highly relevant ethical category is a modern one, not shared by the members of societies where violent cannibalism was socially accepted. From their viewpoint, the argument "but they are humans like you!" would have been similarly irrelevant as the argument "but they are mammals like you!" is for us. Except for ethical vegetarians, most people today consider some mammals as edible, others not. The cannibals made the same distinction, but they drew a smaller circle of non-edibility around themselves than we do.

But if they did not agree that other people were necessarily inedible, did they eat them regardless of their humanity—or because if it? The answer here may vary from place to place. In at least parts of the Congo, as we have seen, "meat that talks" was considered as higher and nobler than other meat—though, of course, it was not the meat that talked, but the person who had been killed to provide it. In Fiji, where meals of human flesh were highly prestigious affairs held by the powerful to entertain their guests and followers, it also seems clear that human flesh was considered superior to other meat for those who could get it. In these regions at least, the cannibals were well aware that their victims were more than mere animals—and they preferred to eat them because of that. They ate higher up the food chain than those who lacked access to human flesh.

Were there other regions where the humanity of the victims was considered entirely irrelevant, where people were eaten in just same way and with no more emotion or elation than animals were? Such an attitude may have existed in other parts of the Congo—especially around the Kasai River, where people spoke with less enthusiasm than elsewhere about their cannibal practices and where the prices of human and animal flesh seem to have been quite similar. It may also have existed in some New Guinean regions, where human flesh was considered "an agreeable change of diet," but not necessarily superior to other meat.[16] In many other regions, however, it seems that the humanity of the victims did matter for the cannibals—but as a point in favor of cannibalism, not against it.

In this context it may be asked whether the outspoken preference for human flesh—in nearly all the regions we have encountered it was praised as better than most or all animal meat—was a (possible unconscious) derivative of the notion that the very humanity of victims made them preferable to eat? Emil Torday, who like other observers noted the widespread and clearly voiced culinary preference for human flesh in the Congo, comments "there is no arguing about taste,"[17] and as non-cannibals we cannot join any arguments about this taste in the first place. But a notion that human flesh was superior because those who had provided it were superior might well have provoked a feeling that it was also better in taste, thus making its acquisition and distribution a worthwhile goal.

Human and Animal Flesh

While it is a special case, cannibalism cannot be considered in isolation from meat eating in general. Nick Fiddes analyzes meat as a "natural symbol" for "dominance" and "power over nature." He points out that across many "different contexts, cultures, social groups, and periods of history" meat has been considered the "supreme" food. Though the spreading of vegetarianism and veganism might be slowly changing this, wealthier people in most modern nations tend to consume a higher "proportion of animal products in [their] diet" than poorer ones. The high significance attributed to meat is not limited to the modern world—some hunting/gathering/horticulturist peoples spend about as much time with hunting as with gardening and gathering, though animal products account for less than fifteen percent of their total nutrition.[18]

If meat eating in general is an expression of "power over nature" and animals, cannibalism is an expression of power over people—over the eaten and over their relatives and communities who were unable to protect them. That being eaten was seen as humiliating and degrading—and eating others accordingly a sign of power and superiority—has been recorded from New Zealand, Fiji, the Congo basin, and China.[19] While in modern society, cannibalism is seen as a sign of backwardness and primitiveness—in short, of inferiority—in cannibal societies the opposite view prevailed. Cannibalism denial, one may note in passing, may thus be explained as due to a lack of imagination: denialists fail to grasp why anyone would want to label themselves as primitive. They do not seem to realize that attitudes in cannibal societies differed from those in their own.[20]

Another aspect that cannot be neglected is that in several of the societies we have visited—the Congo basin, Fiji, and New Zealand—a lack of animal meat was given as a motive for cannibalism.[21] In all these societies, birds and fish were usually available, but mammals—especially larger ones—were rare. This was also the case in New Guinea and the Bismarck Archipelago—where cattle, pigs, and deer were introduced by Europeans—and quite possibly in other South Pacific islands from which cannibalism has been reported.

It seems highly unlikely that the rarity of large mammals in the regions where foreigner poaching and slave eating were most common could have been mere happenstance. So, does an absence of nonhuman mammals turn people into cannibals? This would be too strong a statement, especially as in several of the concerned areas cannibal and non-cannibal peoples lived side by side.[22] But that a scarcity of large mammals was a factor that allowed cannibal practices to either develop or persist seems highly likely, unless a plausible alternative explanation for why these two phenomena often existed side by side could be found.

Assuming that such a factor exists, one might still wonder why this was the case. Cannibalism cannot simply be explained by a desire for meat, since the meat of small mammals (such as rodents), birds, and fish was usually available. Such meat was rarely eaten on a daily basis—several observers note that the typical diet in the cannibal societies was largely vegetarian and monotonous[23]—but people in other premodern societies also ate meat only occasionally without becoming cannibals. Cannibalism too was (as we have seen) never a daily affair, but an occasional diversion which often took the form of communal feasts. It is conceivable that for festive occasions birds and rodents were considered too insubstantial or that catching a sufficient number of them was too hard. The inhabitants of societies that had pigs or cattle for such occasions were usually satisfied with them, while those who lacked such mammals might have been more inclined to explore the edibility of the human animal.

As has been noted earlier, cannibalism might well have started in warfare, where the consumption of killed or captured enemies promised several benefits: it was a way to humiliate the enemy and get revenge for whatever misdeeds they might have committed; it allowed getting food in a situation where provisioning was often particularly challenging; and it allowed getting rid of and making use of enemies who if kept alive might have brought further trouble in the future. Once human flesh had become "edible" in this way, extending this treatment from enemies to mere "suspects"—such as foreigners who might have meant trouble—and to "persons of no concern"—such as slaves—might have been a fairly minor step. While we might ask "why," from the cannibal's viewpoint the question might rather have been: "why not?"

In the Western world (and these days, probably everywhere), the food taboo prohibiting the consumption of human flesh is so deeply ingrained that we tend to assume it must be universal: considering that *we* have such a strongly felt and crystal-clear standpoint, how could anyone, anywhere, ever have felt differently? Is not a rejection of the possibility of eating other people one of the core traits that makes people human? But this is an utterly ethnocentric standpoint: just because *we* feel strongly about a thing does not give us reason to assume that everybody must feel the same.[24] And without the idea, based in Judeo-Christian thought but ultimately developed and spread during the Age of Enlightenment, that people are utterly distinct from animals, the utter rejection of human flesh as food combined with an acceptance of animal meat is not even all that logical.

There are good reasons to reject the consumption of people and yet to accept the consumption of certain animals, but these reasons must develop, and be developed—it is a misunderstanding and an oversimplification to assume that everybody, throughout all places and ages, must have seen things this way. And it is not unreasonable to assume that in the future the circle of non-edibility may become even bigger than it is today. As Claude Lévi-Strauss says:

> A day may come when the idea that human beings in the past raised and slaughtered living things for food and complacently displayed slabs of their flesh in shop windows will inspire the same revulsion as what travelers in the sixteenth and seventeenth centuries felt about the cannibal meals of American, Oceanian, or African indigenous peoples.[25]

Patriarchy, Male Privilege, and Violence

In any society, the question of what—or who—may be eaten, is more complex than a simple distinction between animals (or "nonhuman animals," if one wants to be pedantic) and people (or humans). While eating people is taboo in the Western world, eating animals typically kept as pets—especially cats and dogs—is considered nearly as shocking and unacceptable; other primates (monkeys and apes) and carnivores such as lions or wolves are usually not eaten either.[26] Other societies draw a different line between "edible" and "inedible." But a line always exists, even in cannibal societies. In addition to asking which animals can be eaten and which cannot, the latter also ask which people can be eaten. In the cases considered in this book, the eaten were nearly always outsiders—enemies, foreigners, slaves, or corpses purchased from other communities.

In a few cases, marginal members of one's own community could be singled out for consumption too: women of foreign or slave origin if their husbands decided they needed punishment or after the death of their husband, as well as captive children who had been tentatively adopted by community members but who had not fully lost their status as former "enemies."[27] It is notable that such a marginal status was given only to women and children—the status of men was never in doubt, they were either inedible insiders (community members) or potentially "edible" outsiders (enemies, slaves, foreigners).

It is also remarkable, and certainly no accident, that all or nearly all the societies covered in this book were highly patriarchal: men were in power and made the rules, including the rules of edibility. A partial exception may have been the Maori, the patriarchal character of whose societies is under discussion[28]—but there can be no doubt that at least those Maori groups that commonly practiced cannibalism were very war- and warrior-focused. It is thus no surprise that men were usually the main beneficiaries of cannibal meals—women were often excluded or limited to getting less attractive pieces, and the same is true of children. In some cases, there was a formal prohibition against women (and children) joining cannibal meals, while elsewhere it seems that men preferred to keep "the best" for themselves, leading to the usual (but not total) exclusion of others.[29]

While such an exercise of "male privilege" might have even more pronounced when it came to cannibal meals, it is actually widespread for meat eating in general. Nick Fiddes notes that in patriarchal societies (that is, in most societies), "children, like women, traditionally are allocated a lesser amount of meat than grown men."[30] Carol Adams stresses the association of meat eating with maleness as well as with status in general, noting that "meat is a symbol of male dominance"[31] as well as of power. "People with power have always eaten meat," while "women, second-class citizens, are more likely to eat what are considered to be second-class foods in a patriarchal culture: vegetables, fruits, and grains."[32]

She notes that "food taboos address[ing] meat consumption" are common and that they usually "place more restrictions on women than on men." In various Asian and African cultures, women were forbidden to eat chicken or certain other kinds of meat.[33] When women were forbidden to eat human flesh or got less of it, this was thus very much in common with typical rules among patriarchal meat eaters in general.

While the cannibals were predominantly men, their victims were much more diverse: women, men, older people, and children are all repeatedly mentioned as victims. If a preference is expressed, it is usually for the flesh of women, children, or both, never (it seems) for that of men. Why was this the case? Was this indeed a gastronomic preference, as proclaimed? Were men deliberately targeting those perceived as weaker than themselves? Or did, especially in the case of female victims, men who were presumably most often heterosexual target those they considered sexually attractive?

None of these explanations can be definitively ruled out, and, indeed, all of them may have played a role. The gastronomic explanation, which is always the explicitly voiced one ("the flesh of the women and children is the best"[34] and similar statements) might be more plausible than immediately obvious. Meat eaters often prefer the meat of young animals, and there is no reason why cannibals should have seen this differently. The preference for women is less clear-cut, since people rarely care about the gender of the animals they eat.

But the meat industry does: to avoid "boar taint," an "unpleasant odor or taste that many consumers would notice if they cooked or ate pork from male pigs that had reached puberty," male pigs sold for meat are usually either castrated or "slaughtered at a young age."[35] The same risk of a tainted flavor also exists if bulls (uncastrated male cattle) are slaughtered for meat. For this reason, as well as for others (castrated animals are considered more docile), eighty percent of the cattle butchered in the United States are steers (castrated males) and heifers (young females), while less than two percent are bulls.[36] If men could possess a similarly "unpleasant odor or taste" this might explain why cannibals often preferred other victims.

Adams draws a parallel between sexual violence and the processing of meat, observing that "women say that they feel like a piece of meat after being raped." As she explains this, "just as the slaughterhouse treats animals and its workers as inert, unthinking, unfeeling objects, so too in rape are women treated as inert objects, with no attention paid to their feelings or needs." She also compares "the penis [when used as] the implement of violation" with "the knife" cutting into "a piece of meat."[37] While she sees both "women and animals" as oppressed beings in a male-dominated world,[38] she also notes that this parallel remains on a metaphorical level: animals are not usually raped before being butchered. In violent cannibalism, this may have been quite different. Sexual violence is rarely mentioned in Western sources describing cannibalism published in the early twentieth century or earlier, but this may be partly due to a puritan attitude of the writers.

The rape of women subsequently killed and eaten has been reported from New Zealand, the Bismarck Archipelago, and China.[39] Works mentioning such events were often published only after World War II and based on oral accounts or originally unpublished diary entries, while European accounts published closer to when these events took place usually pass them over in silence. Particularly revealing is that Simon Haberberger learned nearly a century afterwards that the widow Henat had been raped before being killed, while the two accounts published shortly after her death had covered the murder and subsequent cannibalism but ignored the rape.[40]

Several authors writing from Fiji make allusions that likely refer to sexual violence, but without naming it explicitly. The missionary Thomas Williams states: "In the foregoing details, all colouring has been avoided, and many facts, which might have been advanced, have been withheld. All the truth may not be told."[41] And the ethnologist Lorimer Fison notes that "modes of torture, especially those used in the punishment of women" were "so dreadful and so unutterably revolting, that if a writer had dared pollute his pages with their stain, he would have been branded as a liar, and execrated as a filthy wretch."[42]

How often and how typically the victims of violent cannibalism were sexually violated before their death, and whether men and children were subjugated to this double abuse in addition to women will in many cases remain unclear, due to the tendency of European sources to conceal such violence. In this case it is particularly clear that absence of evidence is not evidence of absence.

Cannibalism Denial and the Neglect of the Evidence

As noted before, the cannibalism taboo seems to be so deeply ingrained in Western thought that many have assumed it to be universal, concluding that cannibalism as a socially accepted practice cannot exist, or have existed, anywhere in the world. The pinnacle of this notion of a presumably universal cannibalism taboo may well be a book first published in 1979, William Arens's *The Man-Eating Myth.* Arens purports to carefully examine the most reliable reports of cannibal practices and asserts that they have no merit. From this he concludes that cannibalism never was an accepted practice in any society, and that even cannibalism in times of famine was extremely rare. Any evidence to the contrary is, in his viewpoint, just baseless rumor, deliberate slander, or bad research with misinterpretation of the actual data. "The legion of existing reports . . . were found to range from highly suspect to entirely groundless."[43]

While by no means the first, Arens became the best-known representative of what might be called *cannibalism denial*—the notion that any reports of socially accepted cannibalism can only be fabrications. He did have a point. There are indeed many allegations of cannibalism that may be no more than hearsay and badmouthing, but which were often quite uncritically accepted by both anthropologists and the general public in Western cultures before he published his influential work. Clearly, a more critical view was needed. Arens's bold claims forced anthropologists, archaeologists, and historians to reevaluate the evidence of cannibalistic practices, with clear results. "Anthropologists working in the Americas, Africa, and Melanesia now acknowledge that institutionalized cannibalism occurred in some places at some times. Archaeologists and evolutionary biologists are taking cannibalism seriously," notes Shirley Lindenbaum.[44]

Kajsa Ekholm Friedman observes that cannibalism denial itself is strongly ethnocentric—"our" taboos are taken so seriously that they are considered universal, usually without further justification of how or why such a universal taboo could actually have emerged. Hidden under the claims of denial, she finds a conviction "that cannibalism is the worst thing of all," meaning that false accusations of cannibalism are better suited to vilify others than any other accusation would be.[45]

But why should a specific treatment of dead bodies be worse than any treatments of living persons humans have come up with? Why should it be worse to eat enemies killed during fighting than to take away, forever, the freedom of those captured alive? It is certainly bad to butcher slaves for food, but is it so much better to systematically work them to death over the course of a few years or to throw them overboard because they are considered unsalable? That Europeans tended to believe (and some still do) that cannibalism (practiced, in most circumstances, only in other cultures) is worse than anything they themselves could come up with, is "a remarkable opinion in a culture that has been capable of the most extreme cruelty and destructive behavior, both at home and in other parts of the world," Ekholm Friedman concludes.[46]

The hidden notion that some of "our" values must be universal also indicates a certain unwillingness to actually study other cultures. Even if one were to carefully investigate many cultures, claims of universal values would be hard to make, considering that any other culture might still provide a counterexample. But in fact, notions such as cannibalism denial rarely seem to seriously consider much evidence from other cultures at all. It is instructive to examine how Arens deals with the Congo basin, a region where (as we have seen) war cannibalism and slave eating were widespread. Ignoring most of the evidence considered for this book, he dedicates less than four pages to the Congo—and these pages are full of distortions.

Arens starts by discussing Herbert Ward's book *Five Years with the Congo Cannibals,* claiming that Ward merely heard from Arab slavers that the natives they had enslaved were cannibals and that Ward believed them when he saw natives with "filed teeth[:] He assumed there could be but one reason for this."[47] Actually Ward heard that people living near the Aruwimi River had filed teeth and were cannibals, but he never drew a causal connection (suspecting people of cannibalism *because* they had filed teeth).[48]

Arens then quotes Ward expressing the hope "that 'white men of upright character' would soon 'put an end to this.'" This is a slight misquotation—the quoted page refers indeed to "white men of upright character," but the rest of the quote is a mere paraphrase of Ward's remark, in spite of the quotation marks which Arens puts around it.[49] But worse than this scholarly detail is that Arens omits mentioning the scene to which the quote refers, namely his visit to a village near the Aruwimi: "On arriving there, almost the first man I saw was carrying four large lumps of human flesh, with the skin still clinging to it, on a stick; and, through Fida, I found that they had killed a man this morning, and had divided the flesh."[50]

Ward had not merely heard vague rumors from Swahilo-Arab slavers, he had been an eyewitness to the distribution and cooking of butchered human body parts and (on other occasions) to the actual eating of human flesh.[51] Arens must have known this, considering that he had found the quote on the next page and knew it referred to cannibalism—but he conveniently chose to ignore it. He then turns to Sidney Hinde, whom he finds—just like Ward—merely "amusing." He paraphrases the following remark from Hinde's book:[52]

> Races who until lately do not seem to have been cannibals . . . have, from increased intercourse with their neighbours, learned to eat human flesh;

> for since the entry of Europeans into the country greater facilities for travelling and greater safety for travellers have come about. Formerly the people who wandered from their own neighbourhood among the surrounding tribes were killed and eaten, and so did not return among their people to enlighten them by showing that human flesh was useful as an article of food.[53]

The assumption that people surrounded by cannibal tribes merely needed "enlightenment" in order to discover a not-yet-thought-of usage of human bodies is indeed doubtful. But Hinde has many more substantial things to say about cannibalism, including eyewitness accounts of war cannibalism practiced by his own allies.[54] Arens ignores all of that, as if one speculative remark made by Hinde were enough to dismiss all his detailed memories as mere fiction.

David Livingstone, on the other hand, finds approval by Arens, who cites him as a supposed witness for his thesis that cannibalism is just a myth: "David Livingstone considered the evidence for cannibalism among an African group he was familiar with, and concluded with the terse comment: 'A Scotch jury would say, Not Proven.'"[55]

This remark is actually from a diary entry Livingstone made in January 1871, when he had been in "Manyuema country" (today, Maniema, Congo-Kinshasa) for just a few months. Adding more context, it reads: "Cold-blooded murders are frightfully common. . . . Their cannibalism is doubtful, but my observations raise grave suspicions. A Scotch jury would say, 'Not proven.' The women are not guilty."[56]

Livingstone suspected the Maniema men (as opposed to the women) of practicing cannibalism, but he was not yet convinced that their deeds had been "proven" enough to satisfy the high standards of a jury trial.[57] Over the subsequent months, his doubts disappeared. By April 1871 he accepted as a "fact that the Manyuema eat only those who are killed in war," while rejecting rumors that captives and slaves were deliberately killed and eaten (in this region) as very doubtful. A few months later a chief admitted "frankly that they ate the man of Moezia," which Livingstone comments as follows: "They seem to eat their foes to inspire courage, or in revenge. One point is very remarkable; it is not want that has led to the custom, for the country is full of food."[58]

Considering that, after several months in Maniema, Livingstone reflected on the reasons for the cannibal practices he now knew to be real, it is curious that Arens considers him a witness for his thesis that no reliable evidence of cannibalism exists. It would have been sufficient to read Livingstone's diary entries from Maniema to find some evidence. Instead, Arens contrasts Livingstone with those who followed in his footsteps, claiming that the latter were much more sensational, producing various doubtful accounts of cannibalism in regions where Livingstone had found none. Referring to Henry

Morton Stanley as a supposedly typical case, he writes that "his own reports portray him as constantly set upon, in the very same areas traversed peacefully by Livingstone, by the most bellicose and savage people. . . . According to Stanley, these groups were more often than not also cannibals."[59]

Once more, Arens distorts the actual situation. Stanley had indeed followed in Livingstone's footsteps; his first journey to Africa had been to "find" Livingstone, who had been traveling for years through the interior of Africa without sending any news to Europe. Like his predecessor, Stanley set out from Zanzibar and finally met Livingstone in a village on the eastern shore of Lake Tanganyika to which the latter had returned, leaving Maniema for good. During this journey, Stanley stayed east of the African Great Lakes, never entering the Congo basin. Neither he nor Livingstone encountered cannibals in these areas. Only when he reached Lake Tanganyika, he heard that the people living on the other, northwestern side of the lake were cannibals.[60] But this refers to the Congolese side and the same area (today the South Kivu and Maniema provinces of Congo-Kinshasa) in which Livingstone had found cannibalism.

In his later journeys, Stanley ventured far deeper into the Congo basin, exploring the whole length of the Congo River. There he did indeed encounter cannibals, both in Maniema and in areas where Livingstone had never been. But the claim that Stanley found cannibals in regions where Livingstone had found none is, once again, a falsehood.[61] With this, Arens concludes his coverage of the Congo, repeating that "the discussion so far may be amusing."[62] In truth, the situation in the Congo was anything but amusing—certainly not for those who fell victim to cannibalism and other acts of violence. Arens did not disprove that truth, he merely distorted and ignored it.[63]

Those who actually look at the evidence tend to see a different picture emerge, where our own notions are by no means as universal as we might have liked. Ekholm Friedman, after doing so, states:

> In many parts of the Congo region there was no negative evaluation of cannibalism. On the contrary, people expressed their strong appreciation of this very special meat and could not understand the hysterical reactions from the white man's side. . . . The Europeans' attitude must have appeared all the more incomprehensible to the Africans since the former were capable, quite scrupulously, of burning, whipping, crippling, devastating, and murdering their cannibal hosts.[64]

Negative reactions to cannibalism are a part of Western culture, but neither logic nor historical evidence justifies thinking they must be universal. Cannibalism denial seems to be based on an (often implicit) assumption that they are, and that therefore all reports of cannibalism—no matter how well-documented—can be nothing but defamations, or, at best, misunderstandings. Ignoring or dismissing all the evidence to the contrary, Arens even suggests

Figure 16.1. King Munza dancing in his impressive throne hall, surrounded by his wives and warriors. From Georg Schweinfurth's *Im Herzen von Afrika*, vol. 2 (Leipzig: F. A. Brockhaus, 1874), opposite p. 80.

that the rejection of cannibalism has always and everywhere been so strong that, throughout human history and prehistory, people usually preferred to starve rather than turning to human flesh in times of dire necessity.[65] This bold claim is particularly surprising considering that a well-publicized case of nonviolent famine cannibalism, committed by members and supporters of a Uruguayan rugby team whose plane crashed in the Andes, happened just a few years before the publication of Arens's book.[66] In general, it seems a better and saner strategy to adjust one's picture of the world and of possible human behaviors to the evidence rather than ignoring or dismissing anything that does not fit one's prejudices.

Cannibal Stereotypes and Realities

In modern imagination, cannibalism is associated with backwardness and a primitive lifestyle. Such stereotypes, however, were not always confirmed in actual encounters between Westerners and cannibal peoples. Georg Schweinfurth, for example, was deeply impressed by the culture of the Mangbetu people, admiring the palace of their King Munza whose main hall "was little short of 150 feet in length and 60 feet in breadth, and rose to the height of about 50 feet. Combined with these imposing dimensions were a lightness of character and solidity of structure that were quite remarkable."[67]

George Brown explicitly addresses cannibal stereotypes: "There is something so repulsive to us in the idea of cannibalism, that most people, I think, picture the people who indulge in it as being particularly ferocious and repulsive." His own experiences in Melanesia, however, contradicted such notions: "The fact is that many of them are no more ferocious than other races who abhor the very idea of eating the human body. Many cannibals, indeed, are very nice people, and, except on very special occasions, there is no apparent difference between them and non-cannibal tribes."[68]

Western travelers in the nineteenth century usually judged the peoples they encountered according to the norms and ideals of their own society, and (unsurprisingly) often found their lifestyle and behavior to fall very short of these ideals. Accordingly, they tended to be convinced of their own supremacy, considering other peoples' ways of life as generally inferior to their own. They also liked to classify peoples as "high" or "advanced" versus "low" or "primitive," depending on how far they deviated from their expectations. While cannibalism is very far from European ideals, they could not avoid accepting some cannibal peoples as otherwise quite "highly" developed.

William Bentley states: "Cannibalism is a bad habit, but it does not necessarily mark out the natives who observe it as being of a lower type than others who do not. It is a well-known fact that some of the cannibal peoples of Africa are far in advance of many tribes who would shudder at the very idea."[69] The French governor François-Joseph Clozel (1860–1918) considers the Central African Gbaya people as "intellectually and morally superior to the generality of the tribes of the coast and the middle basin of the Congo," judging them to have (despite their cannibal habits) a "culture and morality . . . not found in many tribes that manifest the most virtuous horror of human flesh."[70]

Other travelers were impressed by the body shapes and physical condition of the people they encountered. Albert Lloyd writes enthusiastically about the Central African Bangwa people whom he had repeatedly seen practicing cannibalism: "They are a splendid race of people; I was very much taken with them. I have seldom seen such physical development and such symmetry of figure; they are upright as a dart, with heads erect, and bright, intelligent faces."[71] Samuel Lapsley states: "The Zappo Zaps have been cannibals very lately, without doubt. . . . But [they] are the finest people about—magnificent men and handsome women, and carry themselves quite as an aristocracy."[72] And Frederick Migeod very briefly characterizes the M'Baka people on the Ubangi River as "a fine race and much given to eating human flesh."[73]

Some went so far as to suggest that the consumption of human flesh was itself the reason for the perceived superiority of those who practiced it. The Belgian author E. Carlier describes the "Bondjo" people on the Ubangi River as "usually tall, well muscled, breathing vigor and strength. Their appearance seems to show that human meat, which partly makes up their nourishment, gives them a muscular vigor rarely encountered in other peoples."[74] And the English-Portuguese explorer Joachim John Monteiro

(1833–1878) states regarding the practitioners of punitive cannibalism he encountered in Angola:

> I was very much surprised to find that, notwithstanding their cannibal propensities, the natives of Novo Redondo were such an extremely fine race; in fact, they are the finest race of blacks, in every way, that I have met with in Africa.
>
> Cannibalism may possibly be one reason of their superiority, from this custom supplying them with a certain amount of animal food more than other tribes make use of.[75]

Prejudiced and full of strange notions as such statements are, they make it clear that Europeans did not merely "smear" the cannibal (or supposedly cannibal) peoples they encountered.[76] Likewise untenable is the idea that accusations of cannibalism were generally used to justify genocide, enslavement, and suppression. A particularly exploitative colonial regime developed in the misnamed Congo Free State from around 1890.[77] Many Europeans, while not silent on the occurrences of cannibalism and slave eating they encountered, were highly critical of this regime. Guy Burrows denounces the "systematic, comprehensive, and coldblooded misdeeds . . . which, during the past fifteen years, have made of the Congo State a veritable charnel-house."[78] His co-author Edgar Canisius deplores the "continuous massacre of the natives" and the "state of terror" which the colonial government had established.[79] George Grenfell criticizes the regime as having changed "from philanthropy to self-seeking of the basest and most cruel kind."[80] Roger Casement, while more diplomatic, is no less critical of the Free State government.[81]

Universalism, Relativism, and Their Pitfalls

Cannibalism denial may be considered an example of inappropriate cultural universalism: the idea that some of one's feelings and values are so self-evident and obvious that they *must* be shared by all humans who ever lived, across all temporal and cultural boundaries. The corrective is cultural relativism: the acknowledgment that, as formulated by Franz Boas (1858–1942), one of the pioneers of modern anthropology, "civilization is not something absolute, but . . . it is relative, and . . . our ideas and conceptions are true only so far as our civilization goes."[82]

That ideas and values are culture-dependent is, of course, not a new insight. That this even applies to extreme (from our viewpoint) acts such as cannibalism is old news too. In his famous essay *Of Cannibals,* the French Renaissance philosopher Michel de Montaigne (1533–1592) anticipated Boas in observing that "every one gives the title of barbarism to everything that is not in use in his own country. As, indeed, we have no other level of truth and reason than the example and idea of the opinions and customs of the place wherein we live."[83]

The denialists would do well to remember this old insight. Montaigne also knew that people tend to be much better at spotting faults in other people's behavior than in their own (in practices accepted by their own culture): "I am not sorry that we should here take notice of the barbarous horror of so cruel an action [as torturing and eating one's enemies], but that, seeing so clearly into their faults, we should be so blind to our own."[84]

A point already made above. But it leaves a worrisome question: if we accept cultural relativism—and we must accept it if we want to be able to properly understand other peoples and cultures—can we even recognize the faults of others? Can we call an act "bad," "barbarous," or "horrifying" it if is according to our value system, while according to their value system it might be good, appropriate, and called-for?

The step from cultural to moral relativism is small and might even seem necessary—certainly, if "our ideas and conceptions are true only so far as our civilization goes," this likewise applies to our moral ideas and conceptions, our notions of good and bad, right and wrong? The moral relativist Gilbert Harman declares that "there is no such thing as objectively absolute good, absolute right, or absolute justice; there is only what is good, right, or just in relation to this or that moral framework," and "there are many different moral frameworks, none of which is more correct than the others."[85]

This position might sound plausible enough. But it is seriously challenged by the existence of certain practices, including violent cannibalism—most clearly in cases such as "murder for meat." Admittedly, the challenge is somewhat attenuated by the fact that socially accepted cannibalism has almost completely disappeared, largely because it was suppressed by persons who cared little about cultural and even less about moral relativism. Otherwise, what if one were to meet somebody who proudly related how in his country wealthy men sometimes buy enslaved children, fatten them for some time, and then have them slaughtered to regale their friends—maybe adding that someday he hopes to be wealthy enough to do the same? Must one reply something along the lines of: "Well I disapprove of your habits, but I respect that your culture and mine have different moral frameworks, different value systems. I understand that there are habits accepted by my value system which you must consider equally disgusting. So, I'm happy to let you stick to your customs as long as you let me stick to mine."

Or might one say: "What you're doing is really bad, not just according to my culture-specific moral framework, but in some cross-culturally valid way. Your people should immediately free all their slaves rather than exploiting and even butchering them."

Lévi-Strauss might have been inclined to go with the first answer, although he might have added: "Do what you want at home, but don't do it here!" In his essay collection *We Are All Cannibals,* he takes a strongly relativistic position, noting that "beliefs that we ourselves judge barbaric or ridiculous are warranted for those who adhere to them" and that "there is no common measure by which to judge systems of beliefs or, a fortiori, to condemn one or another of them, unless we claim—but on what basis?—that only one (ours, of course) conveys universal values and must be imposed on all."[86] He does not explicitly apply this position to violent cannibalism or to formerly common institutions such as slavery, but argues on its basis that "ritual excision on . . . female children"—female genital mutilation—should be considered as acceptable and "warranted" in regions and countries where it has traditionally been practiced, though not necessarily elsewhere (such as in France).[87]

He dismissed the "grievance . . . that ritual excision supposedly eliminates female sexual pleasure, which our societies have made a new article in the declaration of human rights"—in part by citing a contrary viewpoint and then concluding that "opinions differ."[88] But it still seems pretty clear that he does not consider women's right to "sexual pleasure," or more generally, anyone's right to live a self-determined life and seek pleasure and happiness, as fit to become universal values. If one takes this position to its logical end, the idea that there may be "unalienable Rights, that among these are Life, Liberty and the pursuit of Happiness" (as the US Declaration of Independence has it) is just one opinion among many, and not only slavery, but also the slaughter and consumption of slaves are warranted in societies where they are traditional.

Lévi-Strauss's strict relativism notwithstanding, I would consider the second answer—a clear rejection of such practices with a universal scope—as far more appropriate and satisfying than the first one. But how can it be justified? One might of course compromise and say: "Well, according to my moral framework you're acting really bad, and I don't care whether this view can be cross-culturally justified or not. I have the better weapons and you will do as I say, or else!" This is the way cannibalism (whether violent or not) was dealt with in the past and it certainly has been sufficient to eliminate the practice nearly completely. But it too seems unsatisfying, because weapons make poor arguments.

Certainly, no *complete* set of moral values (no value system or, in Harman's terminology, moral framework) could be defended as universally valid across all cultural boundaries. Some values, at least, will always be culture-specific and appear as arbitrary, unjustified, or outright wrong from the viewpoint of those belonging to other cultures and accepting different value systems. But, on the other hand, it seems essential to be able to identify at least *some* particularly important moral values, or ethical rules, that can be successfully defended and justified across all cultural boundaries.

The most obvious candidate for such cross-culturally valid ethical rules are human rights, as expressed, most famously, in the *Universal Declaration of Human Rights* of 1948.[89] These rights clearly point in the direction we are looking for. But, as written down in that Declaration (and, presumably, in other similar documents as well), they are not without problematic details that make it hard to defend them as being equally valid in any and all cultures. The Declaration assumes that nations, governments, and private (individually owned) property exist—assumptions that can hardly be upheld across all cultural boundaries. It postulates that "elementary education shall be compulsory," a notion criticized by thinkers such as Ivan Illich and John Holt. It also demands that copyright must exist, granting to authors "protection of the . . . material interests resulting from any scientific, literary or artistic production"—another idea that has come under criticism.[90]

The point here is not whether or not such criticism is justified, but rather that human rights, as expressed in the *Universal Declaration* or elsewhere, are inevitably full of details, some of which are more fundamental than others. Postulating universal validity for all these details seems a dubious enterprise, considering that some of them point very specifically to the Western, capitalistic cultures from which they emerged—and have come under scrutiny and criticism even here. Referring to the "spirit" rather than the "letter" of human rights does not help since then the discussion would necessarily turn to what the cross-cultural spirit comprises and what are unimportant culture-specific details. If everybody is allowed to determine their own spirit, then the search for universals has ended before it even started; if not, one would have to state clearly what the "spirit" is and why it can claim universal validity.

Rather than search for a hard-to-find spirit, I would propose that a variant of the Golden Rule might be the most promising candidate of a cross-culturally valid ethical rule. The Golden Rule has received this name since it or some variants of it can be found in many different religious and ethical value systems. Turning to it while searching for "moral universals" is not a new idea—the Ghanaian philosopher Kwasi Wiredu, for one, likewise proposes "a principle of conduct . . . obviously reminiscent of what has been called the Golden Rule."[91] Wiredu's proposal, however, might be too demanding to be practical as a universal moral guideline.[92]

The Golden Rule itself—in its most basic form: "One should treat others as one would like others to treat oneself"—is likewise not without problems. What is good for one person might not always be good for others; moreover, different people might *want* to be treated differently. Hence, I would propose a variant: "One must not do things to people against their will that are disadvantageous for them (except possibly to avoid an even more serious disadvantage to other people)."

The proposed rule deliberately leaves a lot open to discussion: Is it acceptable to do things to people that are disadvantageous for them if they want them to happen? Which things, exactly, are disadvantageous for somebody? Under which circumstances is it acceptable to disadvantage one person to avoid even more serious disadvantages to others? Widely differing viewpoints regarding such questions may exist within one culture and across different cultures.

But the rule serves to identify and prohibit, cross-culturally, things that are "really bad," such as slavery and "murder for meat." Such things happen almost never with the victim's consent, and even the most ardent cannibal could hardly claim that being eaten is advantageous for the victim. It would be equally difficult to claim, convincingly, that not being able to eat a tasty meal (or having a slave's services at one's disposal) is a more serious disadvantage than being killed and eaten (or enslaved for life).

It seems to me that combining cultural relativism with such a cautious, limited form of moral universalism in the best approach to dealing with phenomena that from the modern viewpoint are shocking and ethically unacceptable. Cultural relativism is needed for understanding the diversity of human cultures without falling into traps, such as prematurely concluding "that must be a lie, nobody could ever have done such a thing!" or "what inhuman, evil monsters these people must have been!" But strict moral relativism, which utterly refrains from ethically judging behaviors encountered in other cultures, would amount to silently accepting all kinds of exploitative, abusive, or humiliating behaviors, as long as they happen "elsewhere" and are accepted by a majority in that culture.

Simply applying the values of our own culture to make judgments regarding customs found in other cultures, on the other hand, is equally problematic, since it prevents us from asking whether what we consider bad really was so according to the viewpoints of those affected by the custom. It if was not, does it really make sense to condemn a custom on the basis of our own preconceived notions, or prejudices, a custom which might have seen by all involved as appropriate and good? In a few cases, this might indeed be the case—for example, when the victims of a harmful practice are brainwashed into accepting it as harmless or even good for them. But in other cases, there might be no basis for our preconceived notion except for "that is how we are used to seeing things"—hardly a proper basis for judging others or expecting them to adjust their behavior to match our prejudices. A strictly limited form of moral universalism, as expressed by the rule proposed above, seems the best way out of this dilemma of utterly refraining from judgment versus judging in a prejudiced manner.

Notes

1. See Chapter 5 in this volume for an example.
2. Lévi-Strauss, *We Are All Cannibals*, 87–88.
3. See Chapter 7, this volume.
4. See Chapter 1, this volume.
5. See Chapters 6 and 7, this volume.
6. See Chapter 12, this volume.
7. See Chapter 14, this volume.

8. See Chapter 6, this volume.
9. Ekholm Friedman, *Catastrophe and Creation*, 221; see also Chapter 6, this volume.
10. Sagan, *Cannibalism*, xv.
11. Korn, Radice, and Hawes, *Cannibal*, 192.
12. Hunt, "Slaves," 42, 43 (quote).
13. Ibid., 45.
14. Adams, *Sexual Politics of Meat*, 74.
15. Beef and pork are *carne de vacuno* and *carne de cerdo* in Spanish, *Rindfleisch* and *Schweinefleisch* in German—neither language hides the relationship between the living animal and its meat.
16. Monckton, *Some Experiences*, 221; see Chapter 11, this volume.
17. Torday, *Causeries Congolaises*, 80.
18. Fiddes, *Meat*, 12–13, 230, 233.
19. See especially Chapters 2, 6, 12, and 15, this volume.
20. We will return to this phenomenon in the section "Cannibalism Denial and the Neglect of the Evidence."
21. See Chapters 2, 7, and 12, this volume.
22. See for example the last section of Chapter 6, this volume.
23. See cross-references in note 21 in this chapter.
24. For a defense of the notion that all "mores," including food taboos, are culture-dependent and tend to vary across different places and times, see Sumner, *Folkways*. For a systematic application of this notion to eating habits, including cannibalism, see Harris, *Good to Eat*.
25. Lévi-Strauss, *We Are All Cannibals*, 114.
26. Fiddes, *Meat*, 132, 135, 139.
27. See Chapters 8 and 11, this volume.
28. See Chapter 2, this volume.
29. See Chapters 2, 8, and 11, this volume.
30. Fiddes, *Meat*, 159.
31. Adams, *Sexual Politics of Meat*, 56.
32. Ibid., 48.
33. Ibid., 49 (quotes), 50.
34. Wack, *Story*, 305; see Chapter 4, this volume.
35. John Crane, "What is Boar Taint?" *BoarTaint.com*, accessed 19 October 2020, https://www.boartaint.com/en/what-is-boartaint.aspx.
36. Karin Lindquist, answer to "Why Don't We Eat Bulls as We Do Eat Cows?" *Quora*, 12 April 2018, https://www.quora.com/Why-dont-we-eat-bulls-as-we-do-eat-cows; Beef USA, "Industry Statistics," http://www.beefusa.org/beefindustrystatistics.aspx. Both websites were accessed 9 October 2020.
37. Adams, *Sexual Politics of Meat*, 81–82.
38. Ibid., 219.
39. See Chapters 2, 3, 11, and 15, this volume.
40. See Chapter 11, this volume.
41. Williams and Calvert, *Fiji*, 168.
42. Fison, *Tales from Old Fiji*, xxiii–xxiv.
43. Arens, *Man-Eating Myth*, 181.
44. Lindenbaum, "Thinking about Cannibalism," 491.
45. Ekholm Friedman, *Catastrophe and Creation*, 220.

46. Ibid.
47. Arens, *Man-Eating Myth*, 84.
48. Ward, *Five Years*, 160–61, 198, 230.
49. Arens, *Man-Eating Myth*, 84–85; Ward, *Five Years*, 163.
50. Ward, *Five Years*, 162.
51. For a longer discussion of this incident, see Chapter 5, this volume. For other evidence presented by Ward, see also Chapters 6–8 and 12, this volume.
52. Arens, *Man-Eating Myth*, 84–85.
53. Hinde, *Fall*, 66.
54. Ibid., 134–35. For Hinde's accounts of slave eating and foreigner poaching, see Chapters 6–7 and 12, this volume.
55. Arens, *Man-Eating Myth*, 85.
56. Livingstone, *Last Journals*, 98.
57. Under Scots law, a jury trial can end with one of three verdicts: "guilty," "not guilty," or "not proven." While the latter two verdicts both amount to acquittal, "not proven" can be used in cases where the jury suspects the accused of being guilty but considers the evidence insufficient for a conviction. It is no accident that Livingstone used this careful verdict for the men, reserving the stronger statement "not guilty" for the women.
58. Livingstone, *Last Journals*, 117, 148. For Livingstone's accounts of foreigner poaching, see Chapter 12, this volume.
59. Arens, *Man-Eating Myth*, 87.
60. Stanley, *How I Found Livingstone*, 555–57.
61. Stanley's occasional statements regarding cannibalism usually refer to the consumption of enemies in wartime, not to foreigner poaching or slave eating, therefore his accounts have not been considered for this book. For the close encounters which some members of his last expedition had with cannibalism, see Chapters 5, 9, and 12, this volume.
62. Arens, *Man-Eating Myth*, 87.
63. For similar dissections and refutations of Arens's work in regard to other regions see Brady, "Myth-Eating Man," and Forsyth, "Three Cheers." Nigel Davies likewise concludes: "Whilst I am the first to insist that reports from missionaries and others should be examined with discrimination, too many eye-witnesses accounts of cannibalism survive for Arens' opinions to be taken very seriously" (Davies, *Human Sacrifice*, 15).
64. Ekholm Friedman, *Catastrophe and Creation*, 221.
65. Arens, *Man-Eating Myth*, 135.
66. See Korn, Radice, and Hawes, *Cannibal*, chapter 7. For more on famine cannibalism, see, in addition to Chapter 14 of this book, the sources given in Chapter 1, note 16.
67. Schweinfurth, *Heart of Africa*, 118.
68. Brown, *Melanesians and Polynesians*, 140–41.
69. W. Bentley, *Pioneering on the Congo*, 210.
70. Clozel, *Les Bayas*, 20.
71. Lloyd, *In Dwarf Land*, 295 (quote), 297.
72. Lapsley, *Life and Letters*, 173.
73. Migeod, *Across Equatorial Africa*, 153.
74. Carlier, "Les Bondjo," 415.
75. Monteiro, *Angola*, 157.

76. See the quote from Nate Taskin cited in the Introduction (note 11).
77. Van Reybrouck, *Congo*, 60, 79; see especially Chapter 5, this volume.
78. Burrows and Canisius, *Curse of Central Africa*, 195. Burrows adds that all the colonial "exploiters of Africa—of probably every nation—have much to answer for," but leaves no doubt that he considers the Free State government the worst of all (ibid.).
79. Ibid., 167–68.
80. Quoted in Johnston, *George Grenfell*, 1:381.
81. Casement notes that "soldiers are allowed full liberty to plunder" and concludes that his report, which is full of eyewitness accounts of atrocities and reckless exploitation, gives ample "evidence of the spirit which animates the Belgian Administration, if, indeed, Administration it can be called. The Government, so far as I could judge, is conducted almost exclusively on commercial principles, and, even judged by that standard, it would appear that those principles are somewhat short-sighted" (Casement, *Correspondence and Report*, 2).
82. Dall and Boas, "Museums of Ethnology," 589.
83. Montaigne, *Essays*, chapter 30.
84. Ibid.
85. Harman and Thomson, *Moral Relativism*, 8, 17.
86. Lévi-Strauss, *We Are All Cannibals*, 41–42.
87. Ibid., 39–42.
88. Ibid., 40.
89. United Nations General Assembly, *The Universal Declaration of Human Rights*, 10 December 1948, accessed 1 October 2020, http://www.un.org/en/universal-declaration-human-rights/index.html,.
90. Ibid., articles 8, 15, 22, 26 (nations), 21 (governments), 17 (property), 26 (education), 27 (copyright). For the mentioned criticism, see Illich, *Deschooling Society*; Holt, *Learning All the Time*; and Kinsella, *Against Intellectual Property.*
91. Wiredu, *Cultural Universals and Particulars*, 29.
92. After noting that anyone has interests of some kind, Wiredu suggest the rule: "Let your conduct at all times manifest a due concern for the interests of others." He explains: "A person may be said to manifest due concern for the interests of others if in contemplating the impact of his actions on their interests, she puts herself imaginatively in their position, and having done so, is able to welcome that impact" (ibid.).

    Living according to this rule, if taken literally, would be very challenging. At all times one would have to consider the impact of one's actions on anyone who might even slightly be affected, and refrain from the action unless everyone affected positively welcomes it, rather than considering it neutral ("don't care") or negatively. This rule would, among other things, rule out all efforts to act competitively. If I apply for and get a job, I negatively affect other people who might otherwise have gotten it. If I win a game, the other players might feel less happy than if they had won. Regardless of what one thinks of specific cases, suggesting that competition is cross-culturally bad under any circumstances seems too strong a claim.

BIBLIOGRAPHY

Note: Quotes from foreign-language books and articles have been translated by the author. Most of the URLs listed here are assumed to be stable; in such cases, the access date has been omitted. Full source information for websites, news articles, and films is included in the chapter endnotes.

Adams, Carol J. *The Sexual Politics of Meat: A Feminist-Vegetarian Critical Theory.* 20th anniversary ed. New York: Continuum, 2010.

Andrea, Alfred J. *The Medieval Record: Sources of Medieval History.* 2nd ed. Indianapolis: Hackett, 2020.

Angas, George French. *Savage Life and Scenes in Australia and New Zealand.* Vol. 1. London: Smith, Elder, 1847. https://archive.org/details/savagelifescenes01anga.

Arens, William. *The Man-Eating Myth: Anthropology & Anthropophagy.* Oxford: Oxford University Press, 1980 (1979).

Arnaud, Robert. "Notes sur les Montagnards Habé des cercles de Bandiagara et de Hombori (Soudan Français)." *Revue d'ethnographie et des traditions populaires* 2, no. 8 (1921): 241–314. https://archive.org/details/n8revuedethnogra02sociuoft.

Augouard, Prosper. *28 années au Congo: Lettres de Monseigneur Augouard.* 2 vols. Poitiers: Société Française d'Imprimerie et de Librairie, 1905. http://gallica.bnf.fr/ark:/12148/bpt6k1044507, http://gallica.bnf.fr/ark:/12148/bpt6k104451m.

Austen, Ralph A. *African Economic History: Internal Development and External Dependency.* London: James Currey, 1987.

Avramescu, Catalin. *An Intellectual History of Cannibalism.* Princeton: Princeton University Press, 2009.

Baker, Samuel W. *The Albert N'yanza, Great Basin of the Nile, and Explorations of the Nile Sources.* Vol. 1. Philadelphia: J. B. Lippincott, 1866. https://archive.org/details/albertnyanzagrea01bake_0.

Basden, George T. *Among the Ibos of Nigeria.* London: Seeley, Service, 1921. https://archive.org/details/amongibosofniger00basd.

Bates, Daisy. *The Passing of the Aborigines: A Lifetime Spent among the Natives of Australia.* Adelaide: University of Adelaide Library, 2014. First published in 1938. https://gutenberg.net.au/ebooks04/0400661h.html/.

Beaglehole, J. C., ed. *The Voyage of the* Resolution *and* Adventure, *1772–1775.* Vol. 2 of *The Journals of Captain James Cook on His Voyages of Discovery.* Cambridge: Cambridge University Press, 1969.

Beatty, Kenneth J. *Human Leopards: An Account of the Trials of Human Leopards before the Special Commission Court.* London: Hugh Rees, 1915. https://archive.org/details/humanleopardsacc00beatuoft.

Beaver, Wilfred N. *Unexplored New Guinea: A Record of the Travels, Adventures, and Experiences of a Resident Magistrate amongst the Head-Hunting Savages and Cannibals of the Unexplored Interior of New Guinea.* London: Seeley, Service, 1920. https://archive.org/details/unexplorednewgui00beavuoft.

Becker, Jasper. *Hungry Ghosts: China's Secret Famine.* London: John Murray, 1996.

Benedetto, Robert, ed. *Presbyterian Reformers in Central Africa: A Documentary Account.* Leiden: Brill, 1996.

Bennett, Albert L. "Ethnographical Notes on the Fang." *Journal of the Anthropological Institute of Great Britain and Ireland* 29, no. 1/2 (1899): 66–98.

Bentley, Trevor. *Pakeha Maori: The Extraordinary Story of the Europeans Who Lived as Maori in Early New Zealand.* North Shore, NZ: Penguin, 1999.

Bentley, William Holman. *Pioneering on the Congo.* Vol. 2. New York: Fleming H. Revell, 1900. https://archive.org/details/pioneeringoncon00bentgoog.

Bergemann, P. *Die Verbreitung der Anthropophagie über die Erde und Ermittelung einiger Wesenszüge dieses Brauches.* Bunzlau: Kreuschmer, 1893.

Best, Elsdon. *The Maori: Memoirs of the Polynesian Society.* Vol. 2. Wellington: Polynesian Society, 1941. First published in 1924. http://nzetc.victoria.ac.nz/tm/scholarly/tei-Bes02Maor.html.

Bianco, Lucien. *Peasants without the Party: Grass-Roots Movements in Twentieth-Century China.* Armonk, NY: M. E. Sharpe, 2001.

Boulestin, Bruno, and Anne-Sophie Coupey. *Cannibalism in the Linear Pottery Culture: The Human Remains from Herxheim.* Oxford: Archaeopress, 2015.

Brady, Ivan. "The Myth-Eating Man." *American Anthropologist* 84 (1982): 595–611.

Bride, Thomas Francis, ed. *Letters from Victorian Pioneers: Being a Series of Papers on the Early Occupation of the Colony, the Aborigines, etc.* Melbourne: Robt. S. Brain, 1898. https://archive.org/details/lettersfromvicto00publiala.

Brode, Heinrich. *Tippoo Tib: The Story of His Career in Central Africa, Narrated from His Own Accounts.* London: Edward Arnold, 1907. https://archive.org/details/cu31924028752644.

Brown, George. *Melanesians and Polynesians: Their Life-Histories Described and Compared.* London: Macmillan, 1910. https://archive.org/details/melanesianspolyn00browuoft.

———. *Pioneer-Missionary and Explorer: An Autobiography; A Narrative of Forty-Eight Years' Residence and Travel in Samoa, New Britain, New Ireland, New Guinea and the Solomon Islands.* London: Hodder and Stoughton, 1908.

Burger, Friedrich. *Unter den Kannibalen der Südsee: Studienreise durch die melanesische Inselwelt.* Dresden: Verlag Deutsche Buchwerkstätten, 1923.

Burns, Alan. *History of Nigeria.* 6th ed. London: George Allen & Unwin, 1963.

Burrows, Guy, and Edgar Canisius. *The Curse of Central Africa.* London: R. A. Everett, 1903. https://archive.org/details/cursecentralafr01canigoog.

Carlier, E. "Les Bondjo." *Le Mouvement Géographique* 1899: 413–16.

Casati, Gaetano. *Ten Years in Equatoria.* London: Frederick Warne, 1898. https://archive.org/details/tenyearsinequato00casa.

Casement, Roger. *Correspondence and Report from His Majesty's Consul at Boma Respecting the Administration of the Independent State of the Congo.* London: House of Commons, 1904. https://archive.org/details/CasementReport.

Castillo, Bernal Díaz del. *The True History of the Conquest of New Spain.* Indianapolis: Hackett, 2012.

Cayley-Webster, H[erbert]. *Through New Guinea and the Cannibal Countries.* London: T. Fisher Unwin, 1898. https://archive.org/details/throughnewguine01websgoog.

Chapaux, Albert. *Le Congo: Historique, diplomatique, physique, politique, économique, humanitaire & colonial.* Brussels: Charles Rozez, 1894. http://bildsuche.digitale-sammlungen.de/index.html?c=viewer&lv=1&bandnummer=bsb00073006.

Chavannes, Charles de. *Albert Dolisie: Sa correspondance avec l'auteur.* Paris: Editions du Comité de l'Afrique française, 1932. http://gallica.bnf.fr/ark:/12148/bpt6k5549697g.

Chevalier, Auguste. *Mission Chari–Lac Tchad, 1902–1904: L'Afrique centrale française.* Paris: Augustin Challamel, 1907. https://archive.org/details/lafriquecentrale00chev.

Cheyne, Andrew. *A Description of Islands in the Western Pacific Ocean, North and South of the Equator.* London: J. D. Potter, 1852.

Chong, Key Ray. *Cannibalism in China.* Wakefield, NH: Longwood, 1990.

Clozel, François-Joseph. *Les Bayas: Notes ethnographiques et linguistiques.* Paris: Joseph André, 1896. http://gallica.bnf.fr/ark:/12148/bpt6k82020q.

Cole, James. "Assessing the Calorific Significance of Episodes of Human Cannibalism in the Palaeolithic." *Scientific Reports* 7, art. no. 44707 (2017). http://www.nature.com/articles/srep44707.

Conklin, Beth A. *Consuming Grief: Compassionate Cannibalism in an Amazonian Society.* Austin: University of Texas Press, 2001.

Coombe, Florence. *Islands of Enchantment: Many-Sided Melanesia.* London: Macmillan, 1911.

Copet-Rougier, Élisabeth. "Tu ne traverseras pas le sang: Corps, parenté et pouvoirs chez les Kako du Cameroun." In *Le corps humain: Conçu, supplicié, possédé, cannibalisé,* edited by Maurice Godelier, 469–90. Paris: CNRS Éditions, 2009.

Coquilhat, Camille. *Sur le Haut-Congo.* Paris: J. Lebègue, 1888. https://archive.org/details/surlehautcongo00coqu.

Coulbois, François. *Dix Années au Tanganyka.* Limoges: Dumont, 1901. https://archive.org/details/dixannesautanga00coulgoog.

Crocombe, Ron G., and Marjorie Crocombe. *The Works of Ta'unga: Records of a Polynesian Traveller in the South Seas, 1833–1896.* Canberra: Australian National University Press, 1968.

Cruise, Richard A. *Journal of a Ten Months' Residence in New Zealand.* London: Longman, Hurst, Rees, Orme, and Brown, 1823. https://archive.org/details/journalatenmont00unkngoog.

Dall, W[illia]m H., and Franz Boas. "Museums of Ethnology and Their Classification." *Science* 9, no. 228 (1887): 587–89. https://www.jstor.org/stable/1762958.

Davidson, James W. *The Island of Formosa, Past and Present.* London: Macmillan, 1903. https://archive.org/details/islandofformosap00davi.

Davies, Nigel. *Human Sacrifice: In History and Today.* London: Macmillan, 1981.

Deacon, A. Bernard. *Malekula: A Vanishing People in the New Hebrides.* London: George Routledge, 1934.

Deacon, A. Bernard, and Camilla H. Wedgwood. "Notes on Some Islands of the New Hebrides." *Journal of the Royal Anthropological Institute of Great Britain and Ireland* 59 (1929): 461–515.

Dien, Albert E., and Keith N. Knapp, eds. *The Six Dynasties, 220–589.* Vol. 2 of *The Cambridge History of China.* Cambridge: Cambridge University Press, 2019.

Dillon, Peter. *Narrative and Successful Result of a Voyage in the South Seas.* Vol. 1. London: Hurst, Chance, 1829.

Donnelly, Mark P., and Daniel Diehl. *Eat Thy Neighbour: A History of Cannibalism.* Stroud, Gloucestershire: Sutton, 2006.

Du Chaillu, Paul B. *Explorations & Adventures in Equatorial Africa.* London: John Murray, 1861. https://archive.org/details/explorationsadv00chaigoog.

Dumont d'Urville, Jules. *Voyage au pôle Sud et dans l'Océanie, sur les corvettes l'Astrolabe et la Zélée*. Vol. 3. Paris: Gide, 1842. https://gallica.bnf.fr/ark:/12148/bpt6k97680n.image.f3.langFR.

d'Uzès, Duchesse Marie-Clémentine. *Le voyage de mon fils au Congo.* Paris: E. Plon, Nourrit, 1894. http://gallica.bnf.fr/ark:/12148/bpt6k5719226p.

Dybowski, Jean. *La route du Tchad: Du Loango au Chari.* Paris: Firmin-Didot, 1893. http://gallica.bnf.fr/ark:/12148/bpt6k1049816/.

———. *Le Congo méconnu.* Paris: Librairie Hachette, 1912. http://gallica.bnf.fr/ark:/12148/bpt6k6541368f.

Earle, Augustus. *A Narrative of a Nine Months' Residence in New Zealand, in 1827.* London: Longman, Rees, Orme, Brown, Green & Longman, 1832. http://www.enzb.auckland.ac.nz/document?wid=297.

Edgerton, Robert B. *The Troubled Heart of Africa: A History of the Congo.* New York: St. Martin's Press, 2002.

Edgerton-Tarpley, Kathryn. *Tears from Iron: Cultural Responses to Famine in Nineteenth-Century China.* Berkeley: University of California Press, 2008.

Edwards, E[vangeline] D., ed. *Chinese Prose Literature of the T'ang Period, A.D. 618–906.* Vol. 2. London: Probsthain, 1938.

Ekholm Friedman, Kajsa. *Catastrophe and Creation: The Transformation of an African Culture.* Amsterdam: Harwood, 1991.

Erskine, John Elphinstone. *Journal of a Cruise among the Islands of the Western Pacific.* London: John Murray, 1853. https://archive.org/details/bub_gb_giq0cXRgttsC.

Evans-Pritchard, E. E. "Cannibalism: A Zande Text." *Africa: Journal of the International African Institute* 26, no. 1 (1956): 73–74.

———. "Zande Cannibalism." *Journal of the Royal Anthropological Institute of Great Britain and Ireland* 90, no. 2 (1960): 238–58.

Festetics de Tolna, Rodolphe. *Chez les cannibales: Huit ans de croisière dans l'Océan Pacifique à bord du yacht "le Tolna."* Paris: Plon-Nourrit, 1903. http://gallica.bnf.fr/ark:/12148/bpt6k6549123n.

———. *Vers l'écueil de Minicoy, après huit ans dans l'Océan Pacifique et Indien à bord du yacht "le Tolna."* Paris: Plon-Nourrit, 1904. http://gallica.bnf.fr/ark:/12148/bpt6k6550328w.

Fiddes, Nick. *Meat: A Natural Symbol.* London: Routledge, 2004. First published in 1991.

Fison, Lorimer. *Tales from Old Fiji.* London: Alexander Moring, 1904. https://archive.org/details/talesfromoldfiji00fisouoft.

Forsyth, Donald W. "Three Cheers for Hans Staden: The Case for Brazilian Cannibalism." *Ethnohistory* 32, no. 1 (1985): 17–36.

Fox, Greg J. "Big Nambas Custom Texts." *Journal de la Société des Océanistes* 35, no. 65 (1979): 286–93. http://www.persee.fr/doc/jso_0300-953x_1979_num_35_65_3018.

François, Curt von. *Die Erforschung des Tschuapa und Lulongo: Reisen in Centralafrika.* Leipzig: Brockhaus, 1888.

Fräßle, Josef. *Meiner Urwaldneger Denken und Handeln.* Freiburg i. Br.: Herder, 1923.

Friedmann, S[igwart]. *Die Ostasiatische Inselwelt.* Vol. 1, *Sumatra, Borneo, Celebes, die Molukken und Neu-Guinea.* Leipzig: Otto Spamer, 1868.

Frobenius, Leo. *Im Schatten des Kongostaates: Bericht über den Verlauf der ersten Reisen der D.I.A.F.E. von 1904–1906, über deren Forschungen und Beobachtungen auf geographischem und kolonialwirtschaftlichem Gebiet.* Berlin: Georg Reimer, 1907. https://archive.org/details/imschattendesko01frobgoog.

———. *Und Afrika sprach. . . .* Vol. 3. Berlin: Vita, 1913. https://archive.org/details/bub_gb_MJYPAQAAMAAJ.

Froment, Ed. "Un Voyage dans l'Oubangui." *Bulletin de la Société de Géographie de Lille* 11 (1889): 180–216.

Gardner, Don. "Anthropophagy, Myth, and the Subtle Ways of Ethnocentrism." In *The Anthropology of Cannibalism,* edited by R. Goldman, 27–49. Westport, CT: Bergin & Garvey, 1999.

Gardner, Jane F. "Slavery and Roman Law." In *The Cambridge World History of Slavery,* vol. 1, edited by Keith Bradley and Paul Cartledge, 414–37. Cambridge: Cambridge University Press, 2011.

Garnier, Jules. 1868. *Voyage à la Nouvelle Calédonie, 1863–1866.* Cadeilhan: Zulma, 1992. First published in 1876. http://gallica.bnf.fr/ark:/12148/bpt6k261394.

Gero, F[iliberto]. *Cannibalism in Zandeland: Truth and Falsehood.* Bologna: E.M.I. – Editrice Missionaria Italiana, [1980?].

Gill, William. *Gems from the Coral Islands, Western Polynesia, Comprising the New Hebrides Group, the Loyalty Group, New Caledonia Group.* London: Ward, 1855. https://archive.org/details/gemsfromcoralis03gillgoog.

Glave, Edward J. *In Savage Africa; or, Six Years of Adventure in Congo-Land.* New York: R. H. Russell & Son, 1892. https://archive.org/details/insavageafricao00glavgoog.

———. "The Slave Trade in the Congo Basin." *Century Magazine,* Apr. 1890: 824–38. http://www.unz.org/Pub/Century-1890apr-00824?View=PDF.

Gordon-Grube, Karen. "Anthropophagy in Post-Renaissance Europe: The Tradition of Medicinal Cannibalism." *American Anthropologist* 90, no. 2 (1988): 405–9.

Guzman, Gregory G. "Reports of Mongol Cannibalism in the Thirteenth-Century Latin Sources: Oriental Fact or Western Fiction?" In *Discovering New Worlds: Essays on Medieval Exploration and Imagination,* edited by Scott D. Westrem, 31–68. New York: Garland, 1991.

Haberberger, Simon. *Kolonialismus und Kannibalismus: Fälle aus Deutsch-Neuguinea und Britisch-Neuguinea 1884–1914.* Wiesbaden: Harrassowitz, 2007.

Hagen, A., and A. Pineau. "Les Nouvelles Hébrides." *Revue d'Ethnographie* 7 (1889): 302–62.

Hahl, Albert. *Governor in New Guinea.* Canberra: Australian National University Press, 1980.

Harley, George W. *Masks as Agents of Social Control in Northeast Liberia.* Papers of the Peabody Museum. Cambridge, MA: Peabody Museum of American Archaeology and Ethnology, 1950.

Harman, Gilbert, and Judith Jarvis Thomson. *Moral Relativism and Moral Objectivity.* Cambridge, MA: Blackwell, 1996.

Harms, Robert W. *River of Wealth, River of Sorrow: The Central Zaire Basin in the Era of the Slave and Ivory Trade, 1500–1891.* New Haven: Yale University Press, 1981.

Harris, Marvin. *Good to Eat: Riddles of Food and Culture.* Prospect Heights, IL: Waveland, 1985.

Harrisson, Tom. *Savage Civilisation.* London: Victor Gollancz, 1937.

Hecquard, Hyacinthe. *Voyage sur la côte et dans l'intérieur de l'Afrique occidentale.* Paris: Bénard, 1855.

Hilton-Simpson, Melville W. *Land and Peoples of the Kasai.* London: Constable, 1911. https://archive.org/details/landpeoplesofkas00hiltrich.

Hinde, Sidney Langford. *The Fall of the Congo Arabs.* London: Methuen, 1897. https://archive.org/details/fallofcongoarabs00hind.

Hiroa, Te Rangi. *The Coming of the Maori.* Wellington: Whitcombe and Tombs, 1950. http://nzetc.victoria.ac.nz/tm/scholarly/tei-BucTheC.html.

Hogg, Garry. *Cannibalism and Human Sacrifice.* London: Robert Hale, 1958.

Holt, John. *Learning All the Time.* Cambridge, MA: Perseus, 1989.

Howitt, Alfred W. *The Native Tribes of South-East Australia.* London: Macmillan, 1904. https://archive.org/details/nativetribesofso00howiuoft.

Human Rights Watch. *The Curse of Gold: Democratic Republic of Congo.* New York, June 2005. Accessed 27 November 2020. https://www.hrw.org/reports/2005/drc0505/drc0505.pdf.

———. *Ituri: "Covered in Blood": Ethnically Targeted Violence in Northeastern DR Congo.* New York, July 2003. Accessed 27 November 2020. http://www.hrw.org/sites/default/files/reports/DRC0703.pdf.

Hunt, Peter. "Slaves in Greek Literary Culture." In *The Cambridge World History of Slavery,* vol. 1, edited by Keith Bradley and Paul Cartledge, 22–47. Cambridge: Cambridge University Press, 2011.

Hutchinson, Thomas J. *Ten Years Wanderings among the Ethiopians.* London: Hurst and Blackett, 1861.

Illich, Ivan. *Deschooling Society.* London: Marion Boyars, 2002. First published in 1970.

Isichei, Elizabeth. *A History of African Societies to 1870.* Cambridge: Cambridge University Press, 1997.

———. *Igbo Worlds: An Anthology of Oral Histories and Historical Descriptions.* London: Macmillan, 1977.

Jaggar, Thomas James. *Unto the Perfect Day: The Journal of Thomas James Jaggar, Feejee 1838–1845.* Edited by Ester Keesing-Styles and William Keesing-Styles. Auckland: Solent, 1988.

Jameson, James S. *The Story of the Rear Column of the Emin Pasha Relief Expedition.* New York: National Publishing, 1891. https://archive.org/details/storyofrearcolum00jameuoft.

Jewsiewicki, Bogumil, and Mumbanza mwa Bawele. "The Social Context of Slavery in Equatorial Africa during the Nineteenth and Twentieth Centuries." In *The Ideology of Slavery in Africa,* edited by Paul E. Lovejoy, 73–98. Beverly Hills: Sage, 1981.

Johnston, Harry. *George Grenfell and the Congo: A History and Description of the Congo Independent State and Adjoining Districts of Congoland.* 2 vols. New York: Appleton, 1910. https://archive.org/details/GeorgeGrenfellAndTheCongoV1, https://archive.org/details/GeorgeGrenfellAndTheCongoV2.

Junghuhn, Franz. *Die Battaländer auf Sumatra.* Vol. 2. Berlin: G. Reimer, 1847. https://archive.org/details/diebattalnderau02junggoog.

Junker, Wilhelm. *Travels in Africa during the Years 1879–1883.* Vol. 2. London: Chapman and Hall, 1891. https://archive.org/details/travelsinafricad02junk.

Kalous, Milan. *Cannibals and Tongo Players of Sierra Leone.* Auckland: Wright & Carman, 1974.
Keeley, Lawrence H. *War before Civilization: The Myth of the Peaceful Savage.* New York: Oxford University Press, 1996.
Kennedy, Philip F., and Shawkat M. Toorawa, eds. *Two Arabic Travel Books.* New York: New York University Press, 2014.
Kerr, George H. *Formosa Betrayed.* Boston: Houghton Mifflin, 1965.
Kilgour, Maggie. *From Communion to Cannibalism: An Anatomy of Metaphors of Incorporation.* Princeton: Princeton University Press, 1990.
Kingdon, Jonathan. *The Kingdon Field Guide to African Mammals.* 2nd ed. London: Bloomsbury, 2015.
Kingsley, Mary H. *Travels in West Africa: Congo Français, Corisco and Cameroons.* 2nd ed. London: Macmillan, 1904. https://archive.org/details/travelsinwestafr00king_0.
Kinsella, N. Stephan. *Against Intellectual Property.* Auburn, AL: Ludwig von Mises Institute, 2008. https://mises.org/library/against-intellectual-property-0.
Kleintitschen, P. A. *Die Küstenbewohner der Gazellehalbinsel, ihre Sitten und Gebräuche.* Düsseldorf: L. Schwann, [1906?].
Knauft, Bruce M. *Exchanging the Past: A Rainforest World of Before and After.* Chicago: University of Chicago Press, 2002.
———. *Good Company and Violence: Sorcery and Social Action in a Lowland New Guinea Society.* Berkeley: University of California Press, 1985.
Koch, Klaus-Friedrich. *War and Peace in Jalémó: The Management of Conflict in Highland New Guinea.* Cambridge, MA: Harvard University Press, 1974.
Korn, Daniel, Mark Radice, and Charlie Hawes. *Cannibal: The History of the People-Eaters.* London: Channel 4 Books, 2001.
Kotze, Stefan von. *Südsee-Erinnerungen.* Berlin: Dom, 1925.
Krieger, Michael. *Conversations with the Cannibals: The End of the Old South Pacific.* Hopewell, NJ: Ecco, 1994.
Kummer, Ludolf. "Kannibalismus auf Neu-Mecklenburg." *Kolonie und Heimat* 6, no. 47 (1913): 12–14.
Lamb, Robert. *Saints and Savages: The Story of Five Years in the New Hebrides.* Edinburgh: William Blackwood, 1905.
Lamotte, Edouard. *Chez les Congolais.* Brussels: Callewaert, 1895.
Lang, John. *The Land of the Golden Trade.* London: Caxton, 1915. https://archive.org/details/landofgoldentrad00john.
Lapsley, Samuel Norvell. *Life and Letters.* Richmond, VA: Whittet & Shepperson, 1893. https://archive.org/details/lifeandletterss00lapsgoog.
Lawry, Walter. *Friendly and Feejee Islands: A Missionary Visit to Various Stations in the South Seas in the Year MDCCCXLVII [1847].* 2nd ed. London: John Mason, 1850. https://books.google.com/books?id=mYBJAAAAIAAJ.
Leak, Stephen G. A. *Tsetse Biology and Ecology: Their Role in the Epidemiology and Control of Trypanosomosis.* Wallingford: CABI, 1999.
Leertouwer, L[ammert]. "The Cannibalism of the Batak." *Nederlands theologisch tijdschrift* 25, no. 3 (1971): 241–60.
Lenz, Oskar. *Skizzen aus Westafrika: Selbsterlebnisse.* Berlin: Hofmann, 1878. https://archive.org/details/skizzenauswestaf00lenz.
Leonard, Arthur Glyn. *The Lower Niger and Its Tribes.* London: Macmillan, 1906. https://archive.org/details/lowernigerandits010284mbp.

Lévi-Strauss, Claude. *We Are All Cannibals, and Other Essays.* New York: Columbia University Press, 2016.

Levtzion, N., and J. F. P. Hopkins, eds. *Corpus of Early Arabic Sources for West African History.* Cambridge: Cambridge University Press, 1981.

Lindenbaum, Shirley. "Thinking about Cannibalism." *Annual Review of Anthropology* 33 (2004): 475–98.

Livingstone, David. "Fragment of 1871 Field Diary (CII–CLXIII), 23 March 1871–11 August 1871." *Livingstone Online*, project ID: liv_000095 (2016). Accessed 21 October 2020. http://livingstoneonline.org/in-his-own-words/catalogue?query=liv_000095.

———. *The Last Journals of David Livingstone in Central Africa, from 1865 to his Death.* Vol. 2. London: John Murray, 1874. https://archive.org/details/lastjournalsofda02livi.

———. "Unyanyembe Journal (1870 Field Diary Segment)." *Livingstone Online*, project ID: liv_015005 (2016). Accessed 21 October 2020. http://livingstoneonline.org/in-his-own-words/catalogue?query=liv_015005.

Lloyd, Albert B. *In Dwarf Land and Cannibal Country: A Record of Travel and Discovery in Central Africa.* London: T. Fisher Unwin, 1899. https://archive.org/details/dwarflandcanniba00lloy.

Lockerby, William. *The Journal of William Lockerby, Sandalwood Trader in the Fijian Islands During the Years 1808–1809.* London: Hakluyt Society, 1925. https://archive.org/details/no52works02hakluoft.

Lovejoy, Paul E. *Transformations of Slavery: A History of Slavery in Africa.* Cambridge: Cambridge University Press, 1983.

Lu, Tina. *Accidental Incest, Filial Cannibalism, and Other Peculiar Encounters in Late Imperial Chinese Literature.* Cambridge, MA: Harvard University Asia Center, 2008.

Lüders, Karl. *Der Bismarck-Archipel und seine Bewohner.* Weimar: Geographisches Institut, [1890?].

Lumholtz, Carl. *Among Cannibals: An Account of Four Years' Travels in Australia and of Camp Life with the Aborigines of Queensland.* New York: Charles Scribner's Sons, 1889. https://archive.org/details/amongcannibalsac1889lumh.

Lyne, Charles. *New Guinea: An Account of the Establishment of the British Protectorate over the Southern Shores of New Guinea.* London: Sampson Low, Marston, Searle & Rivington, 1885.

Magyar, Ladislaus. *Reisen in Süd-Afrika in den Jahren 1849 bis 1857.* Vol. 1. Pest: Lauffer & Stolp, 1859. https://www.wdl.org/en/item/2924/.

Maistre, Casimir. *A Travers l'Afrique centrale du Congo au Niger 1892–1893.* Paris: Librairie Hachette, 1895.

Makulo, Akambu. *La vie de Disasi Makulo: Ancien esclave de Tippo Tip et catéchiste de Grenfell.* Kinshasa: Editions Saint Paul Afrique, 1983.

Mandeville, John. *The Travels of Sir John Mandeville,* edited by C. W. R. D. Moseley. London: Penguin, 1983.

Manning, Patrick. *Slavery and African Life.* Cambridge: Cambridge University Press, 1990.

Marriner, Brian. *Cannibalism: The Last Taboo.* London: Arrow, 1992.

Marsden, Samuel. *The Letters and Journals.* Edited by John Rawson Elder. Dunedin: Otago University Council, 1932. http://www.enzb.auckland.ac.nz/epubs.

Martingale, Moira. *Cannibal Killers: The Impossible Monsters.* London: Robert Hale, 1993.

Mauss, Marcel. *The Gift.* Translated by Jane I. Guyer. Chicago: HAU, 2016.

McNab, Robert, ed. *Historical Records of New Zealand.* 2 vols. Wellington: John Mackay, 1908/1914. https://archive.org/details/historicalrecord01mcnauoft, https://archive.org/details/historicalrecord02mcnauoft.

———. *The Old Whaling Days: A History of Southern New Zealand from 1830 to 1840.* Christchurch: Whitcombe and Tombs, 1913. https://archive.org/details/oldwhalingdayshi00mcnaiala.

Mecklenburg, Adolf Friedrich, Duke of. *From the Congo to the Niger and the Nile: An Account of the German Central African Expedition of 1910–1911.* Vol. 1. London: Duckworth, 1913. https://archive.org/details/fromcongotoniger01adol.

Meek, C[harles] K. *The Northern Tribes of Nigeria.* Vol. 2. London: Oxford University Press, 1925.

Migeod, Frederick W. H. *Across Equatorial Africa.* London: Heath Cranton, 1923.

Mikaere, Annie. "Maori Women: Caught in the Contradictions of a Colonised Reality." *Waikato Law Review* 2 (1994). https://www.waikato.ac.nz/law/research/waikato_law_review/pubs/volume_2_1994/7.

Miller, Joseph C. *Kings and Kinsmen: Early Mbundu States in Angola.* Oxford: Clarendon, 1976.

———. *Way of Death: Merchant Capitalism and the Angolan Slave Trade, 1730–1830.* Madison: University of Wisconsin Press, 1988.

Mills, Lady Dorothy. *Through Liberia.* London: Duckworth, 1926.

Monckton, C[harles] A. W. *Some Experiences of a New Guinea Resident Magistrate.* 3rd ed. London: John Lane, 1921. https://archive.org/details/someexperienceso00monc.

Montaigne, Michel de. *Essays.* London: Reeves and Turner, 1877. http://www.gutenberg.org/ebooks/3600.

Monteiro, Joachim John. *Angola and the River Congo.* Vol. 2. London: Macmillan, 1875. https://archive.org/details/angolarivercongo02mont.

Moon, Paul. *This Horrid Practice: The Myth and Reality of Traditional Maori Cannibalism.* North Shore, NZ: Penguin, 2008.

Moorehead, Alan. *The White Nile.* London: Penguin, 1960.

Morel, Edmund D. *Red Rubber: The Story of the Rubber Slave Trade Which Flourished on the Congo for Twenty Years, 1890–1910.* Manchester: National Labour Press, 1919. https://archive.org/details/redrubberstoryof00more.

MRG and RAPY. *"Erasing the Board": Report of the International Research Mission into Crimes under International Law Committed Against the Bambuti Pygmies in the Eastern Democratic Republic of Congo.* London: Minority Rights Group International (MRG) and Réseau des Associations Autochtones Pygmées du Congo (RAPY), July 2004. Accessed 27 November 2020. http://minorityrights.org/wp-content/uploads/2015/07/MRG_Rep_Twa_ENG.pdf.

Murray, J[ohn] H[ubert] P. *Papua or British New Guinea.* London: T. Fisher Unwin, 1912. https://archive.org/details/papuaorbritishne00murr.

Musy, Maurice. "Correspondance de M. Maurice Musy, chef de poste à Bangui (Congo français), massacré par les indigènes." *Revue de Géographie* 27 (1890): 455–57; 28 (1891): 64–68, 130–33, 291–94, 377–81.

Norden, Hermann. *Fresh Tracks in the Belgian Congo: From the Uganda Border to the Mouth of the Congo.* London: Witherby, 1924.

Northrup, David. "The Ideological Context of Slavery in Southeastern Nigeria in the Nineteenth Century." In *The Ideology of Slavery in Africa,* edited by Paul E. Lovejoy, 101–22. Beverly Hills: Sage, 1981.

Oberländer, Richard. "Die Eingeborenen der australischen Kolonie Victoria." *Globus* 4 (1863): 238–42, 278–82.

Obeyesekere, Gananath. *Cannibal Talk: The Man-Eating Myth and Human Sacrifice in the South Seas.* Berkeley: University of California Press, 2005.

Oliver, Douglas L. *Oceania: The Native Cultures of Australia and the Pacific Islands.* Vol. 1. Honolulu: University of Hawaii Press, 1989.

Parkinson, Richard. *Im Bismarck-Archipel: Erlebnisse und Beobachtungen auf der Insel Neu-Pommern (Neu-Britannien).* Leipzig: Brockhaus, 1887.

Paton, John G. *Missionary to the New Hebrides: An Autobiography.* Vol.1. New York: Robert Carter & Brothers, [1889]. https://archive.org/details/johngpatonmissi o01patouoft.

Peekel, P. G[erhard]. *Religion und Zauberei auf dem mittleren Neu-Mecklenburg, Bismarck-Archipel, Südsee.* Münster: Druck und Verlag der Aschendorff'schen Buchhandlung, 1910.

Peri, Alexis. *The War Within: Diaries from the Siege of Leningrad.* Cambridge, MA: Harvard University Press, 2017.

Petrie, Hazel. *Outcasts of the Gods? The Struggle over Slavery in M ori New Zealand.* Auckland: Auckland University Press, 2015.

Petrinovich, Lewis. *The Cannibal Within.* New York: Aldine de Gruyter, 2000.

Pettersson, Bengt. "Cannibalism in the Dynastic Histories." *Bulletin of the Museum of Far Eastern Antiquities* 71 (1999): 73–189.

Pfeil, Joachim Graf von. *Studien und Beobachtungen aus der Südsee.* Braunschweig: Friedrich Vieweg und Sohn, 1899.

Pigafetta, Filippo. *A Report of the Kingdom of Congo and of the Surrounding Countries, Drawn out of the Writings and Discourses of the Portuguese, Duarte Lopez.* Translated and edited by Margarite Hutchinson. London: John Murray, 1881. https://archive.org/details/reportofkingdomo00lope.

Polack, J[oel] S[amuel]. *New Zealand: Being a Narrative of Travels and Adventures During a Residence in that Country Between the Years 1831 and 1837.* 2 vols. London: Richard Bentley, 1838. https://archive.org/details/newzealandbeingn00pola.

Polo, Marco. *The Travels.* London: Penguin, 2016.

Poutrin, Dr. "Notes ethnographiques sur les populations M'Baka du Congo Français." *L'Anthropologie* 21 (1910): 35–54. http://gallica.bnf.fr/ark:/12148/bpt6k5433880h.

Powell, Wilfred. *Wanderings in a Wild Country; or, Three Years amongst the Cannibals of New Britain.* London: Sampson Low, Marston, Searle, & Rivington, 1883. https://archive.org/details/wanderingsinwild00powe.

Prout, Ebenezer. *Memoirs of the Life of the Rev. John Williams, Missionary to Polynesia.* New York: M. W. Dodd, 1843. https://archive.org/details/memoirsoflife ofrlond00prou.

Rannie, Douglas. *My Adventures among South Sea Cannibals: An Account of the Experiences and Adventures of a Government Official among the Natives of Oceania.* London: Seeley, Service, 1912.

Rascher, Matthäus. *Baining (Neu-Pommern), Land und Leute.* Münster: Verlag der Aschendorff'schen Buchhandlung, 1909. https://sammlungen.ulb.uni-muenster.de/hd/content/titleinfo/2412160.

Redlich, Edwin. "Notes on the Western Islands of the Pacific Ocean and New Guinea." *Journal of the Royal Geographical Society of London* 44 (1874): 30–37.

Reeves, Edward. *Brown Men and Women; or, The South Sea Islands in 1895 and 1896.* London: Swan Sonnenschein, 1898. http://archive.org/details/brownmenwomenors00reevuoft.

Renouard, G. *L'Ouest Africain et les Missions Catholiques: Congo et Oubanghi.* Paris: H. Oudin, 1904. https://archive.org/details/louestafricainet00reno.

Rickett, W. Allyn, ed. and trans. *Guanzi: Political, Economic, and Philosophical Essays from Early China.* Vol. 1. Rev. ed. Princeton: Princeton University Press, 2001.

Rickman, John. *Journal of Captain Cook's Last Voyage to the Pacific Ocean, on* Discovery*; Performed in the Years 1776, 1777, 1778, 1779.* London: E. Newbery, 1781. https://archive.org/details/cihm_40645.

Robson, R[obert] W. *Queen Emma: The Samoan-American Girl Who Founded an Empire in 19th Century New Guinea.* Sydney: Pacific Publications, 1971.

Róheim, Géza. *Children of the Desert: The Western Tribes of Central Australia.* Vol. 1. Edited by Werner Muensterberger. New York: Harper & Row, 1976.

Rotours, Robert des. "Encore quelques notes sur l'anthropophagie en Chine." *T'oung Pao,* 2nd ser., 54, no. 1–3 (1968): 1–49.

———. "Quelques notes sur l'anthropophagie en Chine." *T'oung Pao,* 2nd ser., 50, no. 4–5 (1963): 386–427.

Rowe, William T. *China's Last Empire: The Great Qing.* Cambridge, MA: Harvard University Press, 2009.

Sagan, Eli. *Cannibalism: Human Aggression and Cultural Form.* New York: Harper & Row, 1974.

Sahlins, Marshall. "Artificially Maintained Controversies: Global Warming and Fijian Cannibalism." *Anthropology Today* 19, no. 3 (2003): 3–5.

Sala-Molins, Lluís. "Slavery in Law Codes." In *From Chains to Bonds: The Slave Trade Revisited,* edited by Doudou Diène, 209–15. New York: Berghahn Books, 2001.

Salmond, Anne. *Two Worlds: First Meetings Between Maori and Europeans, 1642–1772.* Auckland: Viking, 1991.

Samarin, William J. "The Linguistic World of Field Colonialism." *Language in Society* 13 (1984): 435–53.

Schnee, Heinrich. *Bilder aus der Südsee: Unter den kannibalischen Stämmen des Bismarck-Archipels.* Berlin: Reimer, 1904.

Scholz, Benno. "Kannibalismus im Bismarck-Archipel." *Deutsches Kolonialblatt* 18 (1907): 804–10.

Schutt, Bill. *Eat Me: A Natural and Unnatural History of Cannibalism.* London: Profile, 2017.

Schweinfurth, Georg. "Dr. G. Schweinfurth's Reise nach den oberen Nil-Ländern: V. Bemerkungen zur Karte seiner Reise im oberen Nil-Gebiete, 1869 und 1870." In *Petermanns Geographische Mitteilungen* 17, no. 4 (1871): 131–39. https://archive.org/details/bub_gb_P7YBAAAAYAAJ.

———. *The Heart of Africa.* Vol. 2. London: Sampson Low, Marston, Low, and Searle, 1874. https://archive.org/details/heartofafricathr02schw.

———. *Im Herzen von Afrika.* Vol. 2. Leipzig: F. A. Brockhaus, 1874. https://archive.org/details/imherzenvonafri00schwgoog.

Seabrook, William B. *Jungle Ways.* New York: Harcourt, Brace, 1931.

———. *No Hiding Place: An Autobiography.* Philadelphia: J. P. Lippincott, 1942.

Segl, Peter. *Ketzer in Österreich: Untersuchungen über Häresie und Inquisition im Herzogtum Österreich im 13. und beginnenden 14. Jahrhundert.* Paderborn: Ferdinand Schöningh, 1984.

Seligmann, C[harles] G[abriel]. *The Melanesians of British New Guinea.* Cambridge: Cambridge University Press, 1910. https://archive.org/details/melanesiansofbri00seli.

Shaloff, Stanley. *Reform in Leopold's Congo.* Richmond, VA: John Knox, 1970.

Sheppard, William H. *Presbyterian Pioneers in Congo.* Richmond, VA: Presbyterian Committee of Publication, 1917. https://archive.org/details/presbyterianpion00shep.

Shi Nai'an and Luo Guanzhong. *Outlaws of the Marsh.* 4 vols. Beijing: Foreign Languages Press, 1988.

Shillington, Kevin, ed. *Encyclopedia of African History.* 3 vols. New York: Fitzroy Dearborn, 2005.

Simms, W. Gilmore. "The Morals of Slavery." In *The Pro-Slavery Argument, as Maintained by the Most Distinguished Writers of the Southern States,* by William Harper, J[ames] H[enry] Hammond, W. Gilmore Simms, and Thomas R. Dew, 175–285. Philadelphia: Lippincott, Grambo, 1853. https://archive.org/details/proslaveryargume00phil.

Simpson, A. W. Brian. *Cannibalism and the Common Law: The Story of the Tragic Last Voyage of the* Mignonette *and the Strange Legal Proceedings to Which It Gave Rise.* Chicago: University of Chicago Press, 1984.

Singer, H. "Woelffels Reisen im Hinterland der Elfenbeinküste." *Globus* 79 (1901): 313–18.

Slade, Ruth. *King Leopold's Congo.* London: Oxford University Press, 1962.

Smith, S. Percy. *Maori Wars of the Nineteenth Century.* 2nd ed. Christchurch: Whitcombe and Tombs, 1910. http://nzetc.victoria.ac.nz/tm/scholarly/tei-SmiMaor.html.

Snelgrave, William. *A New Account of Some Parts of Guinea, and the Slave-Trade.* London: Knapton, 1734.

Somerville, Boyle T. "Ethnological Notes on New Hebrides." *Journal of the Anthropological Institute of Great Britain and Ireland* 23 (1894): 363–93.

Speiser, Felix. *Ethnology of Vanuatu: An Early Twentieth Century Study.* Bathurst, New South Wales: Crawford House, 1991.

———. *Südsee, Urwald, Kannibalen: Reisen in den Neuen Hebriden und Santa-Cruz-Inseln.* 2nd ed. Stuttgart: Strecker und Schröder, 1924.

Speke, John Hanning. *Journal of the Discovery of the Source of the Nile.* 2nd ed. Edinburgh: William Blackwood and Sons, 1864. https://archive.org/details/journal00ofdiscovespekrich.

Spence, Jonathan D. *The Search for Modern China.* 3rd ed. New York: W. W. Norton, 2013.

Stanley, Henry M. *How I Found Livingstone: Travels, Adventures and Discoveries in Central Africa.* London: Sampson Low, Marston, Low, and Searle, 1872. https://archive.org/details/howifoundliving01stangoog.

———. *In Darkest Africa; Or, the Quest, Rescue and Retreat of Emin, Governor of Equatoria.* Vol. 1. New York: Charles Scribner's Sons, 1890. https://archive.org/details/indarkestafrica01henr.

———. *Through the Dark Continent.* Vol. 2. London: Sampson Low, Marston, Searle, and Rivington, 1878. https://archive.org/details/throughdarkconti1878stan2.

Steffen, Paul. "Die katholischen Missionen in Deutsch-Neuguinea." In *Die deutsche Südsee 1884–1914: Ein Handbuch,* edited by Hermann Joseph Hiery, 343–83. Paderborn: Ferdinand Schöningh, 2001.

Stevenson, Robert Louis. *In the South Seas.* London: Chatto & Windus, 1908. http://www.gutenberg.org/ebooks/464.

St. Johnston, Alfred. *Camping among Cannibals.* London: Macmillan, 1883. https://archive.org/details/campingamongcan00johngoog.

Sumner, William Graham. *Folkways.* New York: Dover, 1959.

Surville, Jean François M. de. *Extracts from Journals Relating to the Visit to New Zealand of the French Ship* St Jean Baptiste *in December 1769, under the Command of J. F. M. de Surville.* Edited and translated by Isabel Ollivier and Cheryl Hingley. Wellington: Alexander Turnbull Library Endowment Trust, 1982.

Sutton, Donald S. "Consuming Counterrevolution: The Ritual and Culture of Cannibalism in Wuxuan, Guangxi, China, May to July 1968." *Comparative Studies in Society and History* 37, no. 1 (1995): 136–72.

Swann, Alfred J. *Fighting the Slave-Hunters in Central Africa: A Record of Twenty-Six Years of Travel & Adventure Round the Great Lakes.* Philadelphia: J. B. Lippincott, 1910. https://archive.org/details/fightingslavehu00swangoog.

Talbot, P. Amaury. *The Peoples of Southern Nigeria.* 4 vols. London: Oxford University Press, 1926.

Tannahill, Reay. *Flesh and Blood: A History of the Cannibal Complex.* London: Abacus, 1976.

Tautain, Dr. "Sur l'anthropophagie et les sacrifices humains aux Iles Marquises." *L'Anthropologie* 7 (1896): 443–52. http://gallica.bnf.fr/ark:/12148/bpt6k5442685v.

Thomas, Hugh. *The Slave Trade: The Story of the Atlantic Slave Trade, 1440–1870.* New York: Simon & Schuster, 1997.

Thomson, Arthur S. *The Story of New Zealand: Past and Present—Savage and Civilized.* Vol. 1. London: John Murray, 1859. https://archive.org/details/storynewzealand05thomgoog.

Thornton, John K. *The Kingdom of Kongo: Civil War and Transition, 1641–1718.* Madison: University of Wisconsin Press, 1983.

Thurnwald, Richard. "Nachrichten aus Nissan und von den Karolinen." *Zeitschrift für Ethnologie* 40 (1908): 106–15.

Torday, Emil. *Camp and Tramp in African Wilds.* London: Seeley, Service, 1913. https://archive.org/details/camptrampinafric00tord.

———. *Causeries Congolaises.* Brussels: Vromant, 1925.

Torday, Emil, and T. A. Joyce. "On the Ethnology of the South-Western Congo Free State." *Journal of the Royal Anthropological Institute of Great Britain and Ireland* 37 (1907): 133–56.

Travis-Henikoff, Carole A. *Dinner with a Cannibal: The Complete History of Mankind's Oldest Taboo.* Santa Monica: Santa Monica Press, 2008.

Tregear, Edward. *The Maori Race.* Wanganui: A. D. Willis, 1904. https://archive.org/details/cu31924026469753.

Twitchett, Denis, and Paul Jakov Smith, eds. *The Sung Dynasty and Its Precursors, 907—1279.* Vol. 5, pt. 1 of *The Cambridge History of China.* Cambridge: Cambridge University Press, 2009.

United Nations Human Rights Council. *Rapport détaillé de l'Equipe d'experts internationaux sur la situation au Kasaï.* July 2018. Accessed 21 October 2020. https://www.ohchr.org/EN/HRBodies/HRC/RegularSessions/Session38/Documents/A_HR_38_CRP.1_FR.docx.

Vanka, Surya. *International Color Guide.* Beaverton: Tektronix, 1999. https://www.academia.edu/8996354/International_Color_Guide.

Van Reybrouck, David. *Congo: The Epic History of a People.* New York: Ecco, 2014. First published in 2010.

Vayda, A[ndrew] P. *Maori Warfare.* Polynesian Society Maori Monographs, no 2. Wallington: Polynesian Society, 1960.

Vogel, Hans Ulrich. *Marco Polo* Was *in China: New Evidence from Currencies, Salts and Revenues.* Leiden: Brill, 2013.

Volhard, Ewald. *Kannibalismus.* Stuttgart: Strecker und Schröder, 1939.

Volz, Walter. *Reise durch das Hinterland von Liberia im Winter 1906–1907.* Bern: A. Francke, 1911.

Wack, Henry Wellington. *The Story of the Congo Free State.* New York: G. P. Putnam's Sons, 1905. https://archive.org/details/storyofcongofree00wackuoft.

Walker, H. Wilfrid. *Wanderings among South Sea Savages and in Borneo and the Philippines.* London: Witherby, 1909. https://archive.org/details/wanderingsamongs00walkrich.

Wallis, Mary. *Life in Feejee; or, Five Years among the Cannibals.* Boston: William Heath, 1851. https://archive.org/details/lifeinfeejee00wall.

Ward, Herbert. *Five Years with the Congo Cannibals.* London: Chatto & Windus, 1891. https://archive.org/details/fiveyearswithcon00wardrich.

———. *My Life with Stanley's Rear Guard.* New York: Charles L. Webster, 1891. https://archive.org/details/mylifewithstanle01ward.

———. *A Voice from the Congo.* New York: Charles Scribner's Sons, 1910. https://archive.org/details/voicefromcongoco00ward.

Weeks, John H. *Among Congo Cannibals: Experiences, Impressions, and Adventures During a Thirty Years' Sojourn amongst the Boloki and Other Congo Tribes.* London: Seeley, Service, 1913. https://archive.org/details/amongcongocannib00weekuoft.

———. "Anthropological Notes on the Bangala of the Upper Congo River." *Journal of the Royal Anthropological Institute of Great Britain and Ireland* 39 (1909): 97–136, 416–59.

Westmark, Theodor. "Chez les Bangallas." *Bulletin de la Société de Géographie de Marseille* 8 (1886): 431–37. http://gallica.bnf.fr/ark:/12148/bpt6k105772w.

———. "Quinze mois chez les cannibales de Bangala." *Bulletin de la Société de Géographie de Marseille* 12 (1888): 17–24. http://gallica.bnf.fr/ark:/12148/bpt6k200488d.

Wilkinson, Endymion. *Chinese History: A Manual.* Rev. ed. Cambridge, MA: Harvard University Asia Center, 2000.

Williams, F[rancis] E. *Orokaiva Society.* London: Oxford University Press, 1930.

Williams, Thomas, and James Calvert. *Fiji and the Fijians.* New York: D. Appleton, 1860. https://archive.org/details/fijifijians00will.

Wilson, Charles T., and Robert W. Felkin. *Uganda and the Egyptian Soudan.* Vol. 2. London: Sampson Low, Marston, Searle, and Rivington, 1882. https://archive.org/details/ugandaegyptianso02wils_0.

Wilson, R. Trevor. *Small Ruminant Production and the Small Ruminant Genetic Resource in Tropical Africa.* Rome: Food & Agriculture Organization, 1991.

Winthuis, Jos[ef]. *Heidnische Greuel und christliche Liebe.* Hiltrup in Westfalen: Verlag der Missionare vom heiligen Herzen Jesu, 1918.

Wiredu, Kwasi. *Cultural Universals and Particulars: An African Perspective.* Bloomington: Indiana University Press, 1996.

Wissmann, Hermann von. *My Second Journey through Equatorial Africa from the Congo to the Zambesi in the Years 1886 and 1887.* London: Chatto & Windus, 1891. https://archive.org/details/mysecondjourneyt00wiss.

Witte, Jehan de. *Monseigneur Prosper Philippe Augouard, Archevêque titulaire de Cassiopée, Vicaire apostolique du Congo français: Sa vie.* Paris: Emile-Paul, 1924.

Woodford, Charles Morris. *A Naturalist among the Head-Hunters: Being an Account of Three Visits to the Solomon Islands in the Years 1886, 1887, and 1888.* London: George Philip & Son, 1890.

Yang Jisheng. *Tombstone: The Great Chinese Famine, 1958–1962.* New York: Farrar, Strauss, and Giroux, 2012 (2008).

Yule, Henry, ed. *Cathay and the Way Thither: Being a Collection of Medieval Notices of China.* Vol. 1. Cambridge: Cambridge University Press, 2009. First published in 1866.

Zelenietz, Martin. "The End of Headhunting in New Georgia." In *The Pacification of Melanesia,* edited by Margaret Rodman and Matthew Cooper, 91–108. Ann Arbor: University of Michigan Press, 1979.

Zheng Yi. *Scarlet Memorial: Tales of Cannibalism in Modern China.* Boulder: Westview, 1996.

Zhou Xun, ed. *The Great Famine in China, 1958–1962: A Documentary History.* New Haven: Yale University Press, 2012.

INDEX

www.ingramcontent.com/pod-product-compliance
Lightning Source LLC
LaVergne TN
LVHW012333130926
847902LV00028B/389